D0362205

Jimi Hendrix
THE ULTIMATE EXPERIENCE

JIMI HENDRIX THE ULTIMATE EXPERIENCE

JOHNNY BLACK

Amador County Library
530 Sutter Street
Jackson, CA 95642

THUNDER'S MOUTH PRESS

There are two people without whom this book would never have happened. The first is Lucian Randall at Carlton, who saw some merit in the idea and guided it through to completion. Equally essential was the unflappable Ian Cranna who burned the lamp way beyond midnight on many occasions to edit a giant economy size text into a regular size book.

Thanks guys.

THIS IS A CARLTON BOOK

Published in the United States by
THUNDER'S MOUTH PRESS
841 Broadway, Fourth Floor, New York, NY 10003

Text copyright © Johnny Black 1999
Design copyright © Carlton Books Limited 1999

All rights reserved. No part of this publication may be reproduced, stored in a retrieval system, or transmitted, in any form or by any means, electronic, mechanical, photocopying, recording or otherwise, without the prior permission of the publisher, except for reviewers wanting to excerpt material for review purposes

ISBN 1 56025 240 5

Library of Congress Cataloging-in-Publication data
Black, Johnny
Jimi Hendrix: the ultimate experience/by Johnny Black
p. cm.
Includes bibliographical references
1. Hendrix, Jimi Chronology. 2. Rock musicians—United States
Biography. I. Title.
ML410.H476B53 1999
787.87' 166' 092—dc21
[B] 99-29460
[CIP]

Distributed by Publishers Group West, 1700 Fourth Street, Berkeley, CA 94710

Printed and bound in Great Britain

Project Editor: Lucian Randall
Editors: Graeme Kidd and Sally Newman
Senior Art Editors: Diane Spender and Phil Scott
Design: Joanna Hill and Simon Balley
Picture Research: Catherine Costelloe
Production: Alexia Turner

10 9 8 7 6 5 4 3 2 1

CONTENTS

Hendrix backstage at the UK television show Top Of The Pops, waiting to be summoned to perform 'Hey Joe'

INTRODUCTION

For Carol, Joanna and William. Writing this book might have been just about possible without you guys, but it wouldn't have been half as much fun. I love you.

In putting this book together, I conducted a number of interviews with—among others—Ian Anderson, Miller Anderson, Ronnie Anderson, Rod Argent, PP Arnold, Eric Bibb, Steve Bloom, Colin Blunstone, Tony Bramwell, Rosa Lee Brooks, Arthur Brown, David Bruce, Jack Bruce, Sonja Carigiet, Glen Coulson, Alan Cowderoy, Mick Coyne, Clem Curtis, Roger Daltrey, Dino Danelli, Simon Dee, Jeff Dexter, Donovan, Bobby Elliott, Keith Emerson, Pete Frame, Roger Fullilove, Peter Green, Mike Harrison, Jimmy James, Barry Jenkins, Mike Kellie, Judd Lander, Andrew Lauder, Lulu, John McCoy, George McManus, Barrie Martin, Zoot Money, Jim Moore, David Nash, Graham Nash, Roger Newell, Walt Parazaider, Rob Partridge, Alan Price, Noel Redding, Roland Rennie, Robbie Robertson, Tim Rose, Phil Ryan, Peter Sando, Jimmy Savile, Daniel Secunda, Ravi Shankar, Marc Silber, Billy Sloan, Eddie Shaw, Johnnie Stewart, Dick Taylor, Glenn Tipton, David Torrey, Dave Lee Travis, Chris White, Vicki Wickham and Steve Winwood, but much of the material is, unavoidably, taken from direct quotes found in other sources, including newspapers, magazines and books, TV and radio documentaries and internet sites. (See the acknowledgements at the end of this book.)

I have taken the liberty of editing the various direct quotes in exactly the same way as if they were spoken to me, simply in order to avoid repetition or inclusion of material which seems to me to be irrelevant. Similarly, I have sometimes combined quotes taken from more than one source interview, to make a more coherent and complete account of a specific incident. For example, when Hendrix speaks of his childhood, the quotes are actually from several different interviews, but I have combined them and placed them in chronological order. This is sheer artifice, but it is also no different to biographers who may interview their subject several times about the same incident, then combine the answers to create a coherent composite whole.

I have also taken the further liberty of correcting quotations when it seems obvious a mistake has been made. For example, Hendrix speaks of The Beatles seeing him play at the Savoy Theatre, but the facts suggest he is actually referring to the Saville Theatre. Similarly although Brian Auger recalls playing with Hendrix at The Cromwellian in 1966, most sources suggest it was at Blaises.

Despite this, there remain startling inconsistencies in the text. For example, the discrepancy between photographer Henry Diltz's memory of the coin-toss at Monterey Pop in 1967 and Pete Townshend's recollection of the same incident. The most tangled web of all, though, remains the convoluted tale of Hendrix manager Michael Jeffery's involvement with New York gangsters in late 1969, which led to Hendrix being kidnapped for several days.

Jimi's own accounts of his life are also full of inconsistencies. His explanation, for example, of the May 1961 car-stealing incident doesn't square with the documented fact that he was arrested on two separate occasions.

I have striven to get Jimi's name right at all times. All of his direct spoken quotes are in the name Jimi Hendrix, because he didn't start giving interviews until after adopting that name. Some of the quotes taken from his letters and postcards, however, are attributed to Jimmy Hendrix, the name by which he was then known.

Finally, it is only possible to create a book like this by standing on the shoulders of giants—all those who have written books or run fanzines and websites dedicated to Hendrix. Without them there would be no *Jimi Hendrix Eyewitness*.

1942

27 November 1942: Jimmy Hendrix is born to Lucille Hendrix at King County Hospital, Seattle, Washington. His father, Al, is in the US Army, stationed at Fort Benning, Georgia.
Dolores Jeter (Jimmy's aunt): His mother, my sister Lucille, was only 16 when she married Al, and then Al went into the service right away.

December 1942: Al Hendrix is refused compassionate leave to visit his new-born son, because his unit is preparing to go overseas.
Al Hendrix: I got a telegram from my sister-in-law… I ask my commanding officer about going home. 'No chance,' he said. 'You live too far away.'

7 December 1942: The child is registered with the name Johnny Allen Hendrix by his mother, Lucille, who is now conducting an affair with a certain John Williams.

Freddie Mae Gautier (daughter of Minnie, for whom Lucille's mother Clarice Jeter works as a housekeeper): One day when it was snowing, Mrs Jeter arrived at the house and had this baby in her arms, about two weeks old with its little legs sticking out. It was cold. The baby's legs were just blue. My mother said, 'What in the world have you got there?'

Mrs Jeter said she had Lucille's baby, that she hadn't seen Lucille for a few days, so she had to bring him. I remember my mother going on at Mrs Jeter because she and Lucille lived clear across town on 21st and St James, yet Mrs Jeter had just brought him in a little blanket. He had wet so much and it was so cold that the diaper had frozen and the urine made pockmarks on his skin. Mrs Jeter had no diapers or bottle.

My mother bathed the baby and I put olive oil on him and cuddled him to get him warm. He whimpered but not too bad. My mother made up some milk in a bottle, but he was a little hesitant at first and she asked Mrs Jeter, 'Does he breastfeed?'

'No, she hasn't been home, so I've been giving him whatever milk was around.' Mrs Jeter was going to take him when she'd finished the house, but my mother said, 'No, you're not taking him anywhere. Leave him here and tell Lucille to come and get him. I want to see why she's leaving this baby in this kind of fix.'

Mrs Jeter said, 'Well, she's gonna be mad.'

'Well, let her be mad.' I can't tell exactly when Lucille came. It wasn't like the next day or two but maybe even a month or two. When she did come, my mother said to her, 'It's a shame to leave this baby with your mother and I'm gonna take this baby and keep him.'

Lucille said, 'Okay.' It wasn't any big deal for her.

For the next few years, off and on, we kept Jimmy in our home, with the other foster children that we had. I helped take care of him, babysat him… During that period of time, Jimmy sometimes stayed with his Aunt Dolores, on the maternal side, and his dad's brother's wife, Pearl, who lived in Canada.

Dolores Jeter: I took care of Jimmy for the first four years of his life.

He (John Williams, with whom Lucille is having an affair) would take my sister and the baby all over the country. There was a project (housing estate) down in Vancouver. I went to see her down there, and the conditions she was living in—it was a mess. We tried to get Lucille to come and live with us, but she stayed with him. Another time, we had to go and get the baby because Lucille was in hospital. This man had beaten her half to death.

"ONE DAY WHEN IT WAS SNOWING MRS JETER ARRIVED AT THE HOUSE AND SHE HAD THIS BABY IN HER ARMS, ABOUT TWO WEEKS OLD, WITH ITS LITTLE LEGS STICKING OUT. IT WAS COLD. THE BABY'S LEGS WERE JUST BLUE. MY MOTHER SAID, 'WHAT IN THE WORLD HAVE YOU GOT THERE?'"

1942

Single parent Al Hendrix did his best to care for his sons in very tough circumstances. Here he is with a portrait of Jimi

I took Johnny Allen back with me to Seattle. John Williams was charged and sent to jail.

1943

20 February 1943: Dolores Jeter takes Johnny Allen to a photographer on Jackson Street, Seattle, for a portrait which is sent to Al Hendrix.

7 March 1943: Larry Lee, later to play with Hendrix, is born in Memphis, Tennessee.

5 October, 1943: Model/actress Eva Sundqvist is born. She will become the mother of Jimi's son.

1944

When Dolores Jeter becomes ill, Johnny Allen is cared for by several others, including her sister Nancy, and a Mrs White and a Mrs Walls in Seattle.

1945

Jimi Hendrix: I remember when I was small enough to fit in a clothes basket. You know the straw clothes baskets they have in America? I remember when my cousin and I was in there playing around... musta been when I was about three years old.

Dorothy Harding (family friend): We were over at somebody's house and Al was there with Lucille and the two boys. Jimmy was small and he was learning to tie his shoes and they'd been trying to teach him. And he was so nervous. Al was watching and Jimmy was trying to get it right. But he was so nervous he kept getting it wrong. Al screamed at him and I said, 'He's just a baby, you'll make him nervous, you'll have a problem.' 'It ain't a problem,' said Al. 'He's just hard-hearted like his mother.'

4 July 1945: Johnny Allen is admitted to King County Hospital with pneumonia.
Jimi Hendrix: I had pneumonia when I was young and I used to scream and cry every time they put the needle in me. I remember a nurse putting a diaper on me and almost sticking me. I must have been in the hospital sick, because I remember I didn't feel so good. Then she took me out of this crib and held me up to the window, and she was showing me something up against the sky. It was fireworks and all that, so it must have been the Fourth of July. That nurse turned me on. Being high on penicillin she probably gave me, and I was looking up and the sky was just... *ssschuussSchush!!!*

11 November 1945: Al Hendrix, now discharged, returns to Seattle to learn that Jimmy is in Berkeley, California.
Dolores Jeter: A church woman friend of ours (Mrs Champ) took Jimmy to California with her on a vacation. Nobody took him away. Then, when Al got out of the service, they all stayed with me for a year.

December 1945: Al collects his son from Mrs Champ in Berkeley, California, and they return to Seattle. They move in with Dolores Jeter.
Al Hendrix: When I brought him back to Seattle, we stayed with my sister-in-law. She had three girls and, with Jimmy, we did all right. I was getting my rocking-chair money from the government, $20 a week. I was looking around for some work but there wasn't much going on. But Jimmy was with me from then on.

25 December 1945: David Redding, later to become Noel, is born in Folkestone, Kent.

1946

15 January 1946: Johnny Allen Hendrix has his photograph taken, holding a stuffed toy while sitting in a chair.

17 June 1946: Kathy Etchingham, Jimi's future partner, is born in Derby, England.

9 July 1946: John Mitchell, future drummer for The Jimi Hendrix Experience, is born in Ealing, Middlesex, England.

11 September 1946: Al Hendrix changes his son's name to James Marshall Hendrix.
Al Hendrix: I wasn't divorced yet. I was in the act of gettin' divorced. All I had to do to get the divorce was pay $25 more, but all I was makin'

was $20 a week. I sure wish I'da did it at the time, but Lucille talked me out of it.

Late 1946:
Jimi Hendrix: I remember one time when I was only four, and I wet my pants and I stayed out in the rain for hours, so I would get wet all over and my mom wouldn't know. She knew, though.

Mostly my dad took care of me. He was a gardener, but we weren't too rich. It got pretty bad in the winter when there wasn't any grass to cut. My first instrument was a harmonica, when I was about four. Next though, it was a violin. I always loved string instruments and pianos, then I started digging guitars. Every house you went into seemed to have one lying around.

1947

March 1947: Leon Hendrix is conceived.
Al Hendrix: My wife and I separated when I came home from the service in 1945, then my wife and I got together again and that's when Leon came into the picture. Leon was born in 1948.

15 August 1947: Birth of Jerry Velez in Puerto Rico. He will be conga player for Band Of Gypsys.

5 September 1947: George Allen Buddy Miles is born in Omaha, Nebraska. He will become the drummer for Band Of Gypsys.

Winter 47: The Hendrix family moves to Rainier Vista housing project, Seattle.

1948

13 January 1948: Leon Hendrix is born.
Freddie Mae Gautier: It's my recollection that Al and Lucille weren't even together when that boy Leon was born.

Jimi Hendrix: My mother and dad used to fall out a lot. My dad was very religious and level-headed, but my mother used to like having a good time, and dressing up. She used to drink a lot, and didn't take care of herself. She died when I was ten, but she was a real groovy mother.

Leon Hendrix (Jimi's brother): Dad must've loved Mom a lot. Even when we talk about her today, he cries. He talks about her for hours, then gets mad and says I look just like her. She was beautiful. She had long, reddish hair and light skin, but what I remember is my dad always arguing with her.

Jimi Hendrix: My dad used to cut my hair like a skinned chicken, and all my friends used to call me Slick Bean.

8 September 1948: Jimmy starts kindergarten at Rainier Vista School, 3100 Alaska St, Seattle.
Al Hendrix: He probably would have been left-handed, but when he was a kid I made him do things right-handed, eating at the table, for instance.

1949

Jimmy's brother, Joseph Allen Hendrix is born. Joey was later adopted and did not know Jimi.

June 1949: Jimmy and Leon are sent to live with Al's sister Patricia, in Vancouver.
Jimi Hendrix: My brother and I used to go to different homes because Dad and Mom used to break up all the time... I stayed mostly at my aunt's and grandmother's.

Pearl Hendrix (Jimmy's aunt): As a young child, Jimmy would come to Vancouver with Pat, Al's sister, for a couple of weeks during the summers. But, to my knowledge, he never lived in Vancouver, as some biographies say. It was during those summer visits that he'd see his Grandma Hendrix.

When he'd come to stay with me in the summer, he came in rags. I'd buy him new underwear and get him clean clothes.

5 September 1949: Jimmy enrols at Dawson Annex School, Vancouver.
Jimi Hendrix: When I was small, my grandmother—she's Cherokee—gave me a little Mexican jacket with tassels. It was real good and I wore it to school every day in spite of what people might have thought, just because I liked it.

I used to spend summer vacations on her reservation in Vancouver, and kids at school would laugh when I wore shawls and poncho things she

Kathy Etchingham was only one of Jimi Hendrix's many girlfriends but is thought by many to have been his truest love

made. But, on the whole, my school was pretty relaxed. We had Chinese, Japanese, Puerto Ricans and Filipinos. We won all the football games.

November 1949: Jimmy returns to Seattle and re-enters Rainier Vista School.
Jimi Hendrix: I used to bring a stray dog home every night til my pa let me keep one. Then it was the ugliest dog of them all. It was really Prince Hendrix, but we just called it Dawg.

1950

5 September 1950: Jimmy moves to Horace Mann Elementary School.
Jimi Hendrix: I used to paint at school. The teacher used to say, 'Paint three scenes' and I'd do abstract stuff like the Martian sunset. No bull.

Al Hendrix: I didn't get a lot of chance to play with him when he was very small because I was was working two jobs. So I'd see him in the morning and in the evening he'd be asleep. On Sundays, we'd have time together, too. After, his grandmother would take him to Sunday school.

Jimi Hendrix: The music (at Dunlan Baptist Church) seemed to engulf me and carry me away with it. It kind of went through me from my head to my feet. I really dug the way that preacher weaved his hypnotic spell over the people.

They kicked me out of that Holy Roller Church, when I was only eight years old. They said I wasn't dressed properly. Are you ready for that? I walked out, very embarrassed, because the preacher made a real big thing out of it. A grandstand play. And I swore I would never go in that church again as long as I lived.

27 September 1950: Cathy Ira Hendrix, Jimmy's half-sister, is born to Lucille (Al is not the father). Cathy is later adopted.
Leon Hendrix: I remember one night when she (Lucille) didn't come home and my dad went looking for her. Dad put me and Jimmy in the back of the Pontiac and we went along. He found her with some guy, but she came out and got in the car and we left. I remember driving down Jackson Street and Dad shouting at her, 'Act right! Grow up! Behave y'self!' She kept bugging him back. She was really drunk. Mom got mad and reached over with her foot and hit the gas and then the brake. The car jumped forward and then stopped short, and me and Jimmy flew into the front seat. Now Mom was crying and telling us she was sorry. She helped us get into the back seat again and hugged us and loved us up. That was the most love I ever got from her. Probably Jimmy too.

Dorothy Harding: The kids and I and Jimmy were sitting on the porch. We sang songs and popped some popcorn, but it was getting late. I said, 'Jimmy, I'm going in to give the kids a bath and put them to bed, but I'll be right back.' So I did that, the kids said their prayers and went to bed.

I came back out and Jimmy was crying. It shocked me so bad. I put my arm around him and I said, 'What's the matter, baby?' And he was sniffin' and I said, 'What's wrong? Tell Aunty Dorothy.'

'Aunty Dorothy (sniff), when I get big, I'm going far, far away. And I'm never comin' back. Never.'

I just didn't know what to say. I hugged him and tears were running down my cheek, and I said, 'Let's sing a song, a church song,' and I told him about the Scriptures and said to him that 'Things happen in your life that you don't like but you know what? Children can be stronger spiritually than their parents and one day you're going to reach down and help your parents up.' He looked up at me and said, 'Really?' I said, 'Yeah. You're really smart and you've got a good heart.'

Leon Hendrix: Every day was about the same. I'd wait for Jimmy to get home and then we'd play outside. Mom would invite friends over and they'd drink. Then Dad would get mad. It happened over and over again and so, finally, they got divorced.

Christmas 1950:
Leon Hendrix: We had a tree, we got presents and Mom and Dad were laughing together, turning the little hand-crank on a toy steam shovel. But then they started fighting again.

That Christmas we had before Mom left was the last one. After that, at Christmas and birthdays, there were no presents. Dad said there wasn't any reason to celebrate—it was just another day. The truth is, there wasn't any money for presents.

1951

Lucille Hendrix finally leaves the family home, which is now at 26th Avenue/Yesler St.
Al Hendrix: She'd come by and promise lots of things—she'd do this and she'd do that—and Jimmy would say to me, 'Why does Mama always tell me she's gonna do this and that when she knows she's not gonna be able to do it?' And I said, 'Well, she means well—she wants to do it.' I didn't talk bad about her to him, 'bout the hard time she gave me, 'cos he knew that.

Leon Hendrix: We weren't supposed to see her. We'd walk over to her house. Dad used to threaten to send us to our mom if we were bad, but we had more fun with her. She'd give us all the love she had for a few days, then she'd be gone for a few months.

5 September 1951: Jimmy re-enters Rainier Vista Elementary School for third grade.
Al Hendrix: He was just an ordinary kid as far as I was concerned. He played sports and ran around with his friends. He was a bit on the shy side. A lot of people seem to think I should have seen a halo around his head or something, but he wasn't nothing spectacular or anything like that.

He wrote and drew right-handed... Playing baseball, he'd bat left-handed but he'd throw the ball right-handed.

27 October 1951: Pamela Margerite, Jimmy's half-sister is born to Lucille (Al was not the father). Pamela is adopted at birth.

17 December 1951: Al and Lucille Hendrix are divorced. Al gains custody of the children.
Al Hendrix: It was an on-and-off affair. It didn't work out too well. So we finally got divorced. Leon was about a year old. I stayed on in the projects with the kids and she moved.
Jimmy's mother didn't come by very often. It was a bit of a struggle for us. He got on my nerves at times, like all kids do, but we had good times too.

1952

5 September 1952: The family move to 3022 Genessee St; Jimmy stays at Rainier Vista School.
Leon Hendrix: Dad hired an old Filipino lady who got room and board to cook meals and take care of us. She was really mean. She whipped me all the time. She gave me and Jimmy catsup sandwiches to eat and we told Dad and she gave us a whipping for telling on her.

Al Hendrix: I used to have Jimmy clean up the bedroom while I was gone, and when I would come home I would find a lot of broom straws around the foot of the bed. I'd say to him, 'Well, didn't you sweep up the floor?' and he'd say, 'Oh yeah, I did.' But I'd find out later that he used to be sitting at the end of the bed and strumming the broom like he was playing a guitar.

1953

January 1953
Leon Hendrix: We moved to one-room on Terrace Street. We weren't allowed to cook in the room, but Dad had a hot-plate anyway and the bathroom was down the hall.

27 April 1953: The family is now at 2603 26th Avenue; Jimmy enrols at Leschi Elementary.
Leon Hendrix: He'd take me out. We'd be gone 'til sundown. Al was often none the wiser because he was out so much as well, although every so often a complaint from the neighbors about child neglect would bring the Welfare around.

“WHEN I WOULD COME HOME, I'D FIND A LOT OF BROOM STRAWS AROUND THE FOOT OF THE BED. I'D SAY, 'WELL, DIDN'T YOU SWEEP UP?' AND HE'D SAY, 'YEAH, I DID.' I FOUND OUT LATER HE USED TO BE SITTING AT THE END OF THE BED AND STRUMING THE BROOM LIKE HE WAS PLAYING A GUITAR”

1951

Jimi Hendrix: The first guitarist I was aware of was Muddy Waters. I heard one of his old records and it scared me to death, because I heard all of those sounds. Wow, what is that all about? It was great.

Leon Hendrix: In the summer time, about three in the morning, we would all go and knock on each other's windows and all start heading downtown to pick up fruit from where the fruit picking was, and get donuts. It was like a routine in the summer.

Then we'd get a bus and go pick butter beans for an hour and get a dollar. Sometimes, we'd get down late and miss the bus. The freight train yards were right there and so we'd wait until one of the trains started up and we'd ride out for free to the bean field. We'd make a few dollars until noon, then go swimming. We were vagabonds. There was always somebody to feed us—we stayed with anybody. Jimmy was my whole world, my only friend.

Summer 1953: Jimmy develops a close friendship with Leschi School boys, James Williams and Terry Johnson.
James Williams: I think we were playing basketball at recess. We were just little kids. So he says, 'Hey, you can dribble between your legs!' and I say, 'Yeah, I learned that a while back, practicing in my back yard.' That's how we became friends.

Al Hendrix: Jimmy and James Williams were in the Boy Scouts together. They used to go to Leschi Park and Seward Park together.

James Williams: We became little soul mates. We hung out together, we played marbles, and we shared little thoughts and things the way little kids did in those days. We joined the Safety Patrol together, and all that kind of stuff.

Jimmy and I were really close for about ten years. I considered him my best friend. Our other closest friend was Terry Johnson.

Terry Johnson: He didn't have too many friends. He was quiet, and he was poor. I had to give him all my sweaters to wear, but he was a really outgoing guy after you got to know him. We used to hang around, learning to swim and all that stuff. Then I started letting him come with me on my paper route early in the morning, 'cause he had nothing else to do. He'd come home and he couldn't even get in his house, and he used to come to my house until his father got home and let him in. That's how we became friends, really.

James Williams: When we were in grade school, Jimmy, Terry and I thought of ourselves as the Three Musketeers. We were pretty much inseparable. It was one for all and all for one, just like in the old Gene Kelly film.

1954

Summer 1954: Al treats the boys with visits to the nearby Florence Cinema, and they become fans of Buster Crabbe's *Flash Gordon* movies.
Leon Hendrix: You could see the strings holding up the rocket ships, but it was fantastic for us. Dad used to give us a nickel for popcorn and ten cents to get in. That's where Jimmy got his nickname, Buster. We would dress up in the cape and helmet. Jimmy even jumped off the roof one time—he actually thought he could fly. Jimmy would tell me all about the stars and the planets and make up stories and do drawings.

Al Hendrix: He drew and painted. Since he had the talent and the slender fingers for it, he started thinking he'd be a commercial artist. But then music struck him and he got interested in that. I was glad he did, because it was something he loved.

1955

Leon Hendrix: We were pretty much taking care of ourselves. Dad had to be at work at 3.30 in the afternoon and we got out of school at 3.10 and we'd always be late getting home, so we didn't see him. He made cheese sandwiches and left them in the refrigerator for us for dinner. He got off work at midnight, got home at one o'clock and in the morning he'd be so tired, sometimes he'd burn our breakfast.

Jimi Hendrix: I wanted to be an actor or a painter. I particularly liked to paint scenes on other planets. Summer afternoon on Venus, and stuff like that. The idea of space travel excited me more than anything else.

James Williams: I remember a mural Jimmy did when we were in Mrs Stophenberg's sixth grade class at Leschi. It was a full wall mural, on one of those big wrap-around blackboards that go around the classroom. He did a spectacular piece of art.

It was a Mexican village scene, really vivid and colorful and full of details. In the foreground there was a powerful palomino carrying a rider in full Spanish regalia. Jimmy had this thing about palomino horses. Well, this horse seemed to be charging right at the viewer. In contrast, there was a man leaning up against a building, asleep, wearing an enormous brightly colored sombrero. The contrast of the man asleep and the movement of the horses was startling. The mood that he captured with the use of details and colors was amazing for someone his age. One of the things about Jimmy was his fascination with colors.

Al Hendrix: When I was doing some yardwork, cleaning garages and such as that, I found a ukelele. I took it home. I had to get some strings for it. He'd play that ukelele, sometimes right-handed, sometimes left-handed. I guess he figured he'd do better left-handed, and that's what he did.

June 1955: Jimmy is photographed with his Leschi Elementary classmates.
Leon Hendrix: Lots of times, me and Jimmy got in trouble at school. Nothing serious. The usual stuff. Sassing a teacher. Sometimes Jimmy cut class. Dad would have to come to school and talk to the principal, so he'd be late for work. They took that for a while, and then they fired him.

17 June 1955: Al can no longer pay for the house, so the family move to 1436 29th Avenue.
Leon Hendrix: We had a dog named Prince, and dog food cost nine cents a can. That was a big item in the budget, so Prince got half a can a day. We all shared one tea bag. We got a whipping if we left a light on, because it was wasting money.

Things got real rough. For a long time he couldn't find work. They cut off the electricity, so he bought milk each day and put it in cold water in the sink. He collected electrical wire and burned off the rubber insulation in the furnace and recycled the copper. We ate horse meat hamburger two or three times a week.
The neighbours would come and get us and they would feed us. We were raised by all our friends, all our aunties and uncles.

17 June 1955: The family move to 1434 29th Avenue. Jimmy finishes at Leschi Elementary. School records show that he got a 'C' for scholarship, his citizenship was 'satisfactory' and his attendance 'regular'.

7 September 1955: Jimmy moves to Meaney Junior High; he plays for the football team.
Terry Johnson: Jimmy moved in with his aunt and uncle and went to Meaney Junior High, and Jimmy Williams and I went to Washington Junior High.

Pearl Hendrix: Jimmy came to live with us in Seattle in 1955, near the end of his sixth grade year. We were on Cherry Street, then we moved to the corner of 22nd and East John, a few blocks from Meaney Junior High School. I can't remember dates too well, but I think Jimmy was with me during grades six, seven and eight. We all loved Jimmy, but he wouldn't let anyone get close to him except for my daughter Diane.

Diane Hendrix (Jimmy's cousin): Jimmy would read his poetry to me. Sometimes I'd have to ask him to re-read a line, or maybe an entire poem. He poured his heart into those poems. They were deeply philosophical. I had to concentrate so totally to understand them.

Jimi Hendrix: At school, I used to write poetry a lot and then I was really happy. My poems were mostly about flowers and nature and people wearing robes.

Pernell Alexander (school friend): Jimmy Hendrix loved football, and he would draw football pictures. He liked the Rams and the Eagles.

1956

23 February 1956: Having moved on to 166 25th Avenue, Jimmy joins Jimmy Williams and Terry Johnson at Washington Junior High.

August 1956:
Diane Hendrix: Elvis Presley was really hot when Jimmy was living with us. We liked him. 'You

Space adventurer Flash Gordon was one of young Jimi's earliest heroes, and inspired a lifelong love of science fiction

Ain't Nothin' But A Hound Dog'—that stuff. Bobby (Diane's brother) and Jimmy used to practice to Elvis's records, using brooms as guitars. I loved watching them. They would put on a show for me.

5 September 1956: Having moved again to Yesler Way/30th Avenue, Jimmy returns to Meaney Junior High.
Leon Hendrix: Living downstairs was a guy who had a guitar. Jimmy would go down there and play on his guitar.

John Eng (school friend): He and I became friends in seventh grade at Meaney Junior High. I remember there were two guys he was often with, Wallace Coleman and Frank Love. Sometimes they would talk in class and be a nuisance.

We had an English teacher who used to say, 'Hip, hip, one, two, three, the British are coming!' Then she'd march those three guys to the front of the room and make them all get under her desk. Then she'd ignore them for the rest of the period and we were all supposed to ignore them too.

29 November 1956: Jimmy is photographed wearing his football outfit at his cousin Grace Hatcher's house.

Winter 1956: With very little money coming in, Al is forced to allow Leon to be fostered.
Leon Hendrix: I went to the Wheelers. They were a rich black family and had about eight kids there. They treated us real good—I called her 'Mom' and Jimmy would come over every other day at least. The only thing that kept me going was that Jimmy would come and visit me.

1957

1 September 1957: Jimmy sees Elvis Presley perform at Sicks Stadium, Seattle.

November 1957:
Leon Hendrix: One day there was this big Cadillac, parked outside the front of the house. Jimmy and I ran out and there was Little Richard himself, sitting in the back seat. He had one of those doowop rags around his head and he had stopped just to see us. His mother lived around the corner and she knew how crazy about music we were. We all went to the same church then, Goodwill Baptist at 14th and Spring.

1958

3 January 1958: Lucille Hendrix marries longshoreman Bill Mitchell.
Terry Johnson: It was a forbidden subject, to talk about his mother, between us, so we just —it was a code that we had. It just wasn't something we'd talk about—anything else but that.

2 February 1958: Lucille dies of a ruptured spleen, caused by years of excessive drinking.
Al Hendrix: He was 16 when his mother died. I didn't go to the funeral, but Jimmy did.

May 1958: Al and Jimmy move yet again, to 1715 College Street South, Seattle.
Jimi Hendrix: The Grand Ole Opry used to come on, and I would watch that. They used to have some pretty heavy guitar players, but I didn't try to copy nobody. Those were just the people who gave me the feeling to get my own thing together.

Summer 1958: Jimmy begins his love affair with guitars.
Jimi Hendrix: I learned to play on an old guitar which belonged to one of my father's friends who came to play cards. While the two men played, I would creep out onto the porch with the friend's guitar and see what I could get out of it. One night my dad's friend was stoned and he sold me his guitar for five dollars.

Al Hendrix: Jimmy told me about it and I said, 'Okay,' and gave him the money. He strummed away on that, working away all the time, any spare time he had.

Jimi Hendrix: I didn't know I would have to put the strings round the other way because I was left-handed, but it just didn't feel right. I changed the strings round but it was way out of tune. I didn't know a thing about tuning so I went down to the store and ran my fingers across the strings on a guitar they had there. After that I was able to tune my own. Then I got tired of the guitar and put it aside but, when I heard Chuck Berry, it revived my interest. I learned all the riffs I could.

Terry Johnson: Jimmy Hendrix and I were terrible singers. All he wanted to do was play his guitar and make funny noises.

Jimmy Williams: Our friend Pernell Alexander was the one who got Jimmy playing the guitar.

Pernell Alexander: The first guitar we played belonged to a guy named Robert McLamore—they call him Snake. He had a guitar that he didn't play, so we practiced on it. I wanted a drum set back in those days, and my grandmother and I had a go-around about it. She said my choices were saxophone, guitar or piano, but we couldn't afford a piano. So she bought me a guitar.

Lacy Wilbon (friend): Jimmy was really into the blues in those days. He was way ahead of the rest of us as far as dexterity goes. I used to sit in awe. He used his single-note technique. He wasn't proficient in chord building. I suggested he get some books and teach himself. I said, 'If you do that, you'll be unstoppable.' He said, 'It would take too much time.' So I taught him six chords and six inversions.

Terry Johnson: When Jimmy and I started junior high, the Rotary Boys Club became the perfect place for us to practice. It was hard to find a place to practice rock'n'roll in those days. We could never practice at Jimmy's house. We couldn't practice at my mom's house much any more because we were too loud.

They had an amplifier that you could check out. So Jimmy would check it out, plug in his guitar and hear what he sounded like amplified.

Al Hendrix: He used to practice a lot. I'd come home from work and he'd be there, plunk, plunk, plunk. If I disturbed him or something, he'd go in the bedroom, and he'd be there, plunk, plunk, plunking. I'd say, 'Jimmy, sweep the floor,' and he'd say 'OK, Dad,' and he'd do that. And after he finished doing that he'd go back to plunk, plunk, plunking. I used to hear it constantly.

Terry Johnson: In the back of our house is a room we call the playroom, where my mom has an old upright piano with a few keys missing. For me and Jimmy it was our sanctuary. Jimmy had a little turquoise guitar that he'd re-strung.

We played by ear, listening to 45s and, believe me, we wore out a lot of 45s. First of all, we had to figure out what key the song was in, then we'd let it play for a while, and then we'd take it off and start all over again. Jimmy would listen to the guitar part until he had it figured out and memorized. Then I'd play the piano part.

One of the songs we'd play was 'What'd I Say' by Ray Charles. That was a big one.

Jimi Hendrix: I was good enough then on the guitar to start working with little groups that we got together. We really thought we were something, but we didn't do much more than play at parks and recreation centres for teenage dances.

Pernell Alexander: We got our little band together when we were in junior high school—the Velvetones. Walter Jones was the drummer, Robert Green played the piano, Luther Rabb played tenor and baritone sax, Anthony Atherton played alto sax, and Jimmy and I played the guitar. I think Terry Johnson played with us a couple of times.

Jimi Hendrix: They drowned me out. I didn't know why at first but, after about three months, I realized I'd have to get an electric guitar.

Robert Green (piano, Velvetones): We used to rehearse about every day in my basement.

Pernell Alexander: Forget all those stories about Jimmy discovering electronic sound distortion in

"I LEARNED TO PLAY ON AN OLD GUITAR WHICH BELONGED TO ONE OF MY FATHER'S FRIENDS WHO CAME TO PLAY CARDS. WHILE THE TWO MEN PLAYED, I WOULD CREEP OUT ONTO THE PORCH WITH THE FRIEND'S GUITAR AND SEE WHAT I COULD GET OUT OF IT"

1958

New York or London. The truth is he discovered it here in Robert Green's basement. One of the amplifiers blew a tube, so we were playing with distorted sound. We were too dumb even to know what had happened. We only had one amp, and we had two guitars and a mike coming out of the one amp. We had it overloaded.

One name no one has mentioned in the material printed about Jimmy is Raleigh 'Randy' Snipes. We called him Butch. He was phenomenal. He had great showmanship. He taught Jimmy the stunts. Butch was the first one here to play the guitar behind his back and with his teeth, and Jimmy learned those tricks from him.

Robert Green: We played for an assembly at Meaney. Then we played our first gig for a women's club event at the Polish Hall. I remember we got paid $125.

Pernell Alexander: We played all over—at Polish Hall, Washington Hall, the Boys Club and the YMCA. We also played at a place called The Shrine at 23rd and Madison.

Anthony Atherton (sax, Velvetones): We played in the Battle of the Bands in the Yesler Terrace gym, battling the Rocking Kings.

Lester Exkano (drummer, Rocking Kings): When he was playing with the Velvetones at the Battle Of The Bands, he was amazing. We talked him into playing with the Rocking Kings.

Jimi Hendrix: My first gig (with the Rocking Kings) was at a National Guard Armory. We earned 35 cents a piece. In those days I just liked rock'n'roll, I guess. We used to play stuff by people like The Coasters.

1959

Pernell Alexander: Mr Williams (a neighbor) was the one who introduced Jimmy to the blues. Jimmy loved the blues. They used to sit out on Mr Williams' porch on 27th Avenue, and Jimmy would listen to him play the blues.

James Minor (school friend): Jimmy used to like to play 'Further On Up The Road'—the Bobby Blue Bland piece. He loved 'Lucille', and I remember him playing 'Wishing Well', 'Money', 'New Dance' and 'Candido'. We all got started with music and guitars because of Jimmy. He taught me to play the guitar.

1959

Al Hendrix: Some of his friends had guitars, so they showed him a few riffs. I never did get him an amplifier, which I planned to, but that didn't make no difference. He decided to get music out of it the way it was. His friends would come over and they'd all do their thing.

Benorce Blackmon (school friend): I remember seeing Jimmy around, but I didn't know who he was. He was on his bicycle with all these fox-tails and all these flashes and mirrors on it. He was always kind of stand-offish, you know? You could never get really too close to him.

I'm sitting on my mother's front porch and here comes this guy up the hill. He started playing my guitar and I said, 'Hey man, show me that.' And he just started to show me things. He was real nice, always showing you stuff. Jimmy was always playing. My mother used to drive me away from the porch sometimes 'cos he would just pop up and come to play.

Walter Harris (sax, Rocking Kings): At first we were hesitant, because he didn't have an amp, but he always managed to find someone to plug in with.

Junior (Heath) was one lead guitar and Jimmy was the other. Jimmy was better than Junior, and Junior knew it. They were good friends off stage, but on stage they were total enemies because Jimmy could play better. Plus, Hendrix was plugged into Junior's amplifier, and it wasn't too kosher to plug into someone's amplifier and then show them up. Junior was good, but Jimmy put more into his playing. You could see it in his face.

9 September 1959: Having moved house again to 1314 East Terrace Street, Jimmy enrols at Garfield High School.
Ralph Hayes (teacher): Jimmy was in my fifth-period US history class. He was very personable, but he was also a very shy person. I mean very shy. I can't believe that gentleman went on to make the kind of music that he made, because he was so shy. When, sometimes, he was a bit

Hendrix was 14 when he saw Elvis Presley perform. According to Jimi's niece Diane, he used to mime to Elvis's records

late for class, like a minute or two, he was always apologetic when he'd sit down.

I noticed though, that Jimmy wasn't very interested in class. I wasn't sure whether it was my fault or not.

Janet Nosi Terada (school friend): He was always doodling, especially when he should have been doing something else. He loved to draw and he was good. He was quite an artist.

I remember him shuffling when he walked. It was like his shoes were untied, but that was just Jimmy.

Terry Johnson: His shoes were worn out, turned over on the sides and had holes in the bottoms. He used to walk on the sides of his feet, and I don't know if that was a natural tendency or if he did it because his shoes were worn out.

John Eng: Jimmy enjoyed chess. He and I had a good time playing chess at school.

Fall 1959: Jimmy gets his first electric guitar.
Al Hendrix: I bought him a Supro (Ozark 1560 S) from Myers store in Seattle and I got me a saxophone, one of them old melody C saxophones. We lived in a rough neighborhood, we was pretty poor, but me and Jimmy would play together on sax and guitar. But, y'know, I soon got behind with the payments on the sax, so I had to give it back. I realized that he was going to be better on that guitar than I was ever going to be on the saxophone, so that was okay.

1960

Betty Jean Morgan (Jimmy's soon-to-be girlfriend): I met Jimmy in school. Jimmy was a beautiful person. He was kind and very generous. We'd talk on the phone and, on the weekend, he'd come up to my house... My mother loved Jimmy. He'd sit on our porch and play the guitar.

Caroline Morgan (Betty's mother): He was a typical teenager. He had a nice personality—he took to me like I was his mother. Jimmy wanted Betty to marry him. He bought her a nice ring.

Mike Tagawa (school friend): Hendrix and I were in the same gym class and I remember one day we were all filing into the gym to get suited up and Bill Diambri, who was the gym coach, asked Hendrix to go get his guitar... They had Hendrix bring his guitar into the office and, for the duration of the period, Hendrix sat there and played guitar for them. They'd heard about how great he was.

James Williams: When we played Little League football, all the guys on our team were Japanese or black. Our name was the Fighting Irish. That always made me laugh.

Gordon Shoji (school friend): Jimmy and I met playing football on The Fighting Irish. When I think of Hendrix I see him pointing his finger at me with a look of delight. I think it was our sophomore year of high school football, during a one-on-one tackling drill. First, Jimmy was tackling. I lowered my head and ran straight ahead. Being 'hot stuff' in football, I wasn't surprised when I literally ran over him. Then Jimmy, the 'scrub'—the guy who was too mellow to play an aggressive game like football—ran right over me. 'Hah! Got you back!' Jimmy said. I was flat on my back in disbelief.

20 February 1960: The Rocking Kings play at Washington Hall, Seattle.
Mike Tagawa: Hendrix talked a lot about Webb Lofton and the group called The Rocking Kings. He'd tell me that they were a good group, and that he really enjoyed himself.

Lester Exkano (drums, Rocking Kings): Sometimes Hendrix played rhythm, and sometimes he did bass by tuning his guitar low.

Jimmy didn't smoke and he didn't drink. The rest of us smoked occasionally and drank a little wine, but not Hendrix.

Webb Lofton (sax, Rocking Kings): We all knew Jimmy was good. He played behind his back and between his legs.

Charles Woodbury (piano/vocals, Rocking Kings): Before we got Jimmy, we were just a little, mediocre group but after we got Jimmy, we started to kind of blossom. We started getting a lot of gigs around town.

Ray Charles's 'What'd I Say' was one of the first songs that Hendrix learned to play while practising with his friends

Walter Harris (sax, Rocking Kings): I never saw Jimmy get angry. There was one incident when we were playing at Birdland with a guy from down South, from Louisiana. His name was Waltz and he was a very good piano player. He had been playing with us for a few months. Anyway, this guy proceeded to say that we weren't playing. So I grabbed Jimmy's guitar, and I was going to hit this guy with it. And all the band members were standing there watching me with this guitar and Jimmy said, 'Hey, uh, look, Walter, that's my guitar.' You know, he never got angry, never made any aggressive move toward me. He says, 'Can you just please pick up something else to hit this guy with? Not my guitar.' Many times I've laughed about that.

Spring 1960: Jimmy's Supro Ozark is stolen during a Rocking Kings gig at Birdland, Seattle.
Al Hendrix: He didn't tell me about it for a long time. He said he left it over at James Thomas'. I dropped him over there and said to bring his equipment home and that's when he told me he'd got it stolen. So I says, 'You're gonna have to do without a guitar for a while.'

Webb Lofton: Jimmy had a used guitar when he joined our group. Walter (Harris) and I wanted to help Jimmy get a new guitar. My uncle helped us with the down payment and co-signed the deal at Myer's Music, where we bought the guitar. But when Jimmy took the guitar home, Al told him to take it back. So he didn't have it very long, but that's the story of Jimmy's first new guitar.

June 1960: Al buys Jimmy a Danelectro guitar to replace the stolen Supro Ozark. The family move again to 2606 Yesler Way.

July 1960: James Thomas starts a new band, Thomas & The Tom Cats, with Jimmy on guitar.
Al Hendrix: James charged the band members five dollars for the jacket rental and Jimmy never did make any money. I remember Jimmy saying, 'Man, I'm not gonna play with those cats any more.' I'd laugh and say he was gettin' experience.

They played Vancouver one time, and Jimmy was surprised I let him travel that far. The car broke down and they didn't make any money then either.

September 1960: Shortly after starting a new term at Garfield High, Jimmy is in trouble for stealing clothes from Wilner's Clothing Store.
Jimi Hendrix: I often nearly got caught by the cops. I was always gone on wearing hip clothes, and the only way to get them was through the back window of a clothing store.

Al Hendrix: They didn't press any charges. Jimmy and I had been doing some gardening work at some time, and I knew the owner of Wilner's.

Ralph Hayes (teacher): I remember saying to him, 'Son, you really aren't interested in this class. Why don't you just leave this place, get your guitar and just make music? It's something that you thoroughly enjoy.' But I was shocked to learn shortly after that he had withdrawn.

Al Hendrix: 'Dad, I have been going down to the recruiting office,' Jimmy told me one day. He knew he was 1-A. He knew if he volunteered he would get the category he wanted. He kept going down to see this recruiting officer, and then one day he told me, 'Dad, I'm going in.' I said, 'That's all right, that's all right. There's nothing wrong with that. Get it over with.'

There were no wars going on—it was after the Korean War and before the Vietnam deal. He said he wanted to get into the Screaming Eagles, and I said, 'Oh, wow! You're going on further than ol' Dad did.' That made me feel real proud of him. He was trying to do something.

James Williams: He came to find me in the library to say that he was quitting school to go in the Army. I thought it was kind of strange. 'You've only got a year to go. What are you quitting for?' He says, 'Yeah, I just want to get out of here and go in the Army.'

31 October 1960: Jimmy drops out of Garfield High without graduating.
Al Hendrix: He tried to get a job as a bag boy at a grocery store. He had applications in at various places. But nothing was shaking. So I asked him to come to work with me.

Jimi Hendrix: School wasn't for me. According to my father I had to go working. I had done that for a few weeks with my father. He had a not-so-good running contracting firm and, in me, he saw a cheap labourer. I had to carry stones and cement all day, and he pocketed the money.

1961

1 March 1961: Birth of Janie Hendrix Wright, Jimmy's adopted sister.

April 1961: Jimmy and James Thomas buy a bigger amplifier for Jimmy at Myers Music.

2 May 1961: Jimmy is arrested for being in a car taken without the owner's consent.
James Oliver (friend): In the ghetto, you have guys who are always running their mouth. Jimmy knew all those people and he could get along with them, but he wouldn't really get involved that much. He didn't rip and run like we did. He was a shy-type guy. He went along because it was easy.

5 May 1961: Jimmy is arrested again for taking another vehicle.
Jimi Hendrix: It was the most frightening thing that happened during my childhood. This friend of mine was a guy with a lot of nerve—one of those guys that was always trying to show out, you know what I mean? So one day he came by my house with this fine 'chine and asked me if I wanted to go for a ride. I said, 'Sure,' and hopped in. He told me it was his uncle's car and I believed him. I should have known better...

6 May 1961: After being charged by Seattle police, Jimmy is sent to Rainier Vista 4-H Youth Center, Seattle for seven days.
Jimi Hendrix: I was 18. I didn't have a cent in my pocket. I spent seven days in the cooler for taking a ride in a stolen car. But I never knew it was stolen.

Because I didn't have a cent in my pocket, I walked into the first recruitment office I saw and went into the Army. I figured I'd have to go sooner or later, so I volunteered to get it over with.

16 May 1961: Jimmy's hearing at Seattle court house. Because he has decided to enlist, he is given a two-year suspended sentence.

17 May 1961: Jimmy returns to the Army recruitment office and enlists.
Jimi Hendrix: When I joined, I figured I might as well go all the way, so I signed with the Airborne.

28 May 1961: Jimmy gives Betty Jean Morgan an engagement ring during a dance.

31 May 1961: Hendrix joins the 101st US Airborne Division at Fort Ord, California. He is now Recruit RA19693532.
Al Hendrix: He went to ship out, and I went down there with him and gave him some money—a helper-out. It made me feel real good.

Jimi Hendrix: I went into the Army for a while, and I didn't play much guitar because the only guitars available were right-handed ones.

8 June 1961: Jimmy writes home:

> The Army's not too bad, so far... All, I mean, all my hair's cut off and I have to shave... I won't be able to see you until about two months from now... we're going through Basic Training...

4 August 1961: Having completed basic training, Jimmy is now ranked Private.

11 August 1961: Jimmy writes home:

> The company left last Saturday morning at 0800 and everybody except four of us are gone home. I'm supposed to be going to Fort Lee, Virginia, at a clerical and typing school. They might just change that when my official orders come in.

September 1961: Jimmy returns to Seattle briefly on furlough.

8 September 1961: Jimmy leaves Seattle.

9 September 1961: Jimmy turns up in San Francisco having lost his bus ticket. Military Police take him to Presidio Military Reservation.

11 September 1961: Jimmy finally makes it back to Fort Ord.

October 1961: Betty Jean Morgan writes to Jimmy:

> You're fooling with someone else down there—California girls are tuff, I know, and I know that there's some down there around where you are. You better write and leave those 'sapphires' alone or you just better not come up here to see me.

1 November 1961: Jimmy writes home again:

> I wouldn't mind breaking a leg or something, if I can come out wearing that

1961

Screaming Eagle patch and those Airborne wings. It's a proud outfit… I signed up for clerk, administrative work and stuff like that, because I really don't want to be in that infantry stuff if I can help it. When I get to Fort Campbell, all I do is go to that jump school and, if I graduate, all I will do is be sent or stationed there as a supply clerk or something, then I just have to make that one jump a month for that extra $55 a month.

2 November 1961: Jimmy writes home:
…when you see me again, I'll be wearing the patch of proudness.

8 November 1961: Jimmy transfers to the 101st Airborne at Fort Campbell, Kentucky.

11 November 1961: Jimmy writes home again:
Here I am, exactly where I wanted to go… We jumped out of a 34-foot tower on the third day we were here. It was almost fun… There's nothing but physical training and harassment here for two weeks.

20 November 1961: Jimmy describes beginning jump school in a letter.
When you go to jump school, that's when you get hell! They work you to DEATH! Fussing and fighting everything you do. You have to do 10, 15 or 25 push-ups. They really make the sparks fly, and half the people quit then, too. That's how they separate the men from the boys. I pray that I will make it on the men's side.

November 1961: Billy Cox hears Jimmy play. They form a group, The King Kasuals, and play at The Pink Poodle Club, Clarksville, Tennessee.
Billy Cox: We were both stationed at Fort Campbell and I was walking past one of the service clubs one day and I heard someone playing some incredible guitar inside. When I went in to check it out, it turned out to be Jimmy.

I introduced myself to him and told him I was a bass player. So then I checked a bass out from the service club—they had almost every instrument you could imagine. We had a really nice jam and after we finished we decided to put a group together from the servicemen stationed with us.

We used a drummer named Gary Ferguson and worked Service Club Nos 1 and 2 at Fort Campbell. Then some guys from Clarksville, Tennessee, came on post and heard our playing and wanted us to play in town, so we added a saxophonist, Major Washington.

Major Charles Washington: Somehow, Jimmy would manage to pawn his guitar before a gig and the band would have to re-possess it. Nothing else could be used, he had to have this specific guitar. It appeared that Jimmy was never really with us. He did a lot of concentrating on his music, and a lot of the small talk that the typical group of guys would make—he would not enter into it. We would look over at him occasionally and there he is, staring. You never did get to know him that closely.

Billy Cox: After a few rehearsals, we started playing at the service clubs and different places. We got to be pretty good.

December 1961: Jimmy makes his first real jump from an airplane.
Jimi Hendrix: When you first jump, it's really outtasite. You're just there at the door and all of a sudden: Flop! RUSH! Once you get out there, everything is so quiet. All you hear is the breeze. It's the most alone feeling in the world. Every time you jump, you're scared that maybe this time it won't open. Then you feel that tug on your collar and there's that big white mushroom above you, and the air is going 'sssssshhhh' past your ears. That's when you begin talking to yourself again and you just say, 'Thank the Lord.' That was about the best thing in the Army—the parachute drops. I did about 25.

1962

17 January 1962: Jimmy writes home:
I hope that you send my guitar as soon as possible. I really need it now—it's still over at Betty's house.

May 1962: Having been promoted to Private First Class and graduated as a parachutist in the 101st Division's Screaming, Jimmy breaks his right ankle on his 26th parachute jump.

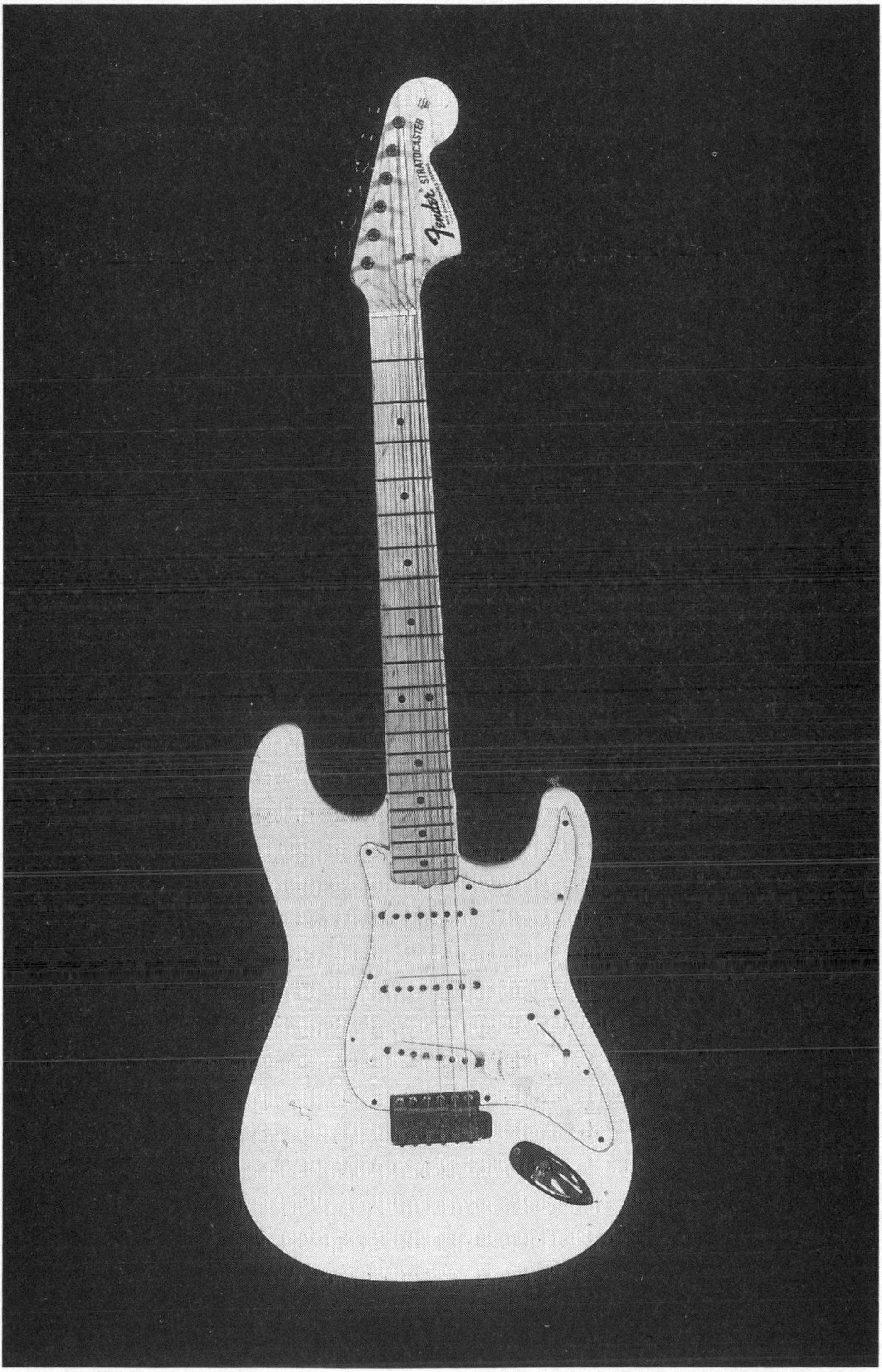

The Fender Stratocaster is the guitar most associated with Hendrix, strung upside down because he was left-handed

Jimi Hendrix: I got my ankle caught in the sky-hook just as I was going to jump, and I broke it. I told them I'd hurt my back too. Every time they examined me, I groaned, so they finally believed me and I got out.

June 1962: With Jimmy's leg still in plaster, The King Kasuals play in the Pink Poodle, Clarksville, Tennessee.
Billy Cox: We were playing blues and R&B. Jimmy was too timid to sing, and they laughed at me when I sang, so we had a singer named Harry Batchelor. We had two guitars, bass, drums and a saxophone.

We were poor musicians. I was the electronics man with the group, so I built Jimmy a 50 or 75ft cord. I used the longest cord they were selling at Radio Shack, and put quarter-inch plugs on the end. It wasn't that large a club—think they could pack in maybe 150—so Jimmy could leave the club and go outside and play on the sidewalk.

He couldn't afford a wah-wah, so he'd feed back by coming back in and playing his guitar on top of the amp, which gave him a lot of feedback. People didn't know whether to clap or walk out.

2 July 1962: Jimmy gets an honourable discharge from the Army because of his broken ankle.
Jimi Hendrix: One morning I found myself standing outside the gate of Fort Campbell with my little duffel bag and three or four hundred dollars in my pocket. I was going back to Seattle which was a long way away, but there was this girl I was kinda hung up on.

Then I thought I'd just look in at Clarksville which was near, stay there that night and go home next morning... I went to this jazz joint and had a drink. I liked it and stayed. People tell me I get foolish good-natured sometimes. Anyway, I guess I must have felt benevolent that day. I must have been handing out bills to anyone who asked me. I came out with $16 left. And it takes more than that to get from Tennessee to Seattle so, no going home, 'cos it's like 2,000 miles.

I first thought I'd call long distance and get my father to send me some money... but I could guess what he'd say if I told him I'd lost nearly $400 in just one day.

All I can do, I thought, is get a guitar and try to find work here. Nashville was only 20 miles away. There had to be something down there.

Then I remembered that, just before I left the Army, I'd sold a guitar to a cat in my unit. So I went back to Fort Campbell and slept there on the sly that night. I found the guy and told him I just had to borrow the guitar back.

Summer 1962:
Betty Jean Morgan: Jimmy and I were engaged to get married, but I was too young. I was still in school, and my mom wanted me to finish school.

Caroline Morgan: He wanted Betty to come to where he was in the service, to get married, but I said no. I'm from the old school and I didn't want her to go without an escort.

Betty Jean Morgan: I don't remember exactly how we broke up... but I sent the rings back.

September 1962: Jimmy and Billy Cox, now also discharged, rent a house in Clarksville.
Jimi Hendrix: I went to Clarksville, where the group I was with worked for a set-up called W&W. They paid us so little that we decided the two Ws stood for Wicked and Wrong.

1 September 1962: Hendrix buys an Ibanez Japanese electric guitar on hire purchase at Collins music store, Clarksville.

October 1962: After a brief stay in Indianapolis, the King Kasuals move to Nashville.
Billy Cox: Someone heard us in Clarksville and said there was a club in Nashville that could use a band. We went up, auditioned for the job, and immediately got hired. This was at the Del-Morocco. They fired the band that was working there part-time and hired us full-time. The fellow who owned the club also owned Joyce's House of Glamour, and Jimmy and I lived upstairs. We were there about a year or so.

Jimi Hendrix: This one-horse music agency used to come up on stage in the middle of a number while we were playing and slip the money for the gig into our pockets. They knew we couldn't knock off to count it just then. By the time the number was over and I got a chance to look in the envelope, it'd be maybe two dollars.

Billy Cox: Back then, Jimmy had a Silvertone that was painted red. He painted the name 'Betty Jean' on it—that was his childhood sweetheart. He used that guitar up to a year after we got out of the service. When we were making a little more money, I co-signed for him and he traded that in for an Epiphone. That Silvertone wound up in a music store in Clarksville.

People nicknamed him Marbles, because he'd walk up the street playing an electric guitar, he'd play it in the show, and he'd play it coming back from the theater.

Jimi Hendrix: Every Sunday afternoon, we used to go downtown and watch the race riots. Take a picnic basket because they wouldn't serve us in the restaurants. One group would stand on one side of the street and the rest on the other side. They'd shout names and talk about each other's mothers. That'd go on for a couple of hours, then we'd all go home. Sometimes, if there was a good movie on that Sunday, there wouldn't be any race riots.

November 1962: Hendrix and Cox do a recording session for local DJ Bill 'Hoss' Allen's Starday-King Records.
Bill Allen: I knew Billy Cox from when he was in the Army and I'd used him on weekends when he'd come to Nashville on leave. He told me he had a guitar-player friend, so I told him to bring him in. This was Jimmy. I told him I wanted a New Orleans chink-chink-chink rhythm thing, nothing fancy. I already had a lead guitar, all I wanted was rhythm. Well, Jimmy played loud, man. I asked him to turn it down. He was ruining the whole thing. Finally, I had to tell the engineer to cut him off, unplug him on the board.

When we played it back, Jimmy was listening and he said, 'Where's my part?' He couldn't hear it because it wasn't there. I said, 'Gee, I don't know, Jimmy. Must be something wrong with your amp.' I tell you the truth, I didn't like his sound.

13 November 1962: The guitar Hendrix bought on 1 September is returned to the store.

Christmas 1962: Jimmy travels to Vancouver, to visit Grandma Nora and Aunt Pat. While there, he plays with The Vancouvers, a Motown-style band led by Bobby Taylor and Tommy Chong (later of Cheech & Chong).

1963

January 1963: Jimmy heads for the South.
Al Hendrix: After he came out of the services, he was playing in a lot of clubs in the South. He wrote me, saying that the bosses at the clubs where his band was playing would have to get them out of jail every once in a while on account that they would go down to the theatre and sit in the white section at the show. Then the police would come in and put them in jail and the boss would have to get them out of jail. And he'd say he'd have to take that out of their wages.

March 1963: Jimmy returns to Nashville and moves in with a girlfriend, Florence Henderson.
Jimi Hendrix: You really had to play 'cos these people were hard to please. It was one of the hardest audiences in the South. Everybody knows how to play guitar. You walk down the street and people are sittin' on the porch playing more guitar. That's where I learned to play really—Nashville.

Larry Lee (rhythm guitarist): I was about the worst guitar player in Nashville and I was searching for somebody in my category, somebody to talk to. I saw the King Kasuals (in the Del Morocco) and they had these two guitars. Jimmy was on the far right... Jimmy caught my eye 'cause he looked like the cat I was looking for. So I sat down and watched him the whole set. He was just doing nothin' with the guitar, man. His guitar was an old Kay with strings about that high, and I was sure that Jimmy was somebody in my calibre that I could talk to.

Jimi Hendrix: Then we got on with a club-owner who seemed to like us a lot. He bought us some new gear. I had a Silvertone amp and the others got Fender Bandmasters. But this guy took our money and he was sort of holding us back.

Larry Lee: When I came back to the club after a few days, I introduced myself, and I saw that he needed a string. I ran home and got him an E-string. He had another guitar, a new Epiphone and a Silvertone amp, and I couldn't believe this was the same cat. I said, 'Wow, he's tricked me!' That's when I found out he really could play.

What really got me was that Jimmy would see a girl dancing and he would drop his guitar and take her to a room and he would always ask me to come and sit in and that kinda got my nerves up. I wasn't a lead guitar player.

13 March 1963: Jimmy sends Al a postcard from Columbia, South Carolina.
Jimi Hendrix: I travelled all the states and played in different groups… Top 40 R&B bands, Jackie Wilson, Wilson Pickett, Isley Brothers gigs. I got tired of feeding back 'In The Midnight Hour'.

19 May 1963: A new line-up of The King Kasuals plays at the Del Morocco, Nashville.
Billy Cox: Nine o'clock, no Jimmy. Ten o'clock, no Jimmy. We're starting to get a little worried, so I run up to the house where he lives. Knocked on the door. He says, 'Come in.' I go in. He's lying there, and I go, 'Hey, Jimmy, you're late for the gig!' He says, 'I dreamed the gig was cancelled so I went back to sleep.'

Jimmy Church (singer, King Kasuals): One time we played in Clarksville and the speaker busted. Jimmy said, 'Listen to the sound man, it's different. Don't change it, man. Listen to the sound.'

He wasn't really a band player. He would take a solo and forget he was in band. It looked like he wasn't gonna quit.

Winter 1963: After being spotted by a promoter in Nashville, Jimmy heads for New York.
Larry Lee: We were playing at The Baron. Some promoter brought in a show from New York. He was a gay cat, a sissy-acting cat. Anyway, this promoter told Jimmy he saw him play, and could get anything he wanted. If he would go back to New York, he could get Jimmy top money.

It was cold, he didn't have a coat, so I told him to take one of mine. He did write me one letter from New York. He asked me to come up there. He said, 'New York is just a big country town and we can take this town, man.' Jimmy had no responsibility, he was just footloose and fancy-free. I knew it couldn't be that easy in New York.

December 1963: Jimmy's does his first recording session, backing saxophonist Lonnie Youngblood, in Philadelphia.

31 December 1963: Jimmy meets Rosa Lee Brooks in the California Club, Los Angeles.
Rosa Lee Brooks (singer): Jimmy and I had met at the California Club in Los Angeles. We were there watching the Ike & Tina Turner Revue.

I was sitting at the bar and I felt like something was tugging at me to make me look around. Eventually, I did and I found myself looking straight at Jimi and he was looking at me. He looked just the way he does on the *Cry Of Love* album cover. He stared at me so long and intense that it became embarassing. I was attracted to him right away, but I turned away and then I got up to go to the ladies room.

He came over and put his hand on my arm and invited me to join him at his table. At the end of the night, we went back to his hotel together. We made love, and I mean extensively, all night long. The next morning, Jimmy was just real limp, and he picked up his guitar as soon as we woke.

1964

1 January 1964: Writes 'My Diary' with Rosa Lee Brooks at the Wilcox Hotel.
Rosa Lee Brooks: Jimmy sang the first verse, 'I know that I will never love again, I know that I will be my only friend' as he started playing what he called a 'love note'. The rest of the words were written by me.

My mother owned a restaurant, with a house in the back. She loved Jimmy right away, and that

"I'D GET A GIG EVERY TWELFTH OF NEVER. SLEEPING OUTSIDE BETWEEN THEM TALL TENEMENTS WAS HELL. RATS RUNNIN' ALL OVER YOUR CHEST, COCKROACHES STEALIN' YOUR LAST CANDY BAR FROM YOUR VERY POCKETS. I EVEN TRIED TO EAT ORANGE PEEL AND TOMATO PASTE"

was where we worked on the song, getting the arrangement together. We knocked on a lot of doors, trying to get hired as an Ike & Tina kind of thing. We were Jimmy & Rose, and this song was our baby.

March 1964: Recording 'My Diary'/'Utee' in Los Angeles.
Rosa Lee Brooks: Jimmy and I were back in the California Club one night and Billy Revis (owner of R&B label Revis Records) was there. I told Jimmy who he was and we both went to him and told him we had a song we would like him to hear. Billy gave us his home address and asked if we would come by the following day, which we did. We played the song for him there, and he loved it. He asked if we could get some additional voices and instruments together.

Major Lance's band was in town, performing at Ciro's on the Strip. Jimmy was the kind of guy who would walk backstage and introduce himself. We wound up partying with them that night, and Big Francis the drummer and Alvin the bass player agreed to come and do it.

I had known Arthur (Lee, later of Love), before I met Jimmy. Arthur was an up-and-coming musician, with a band called The American Four, just started, but he really didn't have much going for him musically at that time. I thought he'd be good to get in on backing vocals, along with the girls from the Honey Cone.

I went to pick Arthur up at his mother's house on 29th and Arlington Street on the day of the session. When Jimmy saw him, he became very jealous. Jimmy hardly spoke to Arthur, thinking that he and I had something more than a friendship going on. Arthur got into the back seat of my 1959 Chevy Impala, and Jimmy was up front. All was quiet during the trip, except when Jimmy spoke to me.

Arthur Lee: Jimmy Hendrix was one of the first long-haired black cats I'd ever seen. He had a suit like a priest, a hoodlum priest, with his hair directly in place and runned-over shoes.

Rosa Lee Brooks: The session took about two hours maximum, in Billy Revis's garage, which he'd converted into a studio, over on Haas Street. We nailed the song in just two takes. If you listen, you can hear that the horns and the backing voices are very loose, because they weren't really familiar with the song. Jimmy and I were the only ones who had much chance to rehearse it. Arthur Lee contributed a nice falsetto backing vocal, and he helped arrange all the back-up vocals, but that was all he did.

When we'd recorded 'My Diary', Billy Revis said, 'Well, we need a b-side.' We didn't actually have any other songs, but Alvin from Major Lance's band had been showing us the steps of a new dance called the U-T, in which you make the shapes of a U and a T, so Jimmy and I just wrote a little dance tune called 'Utee' right there in the garage.

If you listen to Jimmy's lead and rhythm guitar on 'Utee' you hear that he was way ahead of his time. He was playing his own style of rock music long before he went to England.

We spent three beautiful months together. I looked after him. We were so close in spirit, we could communicate without talking.

Late March 1964: Jimmy heads for New York.
Rosa Lee Brooks: The day Jimmy left for New York, towards the end of March, it was raining. He told me later 'One Rainy Wish' was written about that day, and about the things he'd learned while he was with me. If you listen to the intro, it's almost identical to the intro of 'My Diary'.

Jimi Hendrix: I went to New York and won first place in the Apollo amateur contest, you know, $25. So I stayed up there, starved up there for two or three weeks. I'd get a gig once every twelfth of never. Sleeping outside between them tall tenements was hell. Rats runnin' all over your chest, cockroaches stealin' your last candy bar from your very pockets. I even tried to eat orange peel and tomato paste.

March 1964: Jimmy meets Sam Cooke's ex-girlfriend, Faye Pridgeon, in the Palms Café. They go back to the Hotel Seifer, where she lives.
Faye Pridgeon: Nobody was home so we hopped in the sack. He was shy, he was extremely shy. After that first night, he just moved in with me. It wasn't hard because he was carrying all his possessions in his guitar case.

The average day consisted of waking up at noon, but not actually getting up for a couple of hours.

Jimmy loved fooling about with his guitar in bed, and he always slept with it. I used to think of my competition not as a woman, but as a guitar. Many times he fell back asleep with it on his chest. Any time I tried to remove it he woke and said, 'No, no, no, leave my guitar alone!'

All our activity took place in bed. He was well endowed. He came to the bed with the same grace a Mississippi pulpwood driver attacks a plate of collard greens and corn bread after ten hours in the sun. He was creative in bed too. There would be encore after encore, hard-driving and steamy like his music. There were times when he almost busted me in two, the way he did a guitar on stage.

March 1964: Spotted at the Palms Café, Jimmy is invited to audition with the Isley Brothers.
Ronnie Isley: We were at Palms Café, close to the Apollo, talking to a friend, Tony Rice. I told him we were looking for a guitar player, and he started telling me about this guy who had just come in on the bus and he was living at the Hotel Theresa.

Tony said the kid was the best, and that he played a right-handed guitar with his left hand. He tells me the guy's name is Jimmy Hendrix. Tony said Jimmy had sat in with the Palms' band one night and had killed everybody, so we made a date to meet him and hear him.

The night we met Jimmy, Tony went up to the bandstand and asked if Jimmy could sit in, but the guys in the band didn't want to let him on. They said, 'He plays too loud,' and I knew it was jealousy. So I said to Jimmy, 'Come out to my house at the weekend.'

We were living at Teaneck, and the band had rented a house at Englewood. Jimmy came over and I went out and bought him some strings, so he could have a full set.

When he tuned up, it was just like when he played—*wonk, woonk, wheee!* Well, we played some of our tunes, he knew them all from our records, and we hired him that afternoon.

Jimi Hendrix: The Isley Brothers asked if I'd like to play with them... They used to make me do my thing, because it made them more bucks or something. Most groups I was with, they didn't let me do my own thing.

Ernie Isley: He could play wonderfully without an amp. He would play in the hallway of our house while we were in the dining room. With his back to us, no amplifier, the sound and the feeling emanating from him was quite something.

Rosa Lee Brooks: At that time, I received a letter from Jimmy. He was living in New York, calling himself Maurice James. He had joined the Isley Brothers and asked me to send him $60 to get his guitar out of the pawn shop. I sent him the $60.

March 1964: Jimmy records 'Testify Pts 1 & 2' with The Isleys at Atlantic Studios, New York.

April 1964: Jimmy meets Buddy Miles at a gig in Montreal, Canada with the Isley Brothers.
Buddy Miles: We met in Montreal, when he was playing in the Isley Brothers band and I was with Ruby & The Romantics... He had his hair in a pony tail with long sideburns. Even though he was shy, I could tell this guy was different.

He looked rather strange, because everybody was wearin' uniforms and he was eatin' his guitar, doin' flip-flops and wearin' chains. It was really strange, man but, oh boy, he made that band.

I went nuts. We heard each other play, but we didn't have a chance to work together until about three years later.

April 1964: Jimmy and The Isleys play Seattle.
Ronnie Isley: One time we were playing his home town and Jimmy ran into an old girlfriend. He wanted to stay over, and meet us the next day in the next town. We said OK, because we thought he knew where the next gig was. He didn't show up the next day and we didn't see him until a week later in New York. His guitar had been stolen.

April 1964: Jimmy and The Isleys play Bermuda.
Ronnie Isley: We heard what sounded like a riot and figured one of the local acts must have had a big hit. But this guy came into the dressing room and said, 'Who's that out there?' So we all peeked and there was Jimmy down on his knees biting his guitar and the crowd were just going crazy.

23 September 1964: Jimmy records 'Looking For A Love' and 'The Last Girl' with the Isley Brothers at Atlantic Studios, New York. Dionne Warwick sings harmonies on 'The Last Girl'.

September 1964: Jimmy sets off with The Isleys on a 35-day tour of the US.
Ernie Isley: He played all the time. All the time. It wasn't like a thing you were listening to though, it was a simple observation—like the sun is shining, Jimmy's playing his guitar. Jimmy would practice phrases over and over again, turn them inside out, break them in half, break them in quarters, play them slow, play them fast... 'How are you doing, Jimmy?' '*Bading dada dooo*' on the guitar. 'Is it cold outside?' '*Wheeoooooow!*'

28 September 1964: Gig with The Isleys in Columbus, Ohio. Jimmy sends a postcard home:

> Dear Dad, I hope everything is fine. Well, here I am again travelling to different places. I'm on a tour which lasts about 35 days. We're about half-way through it now. We've been to all the cities in the mid-west, east and south. I'll write soon, Jimmy.

October 1964: With the Isleys in Jacksonville, Florida, Jimmy sends another card home:

> Dear Dad, Here we are in Florida. We're going to play in Tampa tomorrow, then Miami. We're playing all through the South. We'll end up in Dallas, Texas...

October 1964: Jimmy leaves the Isley Brothers.
Jimi Hendrix: You get very tired playing behind other people all the time, you know? So I quit them in Nashville somewhere...

October 1964: Jimmy visits Stax Studios in Memphis, in search of Steve Cropper.
Jimi Hendrix: I found him at the soul restaurant right across from the studio in Memphis. I was playing on this Top 40 R&B Soul Hit Parade package with the patent leather shoes and hairdo combined. So anyway, I got into the studio and said, 'Hey man, dig. I heard you're all right; that anyone can come down here if they've got a song.' So we went into the studio and did a song and after that it was just with guitar, and he was messing around with the engineering and it's just a demo acetate. I don't know where it's at now. After that we messed around four or five hours, doing different little things. It was very strange. He turned me on to a lot of things. He showed me how he played certain songs and I showed him how I played 'Mercy Mercy' or something.

November 1964: Another visit to Stax Studios.
Roland Robinson (session bassist): Jimmy was at the Satellite Record shop outside of the Stax Recording Studio dressed in a white suit, with his hair all processed. He had come over to Stax wanting to play with Steve Cropper and the guys at the studio. Cropper wasn't there, but Jimmy hooked up his stuff in the studio. He started playing a bit in his wild style and those guys just kind of laughed and walked out of the studio. Jimmy packed up his stuff and left town.

November, December 1964: After meeting Gorgeous George Odell at The Hippodrome, Nashville, Jimmy joins him as a guitarist.
Billy Cox: Gorgeous George was an entertainer that travelled with the Jackie Wilson tour. We went to the Hippodrome in Nashville and talked with Gorgeous George, but I didn't hear what I wanted to hear. But Jimmy took off and wound up on the road with George.

Jimi Hendrix: This guy was on tour with BB King, Jackie Wilson and Sam Cooke, you know, and all these people. So I was playing guitar behind a lot of the acts on the tour.

Larry Lee: He (Odell) was the kind of cat who needed no rehearsal. He would go up there and put on a show. Jimmy learned from a cat with that much courage...

BB King: Jimmy was kind of quiet, shy. He didn't open up too much, but there were questions we all ask one another—how do you do this and why do you do that... we had small discussions.

"JIMMY ALWAYS SLEPT WITH HIS GUITAR. I USED TO THINK OF MY COMPETITION NOT AS A WOMAN BUT AS A GUITAR. MANY TIMES HE FELL BACK ASLEEP WITH IT ON HIS CHEST. ANY TIME I TRIED TO REMOVE IT, HE WOKE AND SAID, 'NO, NO, NO, LEAVE MY GUITAR ALONE!'"

1964

Mid-December 1964: Jimmy misses the tour bus in Kansas City, but gets himself to Atlanta.
Jimi Hendrix: I got stranded in Kansas City without any money when a group came up and brought me back to Atlanta, Georgia, where I met Little Richard and started playing with him for about six months.

Little Richard: I first met Jimmy in Atlanta, Georgia, where he was stranded with no money. He had been working as guitarist with a feller called Gorgeous George, a black guy who sported a blond wig and wore these fabulous clothes which he made himself.

My bus was parked on Auburn Avenue and Jimmy was staying in this small hotel. And so he came by to see us. He had watched me work and loved the way I wore these headbands around my hair and how wild I dressed.

Henry Nash (assistant tour manager): Gorgeous George asked me if I would allow Jimmy Hendrix to come on the tour as his valet. I saw the manager of the package and we gave Jimmy the opportunity to load the bus as Gorgeous George's helper.

I will never forget Jimmy loading his belongings on the bus. His guitar was wrapped in a potato sack. It had only five strings on it.

Mid-December 1964: Gig at Greenville, South Carolina.
Henry Nash: After the concert that night, we went to an after-hours club and began working on the after-the-concert date. George talked me into allowing Jimmy to sit in with The Upsetters (Little Richard's band). He played the entire night with only five strings to his guitar. He made a good impression on the band though, and they welcomed having him on stage with them.

So, throughout the tour, whenever he would have after-hours dates to play, Jimmy would ask to sit in and I would allow him to. Jimmy to me was never a precision guitarist. He was not a reading musician, though he played well by ear.

Hosea Wilson (road manager): Jimmy was really a strong rhythm guitar player. He was a hell of a talent, you could tell even then. The thing is that when Jimmy was with the band, he wasn't on the band stuff, he was all quiet to himself.

1965

January 1965: Hendrix has graduated to being a full-time band member with The Upsetters.
Little Richard: He wanted to come with me, so Bumps (Blackwell), who knew his folks back in Seattle, rang Mr Hendrix to see if it was OK for him to join us. Al Hendrix told Bumps, 'Jimmy just idolises Richard. He would eat ten yards of shit to join his band.' So he came with me.

He wasn't playing my kind of music though. He was playing, like, BB King blues. He started rocking though, and he was a good guy. He began to dress like me and he even grew a little moustache like mine.

Jimi Hendrix: Little Richard wouldn't let us wear frilly shirts on stage. Once, me and Glyn Wildings got some fancy shirts because we were tired of wearing the uniform. After the show, Little Richard said, 'Brothers, we got to have a meeting. I'm Little Richard and I'm the King of Rock & Rhythm and I'm the only one who's going to look pretty on stage. Glyn and Jimmy, will you please turn in those shirts or else you will have to suffer the consequences of a fine.'

He had another meeting over my hairstyle. I said I wasn't going to cut my hair for nobody. That was another five-dollar fine. If our shoelaces were two different types we'd get fined another five bucks. Everybody on the tour was brainwashed.

25 January 1965: In Lafayette, Louisiana, Jimmy sends a card home to his father:

> Dearest Dad, I received your letter while I was in Atlanta. I'm playing with Little Richard now. We're going toward the West Coast. We're in Louisiana now, but my address will be Los Angeles when I write again, Jimmy.

27 January 1965: Jimmy plays with Little Richard at Club 500, Houston, Texas.
Albert Collins (guitarist): I met Hendrix when he was playing with Little Richard. Oooh man, he was powerful even then, he could play some blues. I was in this little club called the Club 500 in Houston. So Little Richard says, 'I got this guy with me, I want you to hear him play, he can play so good.' So I said, 'Bring him around tomorrow

night.' Then Little Richard come up and introduced us, and Jimmy asked if he could sit in.

28 January 1965: While in Dallas, Texas with Little Richard, Jimmy sends a card home:

> Dear Dad, Well, we just left Houston and we're now in Dallas. We'll play around here and Fort Worth, Tulsa, Oklahoma, and Louisiana for a while, then we'll head for California...

February 1965: After moving into the Wilcox Hotel, Hollywood, Jimmy appears on TV for the first time. He is backing Long Island vocal duo Buddy & Stacey as they perform 'Shotgun', on the US show *Night Train.*

April 1965: Jimmy returns to the Little Richard entourage in time for a gig at the Whiskey-a-Go-Go, Atlanta.
Marquelle (Little Richard's road manager): Richard used to allow him to do that playing with his teeth onstage, and take solos. It became part of the act, all that playing behind his back and stuff. Richard taught Hendrix a lot of things, and Hendrix copied a lot of things from Richard. Richard used to say, 'Look, don't be ashamed to do whatever you feel. The people can tell if you're a phoney. They can feel it out in the audience.'

April 1965: Jimmy returns to New York with Little Richard, and moves into the Theresa Hotel.

17–19 April 1965: Little Richard plays the Paramount Theater, New York.
Pat Hartley (model, friend of Hendrix): The curtain opens and there's a huge gold throne and lots of red carpet and out come two belly-dancers who couldn't belly-dance their way out of anywhere, in amazing costumes. These four guys come out and one of them was Jimmy and he was really gorgeous with his long hair and played electric guitar in between the 'bellies'.

Chuck Rainey (bassist, King Curtis Band): Throughout the whole engagement at The Paramount, I remember constantly going to my bass and trying to play lines the way I had just heard Hendrix play them. His lines were played with a lot of character—he didn't play them straight-ahead and simple: he added feeling by using dynamics, finger tremolo and, of course, his natural showmanship.

May 1965: Jimmy plays with Little Richard at various New York venues.
Peter Sando: My band, The Rahgoos, played at a club in Greenwood Lake, NY. There were many clubs there and we once saw Little Richard and his band at the Long Pond Inn. He had a big band with horns and two lead guitarists. To the left was Jimi, with sort of a processed Beatle haircut and Beatle boots, as we called them at the time. Right away I knew there was something special about this guy – his playing was unique; so fluid and thematic. He even did his playing with his teeth!

June 1965: Jimmy plays at The Apollo Theater, Harlem, with Little Richard.
Rosa Lee Brooks: Jimmy was writing and phoning me all the while. He used to make fun of Little Richard's camp mannerisms. He thought it was very girly. There were a lot of things he didn't like about being in that band, but one of the final straws was getting locked out of his hotel room one night because Little Richard's people hadn't paid the bill. It was right after that he left them.

June 1965: Jimmy leaves Little Richard's band.
Robert Penniman (Little Richard's brother): I fired Hendrix. He was a damn good guitar player, but the guy was never on time. He was always late for the bus and flirting with the girls and stuff like that. It came to a head in New York, where we had been playing the Apollo, and Hendrix missed the bus for Washington DC. I finally got Richard to cut him loose.

Jimi Hendrix: He didn't pay us for five-and-a-half weeks, and you can't live on promises when you're on the road, so I had to cut that mess loose.

I went back to New York and played with King Curtis and Joey Dee. I was trying to play my own thing but working with people like Little Richard, the Isley Brothers and Wilson Pickett, and they didn't like too much of that feedback. I was kept in the background, but I was thinking all the time about what I wanted to do.

July 65: Hendrix rejoins the Isley Brothers and plays with them at Small's Paradise, Harlem.

27 July 1965: Jimmy signs a contract with Sue Records and Copa Management, NYC.
Juggy Murray (record producer): I thought he was great. He came down to my studio a couple

of times before he signed a management and recording contract with me. At that time Jimmy wasn't playing the way that he ended up playing, but I knew the guy was going to be great.

When he was around, we would rehearse but we never completed anything. You wouldn't see him for two or three months. All this guy did was play his guitar for anybody and everybody, from when he woke up in the morning to the last thing he did before he went to bed.

5 August 1965: Jimmy records 'Move Over And Let Me Dance' and 'Have You Ever Been Disappointed' with the Isley Brothers at Atlantic Studios, New York.

8 August 1965: Jimmy writes a letter home:

> I still have my guitar and amp and as long as I have that, no fool can keep me from living. There's a few record companies I visited that I probably can record for. I think I'll start working toward that line because actually when you're playing behind other people you're still not making a big name for yourself as you would if you were working for yourself. But I went on the road with other people to get exposed to the public and see how business is taken care of...
>
> Nowadays people don't want you to sing good. They want you to sing sloppy and have a good beat to your songs. That's what angle I'm going to shoot for. That's where the money is...
>
> I just want you to know I'm still here, trying to make it. Although I don't eat every day, everything's going all right for me.

Albert Allen (friend of Faye Pridgeon): He was very self-conscious about himself... about the things he wore, because he was kind of different, you know, kind of freaky, especially in comparison to a lot of brothers at that time. He was very sensitive to the places that he liked to be in... He always stood out, he was always a stand-out person. We used to call him the Wicked Witch from the East, because of the hat he used to wear.

1 September 1965: Jimmy writes a letter to Faye Pridgeon. Their relationship is ending.
Faye Pridgeon: Jimmy and I had gone through some hard times. We were down to our last dollar and debating whether we should buy the cat some food or share a hot dog. The ASPCA made the decision for us: they charged us our last dollar to take the cat away because we couldn't feed it.

September 1965: Hendrix and Curtis Knight introduced to record producer Ed Chalpin.
Curtis Knight: I stopped in at a cheap hotel on 47th Street (Hotel America) which had a small recording studio in the lobby. As I stood by the elevator, I met Jimmy Hendrix. He said that he played guitar, but he had to pawn it to pay the rent, which was again overdue. I told Jimmy to return to his room while I went to fetch a guitar.

I entered the room, and laying on the bed was a girl who Jimmy introduced as Faye Pridgeon. He plugged in the guitar and in a matter of minutes did things that I had never imagined possible. I told him that the guitar was my gift to him.

October 1965: Jimi joins Curtis Knight & The Squires, and plays with them on and off.
Curtis Knight: Many was the night that he would say to me at the end of the gig, 'Well, ah, Curtis, I don't think I'll be riding back to the city with you. Someone has invited me for breakfast.'

Arthur Allen (friend): I remember Jimi with all of his records, stacks of Elmore James, Lightnin' Hopkins and all of the blues greats. In those days, most black entertainers were not getting into the depths of black music, its roots. Most performers thought, 'It's me!' Totally an ego thing. Hendrix, even though he couldn't read music, would still study it and take you into areas that nobody really knew. He would even get into white music and, when you found a black entertainer would study white music, you knew the guy was serious.

15 October 1965: Hendrix signs a contact with Ed Chalpin's PPX Enterprises, New York
Ed Chalpin: In almost 40 years of my career as a producer and manager, I have at most taken eight acts under contract. They had to be something special. One of them was Jimmy Hendrix. Jimmy was to sing, play and arrange for me exclusively. The contract was signed in the Hotel America on the night of the 15th October 1965. At that time it was usual to insert the clause 'For one dollar and other good and valuable consideration' in contracts.

Nashville, home to so many skilled Country pickers, was where Hendrix said he really learned how to play the guitar

The Isley Brothers were one of the bands with whom Hendrix gained early professional experience as backing musician

October 1965: Jimmy records 'Suey' with Jayne Mansfield at Dimensional Studios, New York.
George 'King George' Clemons: When I went to New York, Jimi was one of the first people I started to talk with. In fact, we were living next door to each other. He used to lose his key and come and sleep in my house. Jimi turned me on to Bob Dylan. In Harlem they were only playing soul music. Jimi brought in a record and said, 'You've got to listen. This guy is really great.' I didn't think very much of his voice. Then I found out that he was more or less a poet, where Jimi was getting into. He was right into these poetic things, that a lot of people around him didn't seem to understand. Especially in the black community.

Once Jimi came into a black club, and they were playing Wilson Pickett. So Jimi takes it off and he puts on a Bob Dylan record, 'Blowin' In The Wind'. So all the black guys standing there are saying, 'What are you doing? Are you crazy?' To many blacks back then, Dylan sounded like a hillbilly, a redneck. And Jimi didn't care about this, so he played that record. So this guy told him, 'I'm going to cut your throat.' So I said, 'Wait a minute now! Stop! We take the record off.' And I took Jimi into this other room, and I said, 'Why are you doing that? You know there is gonna be trouble about that.' He said, 'These people in Harlem have to learn. They can't go around like this without knowing what's going on.'

23 November 1965: During a ten-day tour with Joey Dee & The Starliters, Jimmy arrives in Revere, Massachusetts and writes a letter home:

> Dear Dad, We're in Boston, Mass. We'll be here for about ten days. We're actually playing in Revere… I'm playing up here with Joey Dee & The Starlighters. I hope everything's alright. We're right next to the ocean, across the street! Jimmy.

December 1965: At a nightclub in Lodi, New Jersey, Hendrix is seen by Les Paul.

Les Paul: It was one of those funny nights. My number two son, Gene, and I were taking master tapes from our home in Mahwah, New Jersey to Columbia Records in New York.

We decided to drive by a nightclub in Lodi, New Jersey, which usually had good talent. I stopped the car and, as usual, Gene looked in. He came back out and said, 'Father, you better look for yourself. There's a guy playing all over the guitar.'

I went in and stood in the doorway to listen. I was really impressed by what I heard. Yes indeed, that dude was really working his guitar over. He was bending string, playing funky as hell. I'd never seen anyone so radical.

We had to push on to New York, but we decided that after we'd dumped those tapes, we'd hurry back to the club and nail that guy.

A couple of hours later, that's what we tried to do. When we got back and asked around, the bartender told me some black dude had come in earlier to audition but that his playing was too crazy for them—too wild and too loud, so he and the group he was with hadn't been hired. When last seen, about an hour before Gene and I could get back, the guitarist had been fooling around on the piano in the club. That's all anyone could tell us. No one there knew his name or where he could be found.

Gene and I called musicians' locals all around New York and New Jersey—no one knew who we were talking about. Finally, we decided to look in every single nightclub in north and central Jersey, and also in Harlem, uptown. But, with no name and only a description of a wild man with a guitar—different than what's around, more funky, raunchy—people just looked at us.

December 1965: Jimmy meets Devon Wilson.
Al Aronowitz (journalist, New York Post*):* She was

"ONCE JIMI CAME INTO A BLACK CLUB AND THEY WERE PLAYING WILSON PICKETT. JIMI TAKES IT OFF AND HE PUTS ON A BOB DYLAN RECORD, 'BLOWIN' IN THE WIND'. SO ALL THE BLACK GUYS STANDING THERE ARE SAYING, 'WHAT ARE YOU DOING? ARE YOU CRAZY?'"

1965

one of the most beautiful and sensuous of the groupies, and one of the most successful too. I first met her in the '60s when she was hanging out with I forget which superstar, but whenever a rock hero came to New York, the chances were you'd find Devon in his hotel room. They used to recommend her to one another. Her sex was overwhelming.

Devon Wilson: I was attracted to Jimmy's flamboyance, even though at that time he wasn't an established star. He had a certain visible flair about him: his hair was longer than any other black musician's that I'd ever seen, and in an original style.

I introduced Jimmy to his first acid trip, and he liked it a lot. He tried various pills with me and our relationship became one of excitement and exhilaration. He sniffed cocaine, but he had no desire at all to get into heroin at that time, because he knew that this was a one-way street that led to nowhere.

Curtis Knight: There were a number of things about Devon which Jimmy felt attracted to. She was, above all, magnetic, and she was also attractive, and totally into sex...

Alvenia Bridges (friend of Hendrix): She was a pretty wild lady, but she loved Jimi and he loved her and she ran the show. She told people where to sit at clubs.

26 December 1965: Live recording, including 'I'm A Man', with Curtis Knight at George's Club 20, Hackensack, New Jersey.

1966

January 1966: Jimmy joins King Curtis' band for about six months.
Cornell Dupree: Jimmy and I played together for about six or eight months, sharing lead guitar with King Curtis. When I knew him, Jimmy was a pretty quiet guy. He never really had too much to say unless something was drastically wrong—unless you stepped on his foot or harmed him. He would go off by himself or just disappear. You'd never see him 'til it was time to go to work.

Bernard Purdie (drummer): On a lot of songs that Jimmy didn't know the bass player had to whisper the chords to him. But I never in all my life saw anybody pick up songs as fast as Jimmy did that night. In a couple of days he knew everything, so he didn't have any problem.

Ellen McIlwane (Greenwich Village performer): I used to play with Jimmy Hendrix. I don't think Jimmy ever played with women before. There weren't that many women around. I played piano. I didn't play guitar when he was with me. He played lead guitar. He sat on a barstool and he played and didn't try to steal the show and act macho and everything.

It was real interesting getting to know him, because he was real difficult to get to know. I don't know if anybody ever really did. He was withdrawn. Music was the way he communicated. Music was everything. He lived it and breathed it. He was always interested in hearing everybody. I never heard him put anybody down.

When I was playing with him, I called my manager and I said, 'I've found a guitar player.' And he said, 'Well, who is he?' I said, 'You've got to come down and hear him, his name is Jimmy Hendrix and he's really good.' He said, 'I heard about him.' I said, 'Well, come hear him.' He said, 'No, no. You don't want him in your band, he's black.' I said, 'I don't want you to be my manager.'

13 January 1966: Jimmy sends a postcard back home to Seattle:

> Everything's so-so in this big raggedy city of New York. Everything's happening bad here—I hope everyone at home is all right... Tell Leon I said hello... Tell Ben and Ernie I play the blues like they never heard.

21 January 1966: Jimmy adds guitar to Ray Sharpe's 'Help Me (Parts One & Two)' at Atlantic Studios, New York.

24 January 1966: Jimmy records with King Curtis Band in New York.
Mike Quashie (singer and dancer): Jimmy would come into the African Room, and the owners of the place would freak. He'd have these three hookers with him. At least they looked like hookers, and the owners thought Jimmy was a

The great BB King was another of Hendrix's ealiest and most enduring influences. Later he would get to jam with him

pimp, with his wild clothes and his processed hair and his do-rag. They didn't want him in the place, didn't want that crowd at all.

14 February 1966: Jimmy plays at The Cheetah Club, New York.
Curtis Knight: The couches and wall decor were in a fabric that really looked like the coat of a cheetah. (Jimi and I) went down the Village and found some material that was almost the same as the decor at the club and we designed ourselves shirts and jackets out of it. We added white bell-bottoms and we looked like we were coming out of the walls.

Tom Flye (Lothar & The Hand People): You knew there was something about that guy. He would walk down Bleecker Street with his guitar over his shoulder like a lumberjack.

April 1966: Jimmy plays at The Cheetah, supporting Richie Havens and Carl Holmes.
Richie Havens: I walked in the door, it's early at night… it's empty. This place was a ballroom and there were about 50 people there. I see this guy standing on the stage biting his guitar. Like, what the heck is he doing? What is that, you know? And I look for the other guitar player, 'cause I'm saying he can't be making those notes. Where's the other guitar player? No other guitar player! I was up under that stage man, and it's only about three feet from the floor. I was on my knees, trying to look under the guy's guitar, 'What is he doing?'

28 April 1966: Jimmy records 'Linda Lou', 'Baby How About You?' and 'I Can't Take It' with King Curtis at Atlantic Studios, New York.
Carol Shiroky (girlfriend): I met him at a friend's house and he was sitting in the middle of the living room on an amp, strumming, and I didn't like him. I thought he was on an ego trip. It was like 'hi' and that was that.

May 1966: Jimmy attends a party at Atlantic Records, New York.
Wilson Pickett: Atlantic Records was giving us a party and Jimmy was playing with King Curtis, who attended the party in New York.

Mid-May 1966: Jimmy moves into Hotel Lennox with Carol Shiroky.
Carol Shiroky: 'Wild Thing' was born in the Hotel Lennox. He came home one night and asked me if I'd heard that song. It was on the radio a day or so later. He came flying out of the bathroom, butt-ass naked, hair in rollers, listening to the radio, picked up the guitar and started playing it. He loved that song. He listened to it once or twice and that was it—music came so easy to him.

13 May 1966: Jimmy begins two-week stint at The Cheetah club, New York with Curtis Knight & The Squires.
Carol Shiroky: He came over to my table and he said, 'I wanna tell you something, but I bet you're gonna laugh.' I said, 'I won't laugh.' He said, 'No, you're gonna laugh.' 'I promise I won't laugh.' 'Well, I wanna kiss you on your knee.' So, of course, I laughed. Three days later we moved in together. It was like an instant fire kind of thing.

Jimmy used to always say he was not from this planet, he was from somewhere out in space. That was his great line when he got in a crazy-ass mood… You know what he ate for breakfast? Spaghetti and garlic. I said, 'What do you want for breakfast? Eggs?' 'Eggs? Damn! I want spaghetti and garlic—no sauce.'

He was having a lot of problems with Curtis. He was unhappy, having fights about not being paid, or being paid a pittance, you know? Just enough to keep him fed and that was about it.

May 1966:
Linda Keith (then Keith Richards' girlfriend):
I was sitting near the back of The Cheetah when I noticed a guitarist in the back line of Curtis Knight's band whose playing mesmerized me. After the set, I had Mark check him out to see if he wanted to come have a drink with us. Fortunately, he did.

He was very naïve, very shy and nervous, and he didn't look at you when he spoke to you. And he came back to the apartment and played a lot of Dylan.

20 May 1966: At The Cheetah, New York, Jimmy plays his final gig with Curtis Knight.
Carol Shiroky: I asked him one night, I said, 'Why are you with Curtis? You don't need him—he needs you.' And he said, 'Because it's his guitar.' Two days later I bought him a white Fender Stratocaster. That's what he wanted. That

Little Richard was another early employer. His flamboyant outfits and style taught Hendrix much about showmanship

was the love of his life and he sat there for hours filing the frets down so the strings would fit in reverse. That was his baby. Then he left Curtis and Curtis never forgave me for that.

27 May 1966: Start of one-week stint at The Cheetah, New York, with Carl Holmes & The Commanders.
Linda Keith: He was living uptown in Harlem but he would stay at the Red House (an apartment owned by Linda's friends Roberta Goldstein and Mark Kauffman) as we called it for days on end. I would play loads of music, trying to motivate him, something he desperately needed. It seemed silly, me a middle-class white girl playing him the blues.

I was always pushing him to play the blues and he was rejecting that, in part because his great influences were Buddy Guy and Otis Rush, and he felt that he could not match up to them, certainly not in terms of his vocals.

10 June 1966: As a member of Curtis Knight & The Squires, Jimmy signs a recording contract with Jerry Simon of RSVP Records.

June 1966: Jimmy forms Jimmy James & The Blue Flames.
Randy California (guitarist, later of Spirit): I met Jimi in Manny's Music store. He was in the back of the store playing a Strat. Our eyes caught each other and I asked him if I could show him some things I learned on the guitar. He then gave me the Strat and I played slide guitar.

He really liked it and invited me down that night, which I believe was his first night of this gig at the Cafe Wha? I don't think he played anything solo before then. I'll never forget that moment our eyes met and froze on each other. Some type of real spiritual affinity or connection happened between us. It was like we knew each other.

I remember we went back to the dressing room—the boiler room, and this is where Jimi taught me 'Hey Joe', 'Wild Thing', 'Shot Gun' and some standard blues things. I know he showed me the chords to 'Hey Joe' because I had never heard that before.

For three months we did five sets a night as Jimmy James & The Blue Flames. We made about $60 a night and Jimmy split it equally four ways. The bass player was named Randy also, so Jimmy called him Randy Texas and me Randy California, so that's how I got my name.

We were mostly doing cover stuff, like 'Hey Joe', 'Wild Thing' and 'High Heel Sneakers'. We used to jam a lot and some of the songs would turn out to be pretty long. We used to do 'Look Over Yonder' with double lead.

Peter Sando: When my band The Rahgoos played at the Night Owl Cafe in Greenwich Village, all the musicians were buzzing about this cat who was around the Corner at the Cafe Wha?, Jimmy James & The Blue Flames. From the descriptions, I had a feeling he was the same guy I had seen in 1965 with Little Richard. I tried to coerce my bandmates to go with me on our break to see the show, but no one would spring for the $2 cover charge, so I went alone. Wow! He was now playing with only two sidemen and was totally freaky in his dress. It was a sparse crowd in a dinky club, but he did the whole thing anyway – played with his teeth, and burned his guitar on 'Wild Thing'! Amazing.

Carol Shiroky: You couldn't hold him down. If you tried to hold him down, that's when you lost him. There were nights he didn't come home and I knew he was in someone else's bed and I would never question him, because if I did he'd be gone.

Jeanette Jacobs (singer): He used to grab drinks out of my hand and say, 'You've had enough.' His mother used to drink. 'Please, don't drink. You're the only girl who could make me cry, apart from my mother.' He said to me, 'You're going to have all the clothes you want when I'm a big star.' He'd take down the addresses of clothes shops and say, 'You can have this, and that...'

Mike Quashie: I was workin' in the African Room, right across the street from the Lennox Hotel where Jimmy was staying. He was goin' by the name of Jimmy James and he came into the club all the time. I teased him about his Vaselined hair. It was long, but he was wearin' it greased, and I'd say, 'Wha' fo', baby? You tryin' to be Nat King Cole? Woooooo! Wha' kine nigger are you?'

At the time, I didn't know his real name. I only knew him as Jimmy or JJ. Sometimes I called him JC for Jimmy Coon. He'd come in, see my show, and I'd go see him in his hotel room, usually to buy some speed. I was into speed a long time, and I gave Jimmy $10, $20, lots of times.

Jeff Baxter: I met Hendrix when I was working at Manny's Music Shop in New York. Jimmy was playing in the Village at the time with a group called Jimmy James & The Blue Flames, and I had my eye on an old guitar he was using. When he came into the shop, I offered to trade him a white Strat that I'd just done a fret job on, for his axe, and he agreed.

Carol Shiroky: They used to put him on at the end of the evening, 'cos he would go off. The last song would be 45 minutes of feedback and freak everybody out. We'd all be sitting there, the place would be dark, they'd be mucking about with the lights, and he would just get lost in himself. We would leave there exhausted.

Kim King (guitarist, Lothar & The Hand People): We had jammed a bunch of times before (at The Night Owl) but one time he came in with these killer series of chords—no song, no title, no nothing—just a great series of chord progressions. We played this every day for hours, until Jimmy suddenly disappeared. I later found out when, sometime thereafter, I heard him described as 'England's newest sensation', that these chords had been to 'Hey Joe'.

Carol Shiroky: He got very frustrated very easily if things didn't go right. I saw him lay down on the stage and cry during a performance. I've seen him walk offstage because he broke a string and leave the other guys sitting there like 'OK, what do we do now?'

Bob Kulik (guitarist, Random Blues): Even then he definitely had 'Hey Joe' and he used to perform a rough version of '3rd Stone From The Sun'. He broke a string during one show (at The Night Owl) and he threw a fit afterwards. I couldn't understand what the problem was. I figured he just didn't have the particular string he needed, so I opened up my case and gave him one. His eyes lit up, and it was only then that I realized how badly off he was.

Jimi Hendrix: We were making something like $3 a night and, you know, we were starving.

Paul Caruso (Greenwich Village harmonica player who will be namechecked by Hendrix on Axis: Bold As Love*)* : I was looking for people to play with. I saw Jimmy at the Café Wha?. He was playing with The Blue Flames and had Randy California in the band with him. It was the most powerful blues playing I had ever heard. The scene was pretty liberal, and people could jam and get to know each other pretty easily.

He was a Dylan freak. We talked about Dylan a lot, the symbolism and poetry of his lyrics and just how brilliant he was. Jimmy was very self-conscious about his lack of education and his speech. He was impressed by people who could speak well. That's one of the reasons why he got into Dylan, because it was very literate rock'n'roll.

Jimi Hendrix: I love Dylan. I only met him once, about three years ago (1966) back at The Kettle Of Fish on MacDougal Street. That was before I went to England. I think both of us were pretty drunk at the time, so he probably doesn't remember it.

23 June 1966: Al Hendrix marries Ayako June Fujita in Seattle and adopts her daughter Janie.

Late June 1966: Linda Keith tries to interest Rolling Stones manager Andrew Loog Oldham in Jimmy Hendrix.
Linda Keith: From the hotel suite we were sharing, I borrowed a new, white Fender Stratocaster from Keith Richards, though I must admit the circumstances were actually less savoury than

"THEY USED TO PUT HIM ON AT THE END OF AN EVENING, 'COS HE WOULD GO OFF. THE LAST SONG WOULD BE 45 MINUTES OF FEEDBACK AND FREAK EVERYBODY OUT. WE'D ALL BE SITTING THERE AND HE WOULD JUST GET LOST IN HIMSELF. WE WOULD LEAVE THERE EXHAUSTED"

1966

that. I never actually told Keith that I had taken the guitar because he was away on tour. Jimmy used that guitar for his first audition and thereon in. I doubt Keith ever knew it was missing.

I told this record producer there was this fantastic guitar player and singer playing in the village, and would he come down and listen to him because he's really going to like this, a very materialistic man. And he came down. He thought I was mad. He did not see what I was talking about. When he saw Jimmy, he saw this nothing.

Late June 1966: Linda Keith convinces producer Seymour Stein to see Hendrix at the Café Au Go Go.
Linda Keith: He wasn't as negative as Oldham had been, but he didn't want any part of him either. I couldn't believe these people weren't seeing what I was seeing. To me, Jimmy's talents seemed so clear.

Marc Silber (owner, the Fretted Instruments Shop): Jimmy James & The Blue Flames gained quickly in fame and were playing all about the Village, and then further. I was playing electric bass with The Children Of Paradise and running my shop in the daytimes. Jimi would stop in to try out guitars. He was very quiet, shy and polite, and he could play an acoustic like John Lee Hooker or Lightnin' Hopkins, and that really impressed me. Acoustic guitar was my territory, and Jimi did it very well and it surprised me.

Once I asked him for advice on who to study electric blues from. Jimi said, 'It's only a matter of the three Kings.' I remember thinking this was some sort of Christian reference but eventually I realized he meant Albert King, Freddie King and BB King.

After a few visits to my shop, and hanging out a bit after hours in the restaurants and pubs in the Village I felt I sort of knew him. He was getting some fancy clothes made by my then girlfriend, Phyllis Meshover. Phyllis was a waitress in one of the clubs, and we would all be hanging there. She and another girl named Ann had this side business of making special clothing.

2 July 1966: The Rolling Stones see Jimmy James & The Blue Flames perform at Ondine's, New York.

Sheila Oldham (wife of Andrew Loog Oldham): Linda was madly in love with Jimmy and wanted a committed relationship. She was quite desperate to get something going, but Hendrix was involved with somebody else.

Linda Keith: At the point that I met Jimmy, my involvement with Keith was running out. It was almost out and done. Our relationship was maybe hanging from a thread.

Keith Richards: I had a chick run off with Jimi Hendrix once. I think he's a nice cat actually.

4 July 1966: Linda Keith convinces Chas Chandler to see Jimmy at The Café Wha?
Jeff Baxter: We used to get together down at the old Café Wha? and jam for hours. That whole R&B guitar style that we now take for granted grew out of what Jimmy was doing. It's been integrated into most guitarists' work, but in many cases they don't realize how much of it originated with Jimmy.

Chas Chandler: The night before we (The Animals) were to play in Central Park, someone played me Tim Rose's version of 'Hey Joe' which had been out for about nine months in America. I was so taken by it that I vowed, 'As soon as I get back to England, I'm going to find an artist to record this song.' Later that evening, we went out to a club called Ondine's. As we walked in, Linda Keith came walking out and we stopped to talk. She told me she was going out with this guy in the Village, that I had to see.

It hadn't been public, but my friends knew I was getting into record production after The Animals' impending split, and Linda suggested her friend might be just the guy to start with. So I made arrangements to meet her the next afternoon.

5 July 1966: Chandler sees Jimmy at the Café Wha?
Chas Chandler: I went down to the Village and saw Jimmy James & The Blue Flames perform at Café Wha?. It just so happened that the first song Hendrix played that afternoon was 'Hey Joe'.

Ken Pine (guitarist, The Ragamuffins): Chas was so excited that he kept hitting me with his elbow. I thought he was going to crush me. I didn't think he was going to survive the set.

Les Paul and Mary Ford: early guitar innovator Les wanted to sign Hendrix when in New York but couldn't find him again

Chas Chandler: As much as his version of 'Hey Joe' impressed me, what convinced me of his talent was another song he did that day, 'Like A Rolling Stone'. I knew Dylan well and loved his material, but 'Like A Rolling Stone' was the first of his songs which I didn't quite get. It was something about the way Dylan sang the song. I never felt he expressed it properly. When Jimmy sang it, he did it with tremendous conviction, and the lyrics came right through to me.

Bob Kulik: Chandler was so excited by Jimmy's performance that he spilled some of the milk served to him in his lap.

Chas Chandler: I wasn't impressed with the Blue Flames at all. They were a pick-up band who sounded as if Jimmy had met them that day. I didn't bother to make a recording of any of their performances, because the drummer was lousy. Randy California, the other guitar player, was a nice young kid, but all he wanted to do was play blues, and I didn't think that just playing blues was the way to make a hit with Jimmy Hendrix.

Chas Chandler: We just sat and talked for about an hour. I was astonished to hear that nobody had ever signed him, apart from some small labels, where he felt he was actually under contract as a session man. I remember him telling me that he viewed those agreements as a guarantee of session work—not as a recording contract.

Hendrix wanted to know why we couldn't use Randy California. Randy was 15 years old. The first thing that would happen was that we would be arrested. Jimmy genuinely wanted to bring Randy to England but I was adamant that he made space between them. I said, 'Jimmy, how the fuck am I going to get a visa for a 15-year-old runaway? Do you understand what implications there are with something like that? You just can't do it.'

Jimmy was worried about the equipment we had in England and what the musicians were like. One of the first things he asked me was if I knew Eric Clapton. I said I knew Eric very well, and I saw a lot of him socially at that time. He said, 'Well, if you take me to England, will you take me to meet Eric?' I told him that when Eric heard him play, he would be falling over to meet Jimmy, and that clinched it.

I told him I was going off to tour with The Animals but I would be back in a week or so. I left saying, 'I'll come back to New York and, if you still feel like it, I'll take you to England and we'll start.' Jimmy said, 'Fair enough.'

August 1966:
John Sebastian: John Hammond really noticed Jimmy before anybody did. Jimmy was working down at the Café Wha? as Jimmy James & The Blue Flames—three or four fairly terrible musicians and Jimmy, who was just scary, you know?

John Hammond: I met Jimmy in the fall of 1966. One night between shows, my friend who was working in the Players' Theater came over and said, 'John, there's this band playing downstairs that you've got to hear. This guy is doing songs off your old album, and he sounds better than you.' So I thought I'd check this out. I went down there. And he was playing the guitar parts better than Robbie Robertson had.

6 August 1966: The Animals finish their tour.
Terry McVay (The Animals' tour manager): The Animals finished their tour with Herman's Hermits on August 6 in Atlantic City. We were all going to New York to visit friends and catch our breath before leaving for London.

7 August 1966: Chas Chandler returns to New York.
Chas Chandler: I checked into the Gorham Hotel, where Hilton Valentine (The Animals) and I shared a suite, and began running around the village trying to find Jimmy.

Jimmy was very vague about his living situation. I knew that he had a room in a place on Broadway, but he never seemed to stay there.

Linda Keith: He seemed petrified to make an honest commitment to anyone. He would be in Manhattan with me and then uptown with Faye Pridgeon. At first Jimmy would only refer to her as 'Auntie Faye', not in a deceitful way, but nonetheless I was never quite sure if she was his aunt or his girlfriend. There would always be a twinkle in his eye when he would say he'd have to go uptown and see Auntie Faye. As it was, his life in Harlem was strictly off-limits to me, but I think that Faye and I must have provided Jimmy with separate halves of a whole emotional need.

13 August 1966: John Hammond Jr joins forces with Jimmy James under the name The Screaming Night Hawkes. They begin rehearsing.
John Hammond Jr: When my job was through at The Gaslight, Jimmy and I got together and worked out with a little group we had. There was a guy in his band named Randy Wolfe, but he called himself Randy California, he was fantastic, playing slide guitar. I was just playing harmonica and singing because these guys were heavyweight guitar players. Jimmy did one solo number, a Bo Diddley tune, 'I'm A Man', I think. We rehearsed and opened about two weeks later at the Café Au Go Go. We worked out there for two weeks, and it was fantastic. Everybody came to hear us.

Marc Silber: Jimi got to do one song at the end of the last set, which was 'Hey Joe', which I knew because it had been written by a guy I met in Chicago in 1961, named 12-String Billy Roberts. Well, John Hammond had done such good sets all night, but Jimi just stole the show.

27 August 1966: The Screaming Night Hawkes win a two-week booking at the Café Au Go Go.
Jimi Hendrix: I got a break playing guitar for John Hammond Jr at the Café Au Go Go. That was great because the ceiling was really low and dusty. I'd stick the guitar right up into the ceiling. It was like war.

Bob Dylan: First time I saw him, he was playing with John Hammond. He was incredible then. I'd already been to England and beyond, and although he didn't sing, I kinda had a feeling that he figured into things.

Michael Bloomfield: I was the hot-shot guitarist on the block. I thought I was it. I'd never heard of Hendrix. Then someone said, 'You've got to see the guitar player with John Hammond.' I went straight across the street and saw him.

Hendrix knew who I was and, that day, in front of my eyes, he burned me to death. I didn't even get my guitar out. H-bombs were going off, guided missiles were flying—I can't tell you the sounds he was getting out of his instrument. He was getting every sound I was ever to hear him get, right there in that room with a Stratocaster, a twin, a Maestro fuzztone and that was all... He just got right up in my face with that axe and I didn't want to pick up a guitar for the next year.

Robbie Robertson: John Hammond Jr called me, because I had played on a couple of his records, and he said, 'I just got a new guitar player and you should come down and hear us play tonight.' So I went down there, and this guy was playing with his teeth and behind his back, and made an amazing sound. After the gig, we went outside and we were talking and he was asking me a lot about songwriting. He said, 'I want to write songs, but I don't know much about it.' He was looking for advice. He knew I was working with Bob Dylan, and he asked me what sparked his songs—did he write them on the piano? I said, 'No, usually on the typewriter.'

I met him a couple of times after that. I remember him sitting on a bed, showing me how he changed guitar strings. He had the tuning pegs between his legs and he would haul the string through, and keep pulling it and massaging the strings as he did it. He said that he'd found that if he did it that way, then the strings didn't break so soon and the guitar stayed in tune better.

Stefan Grossman: During the two weeks that Hammond and Hendrix performed at the Au Go Go, I caught their set regularly. Hendrix played straight blues. He never used distortions. His lead playing somehow combined R&B sounds with BB King-style lead lines and a John Lee Hooker rhythmic approach. His singing had a touch of Hooker and Muddy Waters, though I had the impression that Hendrix's biggest vocal influence at the time was John Hammond.

John Sebastian: He really dug John Hammond... and he really learned a lot of old blues off John Hammond records. So, in a lot of ways, Jimi is really unique second generation.

Randy California: When we were backing up John Hammond, we used to run back and forth between the Café Wha? and the Café Au Go Go.

There was some good money involved too. I think we made about twenty bucks each on the nights that we worked with John. On the other nights when we just worked at the Cafe Wha?, I think it was only seven or eight bucks.

9 September 1966: Chas Chandler begins working towards bringing Hendrix to the UK.
Abby Schroeder (music publisher): Chandler

Touring was often an exhausting nightmare for the Experience, with gigs hundreds of miles apart on consecutive nights

brought Hendrix to our office in early September. He didn't have a passport, didn't have a birth certificate and didn't even have real shoes. They came to us because we had offices in both New York and London and Chas felt comfortable with that. We signed him up right away even though he didn't have a thing on tape with him. I just knew something was going to happen with that guy.

Leon Dicker (The Animals' US representative/attorney): Chas called me and set up a meeting. There, in my outer office, sitting alongside Chandler, was a gentleman dressed in an Indian-styled outfit. I invited them in and we discussed Chandler's plan. Chandler wanted me to advance him money from his account so that he could take Hendrix to England.

I was immediately impressed with Hendrix. He was shy but well-spoken with a wonderful personality. I gave Chas the money and offered to do everything I could to help them.

12 September 1966: An application is sent to Seattle Records Office, requesting a copy of Jimmy's birth certificate.
Leon Dicker: To obtain a passport for Hendrix, we had to find his birth certificate but the authorities told me no such man was ever born.

Chas Chandler: He had nothing, as he hadn't been home in so long. Finally, when Hilton Valentine left for London, Jimmy and I used the suite we had shared as an office to send letters and telegrams back to his father to get all the details. Jimmy had an address but he didn't even know if his father was still living there.

Mid-September 1966: Chas Chandler devises a name for Jimmy's next band.
Chas Chandler: The first sort of thing was Jimmy Hendrix & The Experience... and I was going 'The Jimmy Hendrix Experience' and that was decided before I even left New York.

19 September 1966: Jimmy's birth certificate is finally located.
Leon Dicker: A couple of weeks passed until one of my old classmates from college, who lived in Seattle, intervened. There was a certificate, but it had been filed under John Allen Hendrix, the name his mother had given him when his father was away in the service.

Chas Chandler: I went down and found Scott English, a songwriter from the Brill Building, who was a big mate of mine. To help us get Jimmy's passport, Scott agreed to say that he had known Jimmy for years.

I got a list of people he had signed agreements with. I started going around, buying them up, including his agreement with Sue Records. Unfortunately, the one he didn't mention was with Ed Chalpin and PPX. Jimmy thought it was nothing more than another session-man agreement.

At the same time as I was buying his contracts up, I was thinking that we had to get some musicians together. I was determined, however, to do this in London.

23 September 1966: Jimmy is issued with US passport, No G 1044108.
Randy California: One day I arrived to find that Jimmy'd split for England. That was the end of it.

24 September 1966: Chas and Jimmy leave New York for London, where they first stop off at the apartment of Zoot Money (UK R&B group leader) and then book into Hyde Park Towers.

Chas Chandler: On the plane, he'd been worrying how his American style of playing would fit with English guys, so I decided when we got to London airport to drive to Zoot Money's, which was on the way into town. I thought, if he met Zoot, it would dispel his fears about English musicians. We arrived at Zoot's house at 11 o'clock in the morning.

Zoot Money: I had known Chas from the days when he and The Animals first came to London. For some reason, when they landed in England, Jimi didn't have a guitar. Chas was planning to show Jimi off around the clubs, but Jimi didn't want to do that without playing.

So Chas brought him round my house because he knew I'd have guitars around. We chatted for about an hour, and the first thing I noticed about him was that he was very courteous, which was uncommon in the music business at that time.

My whole band lived in the house, which had been split up into flats. It was a musician's enclave. I offered Jimi my Wampree, a rather

Randy Califonia, later of Spirit, learned his craft as a 15-year-old working with Hendrix in New York's Greenwich Village

unusual model, which he didn't like the look of so I had to find him something else.

My guitarist, Andy Summers, was out that day, but I could get down to the basement where he kept his guitars, so I nipped down and brought back a Telecaster and gave that to Jimi on loan.

Chas Chandler: Jimi started jamming for two or three hours. The house was full of musicians and it made him feel he could settle in England. He took to Zoot like a fish to water.

Zoot Money: When I heard him play, it was obvious that all forms of blues or black music had gone through him. He was able to play all forms of blues, gospel, whatever you want to call it.

Kathy Etchingham (upstairs neighbor): Ronni (Zoot Money's wife) came running up to my flat and said, 'Kathy, you gotta come down. Chas has just brought this guy back from America and he looks like the Wild Man of Borneo.' So I said, 'All right, I'll come down,' but I wasn't so keen to get out of bed and by the time I got down they were leaving, so I didn't meet him. But Ronnie said they were all going down to the Scotch of St James (club) that evening.

When we got in there, there was a group in the corner on a rostrum, and there was Jimmy and Chas and they all waved and said, 'Over here!' So we all introduced ourselves and Jimmy leaned over towards me and said, 'I want to tell you something,' and I said, 'What is it?' and I put my head forward. He kissed my ear and said, 'I think you're beautiful.'

Zoot Money: As I recall, Jimi was a little reluctant to play with the band that was on that night. He waited until the break, and sat on a stool by himself, and he just played blues. Nothing flashy, none of the showmanship that came later, but just exceptionally good blues guitar.

Pete Townshend: I was very unimpressed with Jimi that day. He was wearing a beat-up US Marines jacket, and he looked scruffy, jet-lagged, and pock-marked. I thought, 'Ugh!' Two days later, I saw him play at Blaises and it was devastating.

Kathy Etchingham: Anyway, we're all sitting there having a drink and a fight broke out between Ronni Money and this girl… who turned out to be Linda Keith.

Zoot Money: My memory is of this so-called fight being on a subsequent night at the Scotch, but the essence of it was that Linda had got the impression that my wife, Ronni, was after Jimi, which she wasn't. Linda grabbed Ronni and a small scuffle came about, which Ronni was well able to deal with.

Kathy Etchingham: Plates started flying across the table. Everybody said, 'Let's go!' so I stood up and Jimmy grabbed my hand. Chas said to me, 'Take him back to the Hyde Park Towers Hotel' 'cos Jimmy wouldn't have known how to get a taxi or anything. He'd only just arrived that day. So we jumped in a taxi and he was terribly polite. I've never met anyone more well-mannered in my life.

Eventually the others turned up, by which time we had a rapport going. We all gathered in the reception area and Jimmy said to me, 'Will you come outside a minute? I want to talk to you.'

And he gave me all this excuse about this girl, how he hardly knew her at all, how she was Keith Richards' girlfriend and he didn't want to interfere—and please don't go. So I didn't. And that's how it all started.

I'll never forget this. Jimmy said, 'Shall we go to my room?' We got up and everyone said, 'Goodnight Kathy, goodnight Jimmy' and we went off to his room.

"HE TOLD ME, 'I'M OVER IN ENGLAND NOW AND I'M AUDITIONING FOR A BASS PLAYER AND A DRUMMER. IT'S JUST GOING TO BE A TRIO AND I'M GOING TO CALL IT THE JIMI HENDRIX EXPERIENCE, AND I'M GOING TO SPELL MY NAME J-I-M-I.' AND I SAID, 'WELL, THAT'S A LITTLE DIFFERENT'"

1966

25 September 1966: At 4am, Jimmy calls home from Hyde Park Towers Hotel, London.
Al Hendrix: He told me, 'Well, I'm over here in England now and I'm auditioning for a bass player and a drummer. It's just going to be a trio and I'm going to call it The Jimi Hendrix Experience, and I'm going to spell my name J-I-M-I.' I said, 'Well, that's a little different.'

Kathy Etchingham: I spoke to him and said, 'Hello, Mr Hendrix.' I spoke a few words and he said, 'Look, my boy's in England? You tell my boy to write me. I'm not paying for collect calls.'

All he had was a guitar in a case, a couple of satin shirts, a jar of Noxema and a bag of rollers. I used to set his hair in rollers.

26 September 1966: Hendrix holds auditions at Birdland, off Jermyn Street, Soho.
Eric Burdon: The first time I heard him play, I was in a rehearsal room putting together the New Animals, and this shadowy figure stepped into the room, wearing a large Western, sombrero kind of hat, beads around it, and he looked almost sort of purple, you know, in the darkness of this club, and he just grabbed hold of Vic Briggs' guitar and in the same instant said, 'Do you mind if I have a jam?' you know, and cracked up into an uptempo blues jam with John Weider.

27 September 1966: Jamming with The VIPs at the Scotch of St James club, London.
Mike Harrison (The VIPs): After our first set, a friend of mine, Chas Chandler, introduced me to a man he was sitting with. He said he was a guitarist and had just arrived from America where he had played with, amongst others, Little Richard, who was one of my favourites.

Chas asked me if this guy, who he introduced as Jimi, could get up and have a jam. We agreed and so, the next set, Jimi came onstage and plugged into Jim Henshaw's amplifier (a Gibson Mercury). Henshaw came off and joined me in the audience.

What happened next was like an explosion! This guy was amazing. He played and sang many of the songs that were later to become famous, including 'Hey Joe'. Jim Henshaw couldn't believe that this sound was coming out of the same amp that he usually used. Everyone in the club simply froze in their tracks that night.

Chas Chandler: Kit Lambert (co-manager of The Who) knocked half the tables in the club over, getting across and wanting to do a deal with Hendrix...

Chris Stamp (co-manager of The Who): We said that we wanted to be involved with this guy as managers, producers or whatever. We couldn't get in as producers, because Chas was producing. We couldn't get in as managers because Michael Jeffery (The Animals' manager) was managing. So we said, 'Fuck it, we have a record company.' And we talked to Jeffery, Chandler and Hendrix about a record deal.

We hadn't actually started the company yet. We had been talking to Polydor about the desperate need for an independent label... One of the things we offered to Jeffery and Chandler straight off—which we didn't have the right to do—was to guarantee Hendrix two performances on *Ready Steady Go!* Michael Jeffery also forced us to give them £1,000 sterling which was a lot of money for us, but we couldn't do the deal without some kind of an advance, just to show good faith.

Chas Chandler: So we did a deal there and then, for £1,000. That was it.

28 September 1966: Jimmy is issued a work permit, valid until the end of the year.
Kathy Etchingham: We started going around all the time together, and I moved into the hotel with him. We were absolutely flat broke, didn't have a bean. We would wake up in the morning, sit in bed with the tea and toast, talking and talking. Then we'd wander round the shops.

Noel Redding: I was on the way up to London on the train from Kent, when I got a *Melody Maker* and saw an advert announcing auditions for Eric Burdon and the New Animals... so I went around to this office, I think it was the Harold Davison Organisation, and they said, 'Oh, yes, the audition is at the Birdland club, turn up tomorrow.'

29 September 1966: Jimi meets Noel Redding, then jams with UK Brian Auger organ-player at Blaises club.
Chas Chandler: Noel turned up with the same haircut as Jimmy's and asked to join the Animals and I said, 'Well, that seat's gone, but I got this guy in from America looking for a bass player.'

Bob Dylan, whose poetic and visionary songs inspired Hendrix to go exploring outside the traditions of blues and pop

I took Noel round to a hall where Jimi was rehearsing and lent him my bass. When I came back an hour later, he was 'in'.

Noel Redding: I played with a drummer, Aynsley Dunbar, a keyboard player, Mike O'Neill, and this American gentleman and myself. The American was Jimi Hendrix. We played three tunes with no vocals and Hendrix only playing rhythm. One was 'Hey Joe', one was 'Need Somebody To Love'. I can't remember the third.

The first impression was that he was obviously good and that he was a gentleman—quiet and very polite, especially if there was a woman in the room.

After we'd played the tracks he asked me to go down the pub with him for a chat. He asked me about English music, which at the time was The Move, The Small Faces, The Kinks and all that. I asked him about American music—I was into Sam Cooke and Ray Charles as well as rock. We had a couple of pints of bitter, got on, and he asked me to join his group. I said, 'Well, give us the old train fare and I'll come back tomorrow.'

Jimi Hendrix: We started playing almost every day for so long, rehearsed for three days.

Chas Chandler: Things started happening incredibly fast after that. Jimi sat in one night with Brian Auger at Blaises and French pop star Johnny Hallyday was in the audience.

Brian Auger: I was the first musician to play with Jimi Hendrix in the UK. Chas had just got in from New York with him. He was so excited about his new discovery and he wasn't wasting any time. He figured the best thing for Jimi would be as few other musicians as possible, so he was looking for a small, tight group to back him. He thought of my group, Trinity, so he brought Jimi straight down to sit in with us at The Cromwellian (actually Blaise's) where we had a residency.

What I remember most is a very polite, seemingly nervous young man who played a series of chords and asked me, 'Could you follow that please?' I could, just about. Much later I realized that what he was playing then was a very raw presentation of his version of 'Hey Joe'.

Andy Summers (guitarist with Zoot Money, later The Police): I walked in and there he was onstage playing with Brian Auger. At the time, it was amazing. He had a white Strat and as I walked in, he had it in his mouth. He had a huge afro and he had on a sort of buckskin jacket with fringes that were to the floor... Yeah, it was intense and it was really great. It turned all the guitarists in London upside down at the time.

Johnny Hallyday: I was there with Otis Redding that evening. When I heard this totally unknown guitar player, this fantastic black guy who even played very good guitar with his teeth, I got up and asked him to become part of my next show.

Chas Chandler: He wanted us for a short French tour which finished up at the Paris Olympia, one of the biggest theatres in the world. That was to be our first gig.

30 September 1966: Chas Chandler tells Eric Clapton about Jimi.
Chas Chandler: Before we even had a rehearsal, I bumped into Jack Bruce and Eric Clapton down at the Cromwellian Club. They had recently formed Cream, and asked what I was doing... so I told them about Hendrix. They said, 'Why don't you bring him to Regent Polytechnic on Saturday for a jam?' I told them that this wouldn't be fair. 'You're mates of mine,' I said. 'You can't let me do this to you. This guy is really extraordinary.' They said if he was that good, I had to bring him.

Jimmy Savile (top UK DJ): Chas had come to me in Carnaby Street and said, 'I've found an amazing guitar player and I'm bringing him over to perform in the UK.' At that time, the idea of a solo guitar player like Jimi was almost unheard of—it was all groups then.

1 October 1966: Hendrix jams with Cream at Regent Polytechnic college.
Jack Bruce: The first time he played in public in London was with us, The Cream, at London University. I was in a pub in Charing Cross Road, and this guy came up to me and said, 'Hi, my name's Jimi Hendrix. I wanna sit in with your band,' which was practically unheard of to us. So I said, 'Yeah, it's all right with me if it's all right with the other guys.' We walked over to the gig

Rolling Stones manager Andrew Loog Oldham was not impressed by Hendrix when he saw him in New York, June 1966

and he did sit in and played incredibly, with his teeth and everything, and really blew us all away.

Eric Clapton: He was very, very flash, even in the dressing room. He stood in front of the mirror combing his hair and asked if he could play a couple of numbers. He did 'Killing Floor', a Howlin' Wolf number I've always wanted to play, but which I've never really had the complete technique to do. Ginger didn't like it and Jack didn't like it. They'd never heard the song before. It was just, well, he just stole the show.

Chas Chandler: Clapton stood there and his hands dropped off the guitar. He lurched off the stage. I thought, 'Oh God, what's happening now?' I went backstage and he was trying to get a match to a cigarette. I said, 'Are you all right?' and he replied, 'Is he that fucking good?' He had heard ten bars at most.

Kathy Etchingham: He walked off stage with this smirk. He knew exactly what he was doing.

2 October 1966: Mitch Mitchell plays his last gig with Georgie Fame & The Blue Flames at the Grand Gala du Disque, Amsterdam, Holland.
Mitch Mitchell: I did the Georgie gig for 18 months. One day, I went to the office and was told, 'You're fired, son.' The whole band was let go, and it was pretty devastating.

Alan Price: Shortly after Jimi arrived in London, he and I went out and picked up a couple of girls and took them back to my mews flat in Belgravia. I was a bit strapped for cash at that point and Jimi certainly didn't have any money so, the next morning, for breakfast we ate dog biscuits. That was the only food in the house at the time, because I had a beagle.

3 October 1966: Chas Chandler confirms to Noel Redding that he has the job as bassist in the Experience.
Noel Redding: I was glad to get the job, but I wasn't sure what it would come to. At the audition Hendrix didn't really sing, and I wasn't too sure about switching from guitar to bass. And then, of course, we were being paid £15 a week each, which was wonderful.

4 October 1966: Mitch Mitchell is offered an audition with Hendrix.

Mitch Mitchell: On the Tuesday, John Gunnell (manager of Georgie Fame) mentioned to me that Chas Chandler and Jimi Hendrix, a friend of his, were over here, and would I care to go and have a play…

5 October 1966: Auditions for a drummer are held with a jam in evening at Les Cousins club.
Mitch Mitchell: He (Jimi) had this Humphrey Bogart Burberry coat and wild hair. He was shy, not quite Clark Kent, but very quiet. You could take him to meet your mum and dad. He was very polite and very funny.

Chas Chandler: We had quite a few drummers lined up, and narrowed it down to Aynsley Dunbar and Mitch Mitchell. Neither Jimi nor I could make up our minds, so we ended up spinning a coin—it's a pity the coin ran the wrong way. I don't like Mitch Mitchell. He was going to get kicked out of that band every week.

Mitch Mitchell: Hendrix said, 'OK. I'll see you around.' And Chas said there was a gig in Paris the next week with Johnny Hallyday and asked if we fancied doing it. So I said 'OK' and spent three days rehearsing. Then off we went and that was how it started.

6 October 1966: Mitch Mitchell joins Hendrix and Redding for the start of rehearsals at Averbach House, London.
Chas Chandler: Mitchell had played it safe during the auditions. He didn't show all he could do. But as soon as he was told the job was his, he started opening up. We decided there and then that we weren't going to bring any other musicians in. It just sounded so clean, so exciting and new.

7 October 1966: Rehearsals continue at Averbach House.
Mitch Mitchell: Chas went out and got a couple of amplifiers—those little Burns 20 Watt amplifiers—and at the second rehearsal we tried to break the bloody things by throwing them down flights of stairs. And they didn't break!

Noel Redding: I was horrified because gear was hard to come by.

Mitch Mitchell: But we knew what we wanted, which was big clout, you know? Big amplifiers, and make it as dramatic as possible.

8 October 1966: The Experience visit the Marshall Amplification factory.
Jim Marshall: I met Jimi through having taught Mitch Mitchell to play drums, and Mitch brought this guy along to the factory one day. This character said to me, 'I'm going to be the greatest' and I thought, Oh no—not another American wanting something for nothing. But his next words were, 'I don't want you to give them to me. I will pay the full price. I just want to know that, wherever I am in the world, I won't be let down.' And Jimi, without doubt, became our greatest ambassador.

9 October 1966: At ANIM Management, London, discussions are held with Mike Jeffery (The Animals' manager) about managing the band.
Chas Chandler: When I came back to England, Jeffery said to me, 'Strictly speaking, you are still signed to me and anything you do, I've got commission on it. I'll tell you what—I'll put Eric Burdon & The New Animals with The Alan Price Set into a pot, and you put Jimi Hendrix and his group into the same pot, and we'll share it 50-50.'

I knew what I wanted to do, and that was produce Hendrix. I knew very little about the business, only what I thought should be done with an artist but, when it came to negotiating contracts, I thought, 'Well, Jeffery can do that, and I'll do this.'

Lulu Appleton (clothes designer): Jeffery had thick pebble glasses; he was distinctly unattractive. He had a little house behind Holland Park—it was always a mess. He never looked you in the eye. Half the time he didn't know what the hell he was doing. He was the quintessential parasite manager who had struck lucky.

Daniel Secunda (producer/manager, Track Records): I was at Track right from the start. I'd known Chas Chandler for years, and he was a real salt of the earth, honest, no-nonsense Newcastle lad. Jeffery, on the other hand, always remained a man of mystery. You'd hear these stories that he'd worked for MI5, or he was involved with the IRA, but nobody seemed to know for sure.

10 October 1966: More rehearsals for the new band at Averbach House.
Chas Chandler: Jimi was an amazing-looking guy in those days—one of the first black musicians to grow his hair long and wear freaky clothes. When he walked into a bar, all the heads turned and that was at a time when almost anything went in 'Swinging London'. We decided to capitalize on that situation and I made sure that all the photos released were the most evil and ugly we could find.

11 October 1966: All three members of The Experience sign management and publishing contracts with Chas Chandler and Mike Jeffery.
Chas Chandler: If I regret one thing, it was getting Mike Jeffery involved. I didn't really have a choice. Jeffery was the one with the money and the contacts. But it was also Jeffery who later pulled us apart.

Trixie Sullivan (Jeffery's personal assistant): I liked Mike very much. He was really something special. He was an incredibly talented man and could see talent in other people. He was shy and always stood back. But he was one tough guy, and bloody clever.

12 October 66: The Jimi Hendrix Experience fly to France.
Kathy Etchingham: He went to France and did a gig there, and he wore a suit, a two-piece suit. I remember it very well, a blue suit which had a button missing on the back. It was one of these sorta French tailored things, and he looked great in this suit and a white shirt.

He hated it. He didn't want to wear those sort of clothes at all.

Mitch Mitchell: We got a few Marshall bits and pieces. We had no road manager and I remember seeing these amplifiers with no covers on them being literally thrown into the cargo hold.

13 October 1966: Opening night of the European tour, at the Novelty, Evreux.
Unknown reviewer (L'Eure Eclair):

> He was a singer and guitar player with bushy hair, a bad mixture of James Brown and Chuck Berry, who pulled a wry face on stage during a quarter of an hour, and also played the guitar sometimes with his teeth. He ended the first half of the concert…

14 October 1966: Gig at the Cinema Rio, Salle Poirel, Nancy, France.

Eric Burdon, who became a close friend of Hendrix, performs on the famous British 1960s TV show, Ready Steady Go!

Noel Redding: We only did three songs a night, which was just as well because the rehearsals weren't really rehearsals. We didn't learn anything. Maybe just ran over a few chords and then go down the pub.

15 October 1966: Gig at the Salle Des Fêtes, Villerupt, France.
Noel Redding: Those first gigs were strange. We were on this tour bus. Hallyday just turned up in his new Mustang or whatever. The rest of us in this rickety old coach.

17 October 1966: Rehearsal at the Olympia Theater, Paris.
Chas Chandler: Johnny Hallyday was a master manipulator of an audience. Hendrix and I used to sit at the back of a hall and say, 'Look what he's doing, look at that.'... And though Hendrix knew all the routines, somehow watching a Frenchman put a little extra grace into the tricks and licks helped him refine his stage act. We benefitted so much from it.

Really, the Hendrix Experience's entire act—the entire basis of the act—was established on that Johnny Hallyday tour, no question about it.

18 October 1966: Show at the Olympia Theater, Paris.
Chas Chandler: We worked out a great entry for him. Mitch and Noel were on the stage, and we announced Jimi, who was standing in the wings. We did an old blues trick... something like, 'Ladies and gentlemen...' and Jimi, still in the wings, let loose a quick burst of notes. 'From Seattle, Washington...' and Jimi's guitar roared again, 'We have a...' and Jimi would play again.

This went on for ages before Jimi walked out with one hand in the air, still playing. When the audience suddenly realized that all of this great guitar sound was being played one-handed, they went bananas.

Barry Jenkins (drummer, The Animals): I remember one of the stunts he was doing that night. He had two guitars, and he put one on the floor of the stage and played it with his foot, while he played the other one with his hands.

19 October 1966: The band return to London.
Chas Chandler: When we got back from France, things were very quiet. It was very hard to get work and no one would touch him. I was fast running out of money.

20 October 1966: Jimi and Chas see a New Animals/Geno Washington/Georgie Fame gig at The Astoria, London.
Gerry Stickells (roadie): Noel (Redding) comes from the same place as me, and I knew him. He got me the job, really... their first gig was in Paris with Johnny Hallyday, and I joined up when they came back.

22 October 1966: Rehearsals in London.
Chris Stamp: No one realized how hip Jimi was. He was super-hip. Hendrix wanted to immediately acclimatize himself with hip London. He wanted to do that. Chandler wasn't really your man for the gig there. This isn't a knock on Chas but, for that area, Jimi went to places like Granny's (Granny Takes A Trip, hip clothes store) and got all of his look together. He just knew all of those things instinctively, and his whole look changed overnight.

23 October 1966: Recording 'Hey Joe' at De Lane Lea Studios, London.
Chas Chandler: That was where The Animals had done almost all of their recording. I knew the studio well. That's why I took them there.

He was very easy to work with in the studio. We only ever had one ruck, the first time we went in to record. We got into quite a row over the sheer volume of the guitar. At one point, he said, 'This is useless, I'll never be able to make a record

"HENDRIX WANTED TO ACCLIMATIZE HIMSELF IMMEDIATELY WITH HIP LONDON. FOR THAT, HE WENT TO PLACES LIKE GRANNY'S [GRANNY TAKES A TRIP] AND GOT ALL OF HIS LOOK TOGETHER. HE JUST KNEW ALL THOSE THINGS INSTINCTIVELY, AND HIS WHOLE LOOK CHANGED OVERNIGHT"

1966

here.' As it happened, I'd just come from the Visa Office and I had his passport and a return ticket to America in my pocket. So I handed them to him and I said, 'Go on then. Fuck off back to America.' And he just burst out laughing. That was the end of that and we never argued again.

I had only enough money to cover the cost for 'Hey Joe'. I couldn't even think of recording a b-side until I had more cash.

Mitch Mitchell: Hendrix was also shy about his voice. He didn't want to be a singer. Chas really had to drag it out of him.

Tim Rose: Hendrix got his arrangement, basically, from my version. Usually rock bands would perform it as an up-tempo thing, like The Byrds or Love, but I first heard 'Hey Joe' in Miami, Florida and it was real slow. It was a friend of Freddy Neil's... Vince Martin, I think. He was singing two verses of this song and I was working in the same club as him with another group, and I said, 'That's an interesting song. I mean, not much to it, but did you write that?' He said, 'No, that's all I know of it. I think it's an old Appalachian tune.' I said, 'Do you mind if I take it and maybe do something with it?' He said, 'Go ahead.' So I did, and I wrote a couple of verses and that arrangement of mine grew out of a living, breathing kind of working art.

24 October 1966: Jimi jams with Deep Feeling, which includes Dave Mason on guitar and Jim Capaldi on drums, at the Knuckles club (owned by Pretty Things drummer Viv Prince). At Hyde Park Towers, Jimi writes 'Stone Free'.
Viv Prince : One night, Chas Chandler came down to the club with this big black American guy and said, 'This is Jimi. I've just brought him over from the USA. Can he sit in with your house band?' I said, 'Yes, sure, what does he play?' Chas said, 'The guitar, but he's a frustrated bass player, actually.' So Jimi sat in with his back to the audience, playing bass.

Dave Mason: Chas used to take him around to all the clubs. It was a conscious effort on Chas's part to get him known, very subtle, because these were members-only clubs, frequented by entertainment business people. Jimi would get up—jeans, suede jacket, big electric hairdo—and just blow everybody away. I remember thinking I might as well take up another instrument.

Chas Chandler: The first song Jimi wrote was 'Stone Free'. When we did 'Hey Joe', he was on about putting 'Killing Floor' on the b-side, and I said, 'There's nothing going on the b-side but one of your own songs,' and he wrote 'Stone Free' that next night, for the next time we went in.

25 October 1966: The Jimi Hendrix Experience play a private showcase at the Scotch Of St James club.
Chas Chandler: I wanted the Harold Davison Agency to book Jimi, so I invited agent Dick Katz down to the Scotch to hear Jimi in a jam session. Jimi broke a string on his first number but still managed an incredible set. I turned to Dick and said, 'He broke a string, you know.' Dick was glued to the stage—he is a musician himself—'That had not escaped my attention,' he said. 'I can't wait to hear him with six.'

Gerry Stickells (roadie): The club owner kept trying to get me to turn down Hendrix's amp. I kept saying I would do so at the end of the next song but, as each one ended, I ran to the bathroom to hide.

Chas Chandler: Paul McCartney was also sitting at our table and leant over to say he hoped Dick had Jimi signed up as he would be a giant.

29 October 1966: Jimi gets his first UK music press mention, with his name mis-spelled, by an unknown journalist in *Record Mirror*.

> Chas Chandler has signed and brought to this country a 20-year-old Negro called Jim Henrix who, among other things, plays the guitar with his teeth and is being hailed in some quarters as main contender for the title of 'the next big thing'.

31 October 1966: More rehearsals at the Knuckles club.
Viv Prince: Chas had asked me if they could use the club in the afternoons to rehearse. I said, 'Yes, go on.' So they did. I still haven't been paid. I used to go down the club in the afternoons to see how the score was going and that's the first time I ever saw Hendrix with a small cassette recorder. He was recording every number, then playing it back to see how it sounded.

Mitch Mitchell: When the band first started, I was the only one who had a car, which I'd nearly paid off. So I did the driving. Eventually the car

Zoot Money (front, left) with his Big Roll Band. Note a young Andy Summers (later of The Police) at the front, far right

“WHEN JIMI PICKED HIS GUITAR UP, HE SAW THAT IT HAD CRACKED AND SEVERAL OF THE STRINGS WERE BROKEN. HE JUST WENT BARMY AND SMASHED EVERYTHING IN SIGHT. THE AUDIENCE LOVED IT AND WE DECIDED TO KEEP IT AS PART OF THE ACT”

“WHEN JIMI PICKED HIS GUITAR UP, HE SAW THAT IT HAD CRACKED AND SEVERAL OF THE STRINGS WERE BROKEN. HE JUST WENT BARMY AND SMASHED EVERYTHING IN SIGHT. THE AUDIENCE LOVED IT AND WE DECIDED TO KEEP IT AS PART OF THE ACT”

1966

conked out. We were skint, of course, and I think it eventually got repossessed. Now, I've always been into cars and, in the end, he (Hendrix) made me a present of a Lotus Elan.

2 November 1966: Rehearsal at Averbach House; recording 'Stone Free' and 'Can You See Me' at De Lane Lea studios, London.
Chas Chandler: 'Stone Free' was recorded and mixed in one day. I couldn't afford to have the band learn the song in the studio, so I booked a rehearsal at the Averbach House beforehand.

Mitch Mitchell: You have to remember that Chas had been in The Animals, and that 'House Of The Rising Sun' had, like, cost four quid or something to make. Rightly or wrongly, he had the attitude that, since it got to Number 1, there was no need to piss around in the studio.

Noel Redding: Chas would come out into the studio to show me various bass techniques. The bass was still new to me, and I was taking in everything I could. Chas told me about little things like different scales and what was classified as a 'walking bass' line, which were very simple but very effective.

8 November 1966: Gerry Stickells is employed as road manager in time for dates in Germany.
Gerry Stickells: As far as I was concerned, it was purely temporary. I was on my way to Spain to work in a bar.

9–11 November 1966: Two shows per night at the Big Apple, Munich, Germany.
Chas Chandler: (On the 9th) Jimi was pulled offstage by a few over-enthusiastic fans and, as he jumped back on, he threw his guitar before him. When he picked it up, he saw that it had cracked and several of the strings were broken. He just went barmy and smashed everything in sight. The German audience loved it and we decided to keep it as part of the act when there was a good press about or the occasion demanded it.

12 November 1966: Jimi sends a postcard to Al Hendrix in Seattle.

> I feel I must write before I get too far away. We're in Munich, Germany now. We just left Paris and Nancy, France. We're playing around London now. That's where I'm staying these days. I have my own group and will have a record out in about two months named 'Hey Joe'. By the Jimi Hendrix EXPERIENCE... I think things are getting a little better. Your loving son, Jimi.

14 November 1966: The Experience toy with the idea of becoming a four-piece, allowing Noel to switch to guitar.
Noel Redding: Jimi actually wanted to have two guitars in the band, so we auditioned Dave Knights from Procol Harum to play bass. But it didn't really work out and Jimi dropped the idea.

18 November 1966: Now that money has come in from the Track deal. 'Hey Joe' is re-recorded at Regent Sound, London.
Mitch Mitchell: We went into Regent Sound to attempt 'Hey Joe' again, but I'm sure we used the one done at Kingsway.

Noel Redding: At that time we would be using one 50W head and one 4x12-inch each in the studio, and the engineers would be going crazy with the baffles trying to separate off the sound. By modern standards we weren't especially loud, but the engineers would be going mad about the volume.

24 November, 1966: Recording 'Love Or Confusion'/'Here He Comes' at De Lane Lea studios, London.
Chas Chandler: There was always trouble with the bank when you recorded at De Lane Lea. There was a bank above the studio, and it was at the time when computers were just coming in. Every time we went in, we would play so loud that it would foul up the computers upstairs. As a result, we would always have trouble getting in there when we wanted.

25 November 1966: Press reception for the Experience at the Bag O'Nails club.
Chas Chandler: I had six guitars and I sold five of them to pay for a reception at the Bag O'Nails.

Keith Altham (journalist, New Musical Express): It was a lunch-time reception and I remember going down into the cellar thinking, 'Do I really want to be down here with it being such a beautiful day outside?' They came on and played at considerable volume for a small club like that. But Jimi was, I think, almost too much, to be absolutely honest. He was overwhelming in that small space. You knew something special was going on, you knew the guy was obviously a brilliant guitarist but I kept thinking that maybe this was just a bit too clever, this guy should be in an avant-garde jazz group or something, although what he was playing was fearsome in its delivery and obviously rock-oriented.

Charles J. Holley (fan): My girlfriend Winifred managed to get two tickets and we were the only people present who weren't part of rock's hierarchy: Donovan, John Mayall, The Beatles plus Epstein, and Clapton sitting opposite Pete Townshend. No one was more gobsmacked than Clapton—I was torn between watching his face and Hendrix's performance.

Terry Reid: We were all hanging out in Carnaby Street, at the Bag O'Nails—Keith, Mick Jagger. Brian (Jones) comes skipping through, like, all happy about something. Paul McCartney walks in. Jeff Beck walks in. Jimmy Page. I thought, 'What's this? A bloody convention or something?'

Here comes Jim, one of his military jackets, hair all over the place, pulls out this left-handed Stratocaster, beat to hell, looks like he's been chopping wood with it. And all these guitar players in the audience, they're all goin', 'Look at this, er, ugh, yeah right, sure, nice try.'

And he gets up, all soft-spoken. And all of a sudden, '*WHOOOR-RRAAAWWRR!!!*' And he breaks into 'Wild Thing', and it was all over. There were guitar players weeping. They had to mop the floor up. He was piling it on, solo after solo. I could see everyone's fillings falling out. When he finished, it was silence. Nobody knew what to do. Everybody was completely in shock.

Keith Altham: I was on my way out when they started into a version of The Troggs' 'Wild Thing' and that did kick me. What Hendrix was doing with that basic, very simple framework was so extraordinary. I came back and sat down and at that point he really did get me and I thought, 'this guy is doing something on another planet.' You could see the visual thing of the three of them and the way he looked was sufficient in its impact to mean that people were going to look twice at them when they saw pictures in the paper or saw them on stage.

I can remember them walking off. He left his guitar playing on the stage. It did create quite an impact, but it wasn't something that initially made me think, 'Oh, this guy is going to be a super-mega star.'

Roger Mayer (electronics expert): It was like everything I had ever imagined. I just went up to him and started talking, telling him what I did. I had been in electronics since 1963 and was totally into avant-garde sounds. Jimi asked me to come down to a gig he was playing at Chiselhurst Caves on December 16...

Noel Redding: Afterwards, in the dressing room, Lennon walked in, which freaked me out. he was saying, 'Fuckin' grand.' He loved it, but I was like 20 years old, John Lennon had walked into our dressing room and said 'That's grand, lads.' And then McCartney walked in and that freaked me out even more.

Charles J. Holley: Two weeks later I saw Cream at the Marquee. Clapton had permed his hair and left his guitar feeding back, leaning against the amp, which he'd seen Hendrix do at the gig.

26 November 1966: Hendrix visits The Who recording at IBC Sound, then plays at The Ricky Tick, Hounslow, earning £25 as support to The New Animals.
Pete Townshend: Jimi sort of wandered in looking peculiar, just really peculiar, and Keith Moon was in a nasty mood and said, 'Who let that savage in here?' I mean, he really did look pretty wild and very scruffy.

Chas Chandler asked me what kind of amplifiers Jimi should buy. And I said, 'Well, I like Hiwatts—or Sound City, as they were then called—but he might prefer Marshall.' And Jimi said, 'I'll have one of each.'

Anyway, he walked around for a bit, gave me a lukewarm handshake and then I never saw him again for a while.

Chas Chandler: They (the Ricky Tick audience) were transfixed by Jimi and you could almost hear a quick intake of breath when he came on stage, and they made a slight movement backwards. They were both frightened and excited and that was exactly what we wanted.

Late November 1966: Hendrix jams at the Cromwellian with Brian Auger, free-improviser Lol Coxhill and others.
John McCoy (guitarist): As well as playing in The Crawdaddies, I ran the Kirklevington Country Club, just outside Middlesbrough, so I knew Chas Chandler well, because we were both part of the music scene up north.

We had a residency at The Cromwellian and, one night, Chas asked if we would stand down and let Jimi play the midnight set in our place. Chas had organised a band that included Brian Auger on keyboards, Mickey Waller on drums and the bass player from a band called The Gamblers.

Lol Coxhill: Jimi came along to sit in with a few friends and myself. We all met prior to the gig in a convenient pub and I left to buy some cold-sore treatment from a nearby chemist. When I returned, I was asked what the bottle contained and explained that if mixed with beer, the liquid created a hallucinatory effect for anyone who might drink it. Then I tipped most of it into my beer, leaving enough for my lip, and drank it.

John McCoy: As soon as we heard Hendrix tuning up, we knew he was special, and we were more than happy to get out of his way. It started with the band Chas had organised, and they were brilliant, then Lol Coxhill and some others got on stage later.

Lol Coxhill: When I went onto the low stage, I imagined that it was about 15ft high and the band were hovering above a crowd of people who were dancing in a pool of blood. Hendrix was transformed into a life-size hardboard replica of himself. I remember the occasion as something which I observed as if watching a film of myself. Apparently it was a very good gig.

John McCoy: When we got back to the hotel afterwards, I told Chas that he owed me one for having stepped down like that. Chas agreed and so he did a deal with me that when Hendrix's first single came out, he would play a gig up at my club for £50.

1 December 1966: Hendrix signs a contract with Yameta, a Bahamas company owned by Mike Jeffery, Kit Lambert and Chris Stamp. Jeffery gets 40 per cent of Hendrix's earnings.
Daniel Secunda (Track Records): Any act that Jeffery signed up would immediately be signed over to Yameta to avoid tax.

John Hillman (solicitor, adviser to Mike Jeffery): They (Mitchell and Redding) would never sign anything. Those guys chose not to be within that structure and nobody encouraged them hard to be in there, because there was always the thought, certainly in Mike's mind, that they would be transient.

Jeffery was very specific as to who Yameta signed to exclusive contracts. Hendrix was the only one to receive a share, and that's just how Jeffery—and Hendrix—wanted it.

6 December 1966: Hendrix moves in to share Chas Chandler's apartment.
Kathy Etchingham: We started off sharing Ringo's old flat in Montagu Square with Chas and his first wife.

Chas Chandler: I had dozens of science-fiction books at home. The first one Jimi read was *Earth Abides*—an end-of-the-world, new-beginning, disaster-type story. He started reading through them all. That's where '3rd Stone From The Sun' and 'Up From The Skies' came from.

7 December 1966: Jimi obtains an extension to his work permit until 15 January 1967.
Chas Chandler: Above all, Jimi was good fun to be with. I don't think of this brooding, menacing person that we hear about now. I think of someone laughing. One of my favourite memories of him was doing his Little Richard impersonation. If he was doing a story that had four characters in it, he would slip into the roles of the four characters.

10 December 1966: The Experience supports John Mayall's Bluesbreakers at the Ram Jam Club, Brixton, London.
Dave Peverett (fan, later of Savoy Brown): The Ram Jam was a fairly large ex-dance hall/ballroom above Burtons (menswear store) and occupied two floors. The second floor was a bar and the third was the venue.

This Hendrix gig stands out in my memory. His set consisted of mostly blues material—'Catfish Blues', 'Dust My Blues' etc—and he ended the show by shoving his guitar through the ceiling and playing slide utilising the remaining bits of ceiling as the ‘bottleneck’. I never saw him play a better show.

11 December 1966: Hendrix visits Little Richard at his hotel in London and borrows $50. After leaving the hotel, Jimi is stopped by the police.
Little Richard: The last time I saw Jimi, I was touring through England and Jimi came up… He came to the hotel and borrowed some money from me, and he introduced me to his little girl he had with him… He says, ‘I have this new record coming out,’ and he says that it's gonna be a hit. Sure enough, when it came out, it was a mighty hit.

Jimi Hendrix: I was about half a block from The Cromwellian Club, wearing this gear. Up comes this wagon with the blue light flashing and about five or six policemen jumped out at me. One of them points to my jacket and says, ‘That's British, isn't it?’ So I said, ‘Yeah, I think it is.’ They said that I was not supposed to be wearing that—men fought and died in that uniform. So I said, ‘What, in the Veterinary Corps, 1898?’ They said that they didn't want to see me with that gear on any more, and they let me go.

13 December 1966: TV recording for *Ready Steady Go!* for a fee of £91 8s 5d; followed by recording of ‘3rd Stone From The Sun’/‘Foxy Lady’/‘Red House’ at CBS Studios, London.
Chris Britton (The Troggs): When we used to frequent the greasy spoon (cafe) up Denmark Street in 1966, we knew Mitch Mitchell as a short-haired mod. At the end of the year, we were on the edition of *Ready Steady Go!* on which the Experience made their TV debut.

Marc Bolan: Everyone else used to use backing tracks, but he was going to play live because they got him on the show the same day. I was in the control room with the producer, just sitting about, when they started ‘Hey Joe’, and this old lady really freaked out and said, ‘Turn the backing track down!’ because it was really loud. All the machines were shaking. And they said, ‘But there is no backing track.’

Chris Britton: They were miming, but both the music and the act were stunning, though I hardly recognized Mitch with this alarming afro, just like Jimi's. A few months later, you'd see that hairstyle everywhere, even back in Andover.

Mike Ross (engineer): Jimi came in (to CBS studios) with four Marshall cabinets, which I couldn't believe. How was I to mike this? Jimi told me to stick a microphone eight feet away from the cabinets and it would sound great. He actually showed me where to place the microphone, and I put a U-67 valve mike where he had instructed me to.

Peter Green (guitarist with John Mayall's Bluesbreakers, later of Fleetwood Mac): John Mayall took me with him to the studio that night, because John had taken some photographs of Jimi playing and he'd blown one of them up to about 20 by 20 and he took it along to show it to Jimi. He seemed to be experimenting a lot in the studio, but we didn't stay to watch him actually record anything.

Mike Ross: Jimi didn't record a live vocal. I recorded Jimi's lead vocal as an overdub, as well as backing vocals from Mitch, Noel and Jimi. Jimi also recorded a second guitar as an overdub.

Chandler was very much in charge. Jimi was very shy and quiet and didn't have much to say. He seemed very much in awe of Chandler.

There was another aspect that very odd. I was used to the band being a team and having some input. My immediate reaction during the Hendrix session was, ‘These two guys are being treated like shit.’ It was very much like, ‘Play, and do what you are told.’

“FIVE OR SIX POLICEMEN JUMPED OUT AT ME. ONE OF THEM POINTS TO MY JACKET AND SAYS, ‘THAT'S BRITISH, ISN'T IT?’ THEY SAID THAT I WAS NOT SUPPOSED TO BE WEARING THAT—MEN FOUGHT AND DIED IN THAT UNIFORM. SO I SAID, ‘WHAT? IN THE VETERINARY CORPS, 1898?’”

1966

Noel Redding: There's no bass on the original version of 'Red House' released on *Are You Experienced*... Jimi said to us, 'This is a blues in B. It was actually in B flat because we were tuned down half-a-step. I borrowed a terrible, awful, hollow-body electric guitar from someone in the studio—it might have been (DJ) Alan Freeman—because I liked to play along in rhythm to familiarize myself with the sequence...
We ended up just recording it. First take, I think. My guitar's bass was turned full up to make a good contrast with Jimi's.

14 December 1966: Hendrix threatened by two men in a Soho bar.
Kathy Etchingham: They both followed us outside. One of them hung back but the other guy kept going on. Chas turned round and tried to warn the guy off, but he wouldn't listen. Chas turned back to us and said, 'Take care of Lotte' (his wife) and then completely laid out this guy in a most astounding way. It took Jimi aback. He'd never seen anything like it even in New York. He certainly wasn't expecting anything like it in England. Chas totally protected Jimi.

15 December 1966: A CBS studio recording session is abandoned when Mitch Mitchell fails to turn up; Hendrix comes up with the riff that will become 'Purple Haze'.
Noel Redding: Mitchell was late for a session once and Chas didn't pay him his wages for that week. He was never late again.

Mike Ross: At that time, I don't think Chandler had the money to pay the studio. When it came to the second day, he still hadn't paid any money. Jake (Levy, co-owner of the studio) came over to Chas and said, 'Look, if you want to book any more time you've got to pay for what you have used up to now.'...

Chandler got quite upset, telling Jake that this was not the way he had done business in the past... and he was sorry, as he would never work in this studio again. It ended on a sour note, which was a shame, as I was enjoying the sessions.

Chas Chandler: I heard him playing it (the 'Purple Haze' riff) at the flat, and was knocked out. I told him to keep working on that, saying, 'That's the next single.'

16 December 1966: 'Hey Joe' is released in the UK. Photo session. Radio Caroline interview. Gig at Chiselhurst Caves, London.
Chris Stamp: As it turned out, Jimi's first record was released on the Polydor label because the Track label wasn't actually ready, though the deal was. We wanted to release it before Christmas to catch that market and coincide with one of the dates we had set for *Ready Steady Go!*

I wasn't absolutely sure that this was going to be a hit record. But we were going to... if it didn't go into the charts, we were gonna buy it in.We would give them (chart-riggers) money to just go to stores that we knew returned chart returns. They would just go into stores and buy records.

Mike Nesmith (The Monkees): I was having dinner in London with John Lennon, Eric Clapton and a group of people. In the middle of dinner John produced this portable tape player and requested that the restaurant turn down the piped-in music. He then proceeded to play 'Hey Joe' on his recorder saying, "you guys gotta check this out.' Everyone was reverential...

David Nash (fan): I was just 17, and some of my mates asked me to come along to Chiselhurst Caves to see this guy. I knew nothing about him. We got some bottles of Merrydown cider and downed them before we went in. It was an amazing place, ancient deep underground caves where they used to take people round on tours, but the higher level was sometimes used for gigs

It was incredibly atmospheric, dank and gloomy. It was crowded and smoky and they had utility lighting, the bare bulbs with the wire frame round them, strung along the walls. The stage was very small, set back in a natural hollow in the cave wall. There were huge iron gates blocking you off from the deeper levels of the caves, but during the gig people were climbing up onto them.

Then, suddenly, there he was on the stage, the most amazing looking man making this incredible music. I was at the back, so I had to stand on tiptoe to see him over people's shoulders, but I was completely blown away.

Roger Mayer (electronics expert): I went there and brought some of my devices, such as the

Octavia. He tried them out backstage and was thrilled. When I had met Michael Jeffery, he was the type of person that I made out very quickly that I didn't want to deal with. I just wanted to make sure that I received expenses for research and development—I never got salary, I just got paid for making the things. I did things for Hendrix, but not for Jeffery.

17 December 1966: The first local newspaper ad to mention Hendrix appears in the *Southern Evening Echo*, advertising the Southampton Guildhall gig on the 22nd. The band is described as The Jimmy Hendricks Experience.
Chas Chandler: We used to play *Risk* for days on end, having a game going all the time. All four of us played: me, Jimi, Kathy Etchingham and my wife Lotte. There was always a table with the game set—if we went out, we used to leave it until we came back and sometimes it would last three, four or five days.

Graham Nash: I lived on the same street as Jimi for a while, and one of the strangest memories I have is of me and Gary Leeds of The Walker Brothers playing *Risk* with Jimi on LSD at his apartment. He was the black army, of course, and he kicked ass on everybody. Stoned out of his mind, and he was absolutely brilliant at strategy games.

18 December 1966: Chas Chandler's birthday party at his flat.
Chas Chandler: I remember a party, it was my birthday and we held it in Ringo's flat, where I had just moved in. We invited a few friends, and 40 people turned up.

*Chris Welch (*Melody Maker *journalist):* Jimi spent most of the time at the party huddled in a corner on the floor.

21 December 1966: Recording 'First Look Around The Corner' at CBS Studios; gig at Blaises club, London.
Jeff Beck: We were out on the town looking around for some girlies. We went down to Blaises and I heard this sound blasting up the road, and then went in there, and there was Jimi and I couldn't believe it. He was singing 'Like A Rolling Stone'. I knew the tune, but the way he treated it was something else. He was going crazy and the people were going crazy.

Pete Townshend: Eric Clapton called me and suggested that we check him out. It was kind of keeping an eye on the competition. We arrived at the show a little late as I was stuck in the studio and, just as we arrived, Jeff Beck was walking out. I asked Jeff, 'What's the matter, mate? Is he that bad?' Beck could only roll his eyes upward and say, 'No, Pete, he's that good!'

When Eric and I saw his show, we knew what Jeff meant. He was doing everything—the blues, rock, and things I still can't name. He was playing the guitar with his teeth, behind his back, on the floor. It was unbelievable.

Chris Welch (in Melody Maker*):*

> Jimi Hendrix, a fantastic American guitarist, blew the minds of the star-packed crowd who went to see him at Blaise's Club, London on Wednesday. Among those in attendance were Pete Townshend, Roger Daltrey, John Entwistle, Chas Chandler and Jeff Beck. They heard Jimi's trio blast through some beautiful sounds like 'Rock Me Baby', '3rd Stone From the Sun', 'Like A Rolling Stone', 'Hey Joe' and even an unusual version of The Troggs' 'Wild Thing'. Jimi has great stage presence and an exceptional guitar technique which involved playing with his teeth on occasions and no hands at all on others. Jimi looks like becoming one of the big club names of '67.

Eric Clapton: After Pete Townshend and I went to see him play, I thought that was it, that the game was up for all of us—we may as well just pack it in. He could do it all. He was like Pete and I combined and much, much more.

Kathy Etchingham: The atmosphere was not good between him and Eric Clapton, no matter what Eric might say. We went round to Eric's one night in the early days, at the top of Gloucester Road, and I remember that the conversation was so difficult and strained. They had nothing to talk about, they just talked a bit about guitarists and who they liked and, when we walked out in the early hours of the morning, Jimi said to me, 'That was hard work.'

22 December 1966: Gig at the Guild Hall, Southampton, supporting Geno Washington,
Geno Washington: I'm a uniform freak, so in

this little old corner street (at Moss Bros men's clothing store in London) I see this jacket. It's the most beautiful jacket I've ever seen in my life. I walked in and talked to the store-owner and he said, 'This jacket ain't shit, it's an original—£100.' I said, 'Fuck, I only got £50. I'll run to the bank and give you the other £50.' 'You got it, give me the £50 right down in my hand.' So I come back, 'Hey man, where's my jacket?' And he said, 'I'm sorry, I sold the jacket to Jimi Hendrix.' I said, 'What?' He said, 'Look, he came in and he gave me £200. Here's your fifty quid back.'

24 December 1966: The first reviews of 'Hey Joe' appear in the UK music press.
Derek Johnson (NME)*:*

> Here's a young man who could make a profound impression in the future. This is a raw, uninhibited, treatment of a traditional number. It's in the insidious r'n'b pattern, with thundering drums, some spine-tingling guitar work and a hypnotic slow beat. It's gutteral, earthy, convincing and authentic... This is a disc for the connoisseurs.

*Peter Jones (*Record Mirror*):*

> Should justice prevail, this'll be a first time hit... Marvellous blues feel to it, well-sung at a slowish tempo, a slow burner of immense excitement.

25 December 1966: Jimi spends Christmas with Kathy.
Kathy Etchingham: We had egg and chips for our Christmas dinner and spent a quiet day in, as everything was closed. Everyone else was away visiting their families. Christmas didn't mean anything very special to either of us.

26 December 1966: Hendrix completes writing of 'Purple Haze' while waiting to go on stage at the Upper Cut club, London.
Chas Chandler: 'Purple Haze'... was actually written in the dressing room of the club that afternoon. The gig was at 4pm, a press function for the club. He started playing the riff and I said, 'Write the rest of that!' so he did.

Jimi Hendrix: It was just a straight dream I had linked upon a story ('Night Of Light' by Philip Jose Farmer) I read in a science-fiction magazine about a purple death ray.

Peter Shertser (mod scenester): He played a very early gig on Boxing Day '66, at Billy Walker's Upper Cut club in Forest Gate. We're all down there, and we've torn the place apart. There was only 20 or 30 of us and that was it. Very few other people realized who he was, and he never forgot that.

29 December 1966: The Experience perform 'Hey Joe' on *Top Of The Pops.*
Jimmy Savile (DJ): At *Top Of The Pops* you'd be stuck in the studio for four or five hours with nothing much to do, so we'd hang out together. We got quite a rapport going but it was very much just casual chat—the weather, where we'd been working, who was around that day and so on. But sitting there having a cup of tea or coffee and chatting was something he really enjoyed.

31 December 1966: Gig at the Hillside Social Club, Folkestone (Noel's home town), followed by a New Year's Eve party at his mother's house.
Vicki Redding (Noel's sister): I remember looking up the stairs and seeing Jimi, and the charisma. I couldn't take my eyes off him. He was so polite and charming and shy.

Margaret Redding (Noel's mother): The man had something special about him. When Jimi was there, you couldn't look at anyone else. You could feel his presence.

It was very cold that night. Jimi asked me if it would be all right to stand next to the fire. That's how he got the idea for the song 'Fire'.

"ONE OF THE STRANGEST MEMORIES I HAVE IS OF ME AND GARY LEEDS OF THE WALKER BROTHERS PLAYING RISK WITH JIMI ON LSD. HE WAS THE BLACK ARMY, OF COURSE, AND HE KICKED ASS. STONED OUT OF HIS MIND, HE WAS ABSOLUTELY BRILLIANT AT STRATEGY GAMES" [GRAHAM NASH]

1966

Hendrix at London's Marquee club. The Experience broke its house record on their first appearance, on 24 January 1967

1967

January 1967: In New York to secure a US deal for Hendrix, Mike Jeffery speaks with Johanan Vigoda of law firm Marshall & Vigoda.
Johanan Vigoda: One day Jeffery came to our office to talk about getting a record deal for this black guitarist he had found. He showed me some reviews from things like *New Musical Express*, as well as these pictures that had Hendrix in a cape and, under his arms, like a wrestler, two white guys' faces. Jeffery was convinced that Hendrix was a great star.

Tony Bramwell (manager, Saville Theatre, London): I was around Chas Chandler for years, in and out of the ANIM management offices all the time, and you'd never see hide nor hair of Mike Jeffery. He was purely a deal-maker.

4 January 1967: Gig at the Bromel Club, Bromel Court Hotel, Bromley, Kent. Jimi interviewed by Richard Green of *Record Mirror*

5 January 1967: Interview by *Rave* magazine
Mike Jeffery: We took him to a club in London where they were playing records, and Hendrix proudly said, 'Hey, listen to this one. I'm on there somewhere.' I got a bit agitated... and said, 'What do you mean you are on it?' He said, 'Oh, it was made when I was playing with this group, The Squires.' I started questioning him in depth about this group and what his relationship was with them. I said, 'Are you sure you have no other pieces of paper around?' He said, 'No, I did sign something, as a session man or something like that... forget it. It doesn't mean anything.'

6 January 1967: Press interviews and photos for *Fabulous 208* magazine

7 January 1967: Gig at New Century Hall, Manchester. After relaxing at The Twisted Wheel, the Experience is set upon by four men.
Andy Scott (later of The Sweet): I was in a band called SilverStone when I was 16, like a 1960s soul band. We were very fortunate in 1967, to be the support act for Jimi Hendrix in Manchester. I say fortunate because, out of the SilverStone band came The Elastic Band, and that happened immediately after seeing Jimi Hendrix. The obvious thing to do, was to change the whole direction, because we had guys in the band that really wanted to do something different.

Mitch Mitchell: We walked over to the car and suddenly Noel and I were grabbed and slung against the railings of the police station. We got slapped around a few times and I was going, 'What the fuck's going on?' They were the police, but we didn't believe it at first—they were all in plain clothes. They took Hendrix's passport off him, but left him alone because he was American.

8 January 1967: Gig at the Mojo Club, Sheffield, billed as The New Weirdo trio Jimi Hendrick's Experience.

9 January 1967: 'Hey Joe' enters UK charts at Number 48.
Chas Chandler: The DJs hadn't been playing it on the radio, but the word had spread through the ballrooms and it started to sell. I think we had about 30 shillings left between us.

Abby Schroeder (publisher): Jeffery was so desperate for airplay (on 'Hey Joe') that he allowed himself to be blackmailed. He explained to me that... to ensure heavy pirate airplay, one had to give up a piece of the action. I told him that splitting publishing copyrights wasn't like cutting up a pie. There were other ways to get airplay without sacrificing your artist's work.

10 January 1967: Hendrix writes lyric for 'The Wind Cries Mary' at 34 Montagu Square.
Kathy Etchingham: He did write 'The Wind Cries Mary' overnight, because that was the result of all the rows we had. All the incidents in it were what happened: I smashed plates on the floor, he swept them up. He locked me in the bathroom for absolutely ages and wouldn't let me out. He

went out and left me locked in the bloody bathroom. Eventually Chas's girlfriend Lotte let me out. I stormed outside and Jimi was sitting there in his black cloak. I ran out to get a taxi and was standing under the traffic lights, and I had red hair and a red dress. I went back after I'd cooled down and he'd already written it. It was one hell of a barney.

Jimi Hendrix: ...'The Wind Cries Mary' is representing more than one person.

11 January 1967: Hendrix signs to Track Records for three years; John Mayall drops in while the Experience record 'Purple Haze', 'Wind Cries Mary' demo and '51st Anniversary' at De Lane Lea studios; gig at Bag O'Nails
Noel Redding: Michael Jeffery and Chas Chandler signed a contract with Track Records two months before Track was fully set up. Only Jimi was mentioned in the contract, which was for three years and called for four singles and two LPs each year. There was a £1,000 advance and recording costs to a point. Had Mitch Mitchell and I known that Jimi was the only one being signed to contracts (and we didn't even know there were contracts) the Experience would have ended.

Roland Rennie (MD, Polydor Records): We did our deal with Kit and Chris of Track, who already had The Who through Polydor. They were very charismatic young guys, bright and good fun to be around. So we would have paid our moneys to Track, who would then presumably pass it along to Chandler and Jeffery.

I was very fond of Chas Chandler, who I'd known since the days when I was at EMI, and he was in The Animals. Mike Jeffery though, was a rather more shifty sort of character, who had previously worked with British Army Intelligence.

Chris Stamp: All the imagery was basically done at Track. We brought in six of the top London photographers. We had these great black-and-white posters, featuring provocative shots of Hendrix posing bare-chested. Track was doing a semi-management job, but that was because Kit and I were managers who operated a record label.

Chas Chandler: 'Purple Haze' took four hours to record, which at that time, represented a long time in the studio.

Mitch Mitchell: Hendrix came in and hummed us the riff and showed Noel the chord changes. I listened to it and went, 'OK, let's do it.' We got it on the third take, as I recall.

Chas Chandler: Hendrix and I were striving for a sound and just kept going back in, two hours at a time, trying to achieve it. A lot of the background sound on 'Purple Haze' is actually a recording being fed back into the studio through the earphones held around the microphone, moving them in and out to create a weird echo.

Chas Chandler: That song ('51st Anniversary') is a good example of Jimi just sitting around the apartment, singing and playing his guitar. I would sit across from him and say, 'That's good' or 'No, change that to something like this.' These were pre-studio edits, if you like. Then we would get together with the band and rehearse the song.

There was quite a bit of overdubbing on '51st Anniversary', and it was the first time where we consciously thought of approaching production that way. There were five guitar overdubs in all, linking in together to sound like one guitar.

We had about 20 minutes or so left, so I suggested that we cut a demo of 'The Wind Cries Mary'. Mitch and Noel hadn't heard it yet. They played it through once and I remember saying that I really liked the feel of the song. Jimi came in and said, 'I have a good idea for an overdub.' So he went back in and played.

One thing about songs like 'The Wind Cries Mary' that people often miss out, and that's how much Country there is in them. I mean Country & Western. Listen to his little two note runs, and the way he uses the chords. It's Country.

12 January 1967: Band mimes at Olympia, 1967 International Racing Car Show for Radio London; gig at the Seven And A Half Club.
Jimi Hendrix: It's so phoney. I felt guilty just standing there holding a guitar. If you want to scream and holler at a record, you can do that at home. I'm strictly a live performer.

Marianne Faithfull: I saw Jimi Hendrix at the Seven And A Half. I'd gone because Mick (Jagger) told me about him. He said he'd seen Hendrix in New York and it had taken his breath away.

I sat in this tiny basement club for hours and watched him play. A Tantric vision in fashionable crushed velvet pants and a ruffled shirt.

He was very awkward. He sang with his back to the stage, or into his guitar, and mumbled so badly that you couldn't understand a word. There were long unexplained gaps, while he discussed what he was going to play next with Mitch and Noel, or fiddled with his amps. He hadn't got his persona together—he wasn't yet the Voodoo Chile—and you could see he was painfully shy.

But once he began playing, he transformed. The music was sexually charged and direct. I had the feeling he was playing just for me which, since the place was empty, was probably true. I'm such a fool. I should have hung around and seduced him but, typically, I ran away.

13 January 1967: Another gig at the Seven And A Half Club.
Noel Redding: We were doing clubs like the Seven And A Half for £7.

14 January 1967: Hendrix is featured in *NME*'s 'New To The Charts' spot; gig at The Beachcomber, Nottingham.
Keith Altham reports in NME*:*

> Hendrix is a one-man guitar explosion with a stage act which leaves those who think pop has gone pretty with their mouths hanging open. What this man does to a guitar could get him arrested for assault.

15 January 1967: Kirklevington Country Club, Yorkshire, supported by Rivers Invitation.
Jim Moore (roadie, Rivers Invitation): The Kirk was a little two-storey place in a little village, with a tiny stage, and maybe a capacity of 400. We'd never even heard of the bloke, but as soon as Hendrix walked in, I could see he was something different. I chatted with him in the dressing room, and he didn't have any attitude or anything.

John McCoy: He started off with 'Wild Thing' which immediately earned him a round of booing from the crowd. The big thing up north then was blues and soul, so a band like The Troggs was about the most naff thing you could imagine. But within a minute, everybody was converted. The volume kept getting louder through the set until all the glasses in our cocktail bar shattered.

Jim Moore: Afterwards I got him in the dressing room and he explained to me about how he tuned his strings to an open major chord, so you could just barre it all the way up, and it somehow also enabled him to reach notes nobody else seemed to get. We just didn't know anything about that sort of technique.

John McCoy: Later on, we were sitting around in the back and we got into playing games. Jimi arm-wrestled my bouncers, big strapping physical culture blokes, and he beat about six of them.

Then they started a game called Walking The Bottles. This involved putting two rows of beer bottles at 90 degrees to the wall, then getting down and doing press ups. As you went towards the wall, you had to balance on one arm and remove a bottle alternately from each row. The guy who got nearest the wall was the strongest. Jimi won that as well.

One of my bouncers was a bit disgruntled and he said, 'So the nigger wins this one too.' Without a second thought, Chas Chandler turned round and decked the guy, laid him out and sent him flying right over the banister.

16 January 1967: 'Hey Joe' hits Number 11 in the UK. Gig at the Seven And A Half Club.
Jimi Hendrix: 'Hey Joe' is a traditional song and it's about a hundred years old. Lots of people have done different arrangements of it, and Timmy Rose was the first to do it slowly. I like it played slowly. There are probably a thousand versions of it fast, by The Byrds, Standells, Love and others.

17 January, 1967: Recording live concert for *Ready, Steady Radio!* at Tiles Club; gig at the Seven And A Half Club; further recording on 'The Wind Cries Mary'.
Noel Redding: We were virtually broke... After a British radio appearance on January 17, we ran up a bar bill of £2.25; even pooling our money we couldn't pay it.

Mitch Mitchell: I'm sure we did 'The Wind Cries Mary' twice. That was at Kingsway—we did a demo version... and it was ragged, to put it mildly. We went off over the weekend, did some gigs, went back the following Tuesday and got it right, but the initial feeling wasn't there. So the original was released, warts and all.

18 January 1967: Hendrix is interviewed by David Frost; The Experience record TV show *Top Of The Pops*; gig at the Seven And A Half Club.

19 January 1967: Gig at The Speakeasy.
Ronnie Wood: Back in those days, all of us skinny white British kids were trying to look cool and sound black. And there was Hendrix, the ultimate in black cool. Everything he did was natural and perfect.

Jo Cruikshank (Speakeasy member): I was sitting at a table in The Speakeasy one night—I'd been off to have a little dance, and I came back and Jimi Hendrix was sitting there. I walked up and said, 'Sorry, this is my table,' and he was so polite and apologetic— 'Have I taken your seat? Here, have it back.' And I thought, My goodness. I became a complete Hendrix fan after that.

20 January 1967: Interview with *NME;* Hendrix is granted a six-month UK work permit; gig at Haverstock Hill Country Club, London. In New York, record producer Juggy Murray receives $750 from Marshall & Vigoda to settle his contractual claims on Hendrix.
Jimi Hendrix (to John King of NME*):* I know I can't sing—I'm primarily a guitarist. Some people think I'm good and that's what I want to find out. I've been working with myself and my ideas for 21 years. Now I want to find out from everyone else if they are any good.

21 January 1967: Gig at The Refectory, London
Richard Thompson: The first time I saw Hendrix was at The Refectory, Golders Green. Everybody was blown away, of course. It changed things completely, because he was so out there, and so accomplishedly out there. It wasn't someone who didn't have control of the noise and technique, he had it absolutely in control. I don't know how tutored he was, but he knew his notes, where they were and what they were called—it wasn't all intuitive. It was also important that he was a guitarist/vocalist—his vocal phrasing was not dissimilar to his guitar phrasing, in the tradition of great jazz soloists like Louis Armstrong.

22 January 1967: Gig at The Astoria, Oldham, Lancashire.

23 January 1967: For $500, Mike Jeffery acquires rights to Curtis Knight & The Squires (including Jimmy Hendrix) material, cut for Jerry Simon's RSVP Records in New York.
Jerry Simon: As a matter of fact, if Jeffery had so requested, I would have sold the master tapes themselves to him at the time, but neither one of us considered that to be essential.

24 January 1967: On their first appearance at The Marquee, London, band breaks the house record. The support band is The Syn.
Pete Banks (guitarist, The Syn, later of Yes): It was a very peculiar gig. All The Beatles were there and The Rolling Stones. Eric Clapton and Jeff Beck and every other guitar player in town came along. They were waiting for Jimi Hendrix but we had to play once, come off and then play another set. People were going, 'Well, thank God they've gone.' Then we came back on again. It wasn't very nice, but it was great meeting Hendrix.

25 January 1967: An out-of-London gig at the Orford Cellar, Norwich.

26 January 1967: Photo shoot with Paul Popper at Montagu Square.
Chas Chandler: We had been scratching money together to pay for sessions at De Lane Lea. With 'Hey Joe' a hit on the charts, I found myself dealing more with Polydor than Track. One day, I finally went storming into Polydor and said, 'Look, we've got money piling up here. We are trying to put an album together, and I want to go to Olympic Studios. They won't fucking accept me because I have no credit history. They wouldn't even let me in without payment in advance.

So Polydor rang them up, opened an account in my name, and guaranteed that the bills would be paid. For the first time, I wasn't worrying about how I was going to pay for sessions.

27 January 1967: Another gig at Chiselhurst Caves, Kent.

28 January 1967: Gig at The Upper Cut Club.
Jimi Hendrix: Some people have told me that they think wearing a military jacket is an insult to the British Army. Let me tell you, I wear this old British coat out of respect. This was worn by one of those cats who used to look after the donkeys which pulled the cannons way back in 1900. This coat has a history, there's life to it. I don't like war, but I respect a fighting man and his courage. Maybe

the guy who wore this coat got killed in action. Would people rather his coat be hung up and go mouldy somewhere, to be forgotten, like him?

Petra Niemeier (photographer, Bravo *magazine):* We did some pictures at his house. It was a very nice, comfortable, three-storey house, and he was quite house-proud. Domesticity seemed to be new to him, and he was enjoying it. He was very shy, but very nice. He was in the mood for clowning around a bit.

We did some shots in the street, shopping and things, then went to a club in the evening where he was doing a show. He wore a blue velvet suit all day—he didn't have a separate outfit to go on stage, just what he happened to be wearing.

29 January 1967: Gig at the Saville Theatre, supporting The Who, The Koobas and Thoughts.
Chris Stamp: Kit and I had a lot to do with who went into the Saville on Sunday nights, because things were much smaller then. We knew Vicki Wickham from *Ready Steady Go!*, and she was working for Brian Epstein, booking the Saville. We booked The Who and brought the Experience in as support for them. This was Hendrix's most prestigious London gig to date.

Brian May (fan, later of Queen): When I saw him supporting The Who, I couldn't believe it. I felt excited, overwhelmed and also completely deflated. I'd put a lot of work into playing guitar and was thinking I was pretty damn good. But Hendrix came along and destroyed everyone.

Pete Townshend: Kit Lambert, our manager, had just signed Jimi up to our label (Track) and put him on backing us up… I thought, Jesus Christ, what's going to happen? So he went on and he did his thing. He knocked the amplifiers over, he practically smashed it up… and I went on afterwards and I just stood and strummed. I'm not ashamed to say he blew us away.

Eric Clapton: Jimi played this gig that was just blinding. I don't think Jack (Bruce) had really taken him in before. I knew what the guy was capable of from the minute I met him. It was the complete embodiment of the different aspects of rock'n'roll guitar rolled up into one. When Jack did see it that night, after the gig he went home and came up with the riff ('Sunshine Of Your Love'). It was strictly a dedication to Jimi. And then we wrote a song on top of it.

Noel Redding: We were invited to some party afterwards. I had my motor, so I took Mitch and Hendrix, and we arrived at this place near the Irish Embassy. I knocked on the door and McCartney opened it, which freaked me out yet again. We went upstairs and they had a professional joint-roller there as well.

31 January 1967: A promotional film is made at the Saville Theatre.

1 February 1967: Gig at The New Cellar Club, South Shields, near Newcastle.
Chas Chandler: Jimi and I were staying at my mother's house in Newcastle. As we were sitting there talking, I decided to walk down to the phone (box), because my mother had not put one in yet, to ring London and see how things were going. 'Hey Joe' had leapt to Number 7 in the charts, and I knew we were really on our way.

Sting: He was like a Venusian, like someone from another planet. All that hair. And there were hardly any black people in Newcastle—I think he actually was the first black person I'd ever seen. It was absolutely electric, almost too awesome to deal with. You felt like you were on the edge of a precipice. 'Hey Joe' had just come out. That was what decided me to become a musician. But seeing a live gig like that was so much more effective than listening to records. I'd been into The Beatles, but this was the beginning of rock music as opposed to rock'n'roll. It was heavy.

"I KNOW I CAN'T SING—I'M PRIMARILY A GUITARIST. SOME PEOPLE THINK I'M GOOD AND THAT'S WHAT I WANT TO FIND OUT. I'VE BEEN WORKING WITH MYSELF AND MY IDEAS FOR 21 YEARS. NOW I WANT TO FIND OUT FROM EVERYONE ELSE IF THEY'RE ANY GOOD"

Lawrence Vasey (fan): The club had a stage that was designed to rotate by an electric motor, but it had never worked since the club was opened a week earlier by The Cream. So the staff of the club and members of The Bond (support group) had to push the stage manually to move The Experience around to face the audience.

Noel Redding: At the end we were taken back round on the revolving stage and, as we went, the audience grabbed us. I was hanging onto Jimi and he was hanging onto Mitch, and we very nearly got crushed against the wall as we went round.

2 February 1967: The R'n'B Club, Imperial Hotel, Darlington. Afterwards, party at the Club A Go Go with The Moody Blues.
Kathy Etchingham: He'd tour around working men's clubs. In the van Jimi and I got places of honour in the front seat and Mitch and Noel had to sit on the equipment at the back. We ended up in a place in Darlington, nobody took a blind bit of notice of him. I think there was bingo before and after. When we got outside, the bloody van had broken down. We had to push it in the snow.

3 February 1967: First session with Eddie Kramer at Olympic Studios, London, completing the recording of 'Purple Haze', then a gig at the Ricky Tick, Hounslow, Middlesex
Eddie Kramer (engineer): When Jimi and the band arrived at Olympic, they'd already had a couple of singles out which had been done at different places. Everything had been done on a shoestring and the sound was pretty raw, but I know that Jimi was thinking of expanding the sound of the band. He came to Olympic because he thought he could get what he wanted there.

Noel Redding: I was in awe of its size. We had recorded in a few studios, but none were this big. Someone told us that The Rolling Stones were in Studio B and then in came Mick Jagger with a lump of hash, with which I got well spaced out.

4 February 1967: Gigs at The Ram Jam Club and The Flamingo clubs, London. 'Hey Joe' hits Number 6 in the UK charts.
Alan Cowderoy (guitarist): I was playing in a band called Gracious so I was interested in new guitarists. The guitar of choice at that time, for people like Clapton and Beck, was the Gibson Les Paul, with that nice fat sound. They had Telecasters and moved on to Gibsons, and nobody wanted to use effects pedals or whammy bars. Then suddenly, that night at the Ram Jam, I was confronted with this guy getting amazing sounds out of a Telecaster. He was also using a lot of effects, which was deeply unfashionable, so he really was changing things around, and he was already fusing blues and psychedelia and rock in his playing. He still looked to me, though, like a guy who'd just come out of a soul revue.

Andrew Lauder (fan, later record label manager): Word had spread about this guy like wildfire, so I got to the Flamingo early because I knew the place would be rammed. The whole band looked great—they had that image sorted out right at the start—and the gig was fearsomely loud. I had seen Buddy Guy playing guitar behind his neck and writhing around on the floor, so I knew where a lot of Jimi's showmanship came from, but the playing was still awesome.

5 February 1967: Jimi attends a Cream gig at the Saville Theatre, then plays at The Flamingo.

6 February 1967: The Star Hotel, Croydon.
Keith Aldridge (local guitarist): The Star was really busy that night... the stage was not more than a foot-and-a-half off the ground and there was a piano over in the corner.

They've got an alcove/French window with the stage slightly to the right. Well, they brought Hendrix in through that window, there was no way they could get him through the hall.

Before he'd even played, you noticed how impressive-looking Hendrix was. I always thought of blues guitarists as little men, especially after seeing Buddy Guy. But Hendrix was an ex-Yankee paratrooper and he looked massive...

They were basically playing stuff off the first album; a really nice bluesy version of 'Rock Me Baby'; I think he did a Buddy Guy song which might have been 'The First Time I Met The Blues', covers like 'Fire', but mainly slow blues like 'Red House' with lots of feedback and distortion. He was really enjoying himself.

Chas Chandler: The audience were shocked. Their reaction wasn't excitement. I think they were numb. They weren't sure what it was about.

7 February 1967: Recording 'Purple Haze' vocal overdubs at Olympic studios.
Chas Chandler: Jimi was paranoid about his voice from the very first day I met him. From my first day in the studio with him to my last, he would always want his voice buried, and I would want to place it more forward in the mix.

8 February 1967: Recording again; gig at The Bromel Club, Bromley.
Mitch Mitchell: There never seemed to be that much time. The sessions were sandwiched between gigs. It really was a case of getting into the studio for an hour or two when you could. There was no question of rehearsing songs. Jimi would show us the riff or tell us roughly what he had in mind and then it was one, two, three and off you'd go,

9 February 1967: More recording at Olympic, followed by a gig at The Locarno, Bristol.

10 February 1967: Gig at The Plaza Ballroom, Newbury, Berkshire.
The Plaza Bulletin, Newbury, reported:

> The Jimi Hendrix Experience roared and romped their way through an hour-and-a-quarter's worth of music that shattered the senses both aurally and visually. Resplendent in red corduroy trousers and antique waistcoat, Jimi proceeded to show just how many positions it was possible to play the guitar in, at the same time showing his own very professional skill which must rate him as one of the most outstanding newcomers on the scene since Jeff Beck or Eric Clapton.
>
> Jimi showed flashes of on-stage humour for which he must be given full credit. 'Hey Joe' was introduced as being written by Mickey Mouse; after a sudden frenzy of excitement in which he attacked his amplifier with his guitar, he announced, 'Anyone wanna buy an ole guitar? This one don't tune so well.' The finish came suddenly in an excess of violence. Mitch Mitchell attacked a cymbal stand and it broke into pieces, then distributed his drum kit round the stage and finally squirted the other two with a handy water-pistol. The bass-guitarist locked his guitar in its case and then kicked it about over the stage. Jimi attacked the huge amplifier with his guitar, breaking all the strings and nearly toppling the amplifier onto his hand. He then squatted on the guitar with both feet and rocked to and fro. Thus the evening came to its conclusion in a storm of feedback, flying microphones and water-pistols.

11 February 1967: Gig at The Blue Moon, Cheltenham, Gloucestershire.
Jimi Hendrix (in The Cheltenham Chronicle*):* Most people believe that, to be a good blues musician, one has to suffer. I don't believe this. I just like the sound of the blues. When I hear certain notes, I feel real happy.

12 February 1967: Photo shoot at Montagu Square; gig at The Sinking Ship, Stockport.
Gerry Stickells: We had a very small amount of equipment. It all went into a station wagon. We didn't carry a lot of spares. For the first year or so, we only carried two guitars on the road.

There was no food at the shows—you went out and got a pizza. There was no lighting—you used the four spots in the house.

13 February 1967: First BBC Radio session, for *Saturday Club*, at Broadcasting House, London.
Bill Bebb (producer): Saturday Club was pulling in nine million listeners on a Saturday morning... Kids normally bought their records on a Saturday afternoon so, if you could get on a programme like *Saturday Club*, it could put anything up to 300,000 on your sales for that day.

Noel Redding: I think the folks at the BBC were a bit taken aback when they saw us. Obviously, they all had smart jumpers on and we came in with pink suits but, before long, they realized we knew what we were doing. They kept complaining that we were too loud, though. Jimi always said, 'Well, there's nothing we can do about that.'

Bill Bebb (producer, Saturday Club*):* The studio manager said, 'Getting a lot of feedback,' so I opened up the talkback and started saying, 'Er, Jimi, we're getting rather a lot...' when Chas, sitting with me in the control room, leans over and says, 'Shut up, man, that's his sound.' So I quickly said, 'No, everything's fine, Jimi, you just carry on.' By now, the SM's having kittens. 'Just shut it right down,' I said, but when he switched off the monitors, we could still hear Jimi through the soundproof glass, and see the glass moving.

14 February 1967: Gigs at Grays Club, Civic Hall, Tilbury, Essex, followed by The St Valentine's Day Massacre at The Speakeasy, London.
Alain Dister (journalist): He played a rather small gymnasium, with a tiny stage at the end. The atmosphere is totally impersonal. Between 500 and 600 people have turned up. From the first notes onwards, it is ecstasy on stage. I never heard anything like this before. It liberates me from a lot of things. Jimi performs a ballet with his guitar... he turns it into a living object. The numbers follow each other in a flow of colors... finally a terrific 'Wild Thing', during which the stage seems to burn. At the end, he throws his guitar on the floor.

15 February 1967: Hendrix interviewed by Kevin Swift of *Beat Instrumental;* gig at the Dorothy Ballroom, Cambridge.
Jimi Hendrix (to Kevin Swift): If I'd had two blues men with me, we would have gone straight into one bag—the blues. That's not for me. This way we can do anything and develop our own music. We might do our own arrangement of a Howlin' Wolf number, followed straight away by 'Wild Thing', or a Bobby Dylan number. We'll do things our own way and make our own sound.

17 February 1967: Gig at the Ricky Tick club, Windsor.

18 February 1967: Photo session, then gig at the Art College, University of York.
Noel Redding: We set off at 5pm (in Mitch's car) and belted off towards Nottingham, but after only a few miles the generator went. We just about made it into Nottingham, left the car at a garage and started to look round for something to get us to York. Eventually we hired a car and about 9.45pm we were on our way again. We turned up at midnight. Fortunately, we weren't due on until 1am.

19 February 1967: Gig at The Blarney Club, London. The band's weekly wage is increased to £30 each.
Noel Redding: We hated to complain but it became obvious that, unless we did, nothing happened. Like most musicians, we hated to speak up, preferring to avoid any form of upset. It's nearly impossible to play music when you're upset. We'd mumble and complain until we were desperate and forced into confrontation.

In early '67, I found out we were earning £200 or £400 a night, and we were still getting paid £25 a week. I wrote a letter to Chas on behalf of the band and we all got a £200 bonus and it went up to £30 a week or something.

Jimi was very concerned about that. We were all very trusting. Hendrix especially so.

20 February 1967: Recording 'Red House' at De Lane Lea; gig at The Pavilion, Bath.
Chas Chandler: The *Smash Hits'* 'Red House' was definitely done at De Lane Lea, not CBS. The 'Red House' on the album *(Are You Experienced)* came about during the last 15 minutes of another session. [13 December 1967]

Josephine Bayne (in The Bath & Wiltshire Evening Chronicle*):*

> As Jimi Hendrix bellowed 'Lord have mercy' from his altar and his worshippers gazed in silent adoration from below, I echoed his sentiments as my ribs reverberated with the intolerable volume of electronic sound... Why he needs to create horrific wailing effects on his guitar and turn the amplifiers to full strength, I cannot imagine. Perhaps someone should tell him that the 'freakier than thou' competition is over and music is on the way back.

21 February 1967: Rehearsing four new songs.
Chas Chandler: We were still rehearsing quite a bit then, because we were still trying to refine the act. We didn't have that many numbers to play, and we were always trying to push new songs in.

22 February 1967: Radio show, *Parade Of The Pops*, at the BBC; a press reception for Soft Machine at The Speakeasy, and finally a gig at The Roundhouse, London.
Noel Redding: The Roundhouse gig was awful. Jimi had his guitar stolen.

Chas Chandler: I was flat broke, so I had to sell my last guitar. I swapped my last bass for a new guitar for Jimi.

23 February 1967: Black and white photo session at Bruce Fleming Studio, London; recording 'I Don't Live Today' at De Lane Lea; gig at The Pier Pavilion, Worthing, Sussex.
Bruce Fleming (photographer): I met Jimi at

Chas's office, very briefly, then he came to my studio with the boys in the middle of London. It was bloody cold, I remember that.

My first job was to photograph Jimi for his record cover, *Are You Experienced*. He was very caring—'What can we do now? Where do you want me to stand?' You know? Very nice guy.

What I wanted to get was an effect shot from the floor, looking up at him so that the boys came out from under his cloak. I also shot some head-on ones, where I raised the camera up higher—it didn't get quite such a dramatic effect.

Mick Coyne (fan): Worthing Pier was like a Sunday afternoon tea-dance place, but it had rock gigs every Thursday, like The Who, Small Faces, Cream, for about five shillings a time. We didn't know much about Hendrix, but he looked great when he came on in his military jacket, and he had a Sunburst Strat with a rosewood neck. The place wasn't full, so you could have easily walked to the front and touched him. He broke a string halfway through, and at the end he did the full guitar-smashing routine, jumping up and down on the tremolo arm and everything.

Gerry Stickells: In the early days, we had a breaking-up guitar, nailed together with bits of wood, which I used to patch up after every show.

24 February 1967: Gig at the University of Leicester.

25 February 1967: Gig at The Corn Exchange, Chelmsford, Essex.

26 February 1967: Gig at St Mary Cray, Southend, Essex, with Dave Dee Dozy Beaky Mick & Tich, The Nashville Teens and The Koobas.
Ian 'Tich' Amey: We were headlining at a one-nighter on Southend Pier, and The Experience closed the first half with 'Wild Thing' which included the whole works—squealing feedback and Jimi setting fire to his guitar—in front of a family audience, ranging from frightened grannies to wailing babes-in-arms. The theatre staff didn't know what to make of it either—particularly as Jimi was such a quiet, polite bloke offstage.

27 February 1967: Color photo session with Bruce Fleming; recording at De Lane Lea studios.
Bruce Fleming: They (the management) picked the wrong (album cover) picture. There was a much better one which I begged them to use. Much more dramatic, but they used a pretty boring one. We would always try to do something different. Jimi was oblivious to everybody else anyway. He didn't pose. A lot of the rock'n'roll people at that time would do big poses for you. Jimi couldn't do that: he thought telling the truth was a better deal than telling lies.

Melissa Chassay (staff at the Brian Morrison Agency): Jimi was the most charming, polite person in the entire world. If you went to his house, he took off your coat, that kind of thing. If you went backstage, there'd be a queue of girls there. One by one they'd go in and Jimi would fuck them, and after an hour he'd go on stage and tear the place apart.

1 March 1967: Recording 'Like A Rolling Stone' at De Lane Lea; gig at The Orchid Ballroom, Purley, Surrey.
Chas Chandler: We did it ('Like A Rolling Stone') a few times but, for some reason, Mitch could never keep the time right. It used to drive them nuts, because Mitch would be either winding up or slowing down... we both wanted to record it, but we were never successful.

2 March 1967: DJ Dave Lee Travis introduces the band on a syndicated TV show, *Beat Club*, filmed at The Marquee, London.
Dave Lee Travis: I was the regular host of *Beat Club*. It was done out of Bremen in Germany, but

"IN EARLY 1967, I FOUND OUT THAT WE WERE EARNING £200 OR £400 A NIGHT, AND WE WERE STILL GETTING PAID £25 A WEEK. I WROTE A LETTER TO CHAS [CHANDLER] ON BEHALF OF THE BAND AND WE ALL GOT A £200 BONUS AND IT WENT UP TO £30 A WEEK" [NOEL REDDING]

BAND AND WE ALL GOT A £200 BONUS AND IT WENT UP TO £30 A WEEK" [NOEL REDDING]

1967

Bruce Fleming's definitive photograph of the early Jimi Hendrix Experience, shot looking up to add drama to the cape

it was syndicated to about 49 countries and had an estimated audience of around 80 million viewers. Usually I'd fly over and do the show in Germany, but on a couple of special occasions, like this one, we did it from London.

The performance was live, not mimed, and they did great versions of 'Hey Joe' and 'Purple Haze', which wasn't out yet. The volume, in that tiny enclosed space of The Marquee, was quite overwhelming, but it was a great performance.

3 March 1967: The Experience fly to Paris.
Chas Chandler: Britain had been our first target and Europe was our second. It was there, in those first few experimental appearances, that I realized his enormous visual attraction and there that the 'smashing routine' really began by accident.

4 March 1967: Gig, radio show and student ball at the Faculté de Droit D'Assas, Paris.
Alain Dister: At the studio (Europe 1 Radio) they let Jimi listen to Johnny Hallyday's version of 'Hey Joe'. Without much embarrassment, he politely makes clear with an economic expression on his face that he is not impressed.

I take him to the flea-market in Saint-Ouen. He seems to enjoy himself enormously, nosing through the old jewellery, curtain ropes, uniforms from the days of the Empire, and all kinds of things he tries without even discussing the price with the merchants. He buys some rings with large sparkling stones. As he leaves, a rocker passes by and whispers to me, 'That guy you are with, is that Little Richard?'

Dick Taylor (guitarist, The Pretty Things): We shared the billing with Jimi that night, and the thing that sticks in my mind is that in the dressing room, he was sitting playing his Strat without having it plugged in and yet the sound seemed to me to be almost exactly the same as if he was on stage. He was that good.

It was quite a small crowd that night. There were other things going on in the building, as I recall. I think there was a dining room and a dance band somewhere. I made a point of going out to see him and he played brilliantly for them.

5 March 1967: Gig at The Twenty Club, Mouscron, Belgium.

6 March 1967: Band mimes 'Hey Joe' for Belgian TV show *Vibrato* in Zoniewoud forest, St Pieters; gig at The Twenty Club, Lille, France.
Jan Waldrop (in Humo *magazine):*

> The big quiet Zoniewoud rustles in the cold spring wind; an old man gathers wood. A frayed cigarette stump hangs out of his toothless mouth, a fact that is clearly in evidence as the aforementioned mouth falls open at the arrival of Jimi Hendrix... Jimi has an overwhelming amount of dark hair; a fantastic,almost picturesque, primitive head. Between his friendly dog eyes lies a nose like a trampled-down rubber hose. And, as if he feared in spite of all this, he would remain unnoticed, Jimi wears cracking red trousers and a fantastic military dress coat.

7 March 1967: Recording *Tienerklanken* TV show in Brussels, Belgium.

8 March 1967: Gig at The Speakeasy, London.
Dick Taylor: Anybody who imagines Hendrix as some totally out of it, drug-crazed wild man of rock, would be totally wrong. Most of the times I met him he was perfectly straight, sharp, lucid and amusing. We used to see Jimi down at The Speakeasy quite regularly, and there was one night we'd driven him down there and he must have taken some acid, because he seemed to be tripping when we took him home. One of our roadies was driving the car, going quite fast and swerving round corners and I think Jimi thought he was in a spaceship. 'Whoa, hold on, there, man! Slow down!' He was almost cowering in the corner of the seat.

9 March 1967: Photo session at Gered Mankowitz's studio, London; gig at The Skyline Hotel, Hull, Yorkshire.
Gered Mankowitz: I was shooting from very high up and very close in to him. But Jimi, being Jimi, was pretty stoned and kept on rocking back and forth. I had to say to him, 'Stand still, you keep on going in and out of focus.' He didn't smile a lot. It's not that he didn't normally, just that he didn't turn it on in a false way for the camera.

10 March 1967: Gig at The Club A Go Go, Newcastle Upon Tyne.

11 March 1967: Gig at The International Club, Leeds.

12 March 1967: Gig at The Gyro Club, Troutbeck Hotel, Ilkley, Yorkshire.
Vince Philpotts (fan): The ballroom was designed for about 200 people but there were about 450 inside, even standing on window-sills and tables. As soon as Hendrix appeared the place went wild. There was shouting and jumping—it was a thrill to watch this fellow walking on stage. He started off with one hell of an instrumental; Noel Redding started with a bassline, then Mitchell came in on drums. It was just a huge bang, straight into the set. It was loud and excellent.

Tom Chapman (police officer): I just walked in and I was met with all these people. The manager said there were over 900. There should have been 250—that's the Fire Service regulation for granting the license—in the hotel. When I looked into the ballroom, they were shoulder-to-shoulder and I had to push my way through to get to the edge of the stage. I spoke to the chap playing the guitar—I didn't know who he was—and he didn't stop playing.

Vince Philpotts: The next thing, this suicidal plain-clothes cop in a gabardine gets up on the stage and tells Hendrix to shut up and says the place is in breach of fire regulations. Everyone had to go home. He just got everybody's back up.

13 March 1967: The Experience flies to Amsterdam; Mike Jeffery flies to New York to confirm a US deal with Warner Bros Records.

14 March 1967: Hendrix walks out of Dutch TV show, *Fanclub*, when he is asked to mime.
Peter Schroeder (TV staff): At that time in TV-land, one was totally not used to the volume... It was so powerful that within one minute most of the TV people in the studio had left.

Jimi Hendrix: They said, 'Play as loud as you like,' and we were really grooving when this little fairy comes running in and yells, 'Stop! Stop! Stop!—the ceiling in the studio below is falling down.' And it was too—plaster and all.

15 March 1967: Flight back to London.

16 March 1967: Launch party for Track Records at The Speakeasy.
Marianne Faithfull: Jimi was by now the toast of the town and on the verge of displacing Mick as the great sex symbol of the moment. After the show, Jimi came over to our table and pulled up a chair next to me and began whispering in my ear. He was saying anything he could think of to get me to go home with him. All the things he wanted to do to me sexually. Telling me he'd written 'The Wind Cries Mary' for me. Saying, 'Come with me now, baby. Let's split. What are you doing with this jerk anyway?'

I wanted more than anything to go with him, but I couldn't do it. Mick would never have forgiven me. Throughout the whole incident, Mick was a model of sang-froid.

17 March 1967: UK release of 'Purple Haze'; press conference in Hamburg, followed by a gig at The Star Club, Hamburg.
Jimi Hendrix (to Chas Chandler at press conference): When am I going to get my money? Is there any money?

18 March 1967: Another gig at The Star Club.
Paul Gadd (later to become Gary Glitter): I was playing then at The Star Club with my band The Bostons, and shared my dressing room with Hendrix. He was the most stoned person I've ever met—very polite, almost humble, but so out of it, I couldn't understand anything he said.

19 March 1967: Third gig at The Star Club, Hamburg, plus interview for *Bravo*

20 March 1967: Flight to Luxembourg.

21 March 1967: Mike Jeffery signs a contract with Reprise Records, subsidiary of Warner Bros, in the US; after a Radio Luxembourg interview, Jimi flies back for gig at The Speakeasy, London.
John Hillman (Yameta lawyer): Jeffery wanted to keep Hendrix cordoned off from everybody. I gave him the opportunity to do that by saying Hendrix couldn't sign the March 21, 1967, agreement for tax reasons. Naturally, Jeffery used this as his shield.

Noel Redding: ...a five-year, million-dollar contract. I couldn't get a copy, but I have heard that the advance was $150,000, with eight per cent artist royalties and two per cent to Jeffery as producer. The advance never showed up in the accounts, but there was money around. Chas couldn't set up his new £330 stereo, so I did it.

Tim Rose: I saw him (Hendrix) at The Speakeasy Club in London when I was promoting 'Morning Dew', and he'd already had 'Hey Joe', so he was introduced to me and the first thing he did was to thank me for that song. I said, 'You're welcome,' gritting my teeth, thinking, 'You're making millions and I'm not,' but what the hell. Literally, he and Chas Chandler bought my record and listened to it. Hendrix put his own style to it, but they did the same arrangement almost, putting Hendrixisms in it.

22 March 1967: Jimi and Kathy move into 23 Upper Berkeley Street, Mayfair, London W1, again sharing with Chas and Lotte Chandler; gig at The Guildhall, Southampton.

Spencer Davis: When Jimi was living in Mayfair, I used to go round there to parties. One night Jimi was sitting on the sofa, just jamming with a bunch of friends, and I was intrigued by a chord he was playing. I liked the way it sounded but I couldn't figure out how he was doing it because, of course, he was left-handed. Eventually I got him to show me how to do it, and that was the chord I play at the start of 'I'm A Man'.

23 March 1967: Jimi sells a Stratocaster; 'Purple Haze' enters the UK singles chart.
Oliver Keen (musician): I got a telephone call from Harry Moore, then manager of Selmer's music shop, Charing Cross Road, London. On arriving in the shop, Harry told me they had just got a second hand Fender Stratocaster in the shop... 'Well,' he says, 'we even have the fellow who's trading it in as well.' Down to the back of the shop where the guitar section was we go. Harry introduces me to Chas Chandler... Chas in turn introduces me to Jimi. 'Play him a few bars,' says Harry. Jimi, dressed in a long black leather overcoat, strolls over to the amplifier, picks up this blue-white guitar and gives us all a blast of some blues... Here was Jimi Hendrix, helping to sell his own guitar, and he did. I signed the hire purchase form. Total cost £89 sterling.

24 March 1967: Mitch Mitchell's hair is re-permed by Gary Craze at Sweeney's, London.
Mitch Mitchell: Noel said there was girl he knew that could perm my hair and it would save money, rather than going to a hairdresser. After she had finished, it was a complete mess. I ended up having to go to the hairdresser anyway.

25 March 1967: Gig at The Starlight Room, Gliderdrome, Boston, Lincolnshire.

26 March 1967: Gig at The Tabernacle Club, Stockport, Cheshire.

27 March 1967: Recording *Dee Time* at BBC TV Studio, Manchester.
Simon Dee: Before we taped the show, I sat and had a cup of tea with Hendrix, and was fascinated to find that, in fairly dramatic contrast to his image, he was quite a deep thinking sort of guy, able to talk about world events and politics very coherently and precisely.

He was a little nervous, because although they'd done *Ready Steady Go!* and *Top Of The Pops,* they really weren't used to early-evening chat shows. They played live for us, which was our policy, and we had a great producer who really miked them up well. Hendrix obviously much preferred playing live rather than miming.

28 March 1967: *Saturday Club*, BBC Radio; gig at The Grosvenor Ballroom, Aylesbury.
Pete Frame (fan): Hendrix was using the house PA system which was distorting horribly, but his guitar sounded great through these huge Marshall stacks he had behind him, pretty much playing the stuff from the first album. I noticed this chubby roadie, lounging about at the side of the stage and towards the end of the set he went behind the stacks and held them in place while Hendrix bludgeoned into them. I learned later that he was Dave Robinson, who went on to found Stiff Records

29 March 1967: Recording 'Manic Depression', 'No No No', 'Remember' and 'Red House' at De Lane Lea.
Chas Chandler: 'Remember' was an end-of-the-session demo, first recorded at De Lane Lea. We made a quarter-inch, seven-and-a-half i.p.s. reel to listen to and work on the song at home. This was something we did often. The De Lane Lea recording was much too raggedy. Jimi tightened it up later at Olympic. [13 December 1967]

30 March 1967: The Experience perform 'Purple Haze' on *Top Of The Pops.*

31 March 1967: First night of The Walker Brothers package tour at The Astoria, London.

Jimi Hendrix: The first night of The Walker Brothers tour was when I started to worry. I knew where it was at when it came to specialist blues scenes, but this was in front of audiences who had come to see The Walker Brothers, Engelbert Humperdinck and Cat Stevens. All the sweet people follow us on the bill, so we have to make it hot for them. We have to hit 'em and hit 'em good. Those who come to hear Engelbert sing 'Please Release Me' may not dig me, but that's not tragic. We'll play for ourselves—we've done it before.

Keith Altham: There was a clutch of us in the dressing room. Chas, Jimi and I were all talking. Various things were being discussed about what they could actually do that night to grab some headlines and capture people's attention. I think it was simply because I had a variflame lighter, I said, 'What would happen if we set light to his guitar?'. I kind of said it as a joke but Chas said, 'That's not a bad idea.' I said that you would never get away with it. I mean, they are solid-bodied guitars. You could light a bonfire under it and it would take 15 minutes to catch. And Chas said, 'Well, if we use lighter fuel, it will just burn the lighter fuel and won't burn the actual guitar.' So we tried a few experimental runs in the dressing room and it worked.

George McManus (Polydor staff): At that stage, they only did the single, the b-side and the next single, and that was it. There were so many acts on the bill. The way they looked was amazing. You can imagine them, next to the clean-cut Walker Brothers, coming on with the afro hair and the whole lot. You thought, Christ, this is really what rock'n'roll should be. When Jimi set fire to his guitar I was absolutely stunned.

Cat Stevens: You'd hear, 'Hey, there's a fire onstage!' And we came rushing down and there was this guy kneeling down burning his guitar. I was incredibly petrified, so petrified I wouldn't wear my new Anello & David high-heeled shoes. I had to put on my plimsolls to actually move.

Keith Altham: It caused an enormous row with one of the security officers in the theater—he threatened that Jimi would never work on his cinema circuit again. He came storming round afterwards looking for the guitar as evidence of what had happened.

1 April 1967: Gig at The Odeon, Ipswich.
Chas Chandler: We had the Rank circuit up in arms over the act. They sent down investigators and when I knew they were there, we toned down the act. When they went away we went back to normal.

Noel Redding: Humperdinck's guitar player left after the first night, so I played guitar for him on that tour, behind the curtain. I'd play bass with Hendrix then walk across the stage and there would be a guitar and a chair for me.

2 April 1967: Gig at The Gaumont, Worcester.
Chas Chandler: For the rest of the tour, they didn't take too kindly to us. John Walker was a bit of a big head, and he would waltz into our dressing room and say, 'I don't want any upstaging tonight. Who do you think you are?' There was a lot of ill-feeling backstage and they would screw up the lights or put the house lights up on the audience during the act. It was quite a tour.

3 April 1967: Recording 'May This Be Love', 'Are You Experienced' and 'Highway Chile' at Olympic Studios, London.
Eddie Kramer: It was really Chas and Jimi's working together that made everything so tight... On the first album Jimi worked within a very tight three-to-four-minute song structure. That was Chas's background, and Jimi had to compact his awesome imagination into that tight, polished format. In hindsight, it was very good for him.

Mitch Mitchell: 'Are You Experienced' was a bit of a production, because of all the backwards solos and other things but 'Manic Depression', 'Remember', 'May This Be Love' and 'Red House' were all one take. Even '3rd Stone From The Sun', which rambled on a bit, the basic track was all wrapped up in one take.

Chas Chandler: We used to sit at our apartment in the evenings and work out who we were going to offend tomorrow. We did nothing but sit home, play *Risk*, and talk about his career.

4 April 1967: The Experience appears on the opening edition of BBC1-TV's *Dee Time*.
Simon Dee: I seem to remember he performed 'Purple Haze' on that transmission, and as it was the first show, it got about two million viewers. If he'd been on the next week, the audience had

Marianne Faithfull and Mick Jagger: a classic 1960s couple but that didn't stop Hendrix trying to make his move on her

shot up to four million. Despite his nerves about being on the show, he played superbly, and you got the feeling that his inner confidence came from knowing just how brilliant he was as a performer.

5 April 1967: Gig at The Odeon, Leeds.
Noel Redding: There was no PA system, you'd just go and play. There was no fiddling about like these days—soundchecks, whatever that means. We'd turn up, Hendrix and I would go to the pub, we'd do the set, sit around, do the second set. We had no sound man, just a road manager, normal house lighting, very basic but very nice.

Jimi Hendrix: The bosses of the tour are giving us hell. The organizers don't give us a chance to tune up before we go on stage. They say we are obscene and vulgar, but we play our act as we have always played it everywhere else, and there have never been complaints before. We refuse to change our act and the result is my amplifier sometimes gets cut off at the funniest times... or I find my guitar is out of tune after I just tuned it.

6 April 1967: Gig at The Odeon, Glasgow.
Noel Redding: The tour sold out, between our popularity and The Walkers. Jimi began to realize that he personally could be successful, which boosted his confidence. Our egos grew and sometimes clashed. After I went home with a girl he fancied, Jimi freaked out and hit her.

7 April 1967: Unplanned photo-session in The Fridge boutique before gig at the ABC, Carlisle.
Mike Huggon (photographer): I was taking some publicity shots for The Fridge boutique when, en route to buy some extra film, I met Mitch by chance in the street. I invited him and Jimi for a drink, followed by coffee in the boutique.

8 April 1967: Gig at The ABC, Chesterfield, Derbyshire. Hendrix's foot requires four stitches after a fuzzbox control breaks during the first house, but he goes on for the second house.

9 April 1967: Gig at The Empire, Liverpool.
Keith Reid (Procol Harum): Jimi was extremely open to other musicians. I actually remember him being complimentary about Engelbert, saying he had a good voice. And there was a Marmalade record out at that time which he said he liked. Most English musicians would have considered it too uncool to admit to things like that.

Jimi Hendrix: I sat down and listened to Engelbert one night—he really has a very good voice—it's flawless. Maybe if you don't have a very good imagination you need good looks and a flawless voice.

10 April 1967: Jimi is interviewed for *Melody Maker;* the band records tracks at the BBC's Playhouse Theatre, London, for the radio show *Monday Monday*; final mixes for the *Are You Experienced* album at Olympic.
Chas Chandler: When we finally finished the mixing and sequencing of the album it was about 3am. I'd promised Polydor Records that I would play it for them at 11 that morning. After we finished, I went home and caught a few hours sleep, because I had a session booked at the cutting room to make a lacquer in the morning, as Polydor didn't want to hear a reel-to-reel tape copy.

I took the lacquer to play for Horst Schmaltze, who was Polydor's head of A&R. As Horst started to put the needle on the record, I broke out in a cold sweat, thinking, Christ, when he hears this, he's going to order the men in white coats to take me away. I was suddenly terrified that I had to play these recordings to someone outside the circle.

Horst played the first side and didn't say a word. Then he turned the disc over and played the other side. I started thinking about how I was going to talk my way out of this. At the end of the second side, he just sat there. Finally, he said, 'This is brilliant. This is the greatest thing I've ever heard.'

I let out a loud, 'Aaaah!' Horst became a great supporter of the band from that point forward. Kit Lambert and Chris Stamp at Track were creative but, from that point on, we had a crusader for us within the Polydor establishment. He and Roland Rennie got behind the marketing and distribution of the album in a big way.

11 April 1967: Gig at The Granada, Bedford.

12 April 1967: The Gaumont, Southampton.

13 April 1967: The Odeon, Wolverhampton.
Noel Redding: We could no longer go out and cool off between shows. We had no option but to sit around in dressing rooms, with nothing to do but get smashed.

14 April 1967: Gig at The Odeon, Bolton.
Jimmy Leverton (bass player for Engelbert Humperdinck, later in Fat Mattress): Cat used to come on and do 'Love My Dog', 'Matthew And Son' and 'I'm Gonna Get Me A Gun', at which point Noel and Mitch sprayed him from the back with water pistols. Humperdinck fired me for hanging out with 'undesirables'.

15 April 1967: Gig at The Odeon, Blackpool.
Noel Redding: We didn't want to hang out in Bolton so we got a train to Blackpool, but we weren't allowed into that hotel. They said, and this happened a lot to us: 'You aren't booked here. Clear off.' This is three in the morning. I vividly remember walking around Blackpool with Mitch. We'd lost Jimi. We checked into this B&B. Same thing happened to everyone on the tour. Because of our appearance.

16 April 1967: De Montfort Hall, Leicester.
Cat Stevens: He (Hendrix) was with his gang and he used to go to clubs afterwards. I hung around more with him than I did with Humperdinck. We used to talk about girls and that was about it. He was actually quite a sincere fellow. Behind it all, he was a little bit introverted, but not as introverted as Scott Walker who used to hide himself away from everybody.

17 April 1967: TV recording in London for *Late Night Line Up;* jam at the Bag o'Nails.
Mike Appleton (TV producer): Late Night Line Up was recorded in studio B, which was basically built for the continuity announcers. It was made for one person, a camera and a vase of flowers. When Jimi came in, we did the session and it filtered in from Floor 4 all the way through to the ground floor, and there were complaints about the sound in the studio directly below us.

Georgie Fame: When I briefly broke up the Blue Flames, Mitch had walked out of my band and straight into Jimi's. One of their first London dates was at the Bag O'Nails, where I had part-ownership. Ben E King was here on tour, a very good mate I'd known for years, and all three of us hung out in each other's pockets. Most of the jamming was with me and Jimi, well after midnight, with Ben E's band—Ben E singing and me on Hammond. We played regular swinging blues things, stuff that Ben E would know, like 'Every Day I Have The Blues'.

Ben E King: He came in and sat down. And before you knew it, he was up there jamming. He was just playing on the stuff that I was doing in those days—'Spanish Harlem', 'Stand By Me'—things like that. It was very free-flowing, because that was his style. He knew the songs and he knew the music, so we just let him do his thing.

19 April 1967: Gig at The Odeon, Birmingham.

20 April 1967: Gig at The ABC, Lincoln.
Un-named reviewer in The Lincolnshire Chronicle*:*

> Hendrix was in a very bouncy mood. His opening remark was, 'I'm going to put a curse on everyone so that all their babies will be born naked.'... During the show, a score of girls rush the stage. The Experience quickly go to their smoky dressing-room and collapse.
>
> His movements were far too suggestive for an audience mostly in the 14-18 age group.

21 April 1967: Gig at The City Hall, Newcastle.

22 April 1967: Gig at The Odeon, Manchester.

23 April 1967: Gig at The Gaumont, Hanley.

24 April 1967: Jimi attends a Donovan concert at the Saville Theatre, London.
Jimi Hendrix: When I saw pictures of this sweet little guy with the lacquered nails and all, I thought, Damn me! But when I met him, he turned out to be really groovy. It shatters me anyone could be that nice. He's really beautiful.

25 April 1967: Gig at The Colston Hall, Bristol.
Jimi Hendrix: Sure, the tour was good experience but our billing position was all wrong. I was setting the stage on fire for everyone else... that Engelflumplefuff hadn't any stage presence. He never got anything going.

26 April 1967: Gig at The Capitol, Cardiff.

27 April 1967: Gig at The ABC, Aldershot.
Alan Clayson (fan, later rock journalist): Noel Redding and Mitch Mitchell drew the beginnings of a crowd by taking the air during the late afternoon when girls from the High School were going home. They made themselves even more conspicuous by Noel wearing the trousers and Mitch the jacket of the same bright orange suit.

28 April 1967: Gig at The Adelphi, Slough; then a jam with Tomorrow at the UFO Club, London; finally The Speakeasy Club.
Roger Newell (fan): I went along with my band, Rainbow Ffolly from High Wycombe, right after our first album. We'd heard 'Hey Joe' but not much else, so we had no idea what to expect.

Jimi came out to close the first half and right away they looked so strange on that big stage. We'd seen rock trios, like Cream, in little clubs but this was different. Jimmy started by trilling one note on the guitar and, while he was doing this he said, 'We'll be here in a minute,' and then the feedback built up and he was into the start of 'Foxy Lady' and it was just incredible. None of us had ever heard a noise as powerful as that from just three guys before.

At one point, he laid his Strat down on the stage and sat on the tremolo arm and made the guitar give out these groaning noises, a blatantly sexual thing, which sent half the girls in the audience into ecstasies.

We all went back to High Wycombe and immediately started changing our act.

Joe Boyd (co-founder of The UFO Club, later producer): We had The Smoke booked in but they got stuck in Germany... I rang up the agency... he sent down The In Crowd... I was pretty nervous at the thought of some group called The In Crowd playing at the UFO. But when they arrived at the club we were informed they'd changed their name to Tomorrow... Jimi Hendrix leapt up on stage and played bass and it was all very amazing.

Steve Howe (guitarist, Tomorrow, later of Yes): In our show, Junior (John Wood) would put down his bass and dance around. This night I was improvizing and Twink (John Adler) was doing things on drums to keep the rhythm going without it being just a backbeat. Suddenly this figure appeared on stage. We all knew who it was, 'cause we'd seen him a lot. Hendrix picked up the bass, and we went somewhere—for the life of me, I don't know where it was. We were just improvizing. He started playing away and I wasn't ever sure we were in the same key, but we were somehow doing something that was electrifying.

Roger Mayer (electronics designer): We were at The Speakeasy until about six in the morning. As I was leaving, I asked Hendrix where he was playing that night and he said, 'Bournemouth'.

29 April 1967: Winter Gardens, Bournemouth.
Roger Mayer: About four that afternoon, I got a phone call from Jimi. 'Where are you?' I asked. 'At the flat in London.' 'What the hell are you doing there?' 'I'm a bit late for the gig tonight.' So I drove him to Bournemouth in my white Midget MG hardtop sports car. There was a crowd of people by the backstage door; I drove through them so that the passenger door was about six feet from the backstage entrance. Security came over and got Hendrix inside.

I didn't park my car far enough away though. After the gig, there was 'I love Jimi' in red lipstick all over it. The windshield wipers were stolen, the petrol cap, the little nuts off the windows... I started her up and drove to the stage door, where Jimi asked me what had happened. I said, 'I don't know. They're your fans!' We had to drive a few miles to a petrol (gas) station, without wipers to clear the lipstick-smeared windshield. While we filled her up, Hendrix and I cleaned the lipstick off and drove on to The Speakeasy.

30 April 1967: The Granada, Tooting, London.
Mitch Mitchell: Cat Stevens became a real snot so, on the matinee of the last show, when he was doing 'I'm Gonna Get Me A Gun', I placed this mechanical robot on stage. Its chest opened up and all these little machine guns started blazing away. He tried to kick it off stage, but the thing refused to die. He didn't take the joke too well.

1 May 1967: 'Hey Joe' is released in the US.

3 May 1967: While Jimi is interviewed by Keith Altham of *NME*, Mitch phones a plumber.
Mitch Mitchell: The top came off the tap and there's a jet of boiling water about six feet high hitting the ceiling and the water's so deep that we can't open the door because of the pressure and the caretaker doesn't know where the stopcock is...

4 May 1967: Miming 'The Wind Cries Mary' on *Top Of The Pops*; recording 'Taking Care Of No Business' and Noel's 'She's So Fine' at Olympic.
Noel Redding: 'She's So Fine' was about hippies. I had seen some bloke walking about with an

UK jazz organist Georgie Fame, who had employed Mitch Mitchell in his band The Blue Flames, went on to jam with Hendrix

alarm clock around his neck, attached by a bit of string. He must have figured that it looked very avant-garde… I wrote that while we were waiting to do *Top Of The Pops*. We went to the studio that night and put it down.

Chas Chandler: Jimi insisted that Noel's song be allowed on the album. He wanted Mitch to put one on as well, because he felt he would get more commitment from them. It was being generous really, just as simple as that.

Noel Redding: I showed Hendrix the riff, and he liked it because it was in A, and there was an open G in it for him to play, which he liked a lot. Hendrix thought of the G solo in the middle, because I couldn't think of anything. I was overwhelmed that my song was being recorded.

Chas Chandler: Jimi was laughing when Noel was singing. Nobody could keep a straight face.

Noel Redding: The session was great. Hendrix and Mitchell were doing those funny vocals in the background, and Chas thought it was wonderful. He also liked it because it was a pop-type record and it had been written by the bass player in his new band, which looked good from a PR point of view.

5 May 1967: UK release of 'The Wind Cries Mary'; work starts on 'EXP' and 'If Six Was Nine' at Olympic Studios.
Jimi Hendrix: We do this blues. It's called 'If Six Was Nine'. That is what you call a great feeling of blues. We don't even try to give it a name. Everybody has some kind of blues to offer.

Terry Brown (substitute engineer): I remember it all being very intense, with quite a few people sitting around listening. We were working so hard for Jimi. He was such a soft, gentle person—it seemed like he knew something we didn't know.

While the song ('EXP') was very experimental, Jimi was on top of what he was doing. We set up to get the sounds Jimi wanted and then worked for a long time trying to record these bizarre noises. The speaker system Jimi was using was pretty abstract. He had a small amplifier stack and this long, six-foot horn, mounted on the side of one of his amplifiers. We dimmed the lights very low in the studio, and he worked on it until he was satisfied, which took a long time.

6 May 1967: Gig at The Imperial Ballroom, Nelson, Lancashire.

7 May 1967: Gig at the Saville Theatre, supported by US R&B singer Garnett Mimms.
Andrew Lauder: This was just three months after I'd seen him at The Flamingo so, musically, the set hadn't changed much. The place was full, so he'd obviously managed to attract a huge audience very quickly. He had no problem adapting to the bigger stage.

Norrie Drummond (in NME*):*

> Unfortunately, Jimi had a lot of trouble with his guitar and at one point quipped 'If Eric Clapton's in the audience, can he come up here and tune this thing?'

9 May 1967: Hendrix is guest of honour at The Variety Club's 'Tribute To The Recording Industry' lunch in the Dorchester Hotel. Later, further work on 'If Six Was Nine' at Olympic Studios.
Graham Nash: Gary Leeds of The Walker Brothers and I were there and Jimi said, 'Ah, perfect. Come over here.' I said, 'Perfect for what?' He said, 'You're my walkers.' I said, 'Uh, Walker Brothers, right?' He said, 'I need somebody to walk. Come here and listen.'

He put a piece of plywood on the floor and put a microphone down there. He said, 'OK, I'm going to play the track. Put the 'phones on. When I nod my head, you start walking.' I thought, Oh, Jimi. He put on 'If Six Was Nine' and we started to walk. I mean, I'm known for my high harmony and tinkling western sky music, here I am walking.

10 May 1967: Recording 'The Wind Cries Mary' for the next day's *Top Of The Pops;* jam with The Amen Corner at The Speakeasy.
Barrie Martin: I joined *Top Of The Pops* as a floor manager, as a result of which I was given membership of The Speakeasy. Usually, when we'd finished *Top Of The Pops*, we'd go down to the Speakeasy, so I frequently saw Jimi there.

The Speakeasy was a small, enclosed, dark club, and it was set up as a hang-out for the music industry. It would be full of TV people, producers, record pluggers, musicians, journalists. In that context, it was very easy to have access to Jimi. He knew me from *Top Of The Pops,* so I would go and sit with him at the bar and we'd chat.

Then maybe he'd decide to get up and jam with whoever was on that night. You'd hear a few notes of tuning up, and everybody's ears would prick up. The conversations would stop, the drinks would go down, the tables of food in the eating area would be abandoned, and everybody would crowd in to see Hendrix play.

12 May 1967: UK release of debut album, *Are You Experienced;* gig at Bluesville 67 Club, London; Hendrix signs a music publishing contract.
Jimi Hendrix: Our new LP was made in 16 days, which I'm very sad about... It depends on so many things... the cutting of it... You can go in there and mix and mix and mix and get such a beautiful sound and, when it's time to cut it, they just screw it up so bad.

David Toop (writer/musician): That night was the first time I saw the Jimi Hendrix Experience play. We queued on the stairs and rushed for the front row. Breathless, we were close enough to touch when the group filed onto the narrow stage.

Max Anthony (fan): After a couple of jeers and whistles, Hendrix mumbled a mock apology with the promise that he was going to 'break a guitar or two'. The set that followed was a blistering, fully-cranked assault on the senses.

David Toop: During the climax of the act, a roadie had to stand behind the amplifiers to prevent Hendrix from pushing them through the pub window into the streets below.

Max Anthony: The final number ended in a crescendo of feedback, the band leaving the stage after turning the amps up full, Hendrix pausing briefly to lob his still plugged-in Strat out of one of the windows at the back of the stage. The band didn't return for an encore but I didn't really care. I was listening to the guitar banging against the outside wall in the wind.

Gary Brooker (Procol Harum): We played our first gig at The Speakeasy the day the record ('A Whiter Shade Of Pale') came out, so nobody knew us. Because we only had ten Brooker/Reid songs, we played those, then we played a few others that we liked. We played a Bob Dylan song, a Rascals song, and one called 'Morning Dew' that Tim Rose had recorded. Hendrix was down at The Speakeasy watching us playing and he suddenly jumped up on stage when we started 'Morning Dew', grabbed the bass off our bass-player, turned it upside down, and joined in. He loved us. He thought we were lovely.

13 May 1967: Gig at Imperial College, London, supported by 1984, a band including future Queen guitarist Brian May.
Dave Dilloway (guitarist, 1984): We were booked to play first for dancing downstairs on that occasion, and we stopped when we knew Hendrix was due on in the main hall.

Brian Jones came out of the dressing room behind Hendrix and went with him to the stage, where he stood quietly watching Jimi perform from the wings. I don't think I'd ever seen anyone look so skeletal and ill as Jones did that night.

14 May 1967: Gig at Belle Vue, Manchester.

15 May 1967: Start of first proper European tour at Neue Welt Club, Berlin, West Germany.

16 May 1967: Gig at The Big Apple, Munich.
Noel Redding: Drink, smoke and pills got us in the right frame of mind for performing, or just to enable us to stay awake long enough to perform. Being The Experience was like making a pact to get at least that stoned every night.

17 May 1967: West German radio interview by Hans Carl Schmidt in Frankfurt.
Jimi Hendrix (to Hans Carl Schmidt): I wish you could send me home, so I could see my parents for a few days. I haven't been home for about five-and-a-half years... I told my dad we have three records out. He said, 'Oh, yeah!' He didn't even know that I was singing, because I was always too scared to sing. Chas has made me sing serious.

18 May 1967: *Beat! Beat! Beat!* TV show, Stadthalle, Offenbach, West Germany, then Jimi jams with Dave Dee and John 'Beaky' Dymond at the K52 club.
Joerg Pompetzki (fan): In 1967, all these people had no bodyguards, they just sat in the restaurant of the Town Hall for lunch and we youngsters disturbed them. Seeing Jimi dining, I asked him for a drawing of himself and he did not hesitate to draw a slim man with wild hair and a guitar. Naturally he signed his work and I also got Noel and Mitch's signatures.

Dave Dee: Jimi and Noel Redding, Beaky and me went out looning in Frankfurt in the evening at the K52... but he (Jimi) refused to play lead guitar, so Noel Redding played lead guitar and Jimi played bass... He said, 'I fancy a jam, but I don't wanna play guitar...' Beaky, who was our rhythm guitar, played drums.

19 May 1967: Gig at Konserthallen, Liseberg Nojespark, Gothenburg, Sweden.
*Keith Altham (*NME *review of* Are You Experienced*):*

> Hendrix is a new dimension in electrical guitar music, launching what amounts to a one-man assault upon the nerve cells. The LP is a brave effort by Hendrix to produce a musical form which is original and exciting.

20 May 1967: Mike Jeffery's Yameta Co. signs a production deal with Warner Brothers' subsidiary label Reprise Records (owned by Frank Sinatra), with $120,000 advance.
Stan Cornyn (Reprise Records): In a way, it seemed ridiculous to sign Hendrix. Absolutely ridiculous. We didn't know anything about the Jimi Hendrix Experience. We didn't know anything about rock'n'roll. But Mo (Ostin, MD of Reprise) was out to change the label's image.

Johanan Vigoda: The deal I did with Warner Brothers was tremendous for that time. First, there was a $20,000 promotion budget—immense for an unknown artist's first album—and that money was just to start this thing in the works. The second part was that I threw in something which, at the time, was completely unheard of—a soundtrack exclusion.

21 May 1967: Gig at Falkoner Centret Sports Arena, Copenhagen, Denmark.
Anders Stefansen (promoter): There were not many tickets sold in advance but people came running Sunday evening and we got sold out. He (Hendrix) was a real musician, he just loved to play. There was never any problems.

22 May 1967: Gig at the Kulttuuritalo, Helsinki, Finland. In New York, Ed Chalpin informs Polydor and Warner Brothers that Hendrix is under contract to his company, PPX.
Hassi Walli (Finnish guitarist): The curtain was still on (at the Kulttuuritalo) and the guys were getting ready behind it. Jimi was tuning his guitar... the sound of the tuning was already so heavy that it would have been enough. It was unbelievable. Visually, it was out of sight, with Jimi and Noel having these enormous afros... I sat right in front of the guitar amps so I didn't hear much of his voice. I had a feeling that they were pretty tired, but the audience was digging them like hell, and that inspired him.

Roland Rennie (Polydor Records): Chalpin, basically, made cover versions of hits, but he had this contract and Hendrix had signed it when he was a session player. So he came out of the woodwork at this time, flourishing his contract. However, Polydor's deal with Hendrix excluded America, where he was signed to Warners, so he had to sue a different company in each country.

23 May 1967: Bongo Club, Malmo, Sweden.

24 May 1967: *Popside* TV show, Stockholm. On his way to today's gig at the Tivoli Gardens, Hendrix asks a girl for directions. Her name is Eva Sundqvist. The band is turned out of its hotel.
Jimi Hendrix: It seems people in Scandinavia just aren't ready for the way we look. The kids are great and the concerts have been much more successful than we could have expected for a first visit.

25 May 1967: Hendrix is interviewed by Klaes Borlin of Swedish Radio. Refused hotel rooms in Stockholm, the band flies on to Gothenburg.

26 May 1967: Star Palace, Kiel, West Germany.
Eddie Shaw (guitarist, The Monks): Larry, our organ player, and I were staying across the street in a small hotel. That evening, he and I were in the tiny dining room, when Mitch and Noel came in. They sat down at the table with us to eat.

Jimi came to the table a little later. He said he had almost missed the ferry from Copenhagen to Germany—as if he had not traveled with the other two. I was struck by his appearance. He wore a brightly colored silk shirt and scarf, and had frizzy hair. The kitchen staff, or one of the hotel guests, would come into the small room to stare at us and then leave quickly.

That evening, I think we played a couple of sets before Hendrix came on. When he began to play, I was completely blown away by his sound and technique. This was probably the first English-

Another appearance for Hendrix on the highly influential Top Of The Pops; there were very few UK TV music shows at the time

based group I had ever heard, who me made yell, 'This is amazing!' As a bit of stage show, he pretended to play the guitar with his teeth, then laid it on the floor as if he was having sex with it. I was struck how he scowled and didn't seem to like this part of the performance.

When Jimi had finished his set, the audience reacted as if they had been in a stupor. We talked in the back room and I made mention of his show. 'The audience thinks you are playing the guitar with your teeth.' He sighed, 'Oh, yeah.' 'Hey, it was great,' I said. 'Not really,' he replied. He then asked what the box was that Gary played with his foot. We had incorporated a lot of fuzz, feedback and wow-wow sounds into our music. Gary showed Jimi his wah-wah pedal and explained how it worked. He didn't seem a very talkative person, but he seemed very intent and observant.

When we played the next set, he sat at a table in the middle of the club and watched us. He sat by himself and there was something melancholy about him, as if he was used to being a loner. There were no groupies. At times he roamed around the room, as if he wished someone would talk to him. Noel and Mitch had left right after their performance, but he stayed. In fact I noticed that he didn't seem to spend much time with the others.

27 May 1967: Braunschweig, West Germany. *Are You Experienced* enters the UK album chart.
Noel Redding: Jimi was out of his head one night in Germany. I apologized, saying he was ill, and even had to tune his guitar. I discovered he'd taken acid before the show. He couldn't do anything but sit there laughing.

28 May 1967: Final gig of European tour, at Jaguar Club, Scala, Herford, West Germany.

29 May 1967: The Experience tops the bill at Barbecue '67, the Auction Hall, Spalding, Lincs, with Cream, Pink Floyd and The Move.
Germaine Greer (feminist, author): The air was hot and rank because all the sliding cattle-doors were shut but one, and there were no windows. As usual, an unlimited number of tickets had been sold and the promoter had split, leaving the kids to struggle in the heat and the dirt while the police snooped around them with dogs trained to sniff out the drugs that none of them had the money to buy. And there was Jimi caught like a little bird underneath the corrugated iron roof in the stink of cattle shit and sweating English youth. The crowd was so dense that those who fainted couldn't even fall down.

Jimi was wrestling to get his guitar in tune, and cursing the gear that they had to use... The kids were restive and abusive. Jimi began to play and the sound was terrible so he stopped. They jeered, so he yelled, 'Fuck you. I'm gonna get my guitar in tune if it takes me all fucking night.'

Then, as now, they didn't even care whether 'Hey Joe' was in tune or not... But Jimi wanted, like he always wanted, to play it sweet and high. So he did.

31 May 1967: Jimi jams at The Speakeasy with Jose Feliciano, Eric Clapton, Jack Bruce and Graeme Edge of The Moody Blues.

Summer 1967: In Los Angeles, work begins on getting the Monterey Pop Festival under way.
Chas Chandler: The first big break we got in the States came courtesy of Paul McCartney, who they were trying to involve in the Monterey Pop Festival. He told them it wouldn't be any kind of music festival without Hendrix. From there, it just burst wide open.

June 1967: In New York, Mike Jeffery appoints a new lawyer, Steve Weiss of Steingarten, Weeden & Weiss.
Howard Krantz (fellow lawyer): He (Weiss) was disliked by a lot of people in the industry, but he was a killer for his clients. An 'ardent advocate'

"THE BIGGEST SINGLE TRIBUTE FOR ME WAS THAT IT [THE 'SGT PEPPER' ALBUM] WAS RELEASED ON THE THURSDAY AND, ON THE SUNDAY, WE WENT TO THE SAVILLE THEATRE AND JIMI HENDRIX OPENED WITH 'SGT PEPPER', AND HE'D ONLY HAD SINCE THURSDAY TO LEARN IT" [PAUL McCARTNEY]

1967

as we lawyers like to say. He had no respect for other lawyers and didn't try to create relationships with them. He was a loner who cut his teeth with Hendrix and it paid off for him.

1 June 1967: Rehearsals at the Saville Theatre.
Tony Bramwell: NEMS, which was owned by my boss Brian Epstein, was the booking agency for Hendrix. Through our connections, Hendrix often used The Saville for rehearsals. We liked to try and groom the acts a bit, suggest ways they could improve their performances. Hendrix was very open to ideas about stage presentation or lighting, so long as they didn't interfere with what he was doing musically.

One thing we did was to make the legs on Mitch's drum riser weaker, by constructing them out of thinner wood, so that when Hendrix hit them with his guitar, they'd break more easily and send the whole thing crashing down.

2 June 1967: More rehearsals at the Saville Theatre, followed by seeing Pink Floyd at the UFO.
Tony Bramwell: Burning the guitar was becoming a standard part of the act, so Jimi warned us that he'd be doing that to climax his gig on the 4th. All the theatres in the West End came under the control of the Lord Chamberlain's Office for safety regulations, so we had to arrange to have a fire blanket, a fire extinguisher, a fireman standing by in the wings, otherwise the show wouldn't be allowed to go on.

4 June 1967: Gig at the Saville Theatre, London, with Denny Laine's Electric String Band, The Chiffons and Procol Harum; followed by seeing The Turtles at The Speakeasy. Roadie Neville Chesters joins the Experience crew.
Noel Redding: Sgt Pepper had just come out. All The Beatles were there so we came on stage and started with 'Sgt Pepper's Lonely Hearts Club Band'. We'd only learned the song in the dressing room.

Paul McCartney: The curtains flew back and Jimi came walking forward playing 'Sgt Pepper'.

Keith Reid (Procol Harum): He blew out the sound system. This was his first number! So they fixed it and then he went and did the same thing again.

Hugh Nolan (journalist): Despite the amplifier hang-up he refused to be flustered, telling the audience, 'This is our last gig here for a long time, so we're gonna make it nice.'

Paul McCartney: The biggest single tribute for me was that it (the *Sgt Pepper* album) was released on the Thursday and, on the Sunday, we went to the Saville Theatre and Jimi Hendrix opened with 'Sgt Pepper' and he'd only had since Thursday to learn it.

Hugh Nolan: It was Jimi's audience and Jimi's night. He started his set with a driving version of 'Sgt Pepper's', then blasted out 'Like A Rolling Stone', 'Hey Joe', 'Purple Haze' and 'The Wind Cries Mary'. Throughout the whole set, Jimi kept up a constant stream of happy talk, achieving a fantastic sense of communication with the star-studded audience. Then, to a smashing, ear-splitting 'Are You Experienced', Jimi was handed a guitar from the wings—a guitar he'd painted in glorious swirling colors and written a poem on the back dedicated to Britain and its audience—and, bathed in a flickering strobe light, crashed the guitar about the stage and hurled what was left to eager souvenir-hunters.

Steve Howe: Backstage at the Saville Theatre one night I witnessed his reckless guitar-throwing. I knew one of his road managers, and he used to stand behind the stacks of Marshalls and wait, and generally this white Strat would come over the amps. Of course, the idea was that he caught it. And usually he did.

5 June 1967: More recording at Olympic; Hendrix's management contract is amended, so that Chas Chandler must receive half of Mike Jeffery's 40 per cent share of earnings.
George Chkiantz: Kramer adopted a strategy with Hendrix of getting the original live sound down on four tracks which, at the time, other engineers including me, thought was crazy.

Eddie Kramer: Jimi had been exposed to eight-track recording in America. He liked hearing the basic tracks across all four tracks. Hearing it this way, four-track recording did not seem like the step backward it really was.

George Chkiantz: Hendrix was a lot happier. He felt the track was never lost, and that his stuff was always down on tape. He and Eddie could just sit there and mix, or listen.

6 June 1967: Jimi interviewed by Norrie Drummond for *New Musical Express*.
Drummond observes:

> The flat Jimi shares with his manager is tastefully furnished with long couches, leather armchairs, a teak coffee table, original paintings and the latest hi-fi equipment.

7-9 June 1967: Photo sessions with Karl Ferris for the US cover of *Are You Experienced* at Royal Botanic Gardens, Kew, London,; more UK press interviews.

10 June 1967: *Are You Experienced* peaks at Number 2 on the UK album charts.

13 June 1967: The band flies into New York.
Keith Altham (NME): We drove to London airport in Mike Jeffery's Rolls Royce... Jimi ransacked the bookstall for a science-fiction novel.

Noel Redding: The first time (I took LSD) was on an airplane going from London to New York. I was sitting beside Brian Jones and he gave me this little tablet and he said, 'Take it.' So I took it because, like, he was Brian Jones. The next thing I remember was that I was on some boat in New York and I said, 'Well, it doesn't affect me.' And the next thing I knew, I was in San Francisco.

Keith Altham: Arriving at Kennedy airport, we were met by a long, sleek, black Cadillac. Without pausing to check into the hotel, Jimi shot down to the Colony record center, just off Broadway, and bought half-a-dozen LPs by people like The Doors and the Mothers Of Invention.

Keith Altham: In the evening, we visited Jimi's old stamping ground, the Village. We ate at a restaurant called Tin Angel, met a couple of the Mothers, and moved on to the Café Au Go Go...

14 June 1967: Hendrix is taken to the offices of booking agency Premier Talent, and fan club organizers Teen Mail Ltd. Later he attends a gig by The Doors at The Scene.
Keith Altham: With Jimi dressed in multi-colored floral jacket, white trousers, emerald green scarf and gold medallion embossed with the words 'Champion Bird Watcher' we discovered he had obtained the honorary title of 'the man most unlikely to get a taxi in New York'.

15 June 1967: The band flies to San Francisco.
Barry Jenkins: We (The New Animals) were on the same flight, and I'll never forget seeing Hendrix sitting in his seat with his ear pushed up against the side wall of the plane. I asked him what he was doing and he said, 'I'm getting inspiration for the next album, man.' He was listening to the sounds of the engine vibrating inside the walls.

16 June 1967: The Experience arrives in Monterey, California.
Keith Altham: Early in the morning, we set out to find an 'indestructible' guitar for Jimi. 'I need a Fender,' explained Jimi. We failed to get the model Jimi wanted but somehow later acquired one in Monterey. It was the wrong color but he remedied that by spraying it white and drawing swirling designs all over it with a felt pen.

17 June 1967: Rehearsals on-site at the Monterey Pop Festival.
Eric Burdon: Jimi was crouched down outside his motel room with several guitars spread out on the tarmac in front of him, a silver conch belt around his hips, white calf-length boots, gypsy waistcoat, a purple shirt, the box of colored inks and oils alongside his guitars. He was quite alone. I stood and watched a minute. It was like a Navajo dream—the warrior before the hunt.

Al Kooper: I found myself onstage helping organize Jimi's soundcheck. Much to my surprise, he knew who I was, and was a fan of my work with Dylan. 'Hey, Al,' he said, 'we're gonna play 'Like A Rolling Stone'. Why don't you play organ with us?' I must have been clinically insane because I refused his offer. 'I'm actually working while you're playing and I don't think it would go over too well with my co-workers, if I just jumped onstage in the middle of my job,' I weakly offered. 'Oh, OK man, but we'll do it some other time soon, OK?' said Jimi, and we shook on it.

18 June 1967: The Monterey Pop Festival.
John Phillips (The Mamas & The Papas): No one in the States knew who he was yet. He was playing as Jimmy James & The Blue Flames at The Café Wha? the first time I saw him, and then I'd seen him in London in November as The Jimi Hendrix Experience. When I talked with Brian Jones before Monterey, he told us the same thing McCartney and Andrew Oldham had said: 'You've got to have this guy—he's tearing Europe to pieces.'

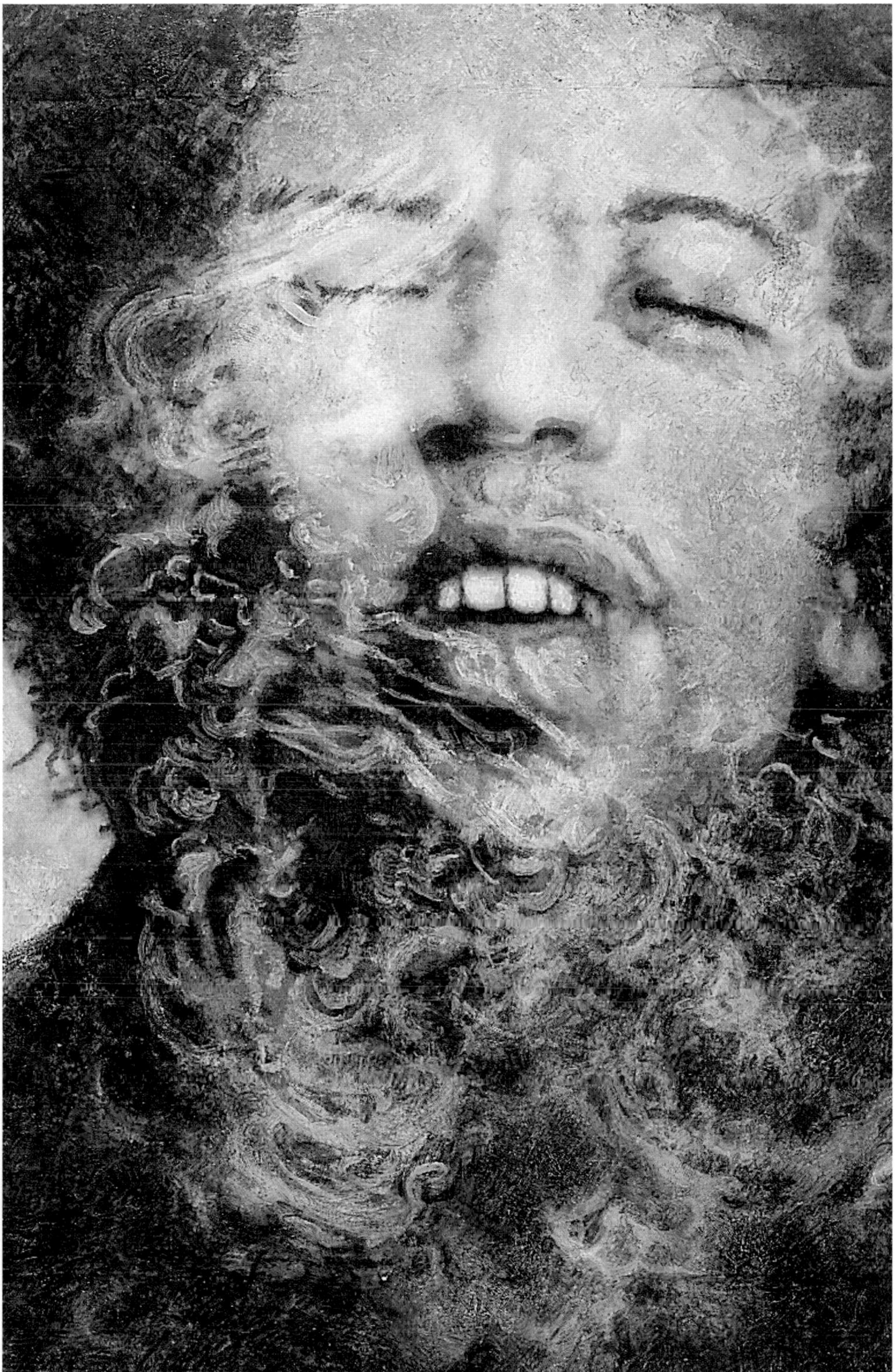

This original painting of Hendrix is by Nic Dartnell, who has done work for Love, Spirit, Genesis and ELP, among others

Zoot Money: "when I heard him play, it was obvious that all forms of blues or black music had gone through him"

Mitch Mitchell: "He was shy, not quite Clark Kent, but very quiet. You could take him to meet your mum and dad"

Chas Chandler: "Jimi was an amazing-looking man—one of the first black musicians to grow his hair and wear freaky clothes"

Chas Chandler: "We decided we weren't going to bring any other musicians in. It sounded so clean, so exciting and new"

Chas Chandler (1938-1996), the man who put Hendrix on the road to fame

Katchy Etchingham, thought to have been Hendrix's truest love, at the launch of her autobiography, Through Gypsy Eyes

Hendrix with (left to right) Carl Wayne (The Move), Steve Winwood, John Mayall and Eric Burdon in Zurich, 3 May 1968

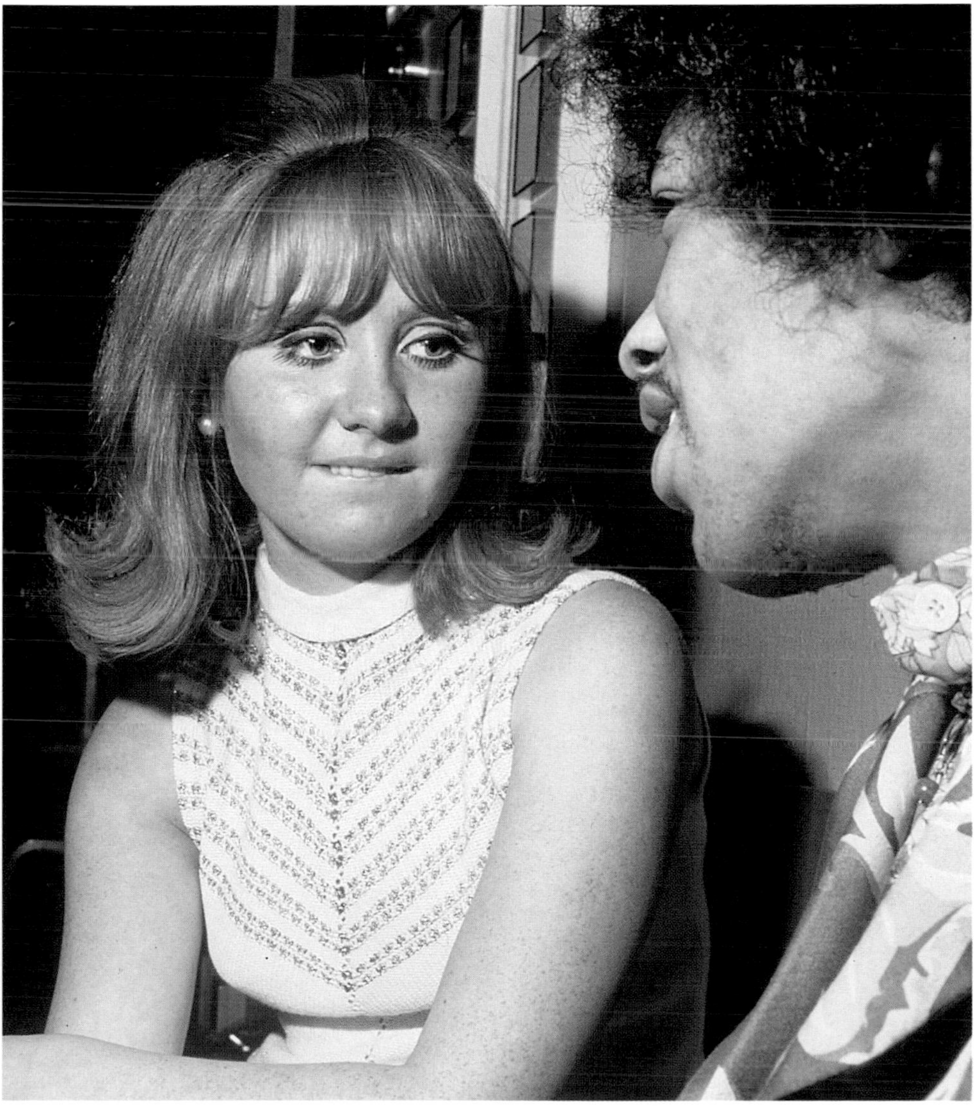

Hendrix and Lulu chat at the Melody Maker readers' poll awards, 16 September 1967; they'd meet again on 4 January 1969

Terry Reid: "All of a sudden he breaks into 'Wild Thing' and there were guitar players weeping. They had to mop the floor up"

Hendrix at Monterey Pop Festival, 18 June, 1967—about to play to thousands just eight months after the band had formed

Margaret Redding (Noel's mother): "When jimi was there you couldn't look at anyone else. You could feel his presence"

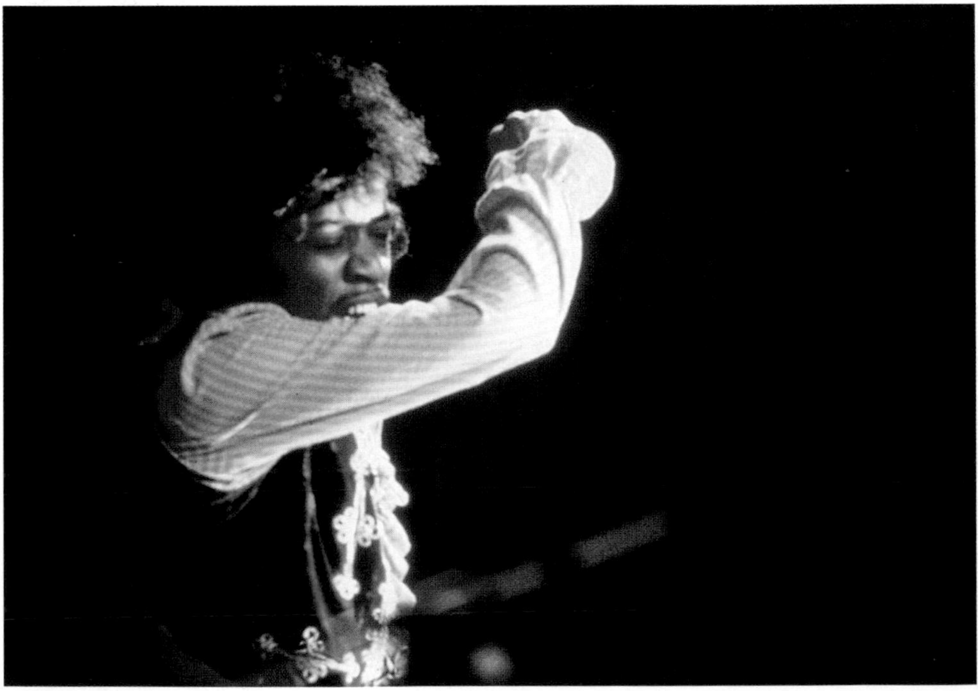

Eric Burdon: "Monterey was really the first time Jimi had the chance to play to his own people. So he just went for it"

Jimi's father, James Allen 'Al' Hendrix, in his home in Seattle, where Jimi's old room remains a shrine to his memory

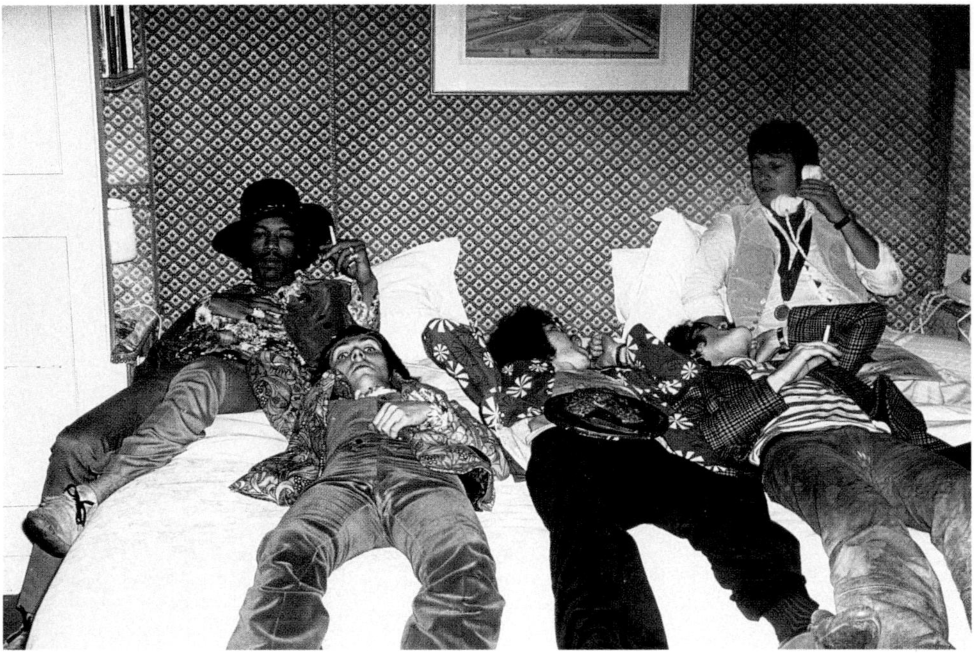

The Experience take it easy at the Duke of Bedford's pad during the Woburn festival, 6 July 1968. Also in the picture are the Duke and DJ Emperor Rosko

Chas Chandler: "Above all, Jimi was good fun to be with. I don't think of this brooding, menacing person we hear about now"

A poster that has adorned many a bedroom wall, from a 1968 silkscreen print of Hendrix by the Australian Martin Sharp

Chet Helms (Family Dog Productions): Hendrix was walking along the road outside the gate, with his guitar case, headed into the fairgrounds. We stopped and gave him a ride, and he and I exchanged hellos, and proceeded into the Festival.

Roger Daltrey: The dressing rooms at Monterey were under the stage and one memory that will live with me forever is of sitting under there with Jimi during the change-over between two acts. Jimi was playing 'Sgt Pepper' on his guitar but, and this was the amazing thing, he was playing all the parts. He would go from a bit of orchestration, to a vocal part, to a solo—the whole thing on one guitar, and he was accompanied by me, Mama Cass, Brian Jones, Janis Joplin and a bunch of other rockers, all of us banging on anything that came to hand.

Henry Diltz (photographer): Backstage, Townshend and Hendrix had been going back and forth about who should follow whom. John Phillips finally resolved the issue by flipping a coin. The Who lost, which is why they came out and played with such a vengeance.

Pete Townshend: They wanted to know what was gonna come first, and we couldn't really decide. I said to Jimi, 'Fuck it, man, we're not going to follow you on.' He said, 'Well, I'm not going to follow you on.' I said, 'We are not going to follow you on and that is it.'

Brian Jones was standing with me, and Jimi started to play. He stood on a chair in front of me and he started to play this incredible guitar, like, Don't fuck with me, you little shit. Then he snapped out of it and he put the guitar down and said, 'OK, let's toss a coin.' So we tossed a coin and we got to go on first. Jimi said, 'If I'm gonna follow you, I'm gonna pull out all the stops.'

John Phillips: The Who knew how good Jimi was and wouldn't be outdone, so they blew the entire stage up with bombs and fireballs. That's why Jimi burned his guitar and made love to his amp.

Peter Pilafan (drummer, The Mamas & The Papas): He took two hits of Monterey Purple just before he went on.

Jerry Wexler (producer): I remember standing in the wings, the air thick with the scent of hemp, when Jimi walked up to me. He was about to go on stage. I'd known Jimi since his back-up days with the Isley Brothers and King Curtis, and I appreciated the revolutionary overhaul he'd given the electric guitar. There he was, however, a veteran of the soul circuit, in crazy feathers and psychedelic regalia. He looked at me almost apologetically, knowing I knew where he came from. 'It's only for the show,' he whispered in my ear before going out.

David Crosby: He looked completely outrageous. He was dressed more crazedly than any of us, and we were all trying to be as 'out there' as we could. He got up on stage and he could play better than our best guys. We said, 'Oh my God!' And he could do it while he was dancing. And he could do it while being completely outrageous.

Abe Jacob (sound engineer): The first thing that went through my mind was that at last someone was doing a theatrical show. As far as rock music was concerned, everybody at that point was very laid back, giving a kind of non-show performance. T-shirts, torn jeans, hair in your eyes, and you looked down at your guitar and played. Hendrix was someone who really was an entertainer.

Pete Townshend: I went out to sit with Mama Cass and watch Jimi and, as he started doing this stuff with his guitar, she turned around to me, she said to me, 'He's stealing your act.' And I said, 'No, he's not stealing my act, he's doing my act.' And that was the thing. For me it was an act, and for him it was something else. It was an extension of what he was doing.

Doug Hastings (Buffalo Springfield): One of my fondest memories was standing at the side of the stage watching Jimi. He was a pretty amazing guitar player, but that was overshadowed by the visceral, animal approach to rock'n'roll he had.

I knew it was R&B and I knew it was Northwest R&B, so I knew where he was coming from and recognized some of the things he was doing that only Northwest guitar players did. But I didn't know where he was going with it. It was so absolutely overwhelming that it frightened me.

Eric Burdon: This was really the first time Jimi had the chance to play to his own people. So he just went for it. And he had special guitars he was going to sacrifice for the gig that he'd been saving. The afternoon before, he painted them out in the sun.

He looked more and more like a Native American to me as the weekend went on. He started out as a black American on Friday night. Saturday night he was Comanche. By Sunday night, he was an Apache warrior, just out to kill.

Ravi Shankar: I liked the music of Jimi Hendrix, but when he started being obscene with his guitar and started burning it, I felt sad. In our culture, the instrument is something which we respect. What he did was like sacrilege to me.

John Phillips: I was standing in the wings when he brought out a can of lighter fluid, squirted it all over his guitar, and then lit it. The Monterey Fire Chief was right next to me. The stage was catching fire behind us and I was trying to distract this man wearing the fire helmet, saying, 'Look at the crowd over there, aren't they wonderful?'

Stan Cornyn (Reprise Records): I do remember Mo (Ostin) saying how embarrassed he was by the spectacle of it, because it was not yet what the sincere record company executive would want to bring home to his peers. Also, I had the strange feeling of deja vu, because we'd already seen Pete Townshend smash his guitar an hour before. So it was not the hottest, most original thing I'd ever seen. None of us was into the aesthetics of chainsaw psychedelic guitar either, so it was funny to look at and excruciating to hear. Clearly, Jimi Hendrix was, for all of us, an acquired taste, and I'm not sure that many finally acquired it.

Nico (Velvet Underground vocalist; who kissed Hendrix as he left the stage): He was the most sexual man I ever saw on stage. Even Mick Jagger said so. It was not all the vulgar things he did with his guitar, though I enjoyed it when he burned his guitar at the festival. It was his presence. He was like a cat. He moved elegantly for a man. He was suave.

*Pete Johnson (*Los Angeles Times*):* Their appearance at the festival was magical: the way they looked, the way they performed and the way they sounded were light years away from anything anyone had seen before. The Jimi Hendrix Experience owned the future and the audience knew it in an instant. When Jimi left the stage, he had graduated from rumor to legend.

Chas Chandler: When I got to the dressing room, there was a blazing row going on between Jeffery and Hendrix, because Jimi had broken a microphone on stage. I yelled to Jeffery, 'What the fuck are you going on about? This guy has destroyed America, and the industry is at his feet, and you're giving him hell for breaking a microphone! Piss off!' I threw Jeffery out of the dressing room that night.

Stephen Stills: Jimi blew me away so bad at Monterey that, through sheer force of personality I just bullied my way past all the security and sycophants to meet him. He was delighted to meet a Southern boy who knew all the same people from New York and actually knew something about blues. He was very intrigued by my acoustic guitar playing. So there was a lot to give and take between us. I wasn't that accomplished a player on electric yet, but all that Travis-picking stuff, he was interested to know how all that went, how I made the guitar sound like that on record. I'd tell him, 'Well, first you get a 50-year-old Martin...'

Rock Scully (Grateful Dead manager): I helped arrange impromptu jam sessions at the free campground we organized at Monterey College. We set up a stage and, after the shows, the various bands would put on jam sessions. Jimi Hendrix, Eric Burdon, Jerry Garcia, Phil Lesh, the Airplane. We hadn't met Hendrix and we didn't know The Who. We got to know them there. We all took acid together and played all night.

Chet Helms (owner, Family Dog Productions): One jam involved Jimi Hendrix on guitar and David Freiberg (of Quicksilver Messenger Service) on bass; they played for several hours. We were out of our minds on acid, and it was wonderful.

Gary Duncan (of Quicksilver Messenger Service): Jack Casady and Jorma Kaukonen (of Jefferson Airplane) were playing real loud. Hendrix walked in, looked over at me and said, 'Hey,' and I said, 'Hey' to him. Then he reached in his pocket, took out this little candy tin, popped the lid and offered me some acid. He had about 20 hits in there: I took about five and he took the rest. He swallowed them all, I swallowed mine. And we stood there for about 15 minutes. Then he started smiling at me and I smiled at him, and we went over and played for two or three hours. That was fun. Somebody should have gotten that on tape.

Boz Scaggs (then with The Steve Miller Band): A big thing happened when the English bands performed at Monterey. It was a wake-up call to all the San Francisco and LA bands. To see the power of Jimi Hendrix and The Who—what those guys were doing was leaps and bounds ahead of anything in San Francisco.

Noel Redding: Bill Graham offered us a Fillmore stint with Jefferson Airplane.

19 June 1967: Hendrix visits the Reprise Records office in Los Angeles.
Stan Cornyn: He had an extraordinary, weak handshake, and that shifting kind of voice, and he was always answering questions a little more cosmically than you were prepared for.

20 June 1967: First of six nights at the Fillmore West, San Francisco, for $500 a night; Mike Jeffery signs a contract with US rock entrepreneur Dick Clark for the Experience to support The Monkees on their upcoming tour.
Mickey Dolenz: I suggested that he would make a great opening act, very colorful, very theatrical. The producers, being rather liberal-minded—we all were—thought that it'd be a great idea. They approached Hendrix's people, and they jumped on it.

Bill Graham: Jimi first came to San Francisco right after Monterey and played The Fillmore with Gabor Szabo and Jefferson Airplane. That was the first night. Afterward, the Airplane asked him if they could open the show. Jimi took the town by storm.

Jimmy Stewart (guitarist with Gabor Szabo): I remember Jimi's first tune well—'Purple Haze'. Looking down from our dressing room window, high above the auditorium floor, I saw him pace the stage, moving to the left and then to the right, then getting down on his knees to face his amplifier until it was screaming back at him.

The togetherness and communication level between the musicians created a definite feeling that there were more than just three of them on that stage.

21 June 1967: Second night at The Fillmore.
Chas Chandler: After one night, they gave the top of the bill to Jimi. It was Big Brother & The Holding Company on first, the Airplane as the middle act, and the Experience at the top.

Bill Graham: The second night, I was walking through the house when he started to play. The main thing that night was that he seemed to just play guitar. Whenever his body really felt like moving, it moved. Most times, when Hendrix performed, part of it was, All right, I'm going to push my body around and then move the guitar. But they were pre-ordained moves. When they weren't, there was nobody close. He was supreme.

Chas Chandler: Bill Graham gave us $2,000 each as a bonus... also antique engraved watches.

Bill Graham: He was also a fashion leader. Hendrix came to San Francisco with a scarf tied around his knee. When he left, there was one on the elbow and one around the head. All of a sudden, everyone else was doing just the same.

22 June 1967: Fillmore show, supported by Big Brother & The Holding Company. Hendrix begins a fling with their singer, Janis Joplin.
Linda Carroll (friend of Janis Joplin): She told me she was in love with Jimi and they were doing heroin together. She said her parents wouldn't approve of her being in love with him because he was black.

23–24 June 1967: Two more shows at The Fillmore; Mike Jeffery rings Chas Chandler to advize him of The Monkees tour support slot.
Chas Chandler: We had just walked in, and Hendrix and I were sitting in my room. Jeffery got me on the phone and said he had great news. 'I have just got them on the hottest tour in America as a support act,' he said. I said, 'That's great. Who is it?' 'The Monkees.' I dropped the fucking phone.

I couldn't believe it. While Jeffery was talking, I said to Hendrix, 'Do you fancy playing with The Monkees?' He went, 'What's Jeffery doing?' I had a flaming row with him on the telephone. I went berserk. The tour was opening in Florida. I said, 'You can go on those fucking dates, because I ain't going. I am totally disassociating myself from it. It's your fuck-up. You take care of it.'

25 June 1967: Afternoon gig in Golden Gate Park, San Francisco, final night at The Fillmore.
Noel Redding: During this tour, we were on wages of $200 a week, and living close to the line financially. I could never understand how other bands would have thousands in spending money… If I had to spend $100 on stage clothes, it was a serious investment. I could never afford new guitars, but found out about pawn shops.

27 June 1967: The Experience attends a private screening of the ABC documentary about the Monterey Pop Festival; jamming at Steve Stills' house in Malibu.
Stephen Stills: It was a pretty eclectic bunch—(South African trumpeter) Hugh Masekela, Buddy Miles and Bruce Palmer. Brucey was around my house all the time because he was the bass player in Buffalo Springfield, and Hughie would show up now and then. We went through two sets of players that night, me and Jimi, because we kept going. We played to one dawn, through the morning and next day, all the way into the next dawn.

Doug Hastings (Buffalo Springfield): I did a jam one afternoon at the Malibu house with Jimi Hendrix, Buddy Miles, David Crosby and Stephen Stills. I think Stephen played bass. It was the four of us playing in one part of the room, and Jimi playing about 15 feet away from us, off in a corner with his back to us. We probably played for a couple of hours. Buddy sang and Jimi sat, off in the corner, playing his wah-wah pedal. I was never quite sure if he was playing with us or just playing while we were playing.

He was popping acid like it was aspirin. He was way out there and taking more because he wasn't far enough out. Later on, we went upstairs and there he was with a couple of girls and he was asking for more acid. I watched as he took two more. He had enough to kill a horse.

Stephen Stills: That night, I really started to learn how to play lead guitar.

28–30 June 1967: Recording 'The Stars That Play With Laughing Sam's Dice' at Houston Studios, Los Angeles.
Chas Chandler: I had never recorded there myself. I booked three days because I had been told it was a state-of-the-art studio, but it was dire. The place was like a rehearsal room compared to Olympic. Los Angeles was so far behind at that time.

1 July 1967: Earl Warren Showgrounds, Santa Barbara, supported by Country Joe & The Fish plus Strawberry Alarm Clock.

2 July 1967: Love-in at Elysian Park, Los Angeles, then opening for Sam & Dave at the Whiskey A Go Go, Los Angeles.
Elmer Valentine (club owner): I had Sam & Dave playing, and they were stiffing. I asked them if I could put Jimi on with them. The people started lining up. Mario (manager of The Whiskey) raised the price from $3 to $5—it didn't matter. The kids came right from the park. Sam & Dave arrived that night, saw the crowd and thought it was for them. When Jimi finished his set, the place cleared out. He burned his guitar, he did the whole thing and, when he left, so did everyone else. Nobody stayed for Sam & Dave.

Noel Redding: We were tired and too stoned to care. We could hardly stand up and it didn't help to know we had a 10am flight the next day.

3 July 1967: Flight to New York; jamming at The Scene club.
Jimi Hendrix: I wrote part of the song ('Burning Of The Midnight Lamp') on a plane between LA and New York. There are some very personal things in there, but I think everyone can understand the feeling when you're travelling that, no matter what your address, there is no place you can call home. The feeling of a man in a little old house in the middle of a desert where he is burning the midnight lamp.

Pat Hartley (New York model and friend): Places like The Scene we liked to hang out (at) basically because we could dance all night; the added attraction was having live people performing. Also, being a chick and not having to be taken out was another reason for going there. You didn't have to have a date. Devon Wilson, who had known Jimi forever, she and I gave each other dirty looks in bathrooms all over town for a long time.

4 July 1967: Gig at The Scene, New York, with The Seeds and Tiny Tim.
Michael Wale (Melody Maker): At The Scene Hendrix broke several of his guitar strings on the

second night, while he was playing with his teeth, which caused road manager Gerry to run on stage like a football trainer with a new string every time there was a breakage. At a reckoning, they got through seven that night.

Don Everly: I remember meeting Jimi one night at The Scene, Steve Paul's club. I was working The Latin Quarter at the time, and I had never been to Greenwich Village before, so Steve and Jimi took me on a tour. Here we were, Steve wearing a bathrobe, the three of us smoking a joint in the back seat of his limo. I was worried about getting busted, but they didn't seem to be. We went to The Bitter End, and there was Joni Mitchell. I became friends with Jimi. He invited me to sessions, even came round to The Latin Quarter to see me. Can you believe it?

5 July 1967: Hendrix goes with old friend Arthur Allen to see Faye Pridgeon in Harlem; The Experience supports The Young Rascals at the Rheingold Festival, Central Park.
Faye Pridgeon: He was bragging and waving this album cover, and Jimi was always ashamed to brag. I said, 'Oh, give me a break! I don't believe a word of it!' He said, 'This is my picture. This is me.' I replied, 'You can have that stuff printed down on Broadway.' He kept saying, 'Why don't you believe me?'

Arthur Allen: For him to be famous, it was like, 'Oh, come on, Jimi.' Out of all of us, I believed it, because we had lived together.

Faye Pridgeon: Finally I said, 'OK, OK, I believe you!' Then he said, 'But you're just saying that. You don't really believe me.' I responded, 'Look, you come here with an empty damn jacket sleeve and you tell me that's your record? Yeah, sure.' He said, 'Oh no, the record is back at the hotel.'

Dino Danelli (drummer, Young Rascals): I'd jammed with him in the days when he was Jimmy James, but that was blues. This was the first time we'd seen him since he went to England and he was just on fire. The Experience went on first and we were like, 'How are we ever gonna follow this?' He was doing stuff that we had never heard in our lives! It was just incredible.

We had to let the audience calm down before we went on because no one had ever seen anything like that. We did a great show too, but it was amazing to see something of that intensity.

Albert Allen: Jimi pulled my brother and me aside. He said, 'Let's have a party.' We decided to go over to Faye's house. Jimi said, 'I got some new stuff here you all gonna love.'

6 July 1967: Party at Faye's apartment in Harlem; 'Burning Of The Midnight Lamp' is recorded at Mayfair Studios, New York.
Albert Allen: When we got there, we all took this new drug—acid, Jimi called it. I took more than I should have and he warned me, saying, 'Hey, man, watch what you're doing.' After we got high, Faye started bugging out. She was looking at Jimi, saying, 'Doesn't Jimi look funny over there? We should hang him.' In a complete trance, I said. 'OK.' Jimi was sitting in the corner, whimpering, 'No, no, you can't do that!'

Then Faye flipped out. She bolted out into her apartment building hallway, running up and down, yelling, 'There are men in my house!' She didn't recognize any of us. It's 3am and both Jimi and I were undressed. We ran into the bathroom and hid behind the shower curtain. We turned the water on when Faye started yelling, 'They're in there!' It was crazy.

Chas Chandler: 'Burning Of The Midnight Lamp' had actually begun as a demo at Olympic. We intended to record it there, but Jimi found the solution to the song in America, and we decided to just do it there.

"HE WAS POPPING ACID LIKE IT WAS ASPIRIN. HE WAS WAY OUT THERE AND TAKING MORE BECAUSE HE WASN'T FAR ENOUGH OUT. LATER ON, WE WENT UPSTAIRS AND THERE HE WAS, ASKING FOR MORE ACID. I WATCHED AS HE TOOK TWO MORE. HE HAD ENOUGH TO KILL A HORSE"

We were still trying to make commercial singles, but we always tried to feature a shift in our sound. We had used female vocalists before with 'Hey Joe' and it seemed appropriate that we feature them again. The Sweet Inspirations were a natural fit.

7 July 1967: Jimi attends Frank Zappa concert at the Garrick Theater, New York.
Michael Wale: Off duty, Mitch spent his time trying to hear Gene Krupa play in a bar uptown... Jimi and Noel went down to the village to see the Mothers Of Invention at The Garrick.

Frank Zappa: He came over and sat in with us at The Garrick that night.

8 July 1967: First gig on The Monkees tour, at Jacksonville, Florida.
Peter Tork: Poor Jimi, they booed him off stage. The Monkees were designed to bring rock to the next level below where it was standing. So you had kids who were 16, 17 and 18 years old who liked rock, and The Monkees were designed to bring 13, 14 and 15-year-olds into the fold and not scare the living daylights out of Mama. The Monkees were in the derrière-garde of music, and Jimi was in the avant-garde.

Jimi Hendrix: They gave us the death spot on the show—right before The Monkees. The audience just screamed and yelled for The Monkees.

Tommy Boyce (Monkees producer/songwriter): It was a personal trip. They wanted to watch Jimi Hendrix every night. They didn't care if he didn't fit.

Mike Nesmith: Jimi was just playing through one Marshall stack at the time. I'd just never heard anything like it. You never heard any power like that in your life.

Lynne Randall (US music journalist): When we were in Miami, The Monkees gave us all a tremendous surprise. They rented a gorgeous 71ft cruiser, loaded it with 30 of us Monkee-show people and we put out to sea for a whole day of fun and laughter together.

9 July 1967: Gig at Jackie Gleason Memorial Hall, Miami, Florida.
Vince Martin (1960s singer-songwriter): We (Martin and Peter Tork) went to a fancy hotel. Jimi Hendrix and Circus Boy (Mickey Dolenz) and all the rest of The Monkees were there. It was Jimi's first American tour. He opened for them, he bombed. I said, 'Peter, why are you subjecting Jimi to this?' He said, 'I love him. He's got to work.'

10 July 1967: The touring party flies to Charlotte, North Carolina.
Neville Chesters (roadie): The whole set up of the tour was farcical. The Monkees had their own plane with the Monkees' logo painted on the full length of it, and the staff had these suits with 'Monkees' on them. The Monkees management tried to keep them apart from other artists, but it didn't really work 'cause Mickey Dolenz was a complete lunatic.

Peter Tork: We got high together. We had this DC6, with this lounge in back. There were some reporters on the plane, so we would leave the reporters in the front and go into the back and smoke it up.

Vince Martin: For three weeks I was in the plane with the Monkees' logo and a red guitar on the side. We sat around in the hotel room, bare-ass naked—me, Steve Stills, Jimi Hendrix and Peter—jamming, with detectives outside the door.

11 July 1967: Show at The Coliseum, Charlotte, North Carolina.
Mickey Dolenz: It was a bit embarrassing, because we went early to watch his set all the time which, to be honest, we never did for any other opening act. It must have been a bit difficult for Hendrix with all the kids yelling, 'We want The Monkees!' and 'Where's Davy?' over 'Foxy Lady'. It was bizarre, in retrospect, to say the least.

Noel Redding: In Charlotte, we really died the death. Jimi pulled a moody, which meant he turned his back on the audience and got unreasonably pissed off when his guitar went out of tune or his amp hummed. Mitch and I carried on and pulled it through.

Mike Nesmith: We would typically go in and take over a wing of a hotel. The police would come and block off the wing, and generally stand guard down the hallway... because we would always attract a large number of people to the hotel. The hallway was lined with probably five or six on either side of these stereotypical Southern police with the big beer belly, and different color blue shirts, and a very Southern kind of redneck attitude.

I'd just come out of my room, guess it was one or two in the morning. A door opened and there was this kind of eerie blue-red light that came in from it because of the exit sign over it. Hendrix appeared in silhouette, with this light in back of him, and of course his hair was out to here, and he had on what has become his famous ribbon shirt. And he took a step forward, and it was like it was choreographed. Noel and Mitch both came up on either side of him, and they made the perfect trio. It looked like the cover of *Axis*.

None of those guys was very big, and all those cops were like 6'5", and Hendrix just started walking down the hall with these pinwheels in his eyes. And to see him walk under the nose of these cops, and these guys lookin' at him going by was something to see. Jimi was in absolute control. He had such a command of himself.

12 July 1967: The tour reaches at Greensboro, North Carolina.
Jimi Hendrix: Finally, they agreed to let us go on first and things were much better. We got screams and good reaction, and some kids even rushed the stage. But we were not getting any billing—all the posters for the show just screamed out—MONKEES! Then some parents who brought their young kids complained that our act was vulgar. We decided it was just the wrong audience.

13 July 1967: Show at Forest Hills tennis stadium, Queens, New York.
Lillian Roxon (rock writer): By the time it was over, he had lapped and nuzzled his guitar with his lips and tongue, caressed it with his inner thighs, jabbed at it with a series of powerful pelvic thrusts.

Frank Zappa of Mothers Of Invention: Hendrix appears on the inside cover of their We're Only In It For The Money album

Even the little girls who'd come to see The Monkees understood what this was about.

14 July 1967: Meeting at attorney Steve Weiss's home on Long Island to discuss how to extricate Hendrix from the Monkees tour; second show at Forest Hills.
Chas Chandler: I had this flaming row with Jeffery. It took all day and night to convince Jeffery that we had to get off the tour…
I said, 'Just remember one fucking thing—Jimi is signed to me and you don't have a fucking contract with him.'

I told him I was pulling them off the tour, no matter how I had to do it. He said that we would get sued by Dick Clark, so I rang Dick there and then and I arranged to meet him the next day.

Mickey Dolenz: He asked to be released from the tour, and we said, 'Yes, of course.'

15 July 1967: The Waldorf Hotel, New York.
Dick Clark: The whole thing was a disaster. As I recall, it was the request of The Monkees that Jimi be included in the show and be the opener. They fancied themselves as being an attractive coupling. It wasn't, and the audience was totally lost. So Chas met me in the hotel and said, 'What are we going to do? This is not a compatible combining of talents.'

Chas Chandler: We sat and cooked up the Daughters of the American Revolution story that afternoon. I had to tell all these lies that Hendrix was (considered by the DAR to be) too outrageous and obscene to be seen by The Monkees' pre-pubescent admirers.

Pat Costello (publicist): We wrote irate letters to the Forest Hills Stadium. We wrote to Warner Brothers Records. We wrote the daily newspapers. We tried to think who the general public would write to, and we pretended to be parents. You know, 'My daughter attended a Monkees' concert last night and something really obscene played first. How dare you!' It was Michael's (PR boss Michael Goldstein) idea. He went to Jeffery with it and Jeffery made no objection, so we ran with it.

Chas Chandler: It actually became this massive public relations story overnight. We never expected that, though we did expect to get sued by the Daughters of the American Revolution and we never were. As far as we were concerned, it was just a story for the trade magazines so it wouldn't look as if we'd been jerked off the tour.

16 July 1967: The Experience withdraw from the Monkees tour.
Gloria Stavers (editor, Sixteen *magazine):* There was a girl singer, a blonde from Australia, who was on the tour too, and she was doing a diary of the tour for me. They were in New York, staying at The Warwick hotel, and she called me and said Jimi was depressed. I went over to the hotel with her and Jimi was crestfallen. He was smoking joint after joint after joint and he was a heartbroken man. They'd kicked him off the tour.

17 July 1967: Jimi attends The Seeds' gig at The Electric Circus, New York. Later, with Curtis Knight, he records 'Hush Now' and 'Flashing' for Ed Chalpin of PPX at Studio 76 on Broadway.
Jimi Hendrix: We all went out to see the Electric Circus club in the Village, which just completely blew my mind.

Ed Chalpin: It is not possible that Hendrix did not know he was recording. In addition, we interrupted the session frequently to make balance tests—microphone volume. During these pauses at Hendrix's request, we would play back the material recorded, to hear the previous sound and, after each number, Hendrix personally entered the control room to hear the results in order to judge whether they had been recorded correctly.

"JIMI CAME IN WITH A WAD OF MONEY. CHARLES OTIS HAD LOANED HIM SOME MONEY BEFORE HE LEFT (WAY BACK IN SEPTEMBER 1966) SO JIMI PAID HIM BACK. CHARLES TOLD ME THAT JIMI PULLED OUT A ROLL WITH HUNDRED AND THOUSAND DOLLAR BILLS AND SAID, 'HERE MAN, TAKE WHAT YOU NEED'

Jimi Hendrix: I knew Curtis Knight was recording but, listen, that was at a jam session.

18 July 1967: Frank Zappa attends Hendrix recording session for 'The Stars That Play With Laughing Sam's Dice' at Mayfair Recording Studio, New York. Hendrix is photographed for the inside cover shot of *We're Only In It For The Money* by the Mothers Of Invention. Gig in the evening at The Gaslight Club, New York.
Neville Chesters: Quite a few people dropped in on that session. It was a really shitty studio, about six or eight floors up...

Mitch Mitchell: 'The Stars That Play With Laughing Sam's Dice' was a deliberate joke, you know? STP and LSD. But it was just a filler, done in one take with the background vocals done by people in the studio. They were Jimi's old friends like Devon Wilson.

19 July 1967: Gig at The Gaslight Club; 21 takes of 'The Stars That Play With Laughing Sam's Dice' are made at Mayfair Studios. The final one is declared the master.
John Hammond: He came in with a wad of money, I remember. Charles Otis had loaned him some money before he left (back in September 1966) so Jimi paid him back. Charles told me Jimi pulled out a roll with hundred and thousand dollar bills and said, 'Here man, take what you need.' And Charles took the $40 he had loaned Jimi and said, 'No, that's cool, man.' But it sure impressed Charles forever.

20 July 1967: Gig at The Salvation Club, New York; later, work on 'Burning Of The Midnight Lamp' at Mayfair Studios.
Mike Quashie: One night I spotted this dude at the bar with a big basket-ball sized Afro. Last time I saw him he was wearing his Vaseline conk. Well, I didn't recognize him at first, but when I left the stage I did, and I said, 'Jimmy? What you do to youse'f? You a rill nigger now!'

21 July 1967: Gigs at Café Au Go Go, New York, and jam with Mothers Of Invention.
Frank Zappa: I thought Hendrix was great. But the very first time I saw him I had the incredible misfortune to be sitting close to him at the Au Go Go, and he had a whole stack of Marshalls and I was right in front of it. I was physically ill. It was so packed I couldn't escape. And, although it was great, I didn't see how anybody could inflict that kind of volume on himself, let alone other people. That particular show, he ended by taking the guitar and impaling it in the low ceiling of the club. Just walked away and left it squealing.

22 July 1967: Chas Chandler marries Lotte Lexon at The Warwick hotel, New York.

23 July 1967: Gigs at Café Au Go Go, New York, and jam with Mothers Of Invention.
Buzzy Linhart (percussionist): We had a famous big New York loft where visiting bands from California and England scored from, and we'd have big jam sessions up there. I can remember a session with Mitch Mitchell, Dave Crosby, Jack Bruce, Eric Clapton and Mike Bloomfield. They didn't all score... but certainly the road crews did... but it led to some fantastic jams.

I sat on the floor in tears for three hours watching Jimi Hendrix and Buddy Miles play one night. It was so funny because Buddy kept breaking my drummer's drum heads and he just stood in the corner grumbling, putting new heads on drums.

25 July 1967: When Sly and the Family Stone play at The Generation, Jimi jams with Ted Nugent, BB King and Al Kooper.
Al Kooper: When the late shows finished, the waitresses would begin their clean-ups and the participants of that night's jams would gather in the dressing rooms. The unknowing, paying customers would settle their bills and set out for the suburbs, and then the action would begin. The doors were locked... and then we'd slowly come out, like bats in the night, and take over...

Hendrix loved this. He would show up more often than not, always with his guitar and his trusty Nagra (tape recorder) in tow. He would fastidiously set up the Nagra next to him and record every jam he participated in.

Many's the night you'd find BB King, Jimi, yours truly, Jim Morrison, Tim Hardin and a cast of dozens wailing away on stage literally until the sun came up. Jimi and I would usually walk back home together, as we lived only a block apart.

26 July 1967: Jimi jams with John Hammond at The Gaslight.
John Hammond: Eric Clapton was in New York

Jerry Garcia of The Grateful Dead with manager Rock Scully (left) and author Tom Wolfe at the epicentre of hippiedom

as well, and both of them jammed with us for two nights at The Gaslight. It was amazing. What were the two of them playing? Blues, man, straight, heavy blues.

27 July 1967: Ed Chalpin buys back Jimi Hendrix tapes from Jerry Simon of RSVP Records for $400; Jimi again jams with John Hammond at The Gaslight.
Jerry Simon: I was approached with the request that my company sell them the seven master tapes which I had previously acquired from PPX. They informed me that the purpose of the proposed acquisition of the tapes by them was that Knight was about to enter into an exclusive recording agreement, and both of them desired that there be no competing recordings of Curtis Knight issued.

28 July 1967: Jimi again jams with John Hammond at The Gaslight.

29 July 1967: More recording at Mayfair Studios; Jimi jams once more at The Gaslight with John Hammond.
Noel Redding: Money worries—like the nagging suspicion that something was going wrong—started to bother us. We were getting on each other's nerves. A good distraction was my desire to write songs. On July 29 I tried recording the roots of 'Little Miss Strange'. I had a cash shortage and began to see that writing was a definite help.

30–31 July 1967: Jimi records several tracks with Curtis Knight at Studio 76, owned by PPX.

3 August 1967: Gig at the Salvation club.
Randy Meisner (guitarist, The Poor, later of The Eagles): We were scheduled to play the club that week as the house band. However, we never got on stage on opening night. No one could follow Jimi. He used to burn his guitar on stage and destroy the PA system. When he finally finished, the manager of the club said to us, 'Hey, good news, you guys don't have to go on at all! Come back tomorrow.' We felt like shit.

4 August 1967: While playing at the Salvation club, Hendrix is served with a notice that Warner Brothers is now being sued by PPX, for proposing to issue *Are You Experienced.*

5 August 1967: Gig at the Salvation club.
Jack Bruce: When we (Cream) were recording in New York, he came down to the sessions at Atlantic and was very encouraging about 'White Room', saying, 'Oh, I wish I could write something like that.' He was certainly not egotistical.

7 August 1967: Gig at the Salvation club.

8 August 1967: Gig at the Salvation club; while making further recordings with Curtis Knight at PPX, Hendrix is taped voicing his concern to Ed Chalpin that the recordings must not be issued under his name.

9 August 1967: Gig at the Ambassador Theater, Washington DC.
Nils Lofgren: First night I saw him we were just kids, and we'd just gone to see The Who. In fact, there was a huge show with the Blues Magoos, Herman's Hermits and The Who. This was the original Who with Keith Moon, and they were just spectacular. Then we all rushed over to the Ambassador Theater—our psychedelic ballroom—to see Jimi. And Pete Townshend was in the audience—he had come over.

Hendrix came out and none of us really knew anything about him apart from he was supposed to be this magical guitarist. And he only had three people in his band which we'd never seen and then… It was funny 'cause we were so naive—he announced he was gonna play 'Sgt Pepper's Lonely Hearts Club Band'. And all of us are like, Well, how can he play that? Where's the horns? Where's the strings? Where's all the extra guitars? What's he talking… We were so oblivious to where Jimi was coming from and he was just so amazing to look at. He was just so, you know, gorgeous. Just like this animal athlete kind of thing. And he counted off the song and I'll never forget—everyone was just kind of sitting down wondering what the hell is going to happen.

He had these huge stacks of Marshall amps and you didn't really know how loud it was going to be, and at the end of the count he just disappeared. He dropped back with his ass on his heels, guitar between his legs, and just kinda went out of vision, and the whole audience just leapt up to their feet and he's down there, bumping and grinding doing 'Sgt Pepper's Lonely Hearts Club Band' à la 'Purple Haze'—that kind of rhythm, a little bit slowed down. It was just completely mesmerising and overwhelming and inspiring.

10 August 1967: Gig at the Ambassador Theater, Washington DC. Mitch Mitchell collapses on stage with appendix trouble and the show is cancelled.

11 August 1967: Gig at the Ambassador Theater, Washington DC.
Carl A. Zaner (fan): I saw Jimi Hendrix perform for six concerts—two on Saturday night—over five nights in a row, at Washington DC's Ambassador Theater, in the Adams-Morgan section of the city. The theater was just that—a movie theater which had been gutted of seats, with the stage remaining, leading up to a huge screen onto which oil-pan psychedelics were projected live from the projection room, above and behind the performers' heads. Concerts were scheduled six nights a week and the admission price for each concert was one dollar.

Hendrix had a loyal following in the UK and a growing group of fans on the West Coast, but was basically unheard of on the East Coast. He walked onto the stage, with Noel Redding and Mitch Mitchell. He wore an outfit similar to (if not the same) as the orange ruffle-collared, psychedelic-eyed outfit, as appears on the cover of the *Are You Experienced* album. What a sight!

After his bombastic version of 'Sgt Pepper', Jimi launched into a full-fledged performance of almost the entire *Experienced* album, beginning with an ultra-sonic 'Purple Haze'. The crowd was completely mesmerized.

While performing 'Purple Haze', for six performances in a row, Hendrix, standing to the left of the stage, clearly pointed directly at Noel Redding standing to the right, and they both laughed and made a thing out of it, each time the phrase came up, '...scuse me while I kiss this guy.' This was not a mistake or a 'misheard lyric'. The two of them were clearly 'goofing' with the crowd and having a great time. Hendrix even walked over to Redding during one or two of these performances, and mimed kissing him!

12 August 1967: Gig at the Ambassador Theater, Washington DC.

13 August 1967: Gig at the Ambassador Theater, Washington DC; Jimi is arrested by the police for jaywalking.

15 August 1967: Gig at the Fifth Dimension club, Ann Arbor, Michigan. The first pictures of Jimi using a wah-wah pedal are taken here.
Jimi Hendrix: The wah-wah pedal is great because it doesn't have any notes. Nothing but hitting it straight up using the vibrato and then the drums come through and that there feels like that, not depression, but that loneliness and that frustration and the yearning for something. Like something is reaching out.

16 August 1967: 'Purple Haze'/'The Wind Cries Mary' released as a single in the US.
Joe Perry (Aerosmith): I must've been 16 or 17 when 'Purple Haze' came out. I remember thinking, Now we're getting radio from Mars. The guitar sounded like a monster coming out of the speakers.

17 August 1967: Hendrix is filmed at Falcon's Lair, the mansion formerly owned by Rudolph Valentino, Los Angeles.
Barry Jenkins: Eric Burdon had moved the band (The Animals) to LA, so we were living in Laurel Canyon. When Hendrix came back to LA to play at the Hollywood Bowl, I was going out with a lovely girl called Jeanette Jacobs who played in a band called The Cake. As soon as she met him, she was completely taken by him and ended up going off with him. I never saw her again.

Noel Redding: Scheduled to film a promo clip in Los Angeles, we started by my passing out beyond recall. We were tripping, of course. It was acid, acid, acid. We were spaced constantly.

Pamela Des Barres (groupie): My photographer, Allen Daviau called one morning to ask if I would like to dance in a short film with The Jimi Hendrix Experience. My mission was to wriggle around behind the group for their first American release, 'Foxy Lady'...

I threw on my favourite blue velvet rag, hitch-hiked over the hill to a crumbling Hollywood mansion and for many hours danced on top of a white column behind Hendrix, Noel Redding and Mitch Mitchell, while 'Foxy Lady' blasted down the peeling walls. Jimi kept peering at me from the corner of his eye, but Noel Redding looked a safer bet to me and, by the end of the day, we were holding hands.

18 August 1967: The Experience support

Scott McKenzie and The Mamas & The Papas at the Hollywood Bowl.
Noel Redding: We died a death (at the Bowl).

Abe Jacob (sound engineer): The Experience followed McKenzie. The Mamas & The Papas were the headliners. At the end of the Experience's set, after the mayhem and the total destruction of the stage, out came a classical string quartet, booked by promoter Lou Adler. They walked over the rubble, positioned their chairs, and performed Beethoven while the crew changed equipment during intermission.

Petula Clark: Jimi Hendrix is a great big hoax. If he can get away with it, then good luck to him. I saw him in Los Angeles. I think he's unexciting and he doesn't move me. The fact that he isn't a big success with the general public proves something.

19 August 1967: The Experience's US visit ends at the Earl Warren Showgrounds, Santa Barbara, with Moby Grape, Tim Buckley and Captain Speed; 'Burning Of The Midnight Lamp' is released in the UK, and reviewed in *Melody Maker* by Beach Boy Bruce Johnston.
Jimi Hendrix: That song ('Midnight Lamp') was the song I liked best of all we did. I'm glad it didn't make it big and get thrown around.

Bruce Johnston (in Melody Maker*):*

> The best passages (on 'Midnight Lamp') are when the drums are rock steady and Jimi and his guitar are cooking. But there is a great deal of record time devoted to jew's harp noises and other extraneous effects.

20 August 1967: The band fly back to London.

21 August 1967: When the Experience land at Heathrow Airport, London, Mitch Mitchell's tear-gas gun is confiscated by Customs.
Mitch Mitchell: It was really degrading. I had to be undressed and searched, while all my friends and family were waiting to see me.

22 August 1967: The Experience perform 'Burning Of The Midnight Lamp' on *The Simon Dee Show*, BBC TV.

23 August 1967: Interview with Bob Farmer of *Disc & Music Echo;* the *Are You Experienced* album is released in the US.

24 August 1967: Recording 'Burning Of The Midnight Lamp' for *Top Of The Pops.*
Johnnie Stewart (producer): Jimi and his group were on the set, ready to do 'Burning Of The Midnight Lamp'. Pete Murray was the presenter that night and, in those days, the artists were allowed to mime to a backing track. Unfortunately, at the end of Pete's introduction, the sound supervisor played in the wrong tape. He used the tape of the following band, The Alan Price Set, singing 'The House That Jack Built'. As the track began, Hendrix said, in a rather quiet voice, 'I like the music, man, but I don't know the words.'

Jimi Hendrix: 'Burning Of The Midnight Lamp' is difficult enough as it is, and I was all cued up ready to say the words nice and clear. This really threw me, man—mass confusion.

25 August 1967: Mitch Mitchell becomes engaged to Carolyn Kinsey.

26 August 1967: Jimi sees Dantalian's Chariot (Zoot Money's new band) at The Speakeasy.
Arthur Brown (musician): Whenever you'd see Jimi in The Speakeasy, he had a very winning way with the ladies. He'd just meet one of the waitresses, for example, and a minute later he'd have his arm round her. They didn't mind at all. It wasn't like he was pestering them for sex—he seemed to envelop them in a sort of lovingness.

27 August 1967: Gig at the Saville Theatre, with Crazy World Of Arthur Brown and Tomorrow. A second performance is cancelled when Jimi learns that Brian Epstein has died. Later, at the Speakeasy, Jimi jams with Fairport Convention.
Arthur Brown: This was quite a significant gig for Hendrix because it was his first major public performance where all the underground people, from The UFO club and so on, came to see him. He'd never actually played at The UFO, and they represented a different kind of audience from the pop fans who had been buying the singles.

Tony Bramwell: I'd seen Jimi play so often, that I could tell that his performances were already starting to get a bit out of control by this time. He'd go off into long, jazzy improvisations that made the set difficult to follow. I also knew that part of the problem was that he was mixing a lot with the boys (John Lennon and Paul McCartney) and doing a lot of LSD.

Chas Chandler: I didn't even know they were on acid. It was Tony Bramwell who told me—he was from Liverpool and was the youngest member of the Beatles' entourage, helping Brian Epstein to run the Saville. He was giving me hell in The Speakeasy for letting them do so much LSD. 'Don't you know how much acid they're doing?' I said, 'What the hell are you talking about?' 'Hendrix is with Lennon and McCartney and they're all pouring acid down their throats!' I said, 'What?' I was living in the same flat as Jimi, and I had no idea.

Noel Redding: We were spaced constantly. Chas stayed straight. He leaned towards whisky, his cure for anything, including stage nerves.

28 August 1967: Photo session in Hyde Park, plus various press interviews.
Keith Altham observes in NME.

> We made a brief excursion to see Jimi's bedroom, which is like a kind of Aladdin's cave, hung with lace shawls, tapestries and great coloured balls of cloth, pinned to the ceiling. The colour red predominates. LPs are liberally sprinkled over the flower carpet and, suspended from the lampshade in the middle of the ceiling are the two little gilt figures of cherubs he bought recently in an antique shop.

29 August 1967: Nottingham Blues Festival, Nottingham, supported by Jimmy James & The Vagabonds (multi-racial UK soul group).

Jimmy James: We'd played the Nottingham Blues Festival several times so we were regulars, but it was Jimi's first time. I sat and chatted to him for about half-an-hour before the show and he mentioned he had been using the name Jimmy James when Chas discovered him in America. We were already quite well known in England, so Chas obviously knew it wouldn't be sensible to bring in a new artist with the same name.

30 August 1967: Jimi goes to The Inn Club, London. The club is raided by police carrying out membership checks; 'Burning Of The Midnight Lamp' enters the UK singles chart.
Jimi Hendrix: I really don't care what our records do, as far as chartwise... but to me that was the best one we ever made. Not as far as recording, because the recording technique was very bad. You couldn't hear the words so good.

31 August 1967: The band flies to West Berlin, does a photosession and a live radio show.

1 September 1967: In Berlin, Jimi goes to Bee Gee Barry Gibb's 21st birthday party, then on to the Playboy Club.

2 September 1967: TV recordings in Berlin, for the first color transmissions in West Germany.
Gerry Stickells: Traffic was on the show too, and everybody was swapping around in the bands because the German producers wouldn't know better.

3 September 1967: Gig at Liseburg, Gothenburg, Sweden.
Orjan Ramberg (Swedish scenester): After the concert it was time to visit The Roastery, the best rock club ever in Sweden. When we arrived, Styrbjorn Colliander (local club manager) made sure that everything was arranged in such a way that he could keep himself out of it. Well, that 'everything' was ready—a tiny piece of Red Lebanon. A little wet, but 'smoke stuff' nevertheless.

Jimi turned up and asked if it was 'time to go ahead'. Clem (club DJ), Frasse (dope dealer), Jimi and myself passed through a door leading to the back yard, a safe place according to Styrbjorn. Jimi was tremendously grateful for this opportunity, happy and constantly talking.

4 September 1967: Two shows at Grona Lund, Stockholm, Sweden.

"WE WERE SUPPOSED TO BE ON 'THE MAGICAL MYSTERY TOUR'. THE BEATLES USED TO COME AND SEE US SOMETIMES AND PAUL McCARTNEY TOLD ME THEY WERE PLANNING TO DO A FILM. THEY WANTED US TO BE IN THIS FILM. WE WEREN'T KNOWN THEN. HE WAS TRYING TO HELP US"

5 September 1967: Live gig recording at Radiohuset, Stockholm, Sweden.
George 'King George' Clemons (soul singer, friend of Hendrix): Every time he came (to Stockholm) there was this girl. I don't know if I should mention names or not, but there was a house were Jimi used to stay. I guess it's safe enough—her name was Barbara. She had a little house just outside Stockholm. We used to meet there. Jimi was there when he wasn't doing concerts. Everybody knew it.

6 September 1967: Gig at Versteras, Sweden.

7 September 1967: Jimi jams with local musicians Bo Hansson and Janne Karlsson for four hours at Club Filips, Stockholm.
George Clemons: We had a place in Stockholm called Club Filips. I played drums there. There was a jazz drummer, but he didn't wanna play with Jimi all the time… anyway, he left the drums, so I went up and played them. I'm good for two songs. Jimi also played with the organ player, Hansson.

Goran Samuelsson (brass player, The Strangers): With the volume far beyond the pain limit, Jimi Hendrix got it on with Hansson and Karlsson. Judging from the smell in the premises, they will never be hired by the Lions Club. Stevie Winwood and Traffic had been there earlier, but had gone back to their hotel to sleep.

Jimi Hendrix: I like free-form beat like Hansson and Karlsson.They are truly fantastic.

8 September 1967: TV show in Stockholm; followed later by a gig at Hogbo, Sweden.

9 September 1967: The Experience play two shows at Karlstaab, Sweden; *NME* publishes a Keith Altham interview with Jimi.
Gerry Stickells: We had performing seals as an opening act. The show took place at a fairground, and I said to the promoter, 'Who's going on first?' He couldn't even explain. Then I went out and saw this ramp, and the performing seals went on. They weren't even any good. They couldn't keep the balls on their noses. Hendrix thought it was hilarious.

Jimi Hendrix: All the things I thought were important before I had a hit record are just as important now. Trying to understand people and respect their feelings regardless of your position or theirs. The beautiful things are all the same—the sunset and the dew on the grass. No material wealth changes the way I feel about these things.

10 September 1967: Gig at Malmo, Sweden.

11 September 1967: Gig at Tivoli Gardens, Stockholm, followed by a jam at Club Filips.
Jimi Hendrix: We were supposed to be on *The Magical Mystery Tour.* The Beatles used to come and see us sometimes, like at certain concerts like the Saville Theater, and Paul McCartney told me about this little scene he had. They were planning to do a film and he wanted us to be in this film. We weren't known then when McCartney asked us. He was trying to help us, but we got a nice break before they got the movie together.

12 September 1967: Gig at Stjarnscenen, Gothenburg, Sweden.

13 September 1967: The Experience is asked to leave the foyer of the Park Avenue Hotel, because Princess Alexandra is about to arrive. They refuse. The incident makes the next day's *Daily Mirror.* Later, the band fly back to London.

14 September 1967: The Experience appear on *Top Of The Pops.*

15 September 1967: Hendrix sits in with Eric Burdon & The Animals at the Bluesville 67 club at The Manor House pub, London.

16 September 1967: Jimi collects the *Melody Maker* award for World's Top Musician at the Europa Hotel, London.

Jimmy Savile: I presented Jimi with his award that night. Those award events were like *Top Of The Pops* without cameras. In those days, the pop business was like the Formula 1 (motor-racing) or the tennis circuit is now. There were only about a dozen bands that were really rated world-wide, and so these same bands would all shunt round these various ceremonies and pick up awards and have a laugh. Nobody played, though. It was just a ceremony.

18 September 1967: Recording *Monday Monday* radio show, London.

21 September 1967: Jimi is interviewed at home by Alan Lubin of *Intro* magazine.

22 September 1967: Ed Chalpin begins a legal action against Hendrix for breach of his October 1965 PPX contract.
Janie L. Hendrix: I remember the first time we heard *Are You Experienced*. Jimi had called us to say he was off to the big time and forming a group called The Jimi Hendrix Experience. Shortly after that, we heard this music coming from our neighbor's apartment and Dad said, 'That sounds like Jimi.' So my mom went over and said, 'Can I ask what album you're listening to?' They showed her and she was stunned: 'That's Jimi! That's my husband's son!' They made her take the album and they went and bought another one. We wore out the grooves, just playing it over and over.

23 September 1967: Hendrix goes to see the Mothers of Invention at the Royal Albert Hall.

24 September 1967: Hendrix, accompanied by Noel Redding and Eric Burdon, checks out Traffic and Tomorrow at the Saville Theater.

25 September 1967: The Experience are filmed at the Guitar-In at the Royal Festival Hall. Backstage, Jimi is photographed with Liberal Party leader Jeremy Thorpe.
Bert Jansch: At the Royal Festival Hall there were classical players like Paco Pena, and Jimi and myself. It was like a guitar showcase. I thought he was great. It really opened up my ears to the electric guitar, which I'd never had any interest in until Jimi came along.

He had a bank of speakers at the back, Marshalls or whatever, and for his soundcheck he came in and plugged into a couple of pedals on the floor, turned his guitar up full volume and smashed the guitar—one chord—and then unplugged it. That was the soundcheck. But it was dramatic to watch him in an empty hall. I shook his hand, and I'm very proud that I did.

26 September 1967: Interview for *Newsweek;* Chas Chandler and Mike Jeffery fly to America to meet with Ed Chalpin.

28 September 1967: Jimi and Mitch go to The Upper Cut club.

Photo opportunity: Jimi larks about with Jeremy Thorpe, the Liberal Party leader, at the Guitar-In on 25 September 1967

30 September 1967: Jimi is interviewed by Pamela Townsend of *Fab 208* magazine.

Jimi Hendrix: Ever since I can remember, I have been moody. I can't help isolating myself from the world. Sometimes I just want to be left alone. People think I'm funny. I'm sorry. I can't help it.

1 October 1967: Recording of 'Little Miss Lover' at the start of five-day recording session at Olympic studios.
Jimi Hendrix: ...the secret of my sound is largely the electronic genius of our tame boffin (Roger Mayer) who is known as Roger The Valve. He has re-wired my guitars in a special way to produce an individual sound and he has made me a fantastic fuzz-tone... actually it's more a sustain than a fuzz. He got a special sound out of the guitar on 'One Rainy Wish' and 'Little Miss Lover'. It comes through a whole octave higher, so that when playing the high notes, it sometimes sounds like a whistle or a flute.

2 October 1967: More recording at Olympic.
Andy Johns (tape operator): During the sessions for *Axis: Bold As Love,* Hendrix never really came in with the tunes finished. Chas would pick out a riff for a line and go, 'That's good. Work on that.' Or he would put two things together for him and Hendrix would go off and muck about with it, but when Hendrix wanted a particular sound or effect he would just ask Eddie (Kramer).

George Chkiantz (engineer): Jimi would sit on the edge of a coffee table on Kramer's left, whispering things to him. Chas would sit on Eddie's right and field Kramer's and Hendrix's requests.

3 October 1967: Olympic studios, recording 'You Got Me Floatin'' and 'One Rainy Wish'.
Chas Chandler: That ('You Got Me Floatin'') was one of the weak songs on the record for me. That's why I put it on the second side. I just wanted to get it over with. I never felt that any of us had ever really been into the song. In fact, we added other people's harmonies to the track because we didn't have any other ideas. Trevor Burton and Roy Wood (of The Move) were mates of Noel's, and that's how they came in and sang on that. To me, it just wasn't one of his best works.

I was very keen (on 'One Rainy Wish') from the very first moment I heard him play it to me. Jimi recorded three guitars for that song—not counterplaying, as he had done with 'The Wind Cries Mary'. These guitar parts each picked up where the other one left off. We had some trouble recording it, as there were originally some gaps between the notes, which caused Noel to struggle a bit with the tempo, but it all came together nicely in the end.

4 October 1967: Recording sessions continue at Olympic Studios.
Andy Johns: Jimi was just about deaf in one ear. Eddie did an ear test on him. he put on the oscillator and he couldn't hear past 6k in one ear. The other ear was fine.

5 October 1967: Recording 'Little One' and 'There Ain't Nothing Wrong' at Olympic. Brian Jones, Jeff Beck and Dave Mason visit the studio.
Chas Chandler: Dave Mason came to a lot of our sessions. One time he brought his sitar but, after trying a song, Hendrix put it down and said, 'That's the last goddamn time I play that instrument.' He was awful.

6 October 1967: Session at Playhouse Theater for BBC radio show *Top Gear.*
Bernie Andrews (producer, Top Gear): Jimi always seemed to be stoned, but in the nicest way. He was very gentle, cooperative and easy to work with.

Noel Redding: We'd basically finished our Experience session at the BBC and Mitch popped out to do something—can't remember what—and we found out that Stevie Wonder was coming in to do a show himself. So, Stevie comes in—'Hello, how are you?' —and I'm not sure if Hendrix knew him from before but we just started jamming with Stevie on drums. There were no mics or anything so we just jammed, segued into an instrumental version of 'I Was Made To Love Her', and just stood there mouthing—or rather shouting—the lyrics at each other. It was just a laugh.

Pete Ritzema (engineer): Stevie wanted to play the drums, to calm down before his interview (with Brian Matthew). Jimi and Noel played along with a bit of 'I Was Made To Love Her' for about a minute-and-a-half, and then about another seven minutes of mucking about. I don't remember Stevie singing, though. It's not that wonderful, but it is one of those legendary things. Stevie Wonder did jam with Jimi Hendrix and it's there on tape.

Hendrix I remember as being rather shy, giggly and camp. He was very self-conscious about doing his vocals. He insisted on having screens put up round his mike when he was overdubbing his vocals because, otherwise, he said, Noel and Mitch would make him laugh.

7 October 1967: Gig at the Wellington Club, Dereham, Norfolk.
Lemmy (of Motorhead): I came to London in '67 and immediately got to sleep on the floor of Noel Redding's flat and got a job as a roadie with Hendrix... I was going along to gigs, and the next thing, I was humping on the tour for a tenner a week.

8 October 1967: Gig at the Saville Theatre, London, with Crazy World Of Arthur Brown, The Herd and Eire Apparent.
Miki Slingsby (photographer): I was just a 20-year-old photography student, keen to become a professional, and I had a fake press pass for a Swiss press agency which I used to bluff my way in. I was allowed to take photos from in front of the front seats, and then someone told me I could use an empty box upstairs which gave me another angle.

As if that wasn't enough, I then got back into the dressing room which Hendrix and Arthur Brown were sharing. There seemed to be no security. It was easy to get access to him. Arthur was doing his make up at the mirror, and the pair of them seemed to get along together very well, making erotic jokes about ways to use Johnson's Baby Powder, so the atmosphere was full of laughter and good feelings.

Arthur Brown: We were fooling around a lot that night, and I seem to remember I ended up sitting in his lap at one point. He was very easy to be around, and always full of fun, as were Mitch and Noel.

Miki Slingsby: Hendrix was very stoned and very gentle and friendly. He had an incredible charisma—even to me he seemed really sexy and that's not something I normally say about a man.

Tony McPhee (guitarist, later of The Groundhogs): I saw Hendrix only once, with Eire Apparent at The Saville, and he was so good I couldn't bear to see him again in case it was a disappointment. He did everything you expected but what sticks out in my mind was the way he communicated with the crowd. At one point in 'Purple Haze' he said, 'Yeah, I really like playing this bit,' and later on he pointed into the crowd and said, 'Out there in the audience, that's Bob Dylan. Oh, excuse me, lady.' That just cracked us up.

9 October 1967: The Experience fly to Paris for a gig at the Olympia, part of which is filmed.

10 October 1967: Taping for a French TV show, *Dim Dam Dom;* later the band hangs out with The Small Faces at Rosko's Club.

11 October 1967: The band is filmed miming 'Burning Of The Midnight Lamp' in the semi-derelict Montparnasse railway station. Jimi visits a market nearby.
Mitch Mitchell: Another one of our early morning filming sessions, on some kind of building site. The difference was that we did a live version of 'The Marseillaise'.

12 October 1967: Jimi pretends to play violin and piano while the Experience mime two songs on the *Musicorama* TV show, Paris. Later, the band flies home.

13 October 1967: Jimi records the *Good Evening* TV show, during which he is interviewed by Jonathan King.

14 October 1967: Jimi is interviewed by *Melody Maker*.

15 October 1967: Gig at The Starlight Ballroom, Crawley, Sussex.

17 October 1967: Recording for *The Alexis Korner Show*, BBC Radio.

Jeff Griffin (BBC producer): One of the best moments I can remember was when we did Jimi Hendrix. We'd already got a couple of tracks down and then Jimi said, 'Hey man, I want to do 'Hoochie Coochie Man', and it'd be great if we had slide guitar on it.
Alexis Korner (who ended up playing the slide): Hendrix had this horrible feeling that he wasn't playing the blues. Such an idea, coming from

someone that was able to play the blues as well as he could, I found very strange. The trouble was that he didn't play it in the watered-down form which had come to be accepted as the blues. Amazingly, he felt guilty because he was playing it perfectly.

18 October 1967: Hendrix attends the premiere of *How I Won The War* (featuring John Lennon) at the London Pavilion.

19 October 1967: Jimi is interviewed by Christine Osbourne of *Fabulous 208* magazine.

20 October 1967: London Records in the UK release a single, 'Hush Now'/'Flashing', from the sessions Jimi did with Curtis Knight. Jeffery and Chandler start legal action to have it withdrawn.
Jimi Hendrix: When I played it, I discovered that it had been recorded with a jam session I did in New York. We had only been practicing in the studio. I had no idea it was being recorded.

22 October 1967: Gig at the Pier Pavilion, Hastings, Sussex.

23 October 1967: Anti-Vietnam War riots outside the US Embassy, near Hendrix's flat; rehearsals at De Lane Lea studios.
Eric Burdon: When I first met him, he still had a very military/politicized mind. You know, it was anti-military and anti-Vietnam and all that shit, and he was still like, soldier boy. I'd say to him, as we looked out his apartment window over Grosvenor Square in London, 'Lookit, Jimi, what do you think of those riots against the US Embassy?' And he'd say, 'Well, when the Chinese hordes come screamin' down from China through North Vietnam and South Vietnam, you'll understand why we're trying so hard to stem the tide of Communism.'

24 October 1967: Gig at The Marquee club, London, supported by The Nice.
Keith Emerson (The Nice): Jimi specifically asked for us to support him when he played The Marquee. We did jam together that night, but it was far too noisy, really just a bit of fun for our own amusement. In fact, it was so loud, I couldn't even hear myself playing.

25 October 1967: Rehearsal at Regent Sound; recording 'Little Wing', 'Electric Ladyland' and 'South Saturn Delta' at Olympic studios.
Jimi Hendrix: 'Little Wing' is, like, one of these beautiful girls that come around sometimes. They might be spaced. They might be, you know, kind of strung out on a certain this or that.

'Little Wing' was a very sweet girl that came around and gave me her whole life and more if I wanted it. And me, with my crazy ass, couldn't get it together. So I'm off here and there and off over there.

It is based on a very, very simple Indian style. I got the idea, like, when we were in Monterey, and I was just lookin' at everything around. So I figured that I take everything I'd see around and put it maybe in the form of a girl, or somethin' like that, you know, and call it 'Little Wing', and then it will just fly away.

We put the guitar through the Leslie speaker of an organ, and it sounds like 'Jelly Bread', you know?

Eddie Kramer: There were no meetings in advance and Jimi created things in a very loose sort of fashion. He knew in his own head what he wanted to create. He had pages and pages of lyrics to choose from, but he knew exactly what he was doing. Every overdub, every backward guitar solo, every double-tracked thing was very carefully worked out in his own head. I was not to know what he was going to do until he walked into the studio. I don't think anybody else did.

Take any of the backwards guitar solos, and there are quite a number of them. When the tape was put on backwards... Jimi knew where he was on every inch of that tape. It didn't matter where you started it. And he knew exactly in his own mind as he was doing the solo what it would sound like afterwards. The point is that the man had a firm grasp of what he was doing and what its end result would be.

26 October 1967: Rehearsal at Regent Sound; Bruce Fleming takes pictures during the recording of 'Wait Until Tomorrow' and 'Ain't No Telling' at Olympic studios.

Chas Chandler: 'Wait Until Tomorrow' was originally written as a put-on. When he was first experimenting with it, we saw it as a joke, a comedy song almost.

Eddie Kramer: For no apparent reason, Jimi just could not play the opening notes to his satisfaction.

Bruce Fleming: I was photographing him, running around with a couple of cameras, and Jimi was sitting on this chair, playing, and he broke a string. While he was talking to someone, a roadie rushed up and put a new string in and, as the roadie was winding up the string for him, Jimi started to play the notes—the notes for the string as he was winding it up. And he said, 'I like this. I'm gonna do more of this.'
Eddie Kramer: There was nothing he wouldn't try. He was wonderful in the studio, he was such a funny guy. There was not a moment when we weren't laughing or carrying on because, to him, recording was fun.

27 October 1967: Olympic Studios, recording 'Spanish Castle Magic'.
Eddie Kramer: I was fooling around with those chords on the piano. I was playing some jazz chords when Jimi said, 'Man, what are those chords? Show me those chords.' I showed him what I had been playing, and he said, 'Man, I gotta put those in this song. You play it.' I said no, but I offered to show them to him, and those were the very chords he played on the final record.

Neville Chesters: He was doing the lyrics as the sessions were going… they would start to lay tracks down very roughly and it would all come together and then Jimi would have to go into the control room or somewhere and sit down. Then you'd see him writing things, and he tried them in his mind and played them… it was, I suppose, very natural. I think they did a bit of rehearsing, but very, very little.

28 October 1967: Recording 'Castles Made Of Sand' at Olympic; gig at the California Ballroom, Dunstable, Bedfordshire.
Jimi Hendrix: I like to write songs like 'Castles Made Of Sand', personally. When it comes to the ballads—the ballads I really like to get together. That's what I dig.

Lemmy: I was at all the sessions for *Axis: Bold As Love*. Once, at the management offices, I remember Hendrix coming in backwards with a typewriter in his fucking hands, going, 'Yeah, I'm the backwards man. Yeah!' and going out backwards through the other door.

Andy Pegg (fan): The hall was only one-third full. Hendrix and the band strode past me towards the stage. He picked up his Strat and said, 'Give me an A' to Noel Redding. As he tuned his guitar, he played a flurry of notes, rippling up and down the fretboard and you could hear the collective sucking-in of breath as the audience tingled with anticipation. He was mesmerising, and the band were really hot.

Jimi Hendrix: In the theater at Luton one guy jumped about 20ft from a box onto the stage, just to shake hands with us. We'd step outside the stage door where the teeny-boppers were and we'd think, Oh they won't bother us, and we'd get torn apart. A girl was hanging onto my guitar saying, 'You don't want it.' I said to her, 'You must be out of your mind.'

*Andy Pegg:*At the end of a blistering set, the manager of the Cali asked us to 'Put your hands together for The Jimi Hendrix Experience.' Jimi responded by hurling his guitar towards the promoter and the Marshall stacks, leaving the guitar lying on the floor, howling with feedback.

29 October 1967: Olympic Studios, working on 'Up From The Skies', 'Castles Made Of Sand', 'Bold As Love', 'One Rainy Wish'.
Roger Mayer (electronics engineer): I spent a lot of time with Jimi privately, hanging out and talking about the sounds and maybe bringing a few (fuzz) boxes around the flat so he could jam

"ONCE, AT THE MANAGEMENT OFFICES, I REMEMBER HENDRIX COMING IN BACKWARDS WITH A TYPEWRITER IN HIS FUCKING HANDS, GOING, 'YEAH, I'M THE BACKWARDS MAN. YEAH!' AND GOING OUT BACKWARDS THROUGH THE OTHER DOOR" [LEMMY OF MOTORHEAD]

"ONCE, AT THE MANAGEMENT OFFICES, I REMEMBER HENDRIX COMING IN BACKWARDS WITH A TYPEWRITER IN HIS FUCKING HANDS, GOING, 'YEAH, I'M THE BACKWARDS MAN. YEAH!' AND GOING OUT BACKWARDS THROUGH THE OTHER DOOR" [LEMMY OF MOTORHEAD]

in private. And we would get some general ideas of what we were trying to accomplish in the way of sustain and tone. We were normally using colors to describe the sound.

Eddie Kramer: Mitch had the ability to almost read what Jimi was thinking. Even though Jimi would dictate a lot of things to play... where to put accents and where to fit fills, it was generally left up to Mitch's imagination, which was pretty vivid. Jimi would never cease to be amazed at Mitch's ability to play ridiculous things.

Mitch Mitchell: He had a little apartment around the corner from the studio. As long as he had a big bed, an amplifier and a guitar, he was happy. Hendrix went to the bathroom with his guitar 'cos he liked the acoustics in there. I saw him cooking eggs and bacon one day with a guitar still slung around his neck. He had hot and cold running girlfriends, but nothing came between Jimi and his guitar.

30 October 1967: More recording on 'She's So Fine' at Olympic. Hendrix manages to leave one finished master of *Axis* in a taxi, obliging Eddie Kramer to mix the whole album again.
Chas Chandler: We brought the master tapes home this night from the studio, and Jimi went off to a party and took them with him to play them to some friends... He comes back in a taxi, he's lost the b side somewhere. He got back with only the a-side of the album.

Jimi Hendrix: We cut the record in just 16 days. It was mixed beautifully, but we lost the original mix so we had to re-mix it. Chas and I and the engineer, Eddie Kramer, all of us had to re-mix it the next morning within 11 hours.

31 October 1967: Mixing the b-side of *Axis: Bold As Love* again, at Olympic.
George Chkiantz: We first tried to re-mix it with reference to an acetate made from a pilot cut of the original master, but the record player at Olympic was terrible.

Eddie Kramer: We didn't even know whether we still had a tape copy of that first mix. Noel suddenly piped up, 'Um, I think I do,' and we sent a cab round to his place to get this little three-inch, seven-and-a-half i.p.s. reel of tape, all crumpled. I had to iron it out, put splicing tape on it and copy it onto 15 i.p.s. but, when we heard it, that was it.

Chas Chandler: We had made arrangements for cutting time, and we went back in the studio the next night and mixed the whole album again in four-and-a-half hours.

Eddie Kramer: And that was the mix that came out. That was an almost impossible task.

7 November 1967: David Montgomery photo session at Upper Berkeley Street; playback of *Axis: Bold As Love* at Chas Chandler's flat.
Noel Redding: Thankfully, when we sat down at Chas's to hear the test pressing, it sounded good.

8 November 1967: The Experience play a gig at Manchester University.

10 November 1967: Flight to Rotterdam, to record the TV programme *Hoepla* in the afternoon; in the evening there's a gig—the Hippy Happy Event—at the Ahoy Hallen, Rotterdam.
Rosalie Peters (presenter, Hoepla*):* It all went very cool. That was the intended atmosphere, to foster a certain absurdity. He came across as very soft-hearted. After all those wild stories about The Jimi Hendrix Experience, a trail of destruction, first class riff-raff, he made a very loveable impression. He gave me a box of chocolates... harmless affection. A really sweet guy.

Wim van der Linden (producer, Hoepla*):* He gave a live performance, incredibly loud, but we told him to. We already had trouble with the technicians and this gave them even more reason to put us down.

Leo Riemens (journalist in the Dutch newspaper De Telegraaf*):*

> One of them (the Experience) tried to eat his guitar. *Hoepla* and all these manifestations of complete negativism between 7 and 8 in the evening should disappear. For which young people is all this actually meant?

Gerard Bed (Dutch fan): I guess there were about 500 people (at the Hippy Happy event). Everybody moved close to the stage. Jimi began very nice and modest by saying 'I don't know what you're used to over here, but take care of your ears. You might as well stand back a little' and then, very quickly, the whole pack shoved backwards.

Rosalie Peters: After the show I said, 'Come along to my place. You can do whatever you want to.' Ah, those boys of the Experience, they were so drunk and stoned. They were just sitting on the stairs. They staggered into a taxi.

Jimi stayed the whole night. He thought it was just fine that I didn't have any of his records. A lady who had been hanging around the hotel came to our door. We let her in. She spent the night with him. We didn't hear a thing... that still surprises me. Next morning we put Jimi in a taxi with a raisin bun.

11 November 1967: The Experience fly back to London. Gig at Sussex University, Brighton, supported by Ten Years After.

12 November 1967: Photo session at Sweeney Todd barber shop, London.
Bruce Fleming: He was having his hair done, a very funny set of pictures. I was just called up by the public relations people and told Sweeney Todd's. It might have been a tie-up between Sweeney Todd, who was then quite a well-known hairdresser, and Jimi, you know? Something for the papers. Because the talk was about his afro—that was a pretty crazy haircut, and then he would try to wear a hat on top of that. I don't think they did a lot with it, more crimping and a few snips here and there, rather than cutting it. It was more of a PR exercise.

13 November 1967: Hendrix writes 'Angel' at Olympic studios.

14 November 1967: Gig at the Royal Albert Hall, London—the start of 15-date UK tour with Pink Floyd, The Move, Amen Corner, The Nice, Eire Apparent and Outer Limits.

Kathy Etchingham: They were great people, but none of those bands was really Jimi's type of music at all. You'd never have found a Pink Floyd album in our record collection. He liked Amen Corner, they were kinda bluesy at that time.

Chas Chandler: Noel and Mitch were shaking like leaves and even Jimi was petrified to go on stage. They realized they were part of something bigger than themselves and I had to get a bottle of Scotch to restore some courage all around.

Roger Fullilove (fan): I went with my girlfriend, Ann, and we got seats about five rows from the front. Because it was a package tour, each band only did three or four numbers, and a lot of time was spent watching crews shifting gear around. Pink Floyd weren't that well known yet, The Move weren't very inspiring, but Hendrix and The Nice proved themselves as great as I'd hoped.

The thing that really sticks out in my mind is that, a couple of songs into Hendrix's set, Ann had to go to the toilet. As she's making her way along the row, Hendrix notices her and makes a wolf-whistle noise with the guitar. Then he makes some comment like, 'Hey, where are you going? We're here to play music,' which had the effect of making her head for the toilet rather faster.

15 November 1967: Jonathan King interviews Hendrix for ATV's *Good Evening*; the tour plays the Winter Gardens, Bournemouth.
Noel Redding: Everybody used to hang out with everybody else. Us lot were really close with The Move. Trevor Burton, their rhythm guitarist, always used to travel with us and, if I was running late, I'd travel with The Move. So, after the show, we'd all go to pubs together, get pissed, then attempt to get on the coach at the proper time. We'd miss the coach and have to get buses and trains.

16 November 1967: Photo session for the *Sunday Times* at the Roundhouse. The feature never appears, so the picture becomes the inside gatefold shot on the UK *Electric Ladyland* sleeve.

David Montgomery (photographer): It was actually pretty hairy. We poured a line of petrol about 15ft across and we lit it. He was standing in front of it—he could have had his head blown off. The flames go up about 15ft high.

17 November 1967: The tour plays at the City Hall, Sheffield.
Ace Kefford (The Move): While we were on the Hendrix tour, we got involved in a battle with the prime minister, Harold Wilson. We'd sent out postcards with Wilson on them to promote our single, 'Flowers In the Rain', and he didn't like it. Guys in black limos started following us. It was only later that we discovered they were from MI5.

Tony Secunda (manager, The Move): We'd come out of a show, and there would be this big limo parked across the road. It'd follow us to the greasy spoon, to the next gig, wherever we went. And Hendrix was doing his nut, because he thought it was the FBI or the CIA or someone, coming after him.

It was really bizarre. We'd say, 'Jimi, why would they be after you?' and we were thinking maybe they wanted to send him to Vietnam, maybe this, maybe that, and he'd just go, 'No, you don't understand, they're spooks. It's the secret service. They want to know what I know', like there was some huge conspiracy he was involved in, UFOs and alien earwigs in the White House. He spun this out for hours, then he finally cracked up and said, 'Man, you guys are so gullible.'

18 November 1967: The tour reaches the Empire Theatre, Liverpool.
Henry McCullough: We (Eire Apparent) had the same manager, Chas Chandler, as the Experience and as a result we did a lot of work with them, including the tour with The Move and Pink Floyd. But it was at some one-nighter with a circular dressing room that I saw Jimi, pretty stoned, feeling his way round and round the walls, facing outwards like an upside-down fly. He looked as if he'd never make it onto the stage. But he always did. He always delivered.

19 November 1967: Gig at Coventry Theatre.
Keith Emerson (The Nice): Halfway through the tour Jimi bought himself a Super 8 cine camera and started filming everything. During my organ-trashing routine with the knives, I was about to throw one into the Leslie speaker cabinet when I suddenly noticed Jimi crouching down beside it, filming me. I thought I'd better not throw it, but he started egging me on, waggling his tongue and gesticulating with his hands. He wanted to film the knife coming towards him, so I did throw it. He loved it.

Syd Barrett: I used to sit in the back of the bus, with him (Jimi) up front. He would film us, but we never spoke. It was very polite. Hendrix was a perfect guitarist, and that's all I wanted to do as kid, play a guitar properly and jump around.

Lemmy: When he was playing, I'd watch him on stage from a chair in the wings. You could never tell how he did it. He loved to fuck off all the guitar players in the audience. Graham Nash used to sit backstage with his ear on the stacks all night—none of this gladhanding you get backstage now with the fucking canapes; in those days people wanted to learn and improve.

22 November 1967: The tour plays at the Guildhall, Portsmouth, Hampshire.
Ace Kefford: I was dropping acid for most of the last half of 1967. What I remember chiefly about the Hendrix tour are people with shiny faces, bright lights everywhere, and Jimi being especially kind to me and old Syd (Barrett), because he knew we were both cracking up. He'd come up to me backstage and place a hand on my shoulder, or ruffle my hair, and say, 'Hey, what's happening, Ace?'

23 November 1967: The tour comes to the Sofia Gardens, Cardiff.
Allan Jones (fan, later editor of Melody Maker): Seeing Hendrix in all his raging glory was a kind of consummation, a final surrender to rock'n'roll. We were overwhelmed that night. For a start, none of us had ever heard anything so loud. The noise was terrific. It seemed to suck the air from our lungs, left us scalded, altered. Hendrix was spellbinding, truly a brother from another planet.

24 November 1967: The tour plays the Colston Hall, Bristol.

25 November 1967: During the gig at the Opera House, Blackpool, Lancashire. Hendrix is filmed for a 16mm short movie, *Experience,* produced by Austin John Marshall.
Austin John Marshall: This was just about the first time that anybody had tried to film really loud rock on stage in Britain. The terrified sound recordist, crouching in the orchestra pit of the Opera House, Blackpool, must have thought we'd been caught in a heavy artillery barrage. The techniques just didn't exist—not at our budget level anyway—to get reasonable sound from a group like The Jimi Hendrix Experience in full cry.

Ace Kefford: At Blackpool Playhouse, I flipped, threw my bass in the air and proceeded to kick the PA speakers into the orchestra pit, which stopped the whole show. Then I chinned one of the theater staff, and all his mates started giving me a kicking until the road crew waded in.

Back at the hotel, me, Trev (Burton of The Move) Noel, Jimi and a few of the real heads were acting just like kids. Playing silly games like sitting on the floor, grabbing each other's ankles and trying to tip each other over. We also had this thing called Going Off The Wall where you'd face the wall with the others pushing against you. You'd then try to bend forward, take as much air into your lungs as possible, stand up straight quick and, basically, you'd faint.

26 November 1967: The tour arrives at the Palace Theatre, Manchester.
Tony Secunda: This was before they'd finished building most of the motorways, so you'd be crawling along two-lane roads, one lane north, one lane south. It was exhausting.

Davy O'List (guitarist, The Nice): Immediately after you finished your set, you could leave, which was great. We used to go on third. Sometimes I'd stay back to watch Pink Floyd play but, otherwise, it was off to the nearest pub or whatever, and wait to be hauled out again.

27 November 1967: The tour flies into Belfast for shows at Whitla Hall, Queen's College, as part of the Belfast Arts Festival.
Charlie Hewitt (festival publicist): I booked them for the Festival. The cost was in the region of £250 to £300.

Caroline Nemec (receptionist, Grand Central Hotel, Belfast): We had no advance notice of Jimi coming to the hotel. The booking was done through his agent, obviously, and the Festival people. One of the first things I noticed was how enormous his hands were when he signed the hotel register. The band had one of the very few suites in the hotel at that time, on the second or third floor.

Shortly after Jimi arrived, I remember the mother of a young fan who had been admitted to Forster Green Hospital with asthma, phoned asking to speak with Jimi. I took her telephone number and went up to the room to tell Jimi. He phoned her back and arranged for her son to be sent a copy of his LP which he had autographed.

He was very gently spoken and a mannerly person, in contrast to some other celebrities who stayed at the hotel, and he didn't create any fuss.

Jimi's clothes and hair seemed outrageous at the time in Belfast. The other two band members had been using rollers in their hair, which horrified the chambermaid when she discovered them under the bedclothes.

Liam McAuley (Gown magazine): It was Hendrix's birthday. The audience sang 'Happy Birthday' in a feeble and slightly embarrassed fashion. The compere hurriedly initiated a cry of 'We want Jimi.' The lights dimmed and weaved and Hendrix exploded onto the stage with 'Plug your ears—it's gonna be LOUD!'

Charlie Hewitt: Hendrix's first set drove them wild. Not only was the audience mesmerized, but also the stewards… some of them were even seen to reach out to try and touch the maestro.

Mary McAree (first aid nurse): I was seated on the balcony to the left above the stage with another nurse. We were looking down on this huge, impressive bank of speakers. When Jimi came on, he had an incredible impact on the audience, made more exciting by the colored lighting being used, which was spectacular.

He used several different guitars during the concert, possibly three or four, playing at what seemed enormous volume.

At the end, he knelt down, played his guitar with his teeth and then smashed it off the wall at the side of the stage—it was a cream/yellow colored guitar—which amazed the crowd.

Charlie Hewitt: During the interval between the two performances, I had arranged a publicity photo call. It was Hendrix's birthday, and a cake had been baked. It was to be presented to him before the local photographers. As the cake was carried into the Green Room by my assistant, Anne Pinkney, candles burning, smiles all round, Hendrix was relaxing, nonchalantly strumming his guitar.

Robin Page (photographer): He thought it was a wind-up at first and we weren't sure what he was going to do.

Charlie Hewitt: He looked up at the cake and its carrier and said, 'Fuck off.' Putting her mission and publicity for the Festival before everything else, she bit her tongue and held back from throwing the cake in his face and posed, smiling with the cake and the star.

Robin Page: After he realized it was genuine, he relaxed again.

Charlie Hewitt: It made the papers the next day, but the cake remained uneaten—by Hendrix anyway.

During the second show, I escorted the University safety officer around the hall, with him looking worriedly at the vibrating balcony and supporting pillars. The volume worried him. Nothing like it had been heard in the city before. He was persuaded that no great harm would befall the venerated auditorium or its capacity audience.

Keith Emerson: In responding to the wildness of the crowd, Jimi went over the top, throwing his guitar around and really laying into Mitch's drum kit. This wasn't the usual staged thing, this was really destroying the gear. Mitch was very meticulous about his drums and he got really angry, almost in tears of rage at Hendrix. But Hendrix just laughed.

Trevor Burton: Jimi finished his set by flinging this Flying V through a backstage window about 20ft up a wall. It was hanging outside in the alley by the lead, and still feeding back.

28 November 1967: When the band returns to London, Kathy Etchingham gives Jimi a bassett hound puppy as a birthday gift. He names it Ethel Floon.
Kathy Etchingham: Jimi thought the world of that dog. It would bound around the room, banging head first into the furniture, which used to have Jimi in great fits of laughter. As she got bigger, and because of the constant barking and complaints from the neighbours, we felt that she would be better off living in the country, so Jeff Beck took her for us.

1 December 1967: UK release of *Axis: Bold As Love;* the tour resumes at the Town Hall, Chatham, Kent.
Jimi Hendrix: When I first saw that (cover) design, I thought, 'It's great,' but maybe we should have an American Indian. The three of us have nothing to do with what's on the *Axis* cover.

2 December 1967: The tour moves on to the Brighton Dome, Sussex for two more shows.
Mick Coyne: About five o'clock I was hanging around outside The Dome when a Ford Zephyr pulled up by the stage door and Jimi got out from the passenger side.

His look had changed dramatically. Now he was like an American Indian, with the headband and the fringed jacket. I had my fan club card, and I got him to autograph it. When he handed me the pen back, he dropped it and was very apologetic.

Keith Emerson: My mum and dad came to see the tour in Brighton. They were quite used to the volume of rock bands, but they thought Jimi was just way too loud.

I became aware, as the tour went on, that Jimi was genuinely interested in my playing. I was quite flattered by that, and when we'd meet at The Speakeasy, he'd ask me up to jam with him.

Mick Coyne: My ticket was for the second show and the first surprise was that he came on stage dressed completely differently. He had the black hat, a black shirt and jacket and dark blue trousers. I remember him playing 'Hey Joe', 'Purple Haze', 'I Don't Live Today' and more, but the striking thing was that the show had calmed down a lot. He was really concentrating on playing, and there was hardly any theatrics at all.

3 December 1967: The tour goes north to the Theatre Royal, Nottingham.
Mitch Mitchell: It was actually good fun—lunacy

"JIMI'S CLOTHES AND HAIR SEEMED OUTRAGEOUS AT THE TIME IN BELFAST. THE OTHER TWO BAND MEMBERS HAD BEEN USING ROLLERS IN THEIR HAIR, WHICH HORRIFIED THE CHAMBERMAID WHEN SHE DISCOVERED THEM UNDER THE BEDCLOTHES"

"JIMI'S CLOTHES AND HAIR SEEMED OUTRAGEOUS AT THE TIME IN BELFAST. THE OTHER TWO BAND MEMBERS HAD BEEN USING ROLLERS IN THEIR HAIR, WHICH HORRIFIED THE CHAMBERMAID WHEN SHE DISCOVERED THEM UNDER THE BEDCLOTHES"

most of the time… It was still the standard package tour, short sets and stuff, but at least by that time it was our sort of audience.

Noel Redding: I remember, when The Move were playing once, I rode a bicycle across the stage. Another time we put stink bombs under Bev Bevan's foot pedal.

4 December 1967: The tour plays the City Hall, Newcastle-upon-Tyne.
Tony Secunda: The thing about Hendrix on that tour was that he hadn't bought in to his own legend yet. He still felt he had something to prove. Later he could complain that it didn't matter what he did, or how badly he screwed up, the audience would always applaud. And that got to him, of course it did. But when he toured with us (The Move) he knew he had to pull out all the stops, and that there wasn't room for mistakes. We'd have eaten him alive otherwise.

Roy Wood (The Move): The best thing I ever heard was Jimi Hendrix playing "I Can Hear The Grass Grow" after rehearsal once.

5 December 1967: The tour ends at Green's Playhouse, Glasgow. Jimi is interviewed for *Melody Maker*.
Ronnie Anderson (freelance photographer): Green's Playhouse was the biggest rock venue in Europe—a 3,500 seater, with three tiers.

I got backstage, and had to crawl into their tiny dressing room—it was underneath the stage—through a mass of drum cases and other stuff. I was immediately made welcome by Jimi with a bottle of Newcastle Brown Ale, of which they had several crates.

I was intrigued to notice that he was filming me as I photographed him. He was using a Canon Super 8 portable camera, very advanced for those days, which he had apparently just bought, and it could shoot in low light.

In the early 1990s, I learned that his camera had gone up for sale in an auction, and it still had that film in it. A good friend of mine had seen the developed film, and there was me, sitting on a crate of Newcastle Brown photographing Hendrix. It seems he had never used that camera again.

Gary Brooker (Procol Harum): The gig was an absolute shambles, with Jimi having the curtains closed on him halfway through his set, because he was supposedly doing rude things with his guitar. Then green-clothed, short-haircut, cap-and-gloved staff tried to pull him off stage.

6 December 1967: Back in London, Jimi attends a party for The Foundations (multi-racial UK pop-soul group) at The Speakeasy.
Clem Curtis (singer, The Foundations): We'd had our first hit, starting in September of that year, with 'Baby Now That I Found You', so this was a party to celebrate the fact that it was still a successful record for us. I'd met Jimi on a number of occasions, seen him jam at The Speakeasy and so on, but the party gave me a chance to sit down with him for half-an-hour and really talk. He wouldn't say much until he felt he'd got to know you, but I remember thinking he had quite a sense of humor, he laughed a lot and I got the impression of a kind, generous person.

7 December 1967: Jimi jams with Noel and Aynsley Dunbar—Mitch Mitchell's original rival for the Experience drum stool—at The Speakeasy.

8 December, 1967: The group record 'Spanish Castle Magic' for broadcast appearance on the *Good Evening* TV show two days later.

9 December 1967: Jimi is interviewed at the flat in Upper Berkeley St, by Tom Lopez (aka Meatball Fulton).

10 December 1967: Jimi and Brian Jones see The Moody Blues at The Speakeasy.

11 December 1967: Jimi is interviewed by *Disc and Music Echo*.

> *Jimi Hendrix:* I don't celebrate Christmas too much since I've been away from home. Otherwise I get homesick and feel kinda lonesome. I'll probably just take off and get lost. I may even go to Sweden. You can take a cabin up in the hills and really have a quiet time.

12 December 1967: Jimi jams with Fairport Convention at The Speakeasy.
Richard Thompson (guitar): It was kind of intimidating, when you're young herberts trying to look cool and this extremely urbane,

very bizarre-looking, very handsome black man comes up and says, 'Do you mind if I sit in?'

He just played whatever we were playing, whether it was 'Absolutely Sweet Marie' or 'East-West' or something. He just seemed to want to be one of the boys for a few seconds.

Simon Nicol (guitar): He played Richard's guitar, Richard would grab mine and I would grab a spare to play rhythm.

13 December 1967: Recording at Olympic; 'Foxy Lady' is released as a single in the US.

14 December 1967: Dezo Hoffman photo session at the ANIM office, resulting in the shot used on the *Smash Hits* album cover.

15 December 1967: Recording for BBC *Top Gear*, with party atmosphere, including 'Hear My Train A-Comin'' and a jingle for the BBC's three month-old Radio One.
Bernie Andrews (producer, Top Gear*):* That was probably an unofficial thing, having a bit of a rave... I should have stopped it happening because it was something the BBC wouldn't have officially condoned at the time. Yet there was no way I was gonna stop 'em doing it, 'cos I knew it was right to do it. So I encouraged them in a way but, at the same time, pretended it wasn't happening.

Noel Redding: Hendrix made that (jingle) up on the spot. They'd asked us to do a jingle, he showed us the chords and we did it.

16 December 1967: Filming for *Top Of The Pops* Christmas special; *Axis: Bold As Love* enters the UK album chart.
Jimi Hendrix: I just thought about the title. There might be a meaning behind the whole thing. The axis on the Earth turns around and changes the face of the world, and completely different civilisations come about, or another age comes about. In other words, it changes the face of the Earth and it only takes about one-fourth of a day. Well, the same with love. If a cat falls in love, or a girl falls in love, it might change his whole complete scene. *Axis: Bold As Love*. One-two-three, rock around the clock.

18 December 1967: Jimi is interviewed by BP Fallon for *Melody Maker.*

19 December 1967: Further filming for the short movie, *Experience*, at Bruce Fleming's photographic studio, London.
Austin John Mitchell: There was a feeling that a quiet, simple sequence would help the film and offset the horrendous distortions of the live stage stuff (filmed in Blackpool on 25 November). I really wanted to clear away the strobe lights, the walls of amps, the phasing, fuzz and feedback for a moment and place Jimi, this paradox of gentleness, genius and freak, against a plain white photographer's studio paper background and hear how he played a simple blues.

The acoustic number followed a joke interview scene, which was the group's idea. The film was obviously about Jimi, but we wanted to involve Mitch and Noel somehow. They were to be hard-hitting interviewers, and be allowed to ask what they all agreed were the dumbest questions they'd ever been asked. And Jimi—always far too polite to slag off a reporter—could send up the questions without giving offence.

So, coaxed along by whisky, cokes and bonhomie, Noel, Mitch and Jimi put together a good-natured question/answer routine which included Jimi choking on a Gauloise pretending it was a joint. But this was all a subterfuge, probably unnecessary, because Jimi was the soul of amenability. It was just that the image-building machinery behind him seemed so relentlessly committed to presenting the world with Mister Black Acid, the Rainbow Superstud—so much so that we expected that at any moment someone would lay a heavy hand on our shoulders and say, 'No one's gonna present our Heavy Star sittin' down playin' no 12-string!'

After Mitch and Noel had split, we had about five minutes' worth of film stock in the camera. We turned up this guitar... and my, my what a coincidence, a 12-string strung and tuned left-handed... (a coincidence somewhat helped by director Peter Neal—no mean Old Timey picker himself—restringing the borrowed guitar that morning).

Jimi took the guitar and looked at it as if it would bite him. 'Twelve-string? Shit—what the hell am I gonna do with that?' 'Um... well, we just thought... as a contrast to the rest of the movie you might play a sort of slow, quiet blues... please?' With the absorbed, serene expression of a father who has discovered his old train set in the attic, Jimi perched himself atop the tall stool and hunched over the huge box. He had a tortoise-shell pick with him and started to strum. We hadn't much film left but we took the risk and started turning the camera straight away. Jimi noodled around with an intro for a while then stopped.

Looking up at the camera he said, 'No, I'd rather do that again. Can we stop the film there? 'Cos I was sorta scared to death by this thing.' 'Oh, yeah,' said Peter Neal, but we all knew that there wouldn't be enough film left in the camera to finish the take. When he'd finished Jimi gave a little chuckle and said, 'I bet you didn't think I'd do that...'

Bruce Fleming: We were doing this session, and I asked, 'What are you doing for Christmas?' And he said he wanted to go home and see his dad—'but I can't go, because if I fly out I have to get back quick for a New Year's concert and shows.' So, I'm like, 'What are you doing?' And he's like, 'I think I'll just have dinner in a hotel.' So, I'm like, 'Fuck that. No, you won't. You'll come and eat with me.' So he came to my house with my wife and me and some friends.

Austin John Mitchell: On that freezing afternoon, Jimi had come out in a really thin leopard-skin print jacket and chiffon shirt, and as we decanted the film equipment into Charing Cross Road, I watched Jimi walk off towards a neon-lit Leicester Square—apparently indifferent to the biting cold. And at the risk of appearing wise after the event, I must say that as I watched him I was overcome by the feeling that he wouldn't be around for long.

20 December 1967: Working on 'Crosstown Traffic', 'Dance' and Noel Redding's song 'Dream' at Olympic studios. Dave Mason of Traffic is on hand to contribute backing vocals.
Jimi Hendrix: I was playing piano on it. And then we sang the background, you know?

Eddie Kramer: The piano sound (on 'Crosstown Traffic') was very heavily compressed with a Pye limiter and, as it was going through that, it was also being EQ'd. I also varied the EQ to make it sound like a mini-wah wah. Jimi doubled up the melody line by singing what he's playing on the guitar. Then he put a kazoo on top of that.

Velvert Turner (friend): He couldn't seem to get the sound he was trying to express across and, to someone in the studio, Jimi said, 'Have you got a comb on you, man? Somebody get me some cellophane.' If you take a comb and put cellophane across it and blow through it, it gives a kazoo sound. So the guitar track, the solo on 'Crosstown Traffic', is laced with the sound of a kazoo—Jimi with his paper and comb.

Noel Redding: Hendrix really liked 'Dream'. I played it to him on the guitar, and he picked up the bass. That one was never completed, but it was a good tune with a lot of validity.

21 December 1967: The Experience are interviewed by Linda Eastman (later McCartney); recording on 'Crosstown Traffic' at Olympic; in the US Capitol release *Get That Feeling*, an album of material featuring Hendrix with Curtis Knight, leased to them by Ed Chalpin of PPX.
Jimi Hendrix: The Curtis Knight album was from bits of tape they used from a jam session, bits of tape, tiny little confetti bits of tapes.

Capitol never told us they were going to release that crap. That's the real drag about it... that cat and I used to really be friends. Plus I was just at a jam session and here they just try to connive and cheat and use. It was a really bad scene. I knew Curtis Knight was recording but, listen, that was at a jam session.

"JIMI COULDN'T SEEM TO GET THE SOUND HE WAS TRYING TO EXPRESS, HE SAID, 'HAVE YOU GOT A COMB ON YOU, MAN? SOMEBODY GET ME SOME CELLOPHANE.' SO THE GUITAR TRACK, THE SOLO ON 'CROSSTOWN TRAFFIC', IS LACED WITH THE SOUND OF A KAZOO — JIMI WITH HIS PAPER AND COMB"

22 December 1967: The Christmas On Earth concert at the Kensington Olympia, London, is filmed for TV; it features the Experience, The Who, Eric Burdon & The Animals, The Move , Pink Floyd, Tomorrow and Soft Machine. It is followed by visit to The Speakeasy.

Noel Redding: We didn't like individual dressing rooms, so The Move, us lot and Eric & The New Animals were hanging out in the same room.

Jim Marshall (of Marshall Amplifiers): In the afternoon, they were doing rehearsals and Mitch couldn't quite get something right. So Jimi said, 'Would you sit in and show (him) how to....' So I did... And all of a sudden, this character came up on the stage and complained about the volume. I said to Jimi, 'You have to cut it down a bit—we've got a complaint.' So Jimi went over to the amp and and set it up a bit more.

Then this chap came back again, all red-faced, and it turned out to be the shop steward of the electricians doing the lighting. He threatened to bring the whole crowd out on strike if Jimi didn't stop. I said, 'I think Jim, you gotta stop.' And then he turned it up again!

In the end, the shop steward said, 'Everybody is out. There will be no show tonight!' And I said to Jimi, 'I think this chap is really serious, there's not gonna be a show.' But Jimi thought it was very funny. He did quieten it down a bit, though.

Noel Redding: We went on at two o'clock, and went down a bomb.

It was the first time I'd been exposed to strobes. These things started going, and it was insane. Hendrix loved them, he'd just go mad, but I could not handle strobe lights in those days.

Miki Slingsby (photographer): I wasn't taking pictures that night, so I was able to concentrate on the music. At times they would have two bands playing simultaneously, but the place wasn't too crowded so you could wander between the stages and get close to the bands. The whole place was awash with color and paisley shirts. The Experience set was amazing, with Jimi playing quite beautifully.

23 December 1967: Hendrix dresses up as Santa for a children's party at The Roundhouse.

24 December 1967: As the US release date of *Axis: Bold As Love* draws near, *The Los Angeles Times* reviews the newly released *Get That Feeling: Curtis Knight Sings, Jimi Hendrix Plays.*

> Beware when an album shrinks the featured vocalist's name into small type beneath the twice-as-large name of a back-up musician. Hendrix records for Warner Brothers but, last July, he backed up Knight for what sounds suspiciously like no more than a demonstration record with some after-the-fact engineering tricks.

25 December 1967: Hendrix spends Christmas with photographer Bruce Fleming's family and friends.

Bruce Fleming: We got to talk a lot... architecture, painting, all sorts. He was into everything. We just had a brilliant time and a lot of laughs. Americans like Christmas and we had turkey, the whole thing. He was very radical in his opinions and his ideas: a very original thinker, very laid back, very quiet, very funny. He had a beautiful sense of humor.

30 December 1967: Working on overdubs for 'Dream' at Olympic studios.

31 December 1967: New Year's Eve party at The Speakeasy, during which Jimi participates in a superstar jam session and plays a 30-minute version of 'Auld Lang Syne'.

Phil Ryan (keyboards, Eyes Of Blue, later of Man): We were playing there that night, and it was a special New Year's party, so the audience was full of celebrities like Clapton, Steve Winwood, Ginger Baker, Georgie Fame and, of course, Hendrix.

When midnight struck, my band was shunted off the stage to make way for a sort of supergroup jam. I remember Ginger Baker turfing our drummer, Pugwash, off his kit. I made my mind up that I wasn't leaving the stage, so I stayed put, and up comes Eric Burdon, Jimi Hendrix and the rest, and they launch into a rock'n'roll version of 'Auld Lang Syne'.

Most of them were playing it pretty straight but Hendrix, in his inimitable way, mutated it into something else completely. Everybody was utterly out of it by this time, but what a brilliant way to bring the New Year in.

Paul McCartney, who offered The Experience a part in The Beatles' Magical Mystery Tour before fame overtook them

1968

1 January 1968: Rehearsal at Hillside Club; interview at BBC, Broadcasting House, London.
Mo Ostin (general manager, Reprise Records): The sales of Hendrix's first album have been extraordinarily successful and, up until 31 December, 1967, aggregated in excess of 287,000 albums, and are anticipated to continue at a very satisfactory rate.

2 January 1968: Hendrix writes a deposition attacking Capitol's *Get That Feeling* album; jams with John Mayall at Klook's Kleek, London.
Jimi Hendrix (in his deposition):

> The label creates the impression that Knight and I recorded as at least equal performers, which is untrue. My involvement was completely subordinated and accommodated to Knight's musical personality and ability, which are the obligations of a 'session man'. The record therefore conveys a completely erroneous, unflattering and unfavourable impression of my talents and abilities.

3 January 1968: Flight to Gothenburg, Sweden, where they check in at the Hotel Opalen.
Mitch Mitchell: When he checked into a hotel, it wasn't like being in America where you got security on the floors of the hotel. People would turn up and say, 'Let's have a party.' In Sweden, they could only drink by license a couple of times a year. So it's, 'Excuse me, we're just coming back from doing a concert, you know? Do you mind leaving us alone? We might have some guests.'

4 January 1968: In the early hours, Hendrix becomes involved in a brawl with the rest of the band and is arrested for trashing his hotel room.
Noel Redding: After performing, we headed for the clubs. Jimi didn't usually come with us when we were drinking. He couldn't handle drinking very well, and that night we all got really pissed. Somehow we got back to the hotel and went to Jimi's room. But something went wrong in Jimi's head and he started freaking out at some weird hanger-on…

Mitch Mitchell: …someone trying to get into his room. We heard this commotion out on the landing and myself, Noel and Gerry Stickells appeared to see what was going on and calm things down. I took Hendrix back into my room, whereupon he started trying to smash things up, which didn't go down too well with me.

Somehow, we struggled with him and got him out into the corridor again. I think I threw a very feeble punch at him, which amazed him rather than anything else. Then we got him on the floor and managed to sit on him.

Noel Redding: The noise finally caused someone to call the police.

Mitch Mitchell: He'd smashed a plate-glass window in my room.

Chas Chandler: I asked him what happened but he didn't know himself and I never really got the full story. But I think Noel hit Jimi and Jimi laid out two cops and tried to jump out of the window.

Noel Redding: They arrested Jimi and took him away about 6am, charging him with disturbing the peace.

Chas Chandler: I went to the jail in Gothenburg and he was sitting in a bare cell. He had been in hospital first to have stitches put in two gashes in his hands. Then they put him in a cell.

Jimi Hendrix: Man, I was just drunk. That can happen to anybody. But when a normal person throws a couple of things through a window in sudden madness, it does not hit the front pages. That is the hard side of being a public person.

Usually I can drink a lot of booze. Someone must have put some kind of tablet in my glass, otherwise I would never have become like that. I really hope the Swedish audience overlook this.

5 January 1968: Interview with Claes Hanning of *Expressen*; gig at Jernallen Sports Hall, Sandvikan.

Jimi Hendrix (to Claes Hanning):

> After Stockholm, I intend taking it easy for a while, as I need to calm down. Since my breakthrough, everything has gone so fast, I have never had a chance to relax.

Noel Redding: I felt the band was drifting apart, and discussed it with Mitch before the next show. As if to accentuate my premonition, Jimi had a sore throat and did only 35 minutes when he could have easily jammed instrumentally for much longer.

6 January 1968: On to Copenhagen, Denmark; interview by Casten Grolin for *Ekstra Bladet*.

Jimi Hendrix (to Casten Grolin):

> I have thought about changing our stage-act completely. In the future, I will present a stage play with colors, which is going to play one part, dancers and other groups, who are going to play different parts. And we will play different parts, either with or without instruments.

7 January 1968: Tivoli Konserthalle, Copenhagen, supported by Page One and Hansson & Karlsson.

Niels Pedersen (Page One): I remember very clearly that evening. The first show I saw from behind the drummer, second show we sat among the audience. The thing which really thrilled me about Hendrix was that he had hurt his hand in Gothenburg so he just played with the other hand.

Un-named reviewer (in Politiken*):*

> His playing contains fewer gimmicks than before; he has reduced it to just biting the strings a couple of times… And he has more blues in his fingertips than hair on his head—and that does say quite a lot.

8 January 1968: Flight to Stockholm, Sweden, for two shows at Stora Salen, Konserthuset. Also interview for Swedish radio.

Jimi Hendrix: I'd like to dedicate this show to Eva, who keeps sendin' roses, but we never seen her before. She's a goddess from Asgard.

9 January 1968: Jimi, Chas and Gerry Stickells return to Gothenburg. The rest of the touring party returns to the UK.

Gerry Stickells: We were not allowed to go out, except that once a day we had to report to the police station. We had to stay in our room at the Esso Motel, right behind the gas station, the only place that would take us, though the manager was a fan so he would even lend us his car to go to the police station.

10 January 1968: Hendrix reports to Gothenburg Police HQ, as he is required to do for the next five days.

Gerry Stickells: Hendrix used to put rollers in his hair to get his look and, in our boredom, he would put them in my hair too. I'll never forget that motel, because we had bunk beds and, every night, two girls used to come round with a joint. We would eat and get laid in the bunk beds, which was quite a struggle.

11 January 1968: Interview for *Expressen*.

13 January 1968: 'Foxy Lady' hits its US chart peak of 67.

Wyclef Jean: When I first heard Jimi Hendrix, it was weird, because I was coming from the streets. I heard 'Foxy Lady' and I thought, What the fuck is this shit? What is this cat thinking? And then I kept playing it over and over on this cassette that I had. I became a Hendrix hound.

15 January 1968: *Axis: Bold As Love* is released in the US.

John Hiatt: On *Axis*, you know that opening little salvo, where they interview this guy, Paul Caruso, and he denies the existence of 'space people' and then he says, 'If you'll excuse me, I must be on my way' and then all hell breaks loose with the guitar? I never heard anything like that—none of us had. What a powerful statement. He was just starting to suggest what he had to offer in terms of his musical vision.

16 January 1968: Hendrix appears before Gothenburg Municipal Court and is fined approximately $2,500.

Jimi Hendrix: I think pop groups have a right to their own private lives… people should judge them by what they do on stage… their private life is their own business… You can't expect artists to be goody-goodies all the time.

17 January 1968: Hendrix, Chandler and Stickells fly back to London.

19 January 1968: Hendrix, along with The Beatles and Brian Jones, attends a launch party for Grapefruit, who have just signed to Apple's music publishing side.

20 January 1968: Photo session for *Top Pop* magazine; Hendrix records tracks for McGough & McGear LP, with Paul McCartney producing.
Jimi Hendrix (in Go Go Girl *magazine):* My eyes are very bad and sometimes you might go into a club and you might not see somebody and they might get all funny—'Oh, you're big time now, you won't talk to me.'

21 January 1968: Recording 'All Along The Watchtower' at Olympic studios, with Dave Mason and Brian Jones in attendance.
Kathy Etchingham: He had a great love for Bob Dylan. He liked his lyrics, he liked the way he looked, he liked his work. Jimi actually wanted to do 'I Dreamed I Saw St Augustine' which was on the *John Wesley Harding* album, but he felt that was too personal so he didn't do that. He decided to do 'All Along The Watchtower' instead.

Jimi phoned Dave Mason and Brian Jones and asked them if they'd like to come and play on it. They came round when we lived in Upper Berkeley Street. Brian could hardly get through the door with this huge sitar. We all piled into this taxi to go over to Olympic...

Mitch Mitchell: Jimi had obviously just heard Watchtower and just fancied doing it. I'd never heard it before—it was like a quick play-through of the original, then it was the usual thing—the strummed guitar and 'This is how it goes.'

Dave Mason: Jimi played his six-string and we just sat opposite each other... so we just put it down with the acoustic guitars and Mitch Mitchell.

Eddie Kramer: Brian Jones decided to help out and play some piano. I think he valiantly tried for a couple of takes then it was abandoned and they went back to cutting the basic track without him.

Noel Redding: We were having a few problems within the band already, and I said I didn't like the tune. I prefer Dylan's version.

Velvert Turner (friend): I saw Jimi, frustrated, running around, trying to get a sound out that he had in his head, but not being able to do it, and grabbing bottles—beer bottles, soda bottles, knives and everything trying to get the middle section where there's a Hawaiian guitar sound.

Eddie Kramer: The tapes went to America (Record Plant, New York) and they were overdubbed further. The four-track was transferred to 12—those tracks were filled up, and then 16 came along. That 12-track was transferred to 16. So it went through eight, ten, probably another 12 tracks were overdubbed on top of it.

22 January 1968: At The Speakeasy, Hendrix jams with Sam Gopal's Dream.
David Larcher (underground film-maker): Sam's guitarist, Mick Hutchinson, kept saying he was the fastest guitar player in Britain, and he was keen to see how he would compare with Hendrix.

Pete Sears (keyboards, Sam Gopal's Dream): The place was full of record company people... For certain pharmaceutical reasons, we were out in the ozone that night, playing very weird stuff. Hendrix got up and jammed with us.

Sam Gopal: I thought Jimi must be stoned out of his mind, because the guitar was strung for a right-handed player, but he just turned it over and played it without re-tuning or re-stringing. I started up a rhythm pattern on the tablas, and he picked up on it. For a while he was using the mike stand as a slide, and he was devastating.

23 January 1968: Jimi is interviewed at Upper Berkeley Street for *Hullaballoo* magazine.

24 January 1968: Hendrix's balance at Martin's Bank stands at a meagre £3 17s 6d.

25 January 1968: A High Court injunction is granted against Decca Records for having released the Curtis Knight album; rehearsals at Middle Earth, Covent Garden, London.

26 January 1968: Bass overdubs for 'All Along The Watchtower' and recording 'Tax Free' at Olympic studios.
Bob Dylan: I liked Jimi Hendrix's record of this ('All Along The Watchtower') and ever since he died I've been doing it that way. Funny though, his way of doing it and my way of doing it weren't that dissimilar. I mean, the meaning of

the song doesn't change like when some artists do other artists' songs. Strange though how when I sing it I always feel like it's a tribute to him in some kind of way. He did a lot of my other songs too from that period… 'Drifter's Escape', 'Like A Rolling Stone', 'Crawl Out Your Window', some others I don't remember. He would have done 'Masters Of War' exactly the way I do it now.

Eddie Van Halen: Hendrix blew my mind, like everybody's. One of my favourite guitar solos is the second one in 'All Along The Watchtower'. I get goosebumps every time I hear it.

27 January 1968: Interviewed by Hugh Nolan for *Disc & Music Echo*.

28 January 1968: Working on 'Mushy Name' and 'Tax Free' at Olympic.

29 January 1968: The band travel to Olympia, Paris, for two shows with The Animals.
Neville Chesters: Prior to going anywhere, Mitch used to go and get his stocks. He had an airline bag with three compartments for sleepers, leapers (amphetamines) and creepers (Mandrax, Quaaludes). The airline bag went everywhere—the pills cabinet.

30 January 1968: The band fly on to New York.
Neville Chesters: I was the only one who was smart. I'd got a white suit on and everybody else were complete hippies. We all went through Customs and they said, 'Excuse me…' Strip-searched the lot of us.

31 January 1968: 'The British Are Coming' press conference at the Copter Club, Pan Am Building, New York; meal later at the Pink Teacup on Bleecker St.
Al Aronowitz (journalist): We went out for soul food on Seventh Avenue, the first thing Jimi wanted to eat in America because he could never get any in England.

1 February 1968: US tour begins at The Fillmore, San Francisco with Albert King, John Mayall's Bluesbreakers and Soft Machine.
Hugh Hopper (then roadie for Soft Machine): It wasn't 16 articulated lorries like you have now. It was me and Hendrix's roadie with one van, praying we would get to the venue on time. Hendrix was becoming really big during that period, so as soon as there was a gap in the schedule it got filled, and we ended up touring for months without a break.

Albert King: The first time I saw him after he left Tennessee was in San Francisco. He had this hot record out… I hadn't seen him in about five years. So I went back in the dressing room and saw him and we laughed and talked and hugged one another. I was glad to see him.

That night, I taught him a lesson about the blues. He had a row of buttons on the floor and a big pile of amplifiers stacked one on another. And he'd punch a button and get some smoke, and punch a button and get something else. Then, when he'd get through playing, he'd take his guitar aside and ram it through his amplifier or something, you know? But when you want to really come down and play the blues, well, I could've easily played his songs, but he sure couldn't play mine.

Noel Redding: After we started working more and more in America, to me, it was then that Hendrix gained an attitude. The band just started to fall apart.

2 February 1968: Two shows at Winterland, San Francisco.
John Mayall: He was always getting pretty upset about the fact that people would put pressures on him to play the hits. He would really go onstage… with the feeling that he wants to play for those people because they've presumably come to hear him and his musical mind. And they don't want to know about it. So he would end up, he would

"I LAUGH WHEN PEOPLE TELL ME HOW LOUD THOSE SHOWS WERE. THEY COULDN'T HAVE BEEN LOUD. FOR THE FIRST TOUR OF AMERICA, EVERYTHING, INCLUDING THE PA, FIT INTO A CHEVROLET STATION WAGON. EVEN WHEN WE FLEW, ALL OUR EQUIPMENT WAS CHECKED LUGGAGE OR EXCESS BAGGAGE"

1968

play a couple of things that they knew, and he would play a slow blues for himself, and it would be—to any musician's ears—a completely mind-blowing and really creative thing that would be so complete and good.

And the audience would still shout out for those other things. So, when he hears that, he's really felt that he's poured something out, and that's the real him as a musician, and they haven't even known about it. So he just gets bitter about it—'OK, you want this, you got it, blam, blam, blam! I'm through and that's it.'

Mick Taylor (guitarist, John Mayall's Bluesbreakers): After our show at Winterland with Albert King and Jimi, we went and played somewhere until about five in the morning. It was kind of like The Grateful Dead meets the blues. Jack Casady from Jefferson Airplane was there. I don't think we played songs, just riffs and notes, anything.

3 February 1968: Jann Wenner interviews Jimi for *Rolling Stone;* two more shows at Winterland.
Buck Munger (PR man, Sunn Amplification): My basic mandate was to find one or two artists that the company could support wholly with equipment for nothing, in exchange for the endorsement. And I saw Jimi play and it was obvious that he played his amplifier even more than he was playing his guitar, so my company got involved.

I walked up to Jimi saying, 'I work for an amplifier company in Oregon, and I see you have a bunch of mixed-up, beaten-up, burned-up shit, and we'll give you whatever you want for nothing.'

4 February 1968: Two more shows at Winterland, with Big Brother & The Holding Company replacing Soft Machine.
Ron Newark (fan): A memorable concert... $3.50 a head and no security to speak of. The Winterland gig... was much anticipated in our group of musicians as we'd heard *Are You Experienced* and were wondering if this deal was for real... Well, it was and it wasn't. Jimi was extremely shy around the microphone, not sure of his singing, and the band seemed geared to play singles, not really stretching out. Jimi's playing was restrained by later standards.

5 February 1968: Arizona State University, Tempe, with Soft Machine.

Robert Wyatt (Soft Machine): Hendrix would sometimes get flak for having this weird-sounding band at the beginning of his show (ie Soft Machine), and he always said, 'Look, they're trying to do something, they're not trying to copy anybody else, and I want them on my show, OK? He personally stood up for us, even though we were making a lot of musical mistakes and hadn't got it fully together...

6 February 1968: VIP Club, Tucson, Arizona, with Soft Machine.
Gerry Stickells: It was so different then. We never used to get to the venue until two in the afternoon at the earliest and I laugh when people tell me how loud those shows were. They couldn't have been loud. What did we have for sound? For the first tour of America, everything, including the PA, fit into a Chevrolet station wagon. Even when we flew, all of our equipment was checked luggage or excess baggage. There was no air freight in those days. The amplifiers didn't even have cases, the speakers didn't have cases, the drums had just a fibre case. Our stuff just came rolling out as luggage.

8 February 1968: Men's Gym, Sacramento State College, California.
Steve Avis (fan): We were 14 years old, went first through the door, and we got right in front of the stage. If he had reached down I could touch him. He had his Flying V leaning up against an amp. We could hear him talking to Noel and Mitch. The power went out early in the show and he said, 'Aw, shucks, just when it was gettin' good.'

9 February 1968: Two shows at Anaheim Convention Center, California, with The Animals, Eire Apparent and Soft Machine.
Les Perrin (PR man): We were standing in the entrance and people were coming in and just staring at him... Jimi was dressed in mauve trousers, a wide-brimmed, brown-topped, black hat with brass-ringed holes with matching material woven in and out. He had brass-buckled shoes, a flowered shirt and a metal-worked waistcoat... He turned to me and, out of the corner of his mouth, said, 'Hey man, Les, all these people standin' here starin' at yuh: ah wouldn't have it—ah'd stare right back.'

10 February 1968: Jamming in afternoon with Mike Bloomfield, David Crosby, Harvey

Brooks and Buddy Miles. Gig at The Shrine, Los Angeles, attended by Crosby, followed by a party at Peter Tork's house.
Mike Bloomfield: He was taking the toggle switch of the guitar (during the afternoon jam), tapping the back of the neck and using vibrato, and it came out sounding like a sirocco, a wind coming up from the desert. I have never heard a sound on a Hendrix record that I have not seen him create in front of my eyes.

Buck Munger: As soon as Jimi got all his (Sunn) equipment (at The Shrine) he went directly to the volume and turned it all the way up to 10. We assumed that maybe a third or two thirds of the power is the maximum ever gonna be required. But, because of the approach Jimi had to this thing, I'm in the middle, talking to an engineer on the phone who's saying, 'Nobody does that! Tell him not to do that!' And I'm saying, 'You tell him not to do that!'

Roger Mayer: These Sunn amplifiers—the transformers were falling off the chassis. I was rebuilding these and it was a completely wrong design. Jimi was most unsatisfied with these amps. In fact, I actually had to go out to the factory to see if we could do anything about it... they were constantly burning up.

Gene Youngblood (in the LA Free Press*):*
> There is only one word for Hendrix—inspiring. He's an electric religion. We all stood when he came on and after he hurled his guitar at the screen in a cataclysmic-volcanic-orgasmic finale, we fell back limp in our seats, stunned and numbed.

11 February 1968: Gig at Robertson Gym, Santa Barbara, with Soft Machine and East Side Kids. Jimi is interviewed by Bob White for *The Santa Barbara Argo*.
Kevin Ayers (Soft Machine): On the first part of that tour with Hendrix, there were moments of sheer magic. I found Hendrix a very gentle, very sad guy. He was being ripped off emotionally, financially, and he had to strap on an enormous amount of chemical armour before he could become Jimi Hendrix on stage.

12 February 1968: Center Arena, Seattle—Jimi's first return to Seattle as a star.
Janie Hendrix: When he came home and got off that plane in 1968... I was six years old. I understood that he was a star because we'd heard the records on the radio and then we saw Jimi play in concert.

Al Hendrix: We were all going in the back door and, of course the security were all around, and a lot of fans around there saw Jimi. We were going in and the guy got this big, large door open, and some of the fans just surged forward, and Jimi says, 'You just go on in!' And the security guard said, 'Hey! No!' He was having a hard time holding them back, and ol' Jimi, he's going to let them go on in.

Janie Hendrix: I was there in the front row, and Jimi told me how nervous he was—it was the first time he and the Experience had played in front of the family. But it was all like a big dream, I had to keep pinching myself to make sure I was awake.

Leon Hendrix: There were maybe eight or nine thousand there. Most of them looked like businessmen, and they didn't seem to get it. There were a lot of black people, and they weren't into that kind of show, that kind of music.

Tom Robbins (in Helix *magazine):*
> Listening to rock in the Arena is like making love in a file cabinet. It's a study in frustration.

John Hinterberger (in the Seattle Times*):*
> Hendrix and his two British-born sidemen

"AS SOON AS JIMI GOT ALL HIS EQUIPMENT, HE WENT DIRECTLY TO THE VOLUME AND TURNED IT UP TO 10. I'M TALKING TO AN ENGINEER ON THE PHONE WHO'S SAYING, "NOBODY DOES THAT! TELL HIM NOT TO DO THAT!" AND I'M SAYING, "YOU TELL HIM NOT TO DO THAT!"

are indeed an experience and, from the sounds they made last night, it is an experience that seems likely to be shared by quite a few more listeners before the trio hangs up its amplifiers... So loud were the instruments amplified, that the equipment kept blowing out like candles in a windstorm and the program was interrupted several times to throw in new power units.

Tom Robbins:

He plays it straight—no copulating with his guitar, no shoving the mike up the drummer's ass. After all, it's a long way from Monterey and his mother is in the audience. Jimi's voice is like raspberry preserves—thick and sweet and the seeds stick in your ears—he has a very limited range and not much gradation in tone... On the guitar, Hendrix does not hold up under analysis either. For all his explosive dynamics, his chording is bulky and coarse... Yet despite the shallowness of much of his sound, Hendrix is a hotly exciting performer.

Patrick MacDonald (in the Seattle Post-Intelligencer*):*

A truly triumphant homecoming. Jimi Hendrix, lauded in the British press as the greatest rock guitarist extant, proved it in his Arena concert last night... Not since the Rolling Stones last concert here have I heard rock music so well done. Hendrix blends lyrics and music for a total effect that is devastating.

Janie Hendrix: I remember being really worried about all the people throwing themselves at the limo. I kept thinking that we were going to run over somebody.

13 February 1968: Jimi re-united with his family. Plans to play at Garfield High are scrapped when equipment isn't available. Hendrix makes a brief speech instead. Later, he is given the keys to the city, then flies to Los Angeles for a show at the Ackerman Ballroom, UCLA.
Mitch Mitchell: Jimi was asked to go back to his old school, Garfield High—from which he'd been more or less thrown out—to speak at the morning assembly. I remember him talking about it the day before and he really didn't want to do it, although he could see the humor of it.

Richard Altaraz (student): Jimi came out, acting very shy. He said he was real glad to be back, that it was really nice, but strange. He didn't seem to know what to say. He asked if there were any questions. Someone asked why he was wearing a hat. He laughed and said, 'If I take off my hat, my head will fall off.' Then he added, 'It's been nice to be here' and he walked off the stage.

Jimi Hendrix: Man, that Seattle thing was really something. The only keys I expected to see in that town were from the jailhouse. But I met my family and we were happy for a change. I told my dad, I could buy you a home. I want to buy you a home this winter. I've got a six-year-old sister, Janie, who I'd never seen. She's a lovely little girl. She keeps every article she reads about me and all the pictures. I've got a picture of her, she's so cute.

14 February 1968: Gig at Regis College, Denver, Colorado with Soft Machine; District Judge Charles Metzner issues an order blocking Capitol Records from selling *Get That Feeling* until a trial is held.
District Judge Charles Metzner: Do the words and symbols on the jacket of *Get That Feeling* and in the advertising therefor, tend falsely to describe its contents? I think that they do.

15 February 1968: Gig at the Municipal Auditorium, San Antonio, Texas, with Soft Machine.
Hugh Hopper: He (Bob Cope, gig promoter) was a great guy. He looked after the artists, buying meals for the whole entourage and taking care of all the trivial things... but if anyone went against him, he dropped like a ton of bricks. His famous catchphrase was 'I'll sue you.' I heard it ring out loud and clear within minutes of meeting him at the airport, when Noel pressed the emergency stop button on the escalator taking us down to the limos. Cope was bringing up the rear and hadn't seen Noel race to the bottom with his giggly schoolboy look. The whole lot of us lurched to a sickening stop and then struggled to stay upright as Noel pressed the re-start button.

16 February 1968: Gig at the State Fair Music Hall, Dallas, with Soft Machine, The Chessmen, and Moving Sidewalks. During the day Jimi trades $40 and his own wah-wah pedal to acquire the Vox wah-wah unit belonging to The Chessmen's guitarist Jimmie Vaughan, brother of Stevie Ray.

Jimi Hendrix (on stage): I'd like to say that this is really a groovy city, because I went down and got these real groovy boots. I'm really out of sight, man. Look at those! I got some pointed-toe shoes, wow! Pointed-toe shoes, why, I'm the biggest square in this whole building.

17 February 1968: Gig at the Will Rogers Auditorium, Fort Worth, with same line-up. Meanwhile, in the UK, *Disc & Music Echo* publishes annual readers poll, showing Hendrix as Best Musician In The World.
Neville Chesters: Jimi smashed all his Sunn gear up. He made a terrible mess of it.

18 February 1968: Gig at the Music Hall, Houston (two shows), same line-up. After the shows, Hendrix gives his pink Fender Stratocaster to Billy Gibbons of support band Moving Sidewalks, later to form ZZ Top.
Billy Gibbons: He said the color pink was not conducive to burning, so he gave it to me and said, 'Play on, brother.'

Tommy Shannon (bass, Johnny Winter Band): I saw him while we were playing little clubs around Houston, starving our butts off. Me and Uncle John (Turner), our drummer, and Johnny Winter went to see him. He was so graceful on stage, the way his hands moved, it was almost like slow motion... all that stuff he did on the albums, like the backwards guitars—he was doing that stuff live. And Johnny was sitting there going, 'Nobody can be this good.' We were just totally speechless.

19 February 1968: The band fly on to New York.
Gerry Stickells: He was a problem to get up in the morning. First thing was you had to find him. He'd always be at some girl's house. You'd have to phone the doorman of the club he'd finished up in, or else get hold of the limousine company to find out where they'd taken him. He was a popular item with the girls.

Jimi Hendrix: Like, if I get up at seven o'clock in the morning and I'm really sleepy, but then I open the door and see someone that appeals to me. First of all, I think, What in the world is she doing here? or What does she want?... She says maybe, 'Can I come in?' And I'm standing there and really diggin' her, you know, she's really nice-looking, about 19 or 20, beyond the age of so-and-so. I say, 'Oh well.' I'll probably just stand there and then there I go, I'll be bitin' into an apple maybe.

20 February 1968: Interview by the *East Village Other,* then jam at The Scene club with Electric Flag, Soft Machine and The Tremeloes
Jerry Velez (percussionist): I first met Jimi at a party in 1968 and then he heard me play a couple of times at The Scene. He would come by with his entourage and I would sit there with my conga drums, waiting for my turn to be called up. Jimi was sensitive and insecure to a certain degree offstage. He had this thing with Mike Jeffery that was very intense—like a love-hate relationship. Jimi was trying to get out of his contract.

Chas Chandler: He (Mike Jeffery) got into this idea that he and Jimi were acid buddies. You'd try and talk to them and it was like talking to an alien. I couldn't bear to stay around.

21 February 1968: Gig at The Electric Factory, Philadelphia (two shows), supported by Todd Rundgren.
Hugh Hopper: Amplifiers came off the plane with their innards hanging out, drum cases crushed. It sometimes looked like the loading crews had held an Olympic meet with equipment destruction as the main event.

22 February 1968: Gig at The Electric Factory, Philadelphia (two shows).
Larry Magid (talent booker at The Electric Factory): Jimi played on a dark stage with fluorescent flowers painted on his face and his hands... All you could see was his face, and his hands moving across the guitar. It was amazing.

Neville Chesters: Jimi went on a long time. The second set didn't finish until 3am.

23 February 1968: The Masonic Temple, Detroit, with Soft Machine and The MC5,
Mitch Mitchell: ... we heard on the TV as we were leaving the hotel, 'There's been a problem with snipers today in downtown Detroit...' And we walked out through the revolving doors and we can hear all these ricocheting bullets, some of them really close, and we had to make a dash for the car. It was the first time I felt that my security was really threatened.

24 February 1968: Gig at The CNE Coliseum, Toronto, Canada, with Soft Machine, Eire Apparent and The Paupers.

Marilyn Beker (in the Toronto Globe & Mail*):*

Youngsters in satin Indian jackets, long hair and curls squatted with sit-in determination in a variety of yoga-like positions.

John MacFarlane (in the Toronto Star*):*

When Hendrix finally went on stage, it was 11pm, and for the first time in the evening the audience applauded without reserve...

Marilyn Beker:

Hendrix looked for all the world like an ant dressed in green trousers and print shirt...

John MacFarlane:

Hendrix plays and sings with great bravado, arms swinging and slashing at the guitar, twisting and bending his body as he forces sound from the shoulder-high bank of amplifiers and speakers behind him, lunging at the microphone between runs on the guitar. He sings with a kind of cat-voice, soft yet powerful. He can play the guitar with tremendous feeling—when he wants to, he can make it an other-world electronic orchestra.

Marilyn Beker:

The words of many of his songs, such as 'Hey Joe' and 'Foxy Lady' were unrecognisable and the guitar was an electronic blast... It was impossible not to notice that Hendrix was a competent, exciting musician. All his work was superior, even when he plucked his guitar with his teeth.

John MacFarlane:

And then Hendrix spoiled it by smashing his guitar—as contrived a finale as any The Monkees might have dreamed up.

25 February, 1968: Before the show at the Civic Opera House, Chicago, Hendrix encounters the Plastercasters.

Cynthia Plastercaster: We saw them beckoning to us and we thought they were waving because they knew who we were, but they were actually just waving to any old girl. Anyway, we got in a cab and followed them to their hotel (The Conrad Hilton) and we asked Jimi if we could cast him, and he said 'Sure, come on up to my room.'

Things just got going straight away. I started measuring the ingredients in the bathroom, while my friend Marilyn helped me take notes—she'd never seen a dick before, so Jimi's was the first one she got to see. And Dianne was giving her first plate (partial-fellatio designed to keep the penis erect while being cast) as a partner of mine. Was she nervous? She had such a huge mouthful, I couldn't see any nervousness on her face. I think she was just desperately concentrating on shoving the whole thing in her mouth.

We needed to plunge him through the entire depth of the vase. We got a beautiful mould. He even kept hard for the entire minute. He got stuck, however, for about 15 minutes—his hair did—but he was an excellent sport, didn't panic. In fact, I believe the reason we couldn't get his rig out was that it wouldn't get soft.

We were waiting for Jimi to fall out of his mould, but he didn't, so I had to pull him out. I hadn't put any lubrication on his pubes, so I had to pull out each public hair one by one. But he didn't mind, because the impression he'd created was just the right size for his dick, so he fucked it while he was waiting.

I was really anxious to see the finished product, and I accidentally cracked the mould open and it crumbled into pieces. But I very carefully folded it back together again, and it came out pretty much intact. It's fairly huge, very thick and rather long.

26 February 1968: A rare day off, in Chicago; the band shops for cine cameras; 'Up From The Skies' is released as a US single.

27 February 1968: Gig at The Factory, Madison, Wisconsin (two shows) with Soft Machine and Mark Boyle's Sense Laboratory.

Michael Hecht (accountant): On the 1968 US tour, Stickells would settle at the box office after every Experience performance, and use that money to pay bills. On his arrival in New York, he would walk into our office with suitcases and paper bags full of money. We would do the accountings and then take the money down to the Franklin Bank. They would have countless slips of paper for receipts but would always be close to $10,000 short. Whatever the excuse, it just would not add up. It was an impossible way to work.

28 February 1968: Gig at The Scene club, Milwaukee, Wisconsin, with Soft Machine.
Michael Milewski (local musician) : It was a small ballroom done up in beautiful plush reds. The hotel was getting kind of funky, but The Scene was still a beautiful place.

Neville Chesters: Another bad club. Terrible. Had to carry gear through the hotel lobby, up in the elevator, through the club's kitchen and then carry it the full length of the club. It took us three hours just to get the gear on stage.

Michael Milewski: I remember seeing Jimi walk up to the amps and just run his finger past all the knobs, and just toss them all up to ten... The way he moved: he reminded me of a lava lamp. He didn't move, he slinked around the stage.

29 February 1968: Another gig at The Scene, Milwaukee, with Soft Machine.

March 1968: Mike Jeffery begins persuading Hendrix to buy The Generation Club.
Chas Chandler: Hendrix came to me and said that he wanted to buy The Generation Club. We spent weeks talking about it. I said, 'What the hell do you want a nightclub for?'

Jeffery wanted to put invisible chains around you, he was totally paranoid about everything. I had seen this paranoia right from the early days of The Animals.

John Hillman (Yameta lawyer): Part of his (Jeffery's) trouble was that he was untidy. He did a whole lot of side deals, some on behalf of Yameta, some not. He did divert funds, there's no question of that, but that doesn't necessarily mean he stole anything.

Spring 1968

1 March 1968: Jimi and Noel spend the evening at The Scene club, New York.
Roland Mousaa (Greenwich Village performer/coffee house owner): One night I saw Jimi Hendrix and Janis Joplin walking out of Folk City together. I'll never forget it. I was walking in and they were just walking out. The whole audience was following them out.

2 March 1968: Hunter College, New York.
Eric Bibb (fan, now blues artist): My family was steeped in the folk tradition, but when I was 17, *Axis: Bold As Love* knocked me for a loop, so I went with a bunch of friends to see Jimi for the first time at Hunter College, where he was supported by The Troggs.

There was a line of people around the block. He had a wall of Marshalls and it was undeniably the loudest thing I'd ever heard. It was an assault on the senses and, although he was clearly a great player, I felt it was definitely far too loud.

3 March 1968: Gig at The Veterans Memorial Auditorium, Columbus, Ohio.
Hugh Hopper: Some lucky guy in Columbus, Ohio, has a guitar of Jimi's. We accepted his offer of help because the stagehands had a desperate need to leave ten minutes after the show had finished. On his second trip from stage to truck, he disappeared... carrying a Fender Stratocaster tuned to E flat.

4 March 1968: While Noel Redding and Mitch Mitchell fly off to the Bahamas, Jimi jams with Eric Clapton at The Scene club, New York.
Mitch Mitchell: We actually managed three days off, so I flew to the Bahamas with a girlfriend. Noel joined us, which was odd, because he really doesn't like sunshine, beyond the odd hour lying by the pool. He gave it all of three hours,

"JIM MORRISON HAD TO BE DRAGGED OFF THE STAGE WHEN HE SAT — OR FELL — IN WITH HENDRIX AT THE SCENE CLUB. HE GETS DRUNK AND CAN'T CONTROL HIMSELF, KNOCKING OVER MIKE STANDS AND FALLING ON HIS BACK — THEY TOOK HIM AWAY AFTER HE TRIED TO MAKE LOVE TO JIMI'S GUITAR" whereupon he decided he hated the Bahamas and flew straight back again.

5 March 1968: Jimi is interviewed by Frank Simpson of *Melody Maker*.

Frank Simpson (in Melody Maker) :

> He's relaxing in his hotel room in New York after being thrown out of his first hotel. 'Must have thought I was an Indian,' he says. He's tired, says so, and should be. The other Experiences, Noel and Mitch, are in the Bahamas and the sunshine. Jimi remains behind. 'I want to think about some sessions we're doing in New York. They're in my mind right now, but I've got to think about them.'

5 March 1968: Recording begins on '1983...', 'Somewhere' and 'Moon Turn The Tides' at Sound Center, New York. Later, Jimi jams with The Hollies at The Scene club.

Bobby Elliott (drums). I was in New York with The Hollies, and we'd just done *The Mike Douglas* show the day before. I went down to the Village Vanguard to see some jazz, and I think it was Allan Clarke, our vocalist, who actually got up with Jimi that night.

Arthur Brown: By this time, The Scene had become very important to Jimi, a sort of second home. It was a medium-sized, intimate place, with a small stage, but it was where everybody went down to hang out. It was run by Steve Paul, who was a real music-lover and very good at changing with the musical climate of the times.

7 March 1968: Noel and Mitch are now both back from the Bahamas; Jimi jams with Jim Morrison of The Doors at The Scene club.

Paul Caruso (harmonica): Jimi Hendrix has being doing a great deal of jamming here on the East Coast. During the month of March, he's played with everyone from Mike Bloomfield to Jim Morrison. The jam is probably the best source of new material and the only way to experiment freely with anything. Jimi bought a four-track stereo tape recorder recently and has been taping all his jam sessions for future reference.

Jim Morrison had to be dragged off the stage when he sat, or should I say fell, in with Hendrix at The Scene recently. He gets drunk and can't control himself, knocking over mike stands and falling on his back a few times for show—they took him away after he tried to make love to Jimi's guitar while singing some beautiful blues thing he made up.

8 March 1968: Gig at Brown University, Providence, Rhode Island.

Neville Chesters: The crowd came in, everybody was drunk, a few fights broke out, there were no cops. We told the promoter that the group wouldn't play unless he got some security, which he did. The Experience did their show, which went down very well. Jimi smashed up an old Stratocaster, everybody went mad.

9 March 1968: Gig at Stony Brook, NYU, Long Island, New York.

10 March 1968: Gig at the International Ballroom, Washington Hilton, Washington DC.

David Torrey (fan): The ballroom was designed for a couple of thousand people at best, not a bad venue. The crowd outside the doors were packed in so tightly that you could literally pick your feet up off the floor, and your body would not drop an inch. (I checked.)

I raced in to have a seat in front of the stacks, stage left. The place was jammed. They opened with 'Red House', which I had never heard. I don't remember the complete set list, but 'Fire' finished me off. Thirty per cent faster than the album cut, and just smokin'. I could not believe how tight that performance was. He destroyed the amps and a guitar at the end of the show...

Bruce Remer (fan): There were two shows. We arrived for the second show early and saw Jimi leaving through a back door. After the second show we ran back to the same door, so we could try to get an autograph. Sure enough, he came out after a few minutes. I asked him for an autograph but they were moving fast, getting into the limousine.

At that point, I tried to grab his hat (the one he wore on the first album cover). He held on to it and said, 'Man, don't take my hat.' They jumped into the limo and drove off around the corner.

We started to walk back to the car. To our amazement the limo was waiting at the light as we turned the corner. I ran up, knocked on the window and said, 'Give me your hat.'

Joni Mitchell: the 'fantastic girl with heaven words' who fascinated Hendrix when he met her in Ottawa in March 1968

The window came down and Jimi said, 'Sorry man, I can't give up this hat.' So I said, 'Well, give me something.' He looked at the others, looked around, and finally gave me his lighted cigarette—a Salem 100 that I kept in a baggie for years. The light changed and they drove off. Very exciting night for a 16-year-old rock'n'roller!

11 March 1968: Soft Machine play at The Scene.
Neville Chesters: I had an argument with Jimi for refusing to set up Experience gear for Soft Machine.

13 March 1968: Jam at The Scene with The McCoys; recording 'My Friend' and 'Little Miss Strange' at Sound Center, New York. Steve Stills, Ken Pine (of The Fugs) and Paul Caruso are present.
Rick Derringer (guitarist, The McCoys): Jimi was very nice and a true gentleman. A lot of other guitar players would get up and jam with Jimi. Most of them would take the spotlight and continue playing until somebody said shut up. Jimi would always encourage other people to play and jam, but would always wait until the very last before he played his thing. My guitars were stolen once from The Scene and Jimi lent me four of his guitars, but they were all backwards. That was the only problem.

Ken Pine (guitarist, The Fugs): He called me at home one afternoon, which really surprised me, as I had not spoken to him for some time. He asked if I would play 12-string guitar on a session he wanted to do. He was looking to add a bluegrass, country rock feel. He picked me up,and we parked in a parking garage near the studio. He had the wide-brim hat with the feather in the band. The attendant looked at him as if he was from Mars.

14 March 1968: Hendrix attends a reception for The Soft Machine at The Scene club.

15 March 1968: Gig at Atwood Hall, Clark University, Worcester, Massachusetts; Hendrix is interviewed by BBC film-maker Tony Palmer.
Jimi Hendrix (to Tony Palmer): I play as I feel and I act as I feel. I can't express myself in any conversation. I can't explain myself like this or that. It doesn't come out like that, but when I'm up on stage, it's all the world. It's my whole life.

16 March 1968: Gig at The Lewiston Armoury, Lewiston, Maine.

17 March 1968: Jimi jams at the Café Au Go Go, New York, with Paul Butterfield, Elvin Bishop, Harvey Brooks, Herbie Rich and Buddy Miles.
John Sebastian: I was riding around New York with him and (Mama) Cass, and Cass was rappin' about 'Castles Made Of Sand'—'You son of a bitch, you don't sing that song. You do something else with that song.' And Jimi was saying, 'Yeah,' and he says to me, 'You have to kind of pretend, like you have to sing it like you was almost falling asleep.'

18 March 1968: Jimi jams with Paul Caruso at his apartment in the Warwick Hotel, New York. Later jams at Sound Center with Caruso, Steve Stills, Ken Pine and Jimmy Mayes.
Steve Stills: We would walk in and Eddie Kramer would have everything set up, playing back a really good mix. You could hear everything. Then Jimi would start fiddling, and there was this wall of sound that hit you in the face. I would tell him, 'That sucked.' He would just look surprised and say, 'Oh, really?'

19 March 1968: Gig at the Capitol Theater, Ottawa, Canada. Bill Cosby is in the audience.
Jimi Hendrix (diary entry):

> Arrived in Ottowa - Beautiful hotel - Strange people - Beautiful dinner. Talked to Joni Mitchell on the phone - I think I'll record her tonight with my excellent tape recorder... Went down to the little club to see Joni - fantastic girl with heaven words - we all go to party - OK - millions of girls. Listen to tapes and smoked back at hotel.

Joni Mitchell: I met Jimi Hendrix at the Capitol Theater in Ottawa, and after his set, he came down, and he brought a big reel-to reel tape recorder. He introduced himself very shyly and said, 'Would you mind if I taped your show?' I said, not at all. And later that evening, we went back, we were staying at the same hotel. He and his drummer Mitch, the three of us were talking. It was so innocent. But the management, all they saw was three hippies. We were outcasts anyway. A black hippie! Two men and a woman in the same room. So they kept telling us to play lower. It was a very creative, special night. We were playing like children.

21 March 1968: Gig at the War Memorial, Rochester, New York.

22 March 1968: Gig at the Bushnell Memorial Hall, Hartford, Connecticut.

23 March 1968: Gig at the Memorial Auditorium, Buffalo, New York.

> *Jimi Hendrix (diary entry):* Well we road through the most extreme weather today. From sunshine to blizzards and fog and everything. We're in buffalo now. Gonna take a nap. Played show—great. Girls came round Oh no—must think of Catherina and write my songs. Goodnight everyone. *(Spelling/punctuation as per the diary)*

24 March 1968: Gig at the Masonic Temple, Flint, Michigan.

Bob Levine (Hendrix management staff, New York): Hendrix continually called me for accountings on merchandising sales. Even out on the road, he'd take time to call me and ask about the poster money and what his share was. Don't think for a second that this guy didn't realize how profitable merchandising was.

Michael Goldstein (publicist): Hendrix spent money like a sieve. It ran through his fingers. You know that gold tooth in Buddy Miles' mouth? Jimi paid for that. He bought a tremendous amount of clothes, and then left them all over New York in various girls' apartments. He bought a house for his parents. And on the road it was even worse...

Daniel Secunda (Track Records executive): Hendrix is often painted as a total victim, but he was very shrewd in some ways. He was a very streetwise sort of guy. He was well aware that he was being fucked, so he would go to Jeffery immediately before a gig and say, 'I need a new apartment' or 'I need a new car'. That was his way of bargaining. He wouldn't go on stage until he got Jeffery to agree to what it was he wanted.

25 March 1968: Jimi jams with Good Earth at Otto's Grotto in Cleveland, Ohio; the audience includes Leonard Nimoy (Mr Spock in *Star Trek).*

Leon Dicker (Yameta Management attorney): Hendrix called me from Cleveland. He said that he wanted to buy a Corvette and asked that I wire $5,000 from his Yameta account to the dealer. Now, I knew he didn't have a driver's license, and couldn't see to save his life. $5,000 was a considerable amount of money in those days. 'C'mon Jimi,' I said. 'Whose money is it?' he admonished. So I did as he asked.

26 March 1968: Live radio interviews at WKYC, to promote the gig at the Public Music Hall, Cleveland, Ohio. During the day, Jimi buys a Corvette Stingray from Blaushild's Chevrolet.

Leon Dicker: He drove it at once, down a one-way street. He was cited for that, as well as not having a driving license. The next day, Hendrix left for Indiana and Jeffery had the car shipped to New York.

Anonymous reviewer in Time *magazine:*

> Shouting 'Stoned! Stoned!' his listeners surged forward, clawing at the kicking feet of the policemen who ringed the footlights. After the performance, they shredded curtains, ripped doors off their hinges and generally wreaked the worst havoc on the Music Hall since it was battered three years ago by The Beatles.

27 March 1968: Gig at the Teen America Building, Lion's Delaware County Fairground, Muncie, Indiana.

Jeff Carter (gig promoter): Two days before, they told us they weren't coming unless we gave them an extra $2,000. They held us up. It's as simple as that. And I think ultimately we only made a few hundred dollars.

I was out with the crowd, and my head of security, who is an investigator for the Sheriff's Department, came up to me and he says, 'I'm gonna have to bust Hendrix.' And I looked at him and said, 'Why?' And he says, 'He's back there, smoking a joint.'

So I went back there and I said, 'Jimi, ya can't be smoking that joint.' And he said, 'Well, you got a cigarette?' And so I got him a cigarette, and he passed off the joint. Then he went out there and he put on just one helluva show!

28 March 1968: Gig at Xavier University, Cincinnati, Ohio.

Jimi Hendrix (diary entry):

> Bought a new Jazzmaster here and a practice amp. Got the guitar for recording.

Neville Chesters: I think we did something like nine weeks worth of gigs and we didn't have too many days off... maybe four or five days... and in that nine weeks I think I have recorded in my diary 19,000 miles of driving.

29 March 1968: Gig at Illinois University Hall, Chicago; jam later with the Paul Butterfield Blues Band at The Cheetah club.
Mitch Mitchell: At the back of the stage was this metal sheeting. There was a radio station on campus, close by, and their signal bounced off the metal sheeting, so you got all kinds of shit feeding through the amps.

Neville Chesters: Jimi went on stage after the Soft Machine, but the amps buzzed so badly he walked off and refused to play, so the rest of the gig was cancelled.

30 March 1968: As 'Up From The Skies' hits its US chart peak of Number 82, the band plays at The Fieldhouse, Toledo University, Ohio.
Hugh Hopper: I sat beside (Noel Redding) in the truck, waiting as he took the necessary charge of speed to get us and the music of rock's greatest guitarist to the eager fans of wherever it was. As soon as the powder was down his throat, his body gave a great shudder and shrank into the corner of the seat. I looked at his face and was horrified to see a contorted, staring mask. His hand went to his throat and he was making gurgling noises. I thought, Jesus, he's dying. He's been poisoned. He kept it up for a couple of minutes, while I went through all the emotions around being alone in the middle of America, with a man dying of drug abuse. Then suddenly his face dissolved into a grin: 'Really got you going, didn't I?' I was too relieved even to hit him.

31 March 1968: Gig at The Arena, Philadelphia.
Mitch Mitchell: By this time we were playing 60-minute shows, maybe 75 with encores.

1 April 1968: The Experience arrive in Montreal, Canada, and see Chubby Checker perform in a nightclub.

2 April 1968: Concert at the Paul Suave Arena, Montreal.
Neville Chesters: Riots! They had to get extra police in to keep the kids back. Right at the end, some guy jumped on the stage and stole Noel's mike and stand. Suddenly, all the lights were on in the hall and there was complete chaos—kids everywhere, all over the stage.

Geno Washington: The place was fuckin' packed, the people are going ape shit. Jim Morrison is drinking his drink and staggers up to the front of the stage. 'Hey Jimi! Jimi! Let me come up and sing, man, and we'll do this shit together.' So Jimi goes, 'That's OK, fella, I can handle it myself.' And he said, 'Hey, do you know who I am? I'm Jim Morrison of The Doors.' 'Yeah,' said Jimi, 'I know who you are—and I'm Jimi Hendrix.'

4 April 1968: Gig at The Civic Dome, Virginia Beach, Virginia.
Mark Boyle (stage lighting designer): The woman serving the drinks told us that Martin Luther King had just been assassinated and there were these guys at the bar drinking the health of the assassin. You immediately find yourself wondering what your role should be. You want to go in there and do something, you're so outraged. And I remember turning and looking at Jimi, who was just staring away into space as if nothing had happened. I realized these guys were just waiting, trying to provoke some reaction from Jimi and us, so they could beat us up.

5 April 1968: Gig at the Symphony Hall, Newark, New Jersey; Jimi jams with Buddy Guy at the Generation club in New York.

Noel Redding: I remember this vividly. We got down to Newark, to the venue, and there were tanks in the street. It was the first time I'd actually seen that. We were supposed to do two shows. The police and the Army advised us to do one show and get out of town. So we did exactly that.

"HENDRIX SPENT MONEY LIKE A SIEVE. IT RAN THROUGH HIS FINGERS. YOU KNOW THAT GOLD TOOTH IN BUDDY MILES' MOUTH? JIMI PAID FOR THAT. HE BOUGHT A TREMENDOUS AMOUNT OF CLOTHES AND LEFT THEM ALL OVER NEW YORK IN GIRLS' APARTMENTS. ON THE ROAD IT WAS EVEN WORSE"

1968

Bob Cianci (fan): I come from Bloomfield, which is the next town. There was a lot of trepidation on the part of our parents about us going down to Newark to see the show. The hall was about half-empty, and as soon as Jimi came on, he said, 'Everybody c'mon and move down the front.'

Mark Boyle: Hendrix came out to enormous applause and said, 'This number is for a friend of mine.' And he abandoned completely his normal set. The band played an improvisation which was absolutely hauntingly beautiful. Immediately everyone knew what this was about. This was a lament for Martin Luther King. And within minutes the whole audience was weeping...

Old redneck stagehands came on the side of the stage and they were standing there with tears running down their faces. The music had a kind of appalling beauty.

Bob Cianci: They did 'Fire', they did 'Foxy Lady', 'Red House', and I know they ended with 'I Don't Live Today'. The thing I remember most about their performance was that they were very subdued. There were no histrionics, at least not until the end of the show. Jimi just kind of stood there and played. I feel I was kind of fortunate to see him doing that, under unfortunate circumstances.

At the end there was the big feedback guitar thing and I remember Jimi taking his Strat off and throwing it into his Marshall amps. Then he turned around, grinned at the audience. There was no violence, there was no trouble.

Mark Boyle: When he came to the end, there was no applause. He just put down his guitar, the whole audience was sobbing, and he just walked quietly off the stage.

Noel Redding: It was very short, as far as I can recall, probably about 45 minutes. There had been a lot of rioting going on. It was more of a jam as far as I can recollect, than one of our proper shows. We basically played a load of blues for 45 minutes, then we went straight back to New York.

Marvin Grafton (reviewer, in the RAT *Subterranean News):*

> ...many great rock stars (at the New Generation Club) had decided to pay tribute to Martin Luther King in the way they could best, by having a folk, rock, blues jam session. The next four hours were non-stop great. First Joni Mitchell, then Buddy Guy lent their personal tributes and sounds to the occasion... Next, the space man himself, Jimi Hendrix.

Ted Nugent: Hendrix came walking in, pulled a blue Strat out of the case, plugged it into a Fuzz Face fuzzbox and a rolled and tucked Kustom amp, and all by himself started playing shit that was unbelievable. I was mesmerized. He did this for about 45 minutes and then BB King, Al Kooper and a bass player joined in. BB signalled for me to come up and we jammed until 6am.

6 April 1968: Gig at Westchester County Convention Center, White Plains, New York.
Neville Chesters: Things weren't actually going that well with the group. By that time, I think that was the early days of it... Hundreds of people were hanging around Jimi. You could not speak to him. You couldn't get anything together and everybody was getting angry with each other.

7 April 1968: Jimi jams at the opening of Mike Jeffery's Generation club, New York, with guitarist Roy Buchanan. The gig also features BB King, Janis Joplin, Joni Mitchell, The Paul Butterfield Band, Richie Havens and Buddy Guy.
BB King: We were at a place called the New Generation in New York City. Any guitar player in town would usually get off work long before us, so they'd come by to see if I was really like someone had told them I was. Everybody would have their guitar out, ready to cut me, you know? Jimi was one of the front-runners.

Buddy Guy: Jimi was just a real nice, quiet guy in person. But he put a certain fire into his music, something that you'll never quite be able to put your finger on. But it was there...

8 April 1968: Jimi records various demos at the Drake Hotel, New York.
Larry Coryell: Once, Jimi rented a suite at the Drake Hotel, ordered lots of champagne and put on Wes Montgomery's latest record, which sounded really nice. Then he put on Jeff Beck's latest, which sounded a bit more modern, and finally he played his new record. To me, Jimi was just head and shoulders above the other two.

Dr Martin Luther King, the inspirational civil rights leader whose assassination elicited a moving tribute from Hendrix

9 April 1968: Jimi jams at the Generation with Elvin Bishop, Al Kooper, Paul Butterfield and others.
Mitch Mitchell: The other thing that did upset me, as well as Noel, was that we discovered Jimi was going out and buying guitars, drums, for friends, in fact loads of stuff for virtually anybody, and then charging them to the band's account.

10 April 1968: The LP *McGough & McGear* is released in the UK, featuring Hendrix on two tracks, 'So Much In Love' and 'Ex Art Student'.

12 April 1968: *Smash Hits* compilation LP is released in the UK.

13 April 1968: Jimi does phone interview with Peter Goodman of *Beat Instrumental.*

15 April 1968: Jimi goes to BB King gig at the Generation club, and jams with King, Elvin Bishop, Paul Butterfield, Al Kooper, Buzzy Feiten, Don Martin and Philip Wilson.
Jimi Hendrix (onstage) : I'm sorry for being out of tune that last number, and I'm sorry for being out of tune this next number.

Mid-April 1968: Chandler and Jeffery try to buy out Ed Chalpin of PPX.
Ed Chalpin: They offered $70,000 to buy me out. I wouldn't take it. My lawyer insisted that I take it, but I said no. They were stealing my artist. I was the producer and the original sound was mine.

17 April 1968: Jimi is interviewed by *Life* magazine.

18 April 1968: After recording 'Long Hot Summer Night' at the Record Plant, New York, with Al Kooper on piano, Hendrix gives Kooper his Stratocaster.
Mitch Mitchell: We went there because Gary Kellgren, who we'd worked with at Mayfair, had raised the money with a partner and managed to start the Record Plant.

Al Kooper: When he arrived at the session, I was sitting there, fooling around with it, trying to see if I could make any reasonable noise. I wanted to see if a right-handed guy could play a Strat set up for a lefty.

Jimi came in and said, 'You like that guitar?' I said, 'I don't know. You've got it all fucked up. I can't tell.' He said, 'Well, why don't you keep it?' I said, 'Fuck you. Get outta here.' But he kept on insisting. I told him to forget about it. The next day, it arrived at my house by messenger.

Chas Chandler: It was slow-going from the moment we started at the Record Plant. I was sitting there watching him play the same song over and over again, thinking to myself, What is going on? Jimi had wanted this to be a double album, and I distinctly recall being glad that I had done so much at Olympic because, at this pace, the album would never be finished.

19 April 1968: Gig at the Troy Armoury, Troy, New York.
Mike Jeffery (quoted in NME*):* Jimi's completely knocked out with the success. For the next couple of weeks he's going to rest up a bit. They don't have any more dates until they go back to England, so Jimi's working on some songs.

20 April 1968: Working on 'Little Miss Strange', 'South Saturn Delta', '1983 (A Merman I Should Turn To Be)', 'Moon Turn The Tides' and 'Gypsy Eyes' at the Record Plant, New York.
Eddie Kramer: It ('1983…') was the complete opposite of of Chas's four-minute pop structures, and Jimi could only really do that when Chas moved out of the picture. Any sound that Jimi dreamt of doing, we did.

Jack Adams (Record Plant staff): Sometimes he and the band would come in and jam all night. One song would blend into the next one, but later on he'd remember every single one. On re-mixing, he'd have such a set idea of what he wanted a record to sound like that he'd remix a song 300 times. No fooling. We'd remix a song for ten hours, all night, all week. I'd get tired and say, 'To hell with it. I'm going home.' He'd smile and ask if he could phone me up if he had a question. Then, about ten the next morning, the janitors would phone up and say, 'Hey, get this guy outta here. We gotta clean the place up.'

22 April 1968: Recording at the Record Plant.
Harvey Mandel: Although Jimi and I were not close personal friends, I did have the opportunity to meet him—the first time I was at the Record Plant in New York, where I was just completing my first album. I remember anxiously waiting to

see Jimi play his guitar up close because, from hearing him at live concerts, I thought he might have a magical something-or-other built into his guitar to help give him the incredible sounds he achieved. I soon discovered that he played a regular old Stratocaster through Marshall amps. He did use some gadgets, such as Univibe, Fuzz Face, and Cry Baby, but these items were available for anyone. The magic obviously came from Hendrix's own fingers.

23 April 1968: Recording '1983... (A Merman I Should Turn To Be)', 'Moon Turn The Tides' and 'Gently Gently Away' at the Record Plant.
Ernie Graham (guitarist, Eire Apparent): I was at all the sessions for *Electric Ladyland*. I loved watching him work, and he tolerated me.

He was a very private person. Nobody could really say they were Jimi's friend. I knew one side of him, but we shared a few girlfriends and I heard some hairy stories about violence.

24 April 1968: Work continues on 'Gypsy Eyes' at the Record Plant.
Chas Chandler: Drugs didn't get in the way of shows and it didn't get in the way of recording, but I thought it was getting in the way of his brain... mainly acid. It was fucking madness.

25 April 1968: Mixing 'Little Miss Strange' at the Record Plant.

26 April 1968: Hendrix's relationship with Chas Chandler continues to deteriorate.
Eric Burdon: Would he listen to Chas? No. So Chas got to the point of like, 'Oh, I can't deal with that crazy nigger any more, it's too much of a drain on me.' And so the window of opportunity was there for Mike Jeffery to walk right in and scoop it all up. And I knew that something dodgy was gonna happen. But I never dreamt that it would lead to his death. ?

27 April 1968: Recording at the Record Plant.
Mitch Mitchell (quoted in Melody Maker):
We don't have any set plans as to recording a single or an LP or anything—we're just going to record a few tracks and see what happens.

28 April 1968: A staggering 41 takes of 'Gypsy Eyes' at the Record Plant.
Chas Chandler: Jimi would turn up in the studio with a dozen hangers-on who you've never seen before in your life. You used a sort of shorthand conversation in the studio when there's nobody around but, when there's an audience around, people get uptight. It changes the atmosphere in the studio. He wanted to go over and over songs, some things he'd got in the first take. I just couldn't communicate with him. I felt like an alien.

29 April 1968: Further work on 'Gypsy Eyes' and 'Little Miss Strange' at the Record Plant.
Eddie Kramer: I remember trying to get as big a bass drum sound as possible.

30 April 1968: Mixing at the Record Plant.
Tony Bongiovi (engineer, Record Plant): I remember setting up for a mix of that record ('All Along The Watchtower') at 3am... The song had begun on four-track, progressed to 12-track and finally 16-track. In the transfer process, the tape got lost and we ended up doing more than 15 different mixes.

Hendrix would stop the tape, pick up his guitar or the bass, and go back out and start re-overdubbing stuff. Recording these new ideas meant that he would have to erase something. In the weeks prior to the mixing, we had already recorded a number of overdubs, wiping track after track—and I don't mean once or twice—he would overdub the bass and guitar parts all over, until he was satisfied. He would say, 'I think I hear it a bit differently.'

May 1968: Chas Chandler decides to stop working as producer with Hendrix, but to continue as co-manager.
Chas Chandler: We didn't fall out during the recording of *Electric Ladyland*, so much as the sessions seemed to fall apart out of apathy. In New York, during the recording, I was spending a lot of time trying to stop the intake of illegal substances. There were a lot of hangers-on turning up at the studio and any artist in that situation is inevitably going to start playing to the gallery instead of to the tape machine.

1 May 1968: Working on 'House Burning Down', 'Tax Free' at the Record Plant.
Jimi Hendrix: Like, 'House Burning Down', we made the guitar sound like it was on fire. It's constantly changing dimensions and, up on top, that lead guitar is cutting through everything.

Velvert Turner (friend): I asked Jimi what that song was about, and he explained to me that the song was about a lot of things but, specifically, it was about the Watts riots. First of all, it was about the insanity of people burning their own neighborhood down, about the outrage and anger that the inner city folks felt at that time about having a leader like Martin Luther King killed. At the end of the song, there's something that Eddie does, panning the guitar sound... that sounds like a cat. The sound of a panther at the end of it could mean a lot of things.

2 May 1968: Working on 'Cherokee Mist', and 'Voodoo Chile' with Steve Winwood and Jack Casady (Jefferson Airplane) at the Record Plant.
Noel Redding: It got to the point once in New York when I told him he was a stupid cunt. He depended too much on himself as writer, producer and musician. He was always trying to do it his way. There were times when I used to go to a club between sessions, pull a chick, come back, and he was still tuning his guitar. Oh, hours it took. We should have worked as a team, but it didn't work.

Eddie Kramer: We had been over at The Scene all night when Jimi said, 'Hey man, let's go over to the studio and do this.' The idea was to make it sound as if it was a live gig.

Steve Winwood: We recorded 'Voodoo Chile' down in the Village and out in the corridor were all of these musicians, waiting to be given their chance. Guys like Larry Coryell were out there, hoping to play something.

Jimi came out and said, 'Hi. Come in.' There were no chord sheets, no nothing. He just started playing. It was a one-take job, with him singing and playing at the same time. He just had such mastery of the instrument and he knew what he was and knew his abilities. That's why everybody says he was a humble, polite person, because he just knew what he could do and he didn't think he was better than he was.

Jimi Hendrix: On 'Voodoo Chile' we just opened the studio up and all our friends came down. We wanted to jam somewhere, so we just went to the studio, the best place to jam. Some of the sessions were like superjamming. Al Kooper is on one track, Steve Winwood on another. There were also some cats from Kansas who hung around while we were recording, and I used them too. I'd start with just a few notes scribbled on some paper, and then we get to the studios and the melody is worked out and lots of guys all kick in little sounds of their own.

Larry Coryell: Jimi asked me to play but, for the first time in my life, I said, 'No, there is nothing I can add to this.'

Robert Wyatt (Soft Machine): Coryell played all over the place for about ten minutes racing up and down the fret-board and Jimi steps up for his solo and went '*ba-WO-O-O-OWWWW*' erasing everything he did in the last ten minutes with one note. It was silly for him to even try, like walking into a blowtorch... the fool.

Eddie Kramer: The applause was added as an overdub, so the track would have a party feel.

3 May 1968: Work continues on 'Voodoo Chile' at the Record Plant; Jimi sits in with Joe Tex at the Town Hall, New York. ABC TV begins a 16-day shoot, filming Jimi for a documentary.
Eddie Kramer: The idea that these jam sessions were informal is something that I completely disagree with. They may have seemed casual to the outside observer, but Jimi plotted and planned out nearly all of them. He'd reason that if he had his songs together , if he really wanted to pull off what he heard in his head, he needed the right mix of people... and that's what he did.

Listen to 'Voodoo Chile', possibly the greatest live recording of Jimi in the studio ever, and the playing of Steve Winwood and Jack Casady—what an incredible rhythm section!

Mitch Mitchell: A call comes in from Joe Tex asking Jimi to come down and play at the Town Hall. Hendrix says, 'OK, but on one condition—I bring my drummer.' Tex agreed and Jimi says to me, 'Hey, come on, have a play with Joe Tex.' I'm going, 'Yeah, I'll have some of that!' What he hadn't told me, or maybe didn't know, was that it was some kind of Black Power benefit. I'm the only white person there out of about 4,000 people. Jimi's chortling away, sort of, 'Ho ho, got the sucker now.'

So we get up on stage and there's all of Joe Tex's band up there—about 17 of them—and the drums are set up out front. It was like, 'OK, sonny, let's see what you can do.' I had to deal with it or get the hell out, so I did the best I could and it was OK. I wouldn't have missed it for the world.

4 May 1968: Recording 'House Burning Down' and 'Voodoo Chile' at the Record Plant.
Tony Bongiovi (engineer): Hendrix would be booked for a 7am session and 7pm would come and go. I'd sit there and doze off until he and his entourage would come back from The Scene. Then they'd usually be totally ripped, gone, out the window with drink. One of Jimi's favourite things to do, if I was asleep, was to turn on all his stuff and play it as loud as he could.

5 May 1968: Working on 'Little Miss Strange' at Record Plant.
Eddie Kramer: Jimi had a lot of fun putting the lead guitar on. It was a DI (direct injection) with a wah-wah pedal, recorded on top of a ton of acoustic guitars Noel had already put on.

Noel Redding: The band actually broke up in the summer of 1968, but no one knew about it. See, we'd go down to the studio to start recording at tea time, about 6pm, that was our arrangement. Well, I went down there for two days and no one even turned up. That's when I did 'Little Miss Strange' just to fill in the time.

8 May 1968: Recording 'Straight Ahead', mixing 'Voodoo Chile', 'Three Little Bears' and 'Long Hot Summer Night' , edits and overdubs on '1983...' and 'Moon Turn The Tides' at the Record Plant.
Chas Chandler: I walked out very quickly at Record Plant. I would go in there and wait for Jimi and he would show up with eight or nine hangers-on. When he finally did begin recording, Jimi would be playing for the benefit of his guests, not the machines.

We'd be going over a number again and again and I would say over the talkback, 'That was it. We got it.' He would say, 'No, no, no' and would record another and another and another. Finally I just threw my hands up and left.

Noel Redding: I vividly remember going into the control room to work on some stuff and there was no chair available, so I said to someone, 'Excuse me, can I borrow your chair?' And they looked at me and said, 'Who the fuck are you?' 'Hey, well, I'm only the bass player.' Totally stupid shit like that; so then I had a huge argument with Hendrix and that's when it started falling apart.

9 May 1968: Steve Paul advertises The Scene club with a personal statement in the *Village Voice*.
Steve Paul: We got together the other night. Traffic played. They were great. You could have come. The Jimi Hendrix Experience, Fat Frankie, Zappa, Yardbirds, Chas Chandler... and even I managed to come.

Mitch Mitchell: We had The Scene club just around the corner, two blocks away (from Record Plant) where some of the best jam sessions ever took place. You'd find people like Roland Kirk, Gabor Szabo, playing with Albert King, who was out in the road—with a 400ft lead playing outside in the street. It was a tiny little club in a basement.

Jim Marron: The Scene was like a Paris disco, in that it was cave style. It had three rooms that focussed, like a cross, on the stage.

Noel Redding: When things got a bit silly in the studio, we'd all go down to The Scene at three in the morning. It was like our second home, actually.

10 May 1968: Gig at the Fillmore East, New York, with Sly Stone & The Family Stone.
Al DeMarino (agent, William Morris Agency): In the early days of the Fillmore East, the norm was a three-act bill. I had Sly & The Family Stone come into the Fillmore East as the only other act

"CORYELL PLAYED ALL OVER THE PLACE FOR ABOUT 10 MINUTES, RACING UP AND DOWN THE FRETBOARD. JIMI STEPPED UP FOR HIS SOLO AND WENT "BA-W-O-O--O-W-W-W" — ERASING EVERYTHING HE DID IN 10 MINUTES WITH ONE NOTE. IT WAS SILLY FOR HIM TO TRY, LIKE WALKING INTO A BLOWTORCH"

1968

A classic psychedelic artefact: the poster advertising the Experience's show at Bill Graham's Fillmore East in New York

but the headliner. There was no opening act. We had one hundred percent special guest star billing below the great Jimi Hendrix Experience.

It was four shows that were spoken of for countless months afterwards because Sly drove that audience insane. He was working the Hammond B-3 organ in those days, stage center, and midway through that show, that audience was absolutely insane. Much of that audience was there to see Hendrix. Jimi was the headliner, but Sly marched the audience out on a couple of those shows—literally, marched a good part of that audience out from the audience and into the streets. There had to be a lengthy intermission to bring that crowd down.

17 May 1968: More recording on 'Gypsy Eyes' at the Record Plant.
Gerry Stickells: A lot of the sessions were just an expensive way to have some fun.

Eddie Kramer: By the end of about the 45th take of 'Gypsy Eyes', Chas said, 'See ya!'

Chas Chandler: I just said, 'I'm going. I've had enough. You're not listening to us like you used to. If you decide to start listening to me again, I'll be there. Goodbye, for now.'

Noel Redding: Chas left, and he advised me the same. 'Get out mate, do your own thing.' Everyone says I left the Experience and went to Fat Mattress because I was frustrated at not playing guitar but that's completely untrue—Fat Mattress was a writing outlet for me.

John Hillman (Yameta lawyer): What people like Noel Redding couldn't understand was that he was not a partner. Jeffery wasn't the only one who had signed the contracts. Hendrix knew perfectly well who was getting what, but he could finger Jeffery as the bad guy, just as Jeffery could point to Yameta.

Jeffery was a loveable rogue. He begged, borrowed and stole just to keep his artists going, but his return was only financial. They were his investments and he was entitled to recoup.

Michael Goldstein (publicist): He would stop at nothing to ensure the success of his artists, but he couldn't relate to them personally.

Keith Altham: It's easy to make Mike Jeffery the villain of the piece (but) he didn't pretend to be much more than what he was—a business-oriented manager. Jimi elected to have that kind of representation and, when he lost Chas, he lost a very important part of his direction and care.

18 May 1968: The Underground Pop Festival, Gulf Stream Race Track, Hallandale, Miami, Florida, with John Lee Hooker, Frank Zappa, Blue Cheer, Arthur Brown and Eire Apparent.

Michael Lang (festival organizer): After the music began we realized somebody had forgotten to pick up Hendrix at the airport. I sent cars out to get him, but Jimi had gotten impatient and rented a helicopter. This turned out to be beautiful. Just as Jimi was due on stage, and we were going berserk, this helicopter came hovering over the stage and Jimi comes down a ladder. He played an incredible set.

Arthur Brown: That event seemed to be run by gangsters. I was standing about ten yards away when I saw Jimi go inside to get his money. A few seconds later, he backed out through the door with his arms raised. There was a guy pushing him, with a shotgun stuck into Hendrix's belly. He said, 'I think you'll wait, Mr Hendrix.' Jimi took it quite calmly, but it was a revelation about what was happening to the peace and love movement. Everything was changing.

19 May 1968: Second day of the Underground Pop Festival, Miami; jam after midnight in the Wreck Bar, Castaways Hotel, Hallandale, Miami.
Mitch Mitchell: One of those huge thunderstorms appeared, the sort you only get down there, and the second show was cancelled.

Eddie Kramer: 'Rainy Day, Dream Away' was written in Miami. I was in the back of the car, we were pulling away from Gulf Stream Park. The bloody thing was rained out, and then he started to write it, right there.

Arthur Brown: It was one of those places where they had go-go dancers on the tables, so I got right into the spirit of the thing and started dancing on the table-top, and removing items of clothing. Frank Zappa looked up at me and said, 'Arthur—control yourself.' It did develop into a jam later on though, with Jimi and me and Zappa.

Trixie Sullivan (Mike Jeffery employee): They had a jam session that night. John Lee Hooker, Frank Zappa... music like you never heard. Everyone played each other's instruments. Brilliant.

20 May 1968: Hendrix formally signs with Reprise Records in America, and Noel Redding flies back to England.

21 May 1968: Noel Redding recruits Eric Barrett as a new roadie for the Experience in Blaises club, London.

Eric Barrett: He came over and said, 'I've been looking for you. Our roadie has freaked out in the States. We're going to Milan tomorrow. Do you want the job?' I said we would talk about it later. I got home drunk at 4.30am. Gerry Stickells rang at 7.30am and said, 'Do you want to go to Milan?' I got up with a terrible hangover and went to the office. We caught the plane to Italy and they played at The Piper Club.

23 May 1968: Gig at The Piper Club, Milan.
Eric Barrett: The equipment was in pieces because they had just finished a tour. After every number, Jimi would scream at me. The amplifier tubes were shot and the power kept rising and falling all the time. Jimi kept screaming, 'What's wrong?' I said, 'I don't know! I'm leaving!'

But Gerry told me it was cool. I said the equipment was no good, and Jimi apologized and said he didn't mean to shout at me.

24 May 1968: Gig at the Brancassio Theater, Rome; Jimi jams at The Titan Club with The Folks; in New York, Mike Jeffery acquires the lease on the Generation Club for Jimi.

Dario Salvatori (fan): Almost the entire musical population of Rome had turned up. The Folks gave up their instruments. Hendrix took the bass and Noel the guitar.

Mitch Mitchell: Hendrix nearly got arrested. We had been to the Coliseum and were caught by the police at dawn with several young ladies.

Eddie Kramer: They did nothing with the lease (of the Generation Club) for about six months. Jimi wanted this spacy nightclub recording studio with a tiny control room at one end.

25 May 1968: Two more shows at the Brancassio Theater, Rome.
Jimi Hendrix: Since I've been to Europe, I've met one in a hundred people who let me talk about what I want to. Everybody asks me how old I am, if it is true I have Indian blood, how many women I have had, if I am married, if I have a Rolls, or more of those jokes. The people who dig me, don't want this at all. They want something different, to feel something inside, something real—revolution, struggle, rebellion.

26 May 1968: Gig at the Palasport, Bologna.
Mitch Mitchell: There was a riot, which I think had already started when we arrived... over-priced tickets or something. You never really found out about these things. We did our set, but had to leave pretty damn quickly.

27 May 1968: The band flies to London; Hendrix flies on to New York for legal meetings.
Vicky Redding (sister of Noel): Jimi gave me some money to pay the (airport meal) bill, and said, 'Give the change to the waitress.' I considered that the waitress wasn't very good and there was about £25 left over, which was a bit much, so I gave her £5. We got on the plane and I gave £20 back to Jimi and he went berserk. He really told me off.

Barry Reiss (attorney, Steingarten, Weeden & Weiss): I was one of the people who used to go over contracts and explain them to him. He was never handed a piece of paper and told to sign... We would sit down at the table in his hotel room and I would explain it page by page, asking if he understood what he was signing. I remember the first couple of times that I did it, I was very impressed by how bright he was, how aware he was. When we had to talk to him about the PPX case, he was very articulate. He knew exactly what was going down.

28 May 1968: The PPX case continues to work its way through the US legal system.
Chas Chandler: Mo Ostin came to New York to see how the case was going, and he, Henry Steingarten and I went out to eat that evening. In the middle of the meal, I turned to Mo—who I got on great with—out of sheer frustration and said, 'What the fuck is going on here? We have writs against us, we can't get any cash and we're not getting a bit of help from Warner Brothers. You're not lifting a finger.' Mo threw up his

hands and sighed, 'Chas, it's business. What can I say? At the end of the day, no matter who wins the case—you or Chalpin—Warner Brothers will be left with Hendrix.'

Surprised, I said, 'How do you work that out?' 'It doesn't matter to the business affairs office whether you have Hendrix or Chalpin does,' Ostin replied. 'We have the artist.'

'What do you mean, you have the artist?' When he mentioned Hendrix's March 21, 1967 contract with the label, I blurted, 'You have a contract with Yameta! And Yameta is me!'

'What do you mean?' Ostin asked.

'You haven't got Hendrix's signature on a contract!'

'Of course we have,' Ostin interjected.

I told him, 'You better go back to California and check the fucking contract, because the only contract you have with Jimi Hendrix was signed by Yameta. If I lose, you lose.'

The very next day, I sat down with 14 lawyers from Warner Brothers and told them where they could shove their settlement agreement they had first proposed we sign. I walked out, went straight to Steingarten's office, broke into his desk, pulled out a big bottle of Four Roses from its hiding place and sat there drinking until Steingarten came back from the meeting—some five hours later—with the settlement. Warner picked up the bills, and gave Hendrix a three-point hike in his royalty rate.

29 May 1968: The band flies to Zurich, Switzerland; journalist Keith Altham is on board.
Keith Altham: Noel thought it would be quite amusing to snap an amyl nitrate capsule under my nose. I thought I was dying, and that was the beginning of the trip. I remember seeing Stevie Winwood at one point on his hands and knees in the aisle trying to unscrew an ashtray because somebody had stubbed out a joint which still had a lot of smoke in it.

30 May 1968: Riots break out during the Experience's set at the Beat Monster Concert, Hallenstadion, Zurich (with Traffic, Small Faces, John Mayall's Bluesbreakers and The Move). Party afterwards at the Crazy Girl Club.
Mitch Mitchell: When the riot started, the police got the batons out and started beating the kids.

Keith Altham: They came in all their Nazi paraphernalia and coal-scuttle helmets with their bikes revving at the far end. They made for the stage in a flying wedge shape with people parting like the Red Sea in front of them.

Jimi Hendrix: I don't know why the police react in this kind of way. Maybe because there is such a low crime rate in this country, they have to find something to do. Any kind of action seems to make them over-enthusiastic.

31 May 1968: Second night at Hallenstadion, Zurich, with Traffic, Small Faces, John Mayall's Bluesbreakers and The Move.

Summer 1968

1 June 1968: Discovering that the gig promoter has gone bust and left their hotel bill unpaid, the Experience check out quickly and fly from Zurich to London.

5 June 1968: Recording *It Must Be Dusty* TV show, during which Jimi and Dusty Springfield duet on 'Mockingbird'.
Dusty Springfield: That I remember... I mean, God knows what it was really like, but I remember the occasion and the thrill of it... I know it was 'Mockingbird', but how it came out, I've no idea, because everything was so rushed... I thought he was so great and... just being with that sound. I loved that sound. Just the idea of doing a duet with him was hysterical... I've no recollection of any (vocal) sounds coming out because there was probably so much sound coming out of the amps.

7 June 1968: The Experience fly to New York.

8 June 1968: Jam with The Electric Flag at the Fillmore East, New York.
Richard Kostelanetz (writer): The Electric Flag was rather undistinguished, with too many horns, an unimaginative guitarist, and a lead singer who simply wasn't any good. Jimi Hendrix appeared on stage after the regular concert, not to sing but

solely to accompany (Buddy) Miles (of Electric Flag). Hendrix's guitar playing is so full of wrong notes that I suspect he is less than musical, or that the amplitude of his sound, abetted by four speakers, has made his ear stone deaf. Miles, however, is simply fantastic and, in cahoots with Hendrix, could well emerge as one of the sparkling talents of the new bluesy rock.

10 June 1968: Recording 'Rainy Day, Dream Away' and 'Still Raining, Still Dreaming' at the Record Plant, New York.
Mike Finnigan (organist): Tom Wilson (producer) had discovered my little R&B band. He introduced us to Hendrix, and Jimi asked me, Larry Faucette (congas) and Freddie Smith (saxophone) to jam on this tune he had in mind. In the early 1960s, Jimmy Smith had made these great, obscure organ quintet albums, which featured organ, congas, guitar, tenor sax and drums. Before we started the session, Hendrix reminded me of this and joked, 'We're going to do a slow shuffle in D. You be like Jimmy Smith and I'll be Kenny Burrell.' Having heard his first two albums, I thought he'd be using stacks of amplifiers and electronic toys to get his sound (but) he was using this small blond 30 Watt Fender Showman amplifier. We couldn't believe it.

11 June 1968: Recording with Buddy Miles, Jack Bruce and Jim McCarty (guitarist with Mitch Ryder) at the Record Plant, New York.
Noel Redding: We'd be in the studio for days but we'd just never get any work done 'cos Hendrix would arrive with fourteen hundred hangers-on.

Tony Bongiovi (engineer): I remember Noel being so stoned on a couple of sessions that he couldn't even stand up to play.

12 June 1968: While Noel and Mitch fly to Majorca with friends, Jimi is interviewed by Albert Goldman at the Drake Hotel.
Albert Goldman (in New York *magazine):*

> On the 17th floor, where Mr Hendrix had his suite, the mood was Oriental pleasure dome. When I arrived, mini-skirted cup-bearers were charging chalices with sparkling wine. Hendrix was flitting about like an emperor moth. Dressed in blue velvet bell-bottoms, an open island shirt and no shoes, his famous fright-wig at half-mast, he looked about half as big and as old as he did in his pictures. Far from being a cross between Genghis Khan and Anthony Quinn, Hendrix's offstage appearance is almost girlish.

13 June 1968: Jimi jams with Jeff Beck in aid of Rehabilitation Of Drug Addicts at the Reality House Rehabilitation Center, New York.
Jeff Beck: Hendrix is the best jam I've ever had. Somebody organized the monster jam of all, not from a status point of view. It really worked out perfectly. It was a concert for reformed drug addicts, but that was the least of it. They were fantastic people. They just sat for two hours and Jimi played 'Foxy Lady'. He was playing bass, and he played a couple of my things.

Ron Wood (bassist, Jeff Beck Group): Jimi came up and guested with us, started bossing us about. He was the first person who ever gave me great credibility in the band. He'd stop the music and say, 'Jeff, why don't you shut up and give the bass player a chance?' And Jeff's face just sort of crumpled up.

Jeff Beck: It just went on and on, we were jumping all over the place. Hendrix came to see me at that scene for two nights—people used to come for the great battle.

14 June 1968: Recording on 'South Saturn Delta' with arranger Larry Fallon at the Record Plant.
Larry Fallon: I was recording at the Record Plant. I was doing a session with horns and things and he came by and said, 'What the hell was that?' Jimi liked what he heard, so he sat down and watched the whole session, and he goes, 'I wanna do a session with you. Can we do something?' So I'm like, 'Sure, I'd love to work with you, Jimi.'

It was a very interesting track. We had a lot of fun doing that. He wanted to experiment with something, and then we were going to do a whole album in that particular kind of concept. Of course, the record companies came in and said that the album wouldn't be commercial enough and so forth. I understood it. That's how business goes. So they just put the track aside.

15 June 1968: Jimi jams with Eric Clapton and Jeff Beck at The Scene.

Marc Bolan first met Hendrix on the British TV show Ready Steady Go! in 1966 and later adopted a similar rakish image

16 June 1968: Hendrix and Beck jam again, at Daytop Music Festival, Staten Island, New York.
Ron Wood: Jimi used to give me solos, at Staten Island and later at The Scene club. He used to recognize my guitar playing through the bass… but Jeff really hated me getting that recognition. I mean, here was Jimi, the world's greatest fucking guitarist, telling Jeff to shut the fuck up and let the bass player have a go.

17 June 1968: Working on 'Gypsy Eyes' at the Record Plant.

22 June 1968: Hendrix and Larry Coryell jam at The Scene.

24 June 1968: Hendrix signs a new recording contract with Warner Brothers; an agreement is reached between Ed Chalpin of PPX and ANIM management.
Stan Cornyn (Reprise Records): When you talk about Jimi Hendrix and Reprise, it is an amazing and convoluted story of deals and re-deals and un-deals. I think that was terribly annoying to Mo (Ostin) but Mo is a pragmatist who can say, 'Value is value, even if you're getting screwed.'

28 June 1968: Hendrix takes the stage at the Martin Luther King Memorial Concert in Madison Square Garden, where it is announced that he has contributed $5,000.

29 June 1968: Working on 'And The Gods Make Love' at the Record Plant.
Eddie Kramer: 'And The Gods Made Love' had loads of tape delay. Jimi's voice was slowed way down below three-and-three-quarters i.p.s. then sped up again. We had tape loops running and echo tape feeding back on itself… It was a four-handed mix that we edited together.

1 July 1968: Jamming with Graham Bond (English R&B pioneer) at the Record Plant.

4 July 1968: The Experience fly to England, and Jimi moves into 23 Brook Street, Mayfair, with Kathy Etchingham.
Kathy Etchingham: Jimi had all the carpets and curtains taken out and new stuff put in. We had bright red carpets, flame, and turquoise velvet curtains that completely blocked out the light. He insisted on having the thickest pile carpet, made of pure wool. He was a very extravagant person.

6 July 1968: Gig at Woburn Abbey with Geno Washington, T-Rex and Family.
Pearce Marchbank (graphic designer, Rolling Stone*):* It was the second Festival of the Flower Children. I was recruited as a litter picker-upper. After the first morning, they were in a terrible state backstage and I suppose I looked relatively together and intelligent, and I was recruited to be an assistant stage manager, which meant knocking up Donovan and Hendrix out of their little encampments behind the stage.

Hendrix arrived with two Transit vans. Really big stuff! He went straight on stage. He had these guitars, you could hear the equipment buzzing. The roadies just touched these guitars and it was instant feedback. Hendrix appeared, really beautiful, a physically beautiful man. He picked them up and nothing happened. The guitars didn't make any noise at all but if anyone else went near them, they would start howling with feedback.

Emperor Rosko (DJ and compere for the event): We were just hanging. You'd try interviewing Jimi and you'd get mono answers. 'Are you all ready for this big event?' 'Yes.' 'Are you looking forward to it?' 'Yes.' 'Did you get any last night?' 'No.' He was very difficult to interview.

Tony Wilson (in Melody Maker *review):*

> People standing in their gardens two miles away from Woburn Abbey could hear strains of pop music floating on the air. As dusk

"JIMI HAD ALL THE CARPETS AND CURTAINS TAKEN OUT AND NEW ONES PUT IN. WE HAD BRIGHT RED CARPETS, AND TURQUOISE VELVET CURTAINS THAT BLOCKED OUT THE LIGHT. HE INSISTED ON HAVING THE THICKEST PILE CARPET, MADE OF PURE WOOL. HE WAS A VERY EXTRAVAGANT PERSON"

1968

fell, along with the temperature, the Festival attendance reached a peak of over 14,000. Emperor Rosko compered the evening session and swung things along with records and tapes in between sets from Little Women, New Formula, Geno Washington, Tyrannosaurus Rex, The Family and Jimi Hendrix blasting his way into the midnight hour.

Pearce Marchbank: He was playing the entire stage, this wall of Marshall amps, 30ft long, with roadies at the back holding them up, and he was jabbing them and hitting them with the guitar.

Fred Frith (guitarist with UK band Henry Cow): I can well remember a breathtaking and unusually disciplined eight-chorus solo in 'Red House'.

Mike Griffin (fan): I remember an extended version of 'Red House' with some fantastic blues instrumental parts, just straight blues. It was just beautiful. Because Hendrix was so hyped up with the whole psychedelic thing, it was really nice to hear him play some really, really good blues.

Jimi Hendrix: It was really only a jam. We hadn't played for so long.

7 July 1968: Jimi attends a Traffic/Pretty Things gig in The Roundhouse, London, where he meets journalist Anne Bjorndal who will become a friend.

Kathy Etchingham: When we lived in Brook Street he was quite safe from those people (hangers-on) because I controlled things. I wouldn't let them in. There was no bell on the door, we were three floors up and, with a busy street like Brook Street, you couldn't shout up because of the noise of the traffic. I used to take the phone off the hook. At least that way people couldn't get to him. He had time to recuperate. He was vulnerable because of his affability. He didn't know how to tell them to sod off.

8 July 1968: Jimi is interviewed by Alan Walsh of *Melody Maker*.

9 July 1968: Noel Redding and Mitch Mitchell jam with Tim Rose at Blaises club.

10 July 1968: ANIM's office in London closes.

13 July 1968: Ed Chalpin of PPX wins a $1m settlement in the US High Court.
Roland Rennie (Polydor Records): Warners in America accepted that Chalpin had a valid claim and paid him some money as compensation. When Chalpin came to me, to try to get money out of Polydor, I told him to bugger off. It eventually came to a court case, after Jimi had died, but the judge blew Chalpin out of the water.

14 July 1968: Noel Redding flies to Spain, for the opening of the Sgt Pepper Club, Majorca, with journalist Keith Altham.

15 July 1968: Hendrix and Mitchell fly in.
Keith Altham: The Sgt Pepper Club was a joint venture by Chas Chandler and Mike Jeffery so, naturally, they got Jimi to play the opening night. They had a load of top footballers, including George Best, along for the night. I remember Chas being none too pleased by the end because Jimi put the neck of his guitar through the roof and brought half the ceiling down.

17 July 1968: Jimi goes go-kart racing in Palma, Majorca.

18 July 1968: To give Hendrix greater control over his finances, a new company, Are You Experienced?, is formed to replace Yameta, but Michael Jeffery still gets 40 per cent. An unannounced Experience concert takes place at Sgt Peppers, Majorca.
Michael Hecht (accountant): I remember his (Jeffery's) share being on the high side of what was considered a normal business relationship.

Steve Weiss (attorney to Mike Jeffery): Before we started to self-promote Jimi's concerts, there was a lot of difficulty in his obtaining dates in America because, at that time, he was considered to be a very erotic act. Most of the deals available then were 60 per cent artists, 40 per cent promoter. We hired a promoter and paid him a small percentage (10 per cent) for promoting the concert. That way, if you did very well, the artist made a lot more of the money. You could only do this with an artist of Jimi's stature because, if you guessed wrong, the artist wouldn't make as much or might even lose money.

19 July 1968: The band fly back to London.
Kathy Etchingham: He did have a lot of casual

relationships with other women—thousands of them. It was difficult to deal with at first, but not after a while, because he never brought it home. So I would just turn a completely blind eye to it... I used to lock him out, sometimes for days at a time. But you could be really angry with Jimi and then he'd say something and you'd just melt.

22 July 1968: Hendrix is interviewed by *Black Music* magazine.

25 July 1968: When Jimi arrives in JFK airport, New York, he meets Jerry Lee Lewis, who refuses to shake hands with him.

26 July 1968: Mixing 'Long Hot Summer Night' and 'House Burning Down' at the Record Plant.

27 July 1968: Richard Robinson of *Hullaballoo* magazine interviews Jimi.
Barry Reiss (attorney, Steingarten, Weeden & Weiss): I vividly remember having to go see Jimi in a hotel room and there were five ladies lined up outside. There would be a knock on the door and one lady would answer while another remained in the bedroom... I would interrupt him to say that I had tour contracts that needed his signature.

28 July 1968: The Experience fly to LA.

29 July 1968: Warner Brothers give the Experience gold discs for *Are You Experienced.*
Mo Ostin: When we saw the numbers those records could sell, we said, 'There's something going on here.' We could struggle with middle-of-the-road acts to sell maybe 300,000 albums. We could sell two million Jimi Hendrix albums. Frank Sinatra and Dean Martin never sold two million albums.

30 July 1968: First date of massive US tour, at Shrieveport, Louisiana, supported by Soft Machine; Eire Apparent join the package later.

31 July 1968: Gig at the Lakeshore Auditorium, Baton Rouge, Louisiana, followed by a visit to see aged bluesmen in a small club.
Abe Jacob (road sound engineer): Hendrix was sitting there, listening to these old guys play. The youngest man on stage must have been 55 or 60. He got up and played with them. It was was a wonderful evening.

1 August 1968: Before the gig at City Park Stadium, New Orleans, Louisiana, the band attends a Love-In in Beauregard Square.
Jimi Hendrix (diary entry):

> Weather's beautiful here in New Orleans. Food's OK. Everybody's on fire—but a groovy fire. We could change America—not from white to black, but from old to young. The park scene was great. Can you imagine Southern Police protecting me? The gig was actually great. Turned them onto physical music. Came back to hotel, got stoned and made love to Bootsy—a tall Southern blond.

2 August 1968: Gig at the Municipal Auditorium, San Antonio, Texas.
Abe Jacob: Every time we set up (in Texas), the fire department, police department and mayor's office were all there, saying, 'You can't do this, we don't allow that kind of stuff in our town.' They all thought Hendrix was going to burn the building down.

3 August 1968: Gig at the Moody Coliseum, Southern Methodist University, Dallas, Texas; 'Hurdy Gurdy Man' by Donovan reaches Number 5 in the US.
Donovan: When I wrote 'Hurdy Gurdy Man' I intended it for Jimi, and he agreed to play the guitar for it on my version but, in the event, he wasn't around so (UK jazz guitarist) Allan Holdsworth did it.

4 August 1968: Gig at the Sam Houston Coliseum, Houston, Texas.
Mitch Mitchell: Some of the later gigs weren't that good. I'd be battling against these giant Marshall amplifiers and sometimes I couldn't even hear what I was playing. I'd watch Jimi and hope I'd be playing in the same time.

5 August 1968: The Experience fly to New York.

6 August 1968: At The Scene, Jimi jams with Ten Years After and Larry Coryell.

7 August 1968: Photo session with Linda Eastman (McCartney to be) in Central Park.
Linda Eastman: He said, 'I really want you take this album cover on the Alice In Wonderland sculpture in Central Park. In fact, I want it to be a little black boy and two little white boys.' And I thought, Oh, lovely. That'd be Jimi, a little black

boy, a little white boy... 'No, the little white boy— Mitch.' He kept saying, 'You gotta do this, you gotta do this.'

10 August 1968: Gig at the Auditorium Theater, Chicago, with The Association as guests.

11 August 1968: Gig at the Colonial Ballroom, Davenport, Iowa.
Gerry Stickells: Most nights, it took 45 minutes just to convince Hendrix to go on. Then, when you'd got him on, he didn't want to come off. Every night he'd say, 'Give them their money back. I don't feel like playing tonight. We'll do it tomorrow.' Then he would go on, and we would have to scream at him to stop at 11pm.

12 August 1968: The Experience fly to New York, where Jimi attends the Operation Airlift Biafra Benefit at The Scene; 'Room Full Of Mirrors' is re-recorded at the Record Plant.

16 August 1968: Gig at the Merriweather Post Pavilion, Columbia, Maryland.

17 August 1968: Two shows at the Municipal Auditorium, Atlanta, Georgia; Vanilla Fudge is added to the tour.
Robert Wyatt: Apparently Mike got a call: 'The Fudge haven't made it on the West Coast, they would like to join your little tour.' 'Oh no, sorry, we've got our package tour.' 'You don't understand what I'm saying. The Fudge would like to join your tour. You don't want any trouble. The Fudge join your tour.' And then the Vanilla Fudge arrive accompanied by, and I kid you not, two geezers straight out of *The Godfather* with scars down their cheeks. Everybody, including Mike Jeffery, was frightened. That's the word for it.

Mick Cox (guitarist, Eire Apparent): The first time they arrived on the tour, they walked up to Dave Robinson (roadie) and said, 'We're using your gear. Ours hasn't arrived yet.' Dave Robinson says, 'Oh no, you're not.' And so this guy just walked up to him, ripped his shirt off, pulled out a gun and pushed him up against the wall. 'Right, we're using your gear.' 'Yeah, right, sure you are.'

They (Vanilla Fudge) weren't allowed to do anything at all, you know? Like talk to under-age girls, smoke, drink, take anything. They had to be white as white.

Jimi Hendrix: I didn't feel really up to it (the afternoon show), you know, because we were pretty tired. Very, very tired as a matter of fact. We just got straight off the plane and came over here. Had free time for about an hour-and-a-half. It's just like having recess in school. The first show was a drag—it was a bore.

Steve Ball (local musician): As soon as the band walked out and nonchalantly cranked into the opening chords of 'Fire', kids stormed the stage, knocking over rows of chairs in their frenzy to get closer to this mythological shaman. I took it all in from what had once been the 15th row, standing on a chair to see over the heads of the crazed beings in front of me.

18 August 1968: Gig at Curtis Hall, Tampa, Florida. Mick Cox, Noel Redding and Mitch Mitchell decide to go boating on the hotel lake.
Mick Cox: Me and Noel go out in one of those little paddle boats and, of course, Mitch had to have a speed boat. Mitch is buzzing up and down, doing 90mph, flooding the boat, and then he goes straight for the jetty and smashes it to bits. Within minutes there's these police cars coming from everywhere—all the lights on, sirens going, they've all got guns—and they arrest Mitch. The guy who's handling Vanilla Fudge just comes walking out of the hotel and walks up to the head cop. He has a few words with him and they all drove off—it was unbelievable. I've no idea what he said, but there was a lot of police there... that was real insight into some of the things that went down.

20 August 1968: Concert at The Mosque, Richmond, Virginia.

21 August 1968: Concert at the Civic Dome, Virginia Beach, Virginia.

22 August 1968: In New York, The Experience sign legal documents relating to the PPX court action, and others transferring financial control from Yameta to Chandler & Jeffery.
Noel Redding: All the money from the early days went to this company (Yameta) in the Bahamas, which was owned by another company called Caicos Trust, which was in the care of the Bank Of Nova Scotia, and in care of whoever. It's impossible to find out about these little offshore companies. They're just places where people send money, and then it disappears.

Janis Joplin, singer of Big Brother & The Holding Company: she and Hendrix were later reputed to have had a brief fling

Mitch Mitchell: The early royalties we made apparently went into Yameta, but there are no detailed financial records and, for damn sure, I never saw anything from Yameta.

23 August 1968: New York Rock Festival, Singer Bowl, Flushing Meadow, Queens, New York, with Janis Joplin and The Chambers Brothers.
Elliott Hoffman (attorney, PPX): Two of my clients were staging the show, and one of them whispered into my ear that the security force had not shown. He and his partner had closed the box office, as the concert had sold out, and they were leaving.

I had to do something, so I went downstairs to Hendrix's dressing room. Steve Weiss and Albert Grossman were there, and Steve, unlike Jimi, could be antagonistic. I told them straight out that, outside of a handful of uniformed police officers, we had no security personnel on site.

I didn't know who to blame, but I told them that we could either be responsible for a lot of people getting hurt or we could do something about the situation. I appealed directly to Hendrix, asking him not to incite the crowd in any way, and requested that the house lights remain on.

It was a great show. No one noticed that there weren't any security guards; there were no fights or injuries.

Rae Warner (The Chambers Brothers): Jimi was a changed man. At this time, he wanted everyone's attention in the whole world.

Willie Chambers (The Chambers Brothers): He'd get highly upset on the stage if people wouldn't give him their attention.

Rae Warner: So, at the Singer Bowl, he walked off. Between the first act of the evening and the last act before him—Janis—the energy of the audience was totally drained. There was no hope for him to express anything, and he left the stage. Most shows run 45 minutes and Jimi usually did 60, but he left early. Real early, dragging his guitar behind him.

24 August 1968: Gig at the Bushnell Memorial Hall, Hartford, Connecticut.

25 August 1968: Gig at the Carousel Theater, Framingham, Massachusetts.

26 August 1968: Gig at the Kennedy Stadium, Bridgeport, Connecticut.
Chas Chandler: I went over to a guy that had the walkie-talkie system. We presumed he was in charge. They (the band) just walked on stage and all the lights were on in the stadium, so I said, 'Can you put all the lights out?' He said, 'You'll have to ask him over there.' There's this grossly fat little man, and I walked over and I said, 'Can you turn the lights out in the stalls, please?' And he said, 'Beat it, fatso.' I said, 'What?' He said, 'Arrest him.' The next thing I know I was in the cell. I could hear a voice saying, 'Charge him with being drunk and disorderly.' All I had was a can of Budweiser.

27 August 1968: At the Record Plant, New York, Jimi plays percussion on Fat Mattress song 'How Can I Live?', and records 'Come On'.
Noel Redding: That ('Come On') was done to fill out the album. I was amazed, because it was just a jam in E. It was boring for the bass player. We just played it live, and they took it, thank you. We wouldn't have had a situation like that with Chandler, would we?

Roland Rennie (Polydor Records): When Noel Redding formed Fat Mattress, Chas did a deal for them through me at Polydor. They were a great little band, but I seem to remember they got a great big advance, spent it immediately on who knows what and never really got anywhere.

30 August 1968: Gig at the Langoon Opera House, Salt Lake City, Utah; Eddie Kramer sends the completed *Electric Ladyland* tape to be mastered.

31 August 1968: Hendrix attends an Everly Brothers concert in Salt Lake City.

1 September 1968: Gig at Red Rocks Park, Denver, Colorado
John W. Shipman (fan): Red Rocks is a fabulous place for concerts. The stage backdrop is a vertical cliff face, and the outdoor seating fits in a beautiful natural amphitheater flanked by more cliffs.

Jimi Hendrix: I had a lot of fun at that Denver, Colorado, place. We played out there at Red

Rocks. That was groovy. That was nice, 'cause people are on top of you there, or at least they can hear something. That's where it should be, natural-theater type things.

Tim Bogert (Vanilla Fudge): Mitch and Noel didn't like to do the soundchecks. Carmine and I did. We did hundreds of soundchecks with Jimi, literally. The best one would have been at Red Rocks. I walked into the dressing room and Jimi had some things there which we did, and we all went out on stage and we played for quite some time. It was incredible. I got to play through 11 Sunn cabinets that Noel had set up at the time. It was one of the loudest things I'd ever heard. I thought it was bitchin'.

John W. Shipman: I've never experienced music this intense anywhere else. It was hard just to track it, just to try to hear everything that was going on in the storm of music that came out of the big stacks of Marshall amps. Jimi didn't use a lot of special effects, just a wah-wah pedal—and a lot of feedback.

There were some technical problems with the show. Jimi started out with about nine Marshall amplifiers, and he destroyed at least three of them, although the roadies managed to rescuscitate one of them. Right at the beginning of 'Purple Haze', he broke his high string, but he didn't stop. All he had to do was move up the neck a bit; the song sounded just fine to me. At the end of the song, he asked for a roadie to bring out his spare guitar, then started changing the string. By the time the roadie brought the spare out, he not only had the string replaced but had it in tune as well. This is tricky on a Stratocaster, because the tremolo bar has a big spring in it so that when you tighten one string you loosen all the other ones.

Eric Barrett: If a string would bust, I'd run out with another guitar, and we would change that in fractions of seconds. I would hold it up, he would take it off his neck, and he would play this enormous chord. All of a sudden, I would pull out one jack and go right in with another, and his hands would change down onto the same chord he was on. People very rarely heard a slump.

2 September 1968: 'All Along The Watchtower' is released as the band's fifth single in the US (it will peak at Number 20); the Experience explore the Rocky Mountains near Denver with Eire Apparent.

Mick Cox (guitarist, Eire Apparent): With Mike (Jeffery), it was 'Come in, guys. Hey, try some of this.' Very soon, instead of asking for money it was, 'Oh yeah, er, nice wall you've got, Mike.' That went on so much.

3 September 1968: Gig at the Balboa Stadium, San Diego, California.

Ernie Graham (Eire Apparent): I heard someone whistling at me. It was Jimi, whose room was opposite. He had the white label of *Electric Ladyland*, so I was the first person to hear it, with Jimi, in his room.

4 September 1968: Gig at the Memorial Coliseum, Phoenix, Arizona.

Ron Terry (booking agent): I got a call from Michael Jeffery telling me that Jimi didn't want the Fudge on the bill. I asked Jeffery to let me speak to Hendrix personally. I wanted to try to appeal to his competitive sense. 'Look,' I said, 'you're being a pussy about this whole thing. They had a good night, you had a bad night. Just do your thing.' He first told me to go fuck myself but then offered me a warning—'OK, we'll see what happens tonight.'

That night we were in Phoenix and the Vanilla Fudge's set went over well. Hendrix came out on stage and the fire was coming out of his ears. He was smoking. He showed everybody in the house who Jimi Hendrix was and, as he came off stage, he looked right at me and said, 'That's the way it's supposed to be.'

5 September 1968: Gig at the Swing Auditorium, San Bernardino, California.

Tom Hulett (tour promoter, Concerts West): I give Hendrix credit for introducing a whole new way of doing business, where the artist made most of the money. The booking agencies didn't like it, because Michael Jeffery and Steve Weiss no longer needed a booking agent to get to a Tom Hulett or a Phil Basile. All of a sudden the middle man was cut out and Hendrix made more money.

I would call up and clear the dates with Steve Weiss, who would clear them with Gerry Stickells who, in turn, would let Hendrix know where we were going to play. I knew what Hendrix wanted.

A far cry from arriving in London in 1966, when all he had was a couple of shirts, a jar of Noxema and a bag of hair-rollers

In the offices of the Isle of Wight Festival, 30 August 1970, with Joan Baez. Roy Carr (NME): "In the weeks leading up to Jimi's death, his hair became flecked with grey and his skin took on an unhealthy pallor"

Little Richard: "He loved how wild I dressed... He began to dress like me and even grew a little moustache like mine"

The New Century Hall, Manchester, 7 January 1967: Jimi Hendrix demonstrates the style he learned from Butch Snipes back in 1958

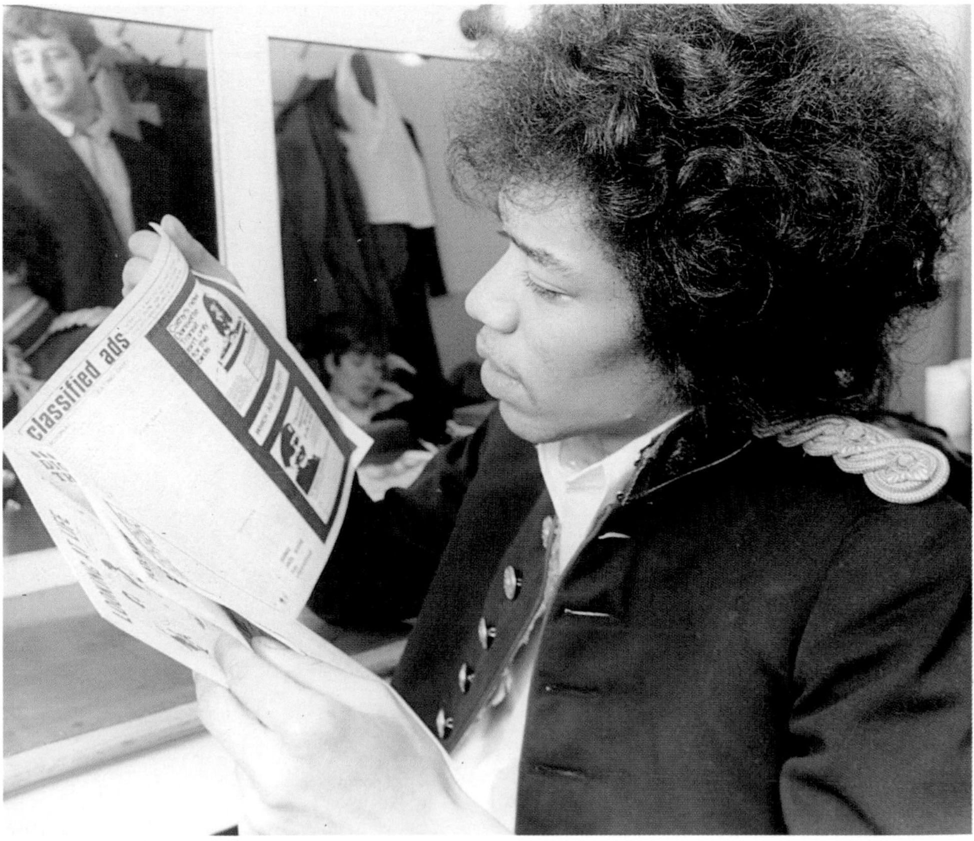

Dressed in his 1898 British Army jacket, Hendrix studies a January 1966 recruiting ad backstage at the Saville Theatre

Hendrix and his Stratocaster, strung upside down because he was left-handed, at the Saville Theatre in January 1966

Hendrix on stage at the New Century Hall, Manchester, 4 July 1967. Chas Chandler: "You could almost hear an intake...

...of breath when he came on stage. They were both frightened and excited, and that was exactly what we wanted"

The Experience play the second Festival Of The Flower Children at Woburn, Bedfordshire, 6 July 1968

Eric Clapton: "After Pete Townshend and I went to see him play, I thought that was it, we may as well just pack it in"

Jerry Velez and Hendrix at Woodstock, 18 August, 1969. It was the Puerto Rican percussionist's first professional gig

Hendrix is honored posthumously with a star on the Hollywood Walk of Fame. Al Hendrix, Jimi's father, holds the plaque

Jimi Hendrix in his 1898 British Veterinary Corps jacket: "I don't like war, but I respect a fighting man and his courage"

Dick Taylor (Pretty Things): "Anyone who imagines Hendrix as some totally out-of-it, drug-crazed wild man, would be totally wrong"

Hendrix receives his Melody Maker award for Top World Musician at the Europe Hotel, London, 16 September 1967

Chas Chandler has a word with his protege over one of the huge amplifiers which were to become a Hendrix trademark

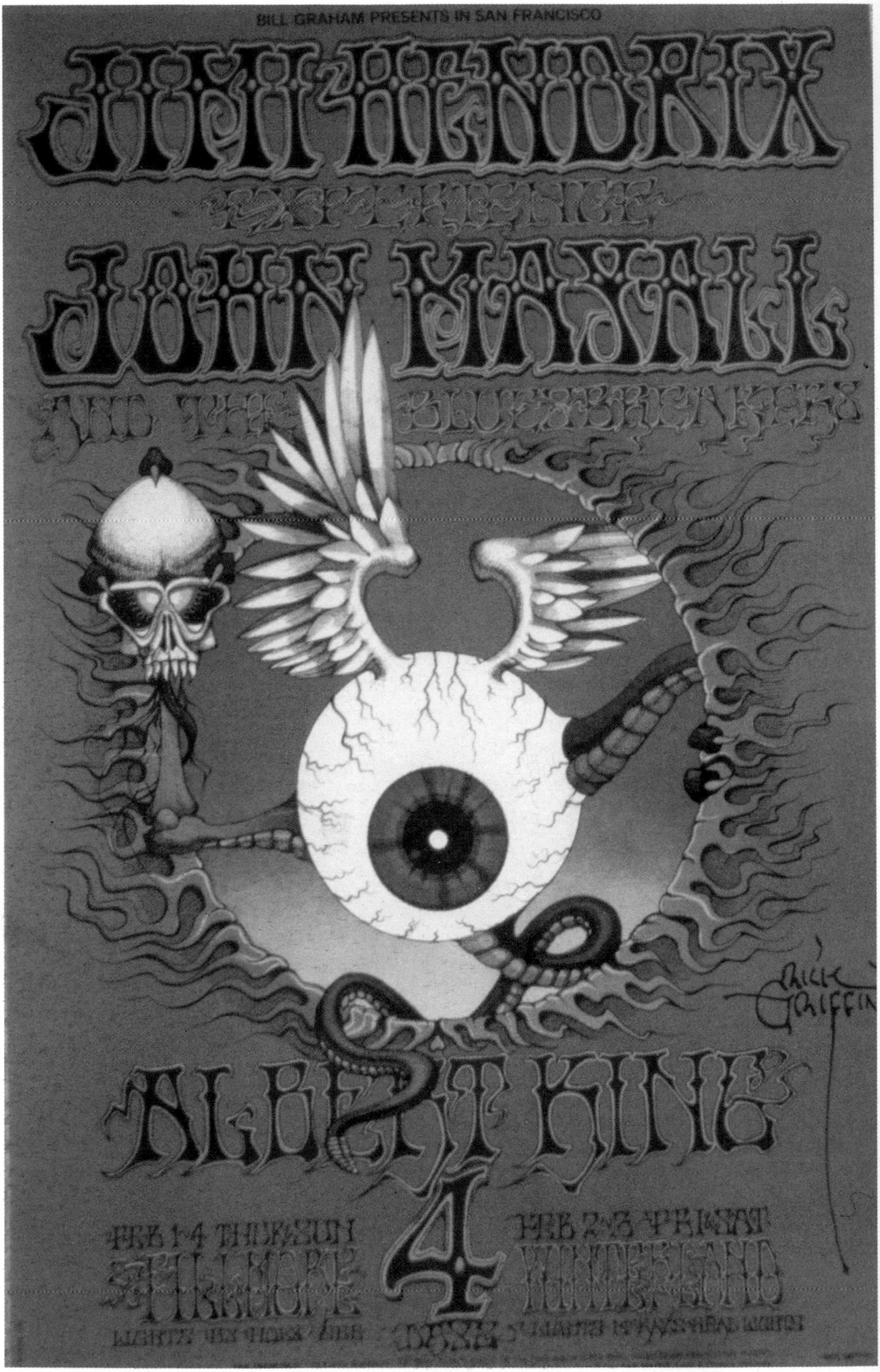

A classic psychedelic artefact: Rick Griffin's poster for The Experience's week of gigs in San Francisco in February, 1968

I knew about his security requests backstage and that he loved 'festival seating' where, unlike reserved seating, kids could move around. We made tours as comfortable as we could for him.

6 September, 1968: Gig at the Center Coliseum, Seattle, Washington.
Pearl Hendrix: Allen and I and Grandma always wore earplugs at Jimi's concerts. And even doing that, I couldn't stand the physical vibrations that would pummel my body from the noise.

Jimi wanted to spend time in Seattle when he came for concerts. The management wouldn't allow it. Jimmy insisted on sleeping one night at his dad's and one of the management people slept right there too, to keep an eye on him.

Janie Hendrix: He had this big cape and, after the concert, he chased me down the hall in the hotel. He knew that I loved Batman, so he chased me down the hall, and he was singing the Batman theme song. Then he scooped me up in the cape and hugged me and tickled me. That was a lot of fun. Then we visited him in his hotel room and, in his ashtray, there was a little agate heart on a chain. I asked him what it was, and he said, 'Oh, that's for you. I got that for you.' So he put it on me. And he drew a little picture of him on my hand.

You know, people used to make comments like, 'He's your step-brother' or 'You're his step-sister' and I asked him what that meant... and he said, 'No. You are my sister. You will always be my sister. You are my only sister.' That was real special.

After that, he held my hand, and we walked through the Coliseum to get to the limo, and all these people were trying to get his autograph. But not at any time did he let go of my hand.

7 September 1968: Gig at the Pacific Coliseum, Vancouver, British Columbia. Jimi refuses to visit his brother Leon, who is in jail, then runs into Spooky Tooth at the airport.
Janie Hendrix: After that (Seattle) concert we went up to Canada. He performed up in Canada. We rode in the car that he bought for my parents the first time he visited. He was so excited to ride in the car with us.

Bob Hicks (journalist): I was a somewhat unwilling member of that Vancouver audience, having witnessed mass hysteria in the past. Even so, there was a kind of deadly fascination at the sight of 500 people, with single-mindedness, trampling forward, animal cries wrenching from their throats, as god-worship, and Hendrix, accustomed to it as he was, responding with a sad contempt, ordering the mob back to its seats before he would play, treating it with the same authority but with none of the love or respect he gave the wild electric forces within his equipment.

Mike Kellie (drummer, Spooky Tooth): We were on tour in Canada when we bumped into The Experience at Vancouver airport. I remember Noel suggesting that we pass the waiting time in a nearby telephone kiosk. Once we were rammed inside the kiosk, I can clearly recall him opening his briefcase and producing a joint! He always has been such a charmingly hospitable chap. I remember being really surprised, and impressed, that he had a briefcase. A true sign of success in those times!

8 September 1968: Concert at the Coliseum, Spokane, Washington.
Ron Terry: The hotel didn't have our rooms ready, so we all sat in the coffee shop. We were sitting quietly when a businessman in a suit and tie said to Mitch, 'Oh, young lady, would you pass me the cream?' Mitch flipped, screaming, 'I'll tell you who's a fucking woman!' He was ready to start whaling on the guy with his travel bag, and we were saying, 'Mitch, cool it.' The guy caught him at the worst possible time, because he was tired and bitchy from the road and wasn't about to take shit from anyone.

"JIMI WANTED TO SPEND TIME IN SEATTLE WHEN HE CAME FOR CONCERTS. THE MANAGEMENT WOULDN'T ALLOW IT. JIMI INSISTED ON SLEEPING ONE NIGHT AT HIS DAD'S AND ONE OF THE MANAGEMENT PEOPLE SLEPT RIGHT THERE TOO, TO KEEP AN EYE ON HIM"

9 September 1968: Press interviews; gig at the Memorial Coliseum, Portland, Oregon.

10 September 1968: The Experience return to Los Angeles and rent a Beverly Hills mansion on Benedict Canyon Road where they hang out with Buddy Miles.
Buddy Miles: Our next door neighbour was Buddy Ebsen. On the other side was Marlene Dietrich's daughter. We partied for days doing some crazy shit. One night I was taking a shower when I heard a knock on the door. And there was Jimi, with a blonde wig and a brassiere. He says, in a female voice, 'Buddy?' I said, 'Come on in, James.' He said, 'Can we go out to the pool?' So we went out to the pool, and I jumped in, and the splash knocked off his wig. He would just do funny shit like that.

11 September 1968: Photo session for *Life* magazine.
Noel Redding: He attacked a few young ladies in LA with bricks and stuff like that. One of them was because she came to my room, not his room, and we heard this screaming, and he'd go on chasing her—batter, batter, batter.

Eric Burdon: There were two black bodyguards standing by watching as he was wading into these girls. There was the beginning of the end.

13 September 1968: Gig at the Coliseum, Oakland, California.

14 September 1968: Concert at the Hollywood Bowl, Los Angeles.
Jimi Hendrix: When we played in the Hollywood Bowl, they were waiting with fire extinguishers.

15 September 1968: Final date of this tour: Memorial Auditorium, Sacramento, California.
Ron Newark (fan): He had, by then, figured out what he thought we wanted to hear and see. By then the other guys in the band had become almost puppets for his hi-jinks, both visual and musical. While there were some brilliant improvisational moments, by and large it was a sideshow kind of a gig—the tongue bit, the feedback, every trick came out that night and it left me with an empty feeling afterwards.

So much talent wasted on goofing around to please who knows whom.

Hugh Hopper (Soft Machine roadie): When I look back now, I think, 'Great! I was on tour with Hendrix.' But I never got to see much of the music and, even when I did, I couldn't appreciate it because I was so knackered... It did Hendrix's roadie's head in completely. He abandoned the van in the streets of New York at the end of it.

16 September 1968: The house on Benedict Canyon Drive, has unwelcome visitors.
Mitch Mitchell: The house came with staff and security dogs and we'd only been there a week when the dogs got stolen. They were found wandering on Sunset Boulevard, doped out of their minds. The burglars also nicked guitars and clothes and stuff. This was the first time that we had seen any kind of money at all. Hendrix had a Stingray he'd ordered earlier. This led us to realizing how bad his eyesight was. He should not have been driving.

Robert Wyatt (Soft Machine): My group broke up, and I ended up staying with them (The Experience) in a stereotypical Hollywood-type place up in the hills. They had a spare room and let me stay because I had nothing to go back to musically.

Once, I was practicing on the guitar, trying to compose 'Moon In June' probably, and Jimi was sitting on a sofa and he said, 'You can get to that note much easier if you go across rather than up...' And I said, 'It's OK, I've got my own way of doing it.' He said, 'Cool,' and I realized I'd just been offered a guitar lesson by Jimi Hendrix and I'd turned it down.

17 September 1968: The *Electric Ladyland* album is released in the US.
Jimi Hendrix: Electric Ladyland was really expensive because we were recording and playing at the same time, which is a whole lot of strain on you. Therefore, you have to go back into the studio and re-do what you might have done two nights ago. That's twice as much strain on you.

The whole LP means so much. It wasn't just slopped together. Every little thing on there means something. It's not a little game we're playing.

Some of the mix came out muddy, with too much bass. We mixed it and produced it but, when it came time for them to press it, quite naturally, they screwed up, because they didn't know what we wanted. There's 3-D sound being used on there that you can't even appreciate because they didn't know how to cut it properly. They thought it was out of phase.

Lenny Kravitz: 'Voodoo Chile' just howls from the soul. It's so intense. Sometimes I put it on, I can't even take it.

18 September 1968: The Experience jams at The Whiskey A Go Go, Los Angeles with Eric Burdon, Graham Bond and Buddy Miles.
Walt Parazaider (saxophonist, Chicago Transit Authority, later Chicago): Hendrix gave us our first big break. The first time I met him was at The Whiskey in LA. This guy came up very quietly and tapped me on the shoulder. He says, 'Hi, I'm Jimi Hendrix. I've been watching you guys and I think your guitarist is better than me. I'd really like to take you guys out on tour to open for me. I thought he was winding me up, but that's how we got in front of big audiences.

19 September 1968: Noel Redding and Mitch Mitchell return to London.

Clem Curtis: When I quit The Foundations, I went out to Los Angeles and lived with The Cowsills for a while, and I ran into Jimi at The Windjammer on Sunset Strip. I hung out with him for a couple of weeks, and it seemed like he didn't socialize much with the guys from the Experience when they weren't working.

So, I'm sitting in this bar with Jimi and Will Chamberlain, the basketball player, and I'm complaining about my current girlfriend. Jimi said I should dump her, because he knows exactly the right girl for me. He introduced me to Barbara Grio, a beautiful dark-haired Mexican schoolteacher, and she was every bit as wonderful as Hendrix promised she would be.

21 September 1968: 'Fire' by The Crazy World Of Arthur Brown enters the US charts.

Arthur Brown: Jimi was instrumental in making 'Fire' a hit in America. We were both on Track Records, so there was that connection, but he actually took the single round personally to a whole bunch of black radio stations who would never otherwise have played it and said, 'Listen to this, you mothers,' and got them to put it on air.

24 September 1968: Chas Chandler returns to London, resolved to end his association with Hendrix and Jeffery.
Bob Levine: He knew there would be destruction if he continued with Jeffery. He specifically requested John Hillman to make some kind of settlement that would not interfere with or hurt Jimi. Chas earned a great deal of respect for that, because a lot of people would have said, 'Never mind Jimi, I'm going to get what's mine.'

John Hillman (Yameta lawyer): I had to referee that split. I tried to do what was fair financially, but there was no way I could settle it emotionally. That would never be settled and Chas remained very bitter.

Noel Redding: Chandler had been there from the beginning. He was a guy you could talk to... Jeffery didn't care about Mitchell or I. To him, Jimi was the star.

3 October 1968: Hendrix flies to Honolulu, Hawaii.

4 October 1968: Mitch Mitchell and Noel Redding fly to Honolulu.

5 October 1968: Gig at the International Center, Honolulu.

6-7 October 1968: Ron Rafaelli's legendary photo-shoot of the Experience in the hills of Maui with two naked blonde girls.

8 October 1968: The Experience return to LA.

10 October 1968: The first of six concerts at the Winterland, San Francisco. Jefferson Airplane's Jack Casady guests on bass.
Mitch Mitchell: We always tried to do something special at Winterland. On these gigs we probably jammed more and had lots of guests up like Jack Casady and Virgil Gonzales and Herbie Rich from Buddy Miles' band.

Jack Casady: His left and right-hand dynamics were fabulous. In his left hand, his vibratos, and his right hand, where he picked to get different overtones out of the guitar, was astounding. He would always be moving that around and you would always be taken to a different place, a little adventure on the guitar.

11 October 1968: Second Winterland concert, with Virgil Gonzales guesting on flute and Herbie Rich on organ.
Chet Helms (Family Dog Productions): Hendrix is back in San Francisco and he calls me and asks me to put together a jam with him and Quicksilver (Messenger Service) and the Grateful Dead. He said he really enjoyed jamming with (David) Freiberg at Monterey and would like to do it again… I told him, 'Sure, I think I can set it up.' I made a few calls and got it together. A friend of mine was managing this restaurant in Sausalito that was on a ferry boat and I set it up for Quicksilver and the Dead to show up and jam with Hendrix… I called Hendrix back and told him to meet us at the ferry boat in Sausalito at 2.00am, and we would jam all night.

We go out to this place, and the Dead are beat and dead tired because they had just played The Avalon but, after all, it's a jam with Hendrix. We sit there from 2.00am until morning, and Hendrix never shows. Everybody in Quicksilver and the Dead were pissed.

12 October 1968: Third Winterland concert.
Chet Helms: The Dead played again at The Avalon that night and Hendrix shows up there while The Dead are playing. Hendrix comes up to me and I told him that The Grateful Dead and Quicksilver and I were waiting for him all night in Sausalito, and I asked him what happened. Hendrix says, 'Oh, I met this broad, and we dropped acid and we fucked all night.'

… Hendrix said, 'Can I jam with The Grateful Dead tonight on the stage?' and I said, 'It's OK with me, but it's their gig, it's their show. If they want that to happen, it's fine with me.' I brought Hendrix into the dressing room and told The Dead that Jimi wanted to jam with them, and they're saying, 'Great! We'll do it.' The Grateful Dead go back out on stage to do their last set of the night and start playing. And keep playing. I tell Hendrix and everybody that no matter what, I'm pulling the plug at midnight. What happened was the Dead kept telling him to wait, and played out their set… So Hendrix never jammed with The Grateful Dead, and the bottom line is that they were pissed at him.

15 October 1968: The Experience listen to the live concert tapes recorded at Winterland.

17 October 1968: Rehearsals at TTG Recording Studios, Hollywood, California, jamming on 'Sunshine Of Your Love' with Jack Bruce on bass and Jim McCarty on guitar.
Angel Balestier (assistant engineer, TTG): When The Experience began rehearsing, Ami Hadami (studio owner) came downstairs and wanted the monitors turned down, because the sound was coming right up through the studio upstairs. I pointed through the control room window and said, 'Ami, that's not the monitors, that's the band.'

18 October 1968: 'All Along The Watchtower' is released as a single in the UK (highest position Number 5); recording 'Izabella' at TTG.
Mitch Mitchell: Marshall Brevitz, who'd done (promoted) the Miami Pop Festival, opened a club in LA at that time called Thee Experience… It became a home from home for us.

Marshall Brevitz: The people at The Whiskey didn't want me to succeed. By performing at the club, Jimi was telling other musicians that The Whiskey blacklist sucked. So, for the next week, ten days, Jimi came in every night. He even told me to call the radio stations to say he was there. Then, at the end of the week, minus $1,000 to cover the beer and wine Jimi and his friends drank, Jimi told Gerry Stickells to be sure that the club got to keep every dollar that came in, which Gerry had been holding. I'm telling you now, Jimi Hendrix kept Thee Experience alive.

19 October 1968: Jimi and Mitch attend Cream's farewell gig at the Fillmore West.
Mitch Mitchell: We went to see Cream and had a party back at the house. The party didn't break up until five and, at about seven, when I'd just got off to sleep, I heard this voice. 'Guess what? I've just crashed my car.' I thought I was dreaming and went back to sleep. Several hours later I discovered it was true.

How the hell Hendrix survived, I've no idea. He'd completely demolished the car. Luckily, he'd turned right and gone into some rocks. If he'd gone left, he'd have gone straight over the edge of the canyon, a 300ft drop.

20 October 1968: Recording 'Messenger' at TTG Studios.
Angel Balestier: Jimi told me that once we started recording, I was never to stop the tape or let the

tape run out. As a result, we recorded every tune as it evolved, changing tape only when people stopped to breathe.

21 October 1968: Recording 'Calling All The Devil's Children', 'Hear My Freedom' and 'Electric Church Jam' at TTG Studios.
Angel Balestier: Jimi asked me if I could get 13 chicks in the studio. I told him that I would make a few calls and see what I could do. Then so many girls came down to the studio it was unreal. There were girls in the studio, in the vocal booth, and even outside the door to Studio B. When he started to put some guitar overdubs on, Jimi walked over to this beautiful girl and asked what her sign was. When she replied, 'Sagittarius,' Jimi said, 'Does that mean I can ball you?'

Zoot Money: I was living up in the hills in Los Angeles around this time, and Jimi had invited me and Andy and Robert Wyatt along to the studio, on a very informal basis.

Andy Summers (guitarist, Zoot Money's band): I walked into the control room and he was just leaning against the glass window on the other side with a cigarette in his mouth, and he was very laconically just shredding on his guitar... I remember the image quite vividly. Anyway, I came in and we sat around for a while then we played for a bit. Noel wasn't there actually—it was Mitch and Jimi.

Zoot Money: He asked me to play a simple riff on the piano, basically a bass line, which Andy doubled on the guitar, while Jimi improvised over the top. I had no idea what he might use it for, and still don't know if it ever appeared on record.

22 October 1968: Recording 'Look Over Yonder' and jamming with legendary session bassist Carol Kaye at TTG Studios.
Mitch Mitchell: Jimi and I had a play with Carol Kaye, the bass player who did a lot of sessions for Motown after it moved to LA. She was brilliant, scared the shit out of me.

23 October 1968: Working on 'The New Rising Sun' and 'Introduction' at TTG Studios.
Angel Balestier: Somebody brought a hash cake to one session. We had Kool-Aid that was laced, marijuana cookies, and Thai cigarettes from Vietnam at others. You name it, it was there. One night, I looked over and saw a cop looking in on the session through the studio door. In a panic, I got Tom Hidley, who was in Studio C, on the phone. Tom escorted the cop into the control room, and he was digging it. He had heard Jimi playing while he was outside walking his beat. He was from the Wilcox station, in full uniform, badge and all, bopping his head, really into it. I was freaked. I thought we were all going in.

24 October 1968: Recording 'Peace In Mississippi' at TTG Studios.

Cream playing at their farewell gig at the Fillmore West, San Francisco, a show attended by Hendrix and Mitch Mitchell

Angel Balestier: Jimi had said he was looking for a certain sound. I stood listening in the studio during a rehearsal, then went back into the control room and heard the playback. To my surprise, I wasn't hearing what Hendrix was hearing out in the studio.

What Jimi had been hearing was the sound bouncing off the glass separating the studio from the control room. I put up a microphone to capture that. He came inside, listened and said, 'I'd like to get a little more of that here.'

That's how Hendrix was. He wasn't like a lot of guys today who would say, 'Give me 3K more and you've got it.' I went back out, put three music stands in a corner to bounce more of his sound, changed my microphone positions slightly, and he said, 'Yeah, that's what I'm looking for.'

25 October 1968: The *Electric Ladyland* album is released in the UK with a different cover from the US version, featuring naked women.
Chas Chandler: When the album came out and I saw that it was 'produced and directed by Jimi Hendrix', I was pissed off. I was especially surprised to see how much of what I had done was on there, because I know how much more time they spent at the Record Plant after I had walked off the project. In all truth, I had expected to see a much different album.

Robert Wyatt: They'd booked studio time almost open-season, go round and try out ideas. I was trying a tune myself, a Mose Allison-ish bluesy thing called 'Slow Walking Talk' and could play all the parts, the drums and the organ, because I could multi-track, but I couldn't play bass. He just appeared at the door, sat around for a bit and then said, 'Need a bass part for that?' He borrowed an old right-handed bass and, upside down, laid down a rock-solid bass line, every chord change and rhythmic twist and turn totally spot on—no rehearsal, no run-through.

26 October 1968: Gig at the Civic Auditorium, Bakersfield, California. Police visit Jimi backstage.

27 October 1968: Recording 'Everything's Gonna Be Alright' at TTG Studios, with Lee Michaels on organ.
Angel Balestier: Lee Michaels had been recording upstairs when he found out Hendrix was going to be working downstairs. I admitted that he was but I told him I was supposed to keep it quiet. Lee laughed and said he was going to come down anyway, so we moved his B-3 organ into Studio B.

The visitors that would come by were incredible. With Hendrix, if someone walked into the room, it wasn't like, 'Get him out of here!' Jimi would say, 'Come on in,' or he'd ask us to make room for people. He was extremely polite. He never said no to anybody and never threw anybody out.

Monika Dannemann: Once, Jimi was in a taxi in New York, and this taxi driver said that he could play bass guitar and could he come in the studio and Jimi said, 'Yes.' Sure enough, this guy came and he played for hours and Jimi just couldn't tell him 'Please go!' It wasn't good enough to be recorded, but Jimi didn't want to hurt him.

Angel Balestier: Ricky Nelson dropped by one of his sessions and he and Jimi got on great. They talked about all kinds of music.

A lot of the guys from the Buffalo Springfield would come by, especially Dewey Martin (drummer) and Steve Stills... that was a great jam... those guys were playing their asses off.

29 October 1968: Recording 'Lover Man', 'Gloria', 'Red House' at TTG Studios. Apart from Noel and Mitch, the session includes Buddy Miles on second drum kit and Lee Michaels on organ. Hendrix referred to this group as Electric Church.
Angel Balestier: The distance between Jimi and Noel was very apparent. It was sad. You could see it, it was so obvious. They kept two different crowds. They both would say hello to each other but would keep to their own corners.

When people would come for Jimi, Noel would withdraw. The sessions were peaceful, however. I never witnessed any verbal or physical confrontations, but the vibe was always there. Once they got to playing, though, it still worked.

30 October 1968: Jimi films a promo clip for 'All Along The Watchtower' in Laurel Canyon.

31 October 1968: Hendrix adds guitar to Eire Apparent's tracks 'Captive In The Sun' and 'The Clown' during their final session at TTG Studios.
Angel Balestier: Eire Apparent was just too sterile. Jimi was looking to give their sound the

same edge he gave his own. Jack (Hunt, engineer) though, was very structured in the studio. Each instrument was to be baffled and recorded on separate tracks. He also did not want to put that much recording level on the tape because of the possibility of distortion—but that was just the effect Jimi was looking for.

1 November 1968: Gig at the Municipal Auditorium, Kansas City, Missouri.

2 November 1968: Gig at the Minneapolis Auditorium, Minneapolis, Minnesota.
Robert Protzman (in the St Paul Pioneer Press*):*

> A raucous rendition of the 'Star Spangled Banner' in this year of the rejuvenation of the anthem brought to a crashing close an electronically charged Jimi Hendrix Experience concert in the Minneapolis Auditorium Saturday night. What an experience it was listening to and watching Jimi Hendrix!
>
> His biggest hangup is that he creates so much excitement that he must compete for attention with the audience and all the security measures to protect him from the audience. There were more than 80 ushers, about 20 police officers, 10 of Hendrix's own security men, some Hennepin County deputy marshals, and according to a crack from Hendrix, some narcotics agents, 'enjoying' the Experience. And some of the loudest sounds in a night of mighty amplification were the sighs of relief heard from the officers when the concert ended and the estimated 7,500 persons in the audience did not charge the stage.
>
> From the moment he appeared onstage with drummer Mitch Mitchell and bassist Noel Redding, the 22-year-old Seattle-born Hendrix had the audience with him. Mostly youngsters, the audience surged to the stage-front as soon as Hendrix appeared, and this move chased us backstage from where we watched and listened to the one-hour performance. Fire marshals tried to get the audience back to their seats... so did a local radio station disc jockey, who sounded as if he would cry if the concert could not continue. 'We'll never be able to get great talent like this back in the Twin Cities if we don't sit down. Please sit down,' he pleaded. No one budged. Hendrix made a half-hearted appeal. No one moved. Guess who won the struggle?
>
> So with kids— thousands of them—jammed against the stage, Hendrix and cohorts rocked into their program (after some delays because of trouble with amplifiers, a source of difficulty for nearly all acid rock groups): 'Are You Experienced', 'Foxy Lady', a gas of a slow blues called 'Red House', and many other Hendrix hits. Then came the star spangled spectacular. As if to rub it into those who have made an issue of the singing of the anthem by Aretha Franklin and Jose Feliciano in recent months, the Hendrix Experience charged wildly into the song.
>
> Drummer Mitchell, a 24-year-old Londoner, went off on his own on a smashing solo; 23-year old bassist Redding (also from England) set the pulsating pace; and Hendrix hurled himself into an atonal, quavering improvisation—barely touching upon the melody of the anthem. This version made those of Aretha and Jose sound like a Sunday school class sing-a-long. Hendrix, often an exciting guitarist and a good blues vocalist, ended things with his biggie, 'Purple Haze', and the throng of kids—their appetites apparently satisfied—stood silently, seemingly stunned for awhile, before trudging slowly from the auditorium.

3 November 1968: Concert at the Kiel Auditorium, St Louis, Missouri.

4 November 1968: The Experience return to New York; UK record-dealers refuse to stock *Electric Ladyland* because of the cover picture.
Noel Redding: I think Hendrix had wanted it (Linda Eastman's photograph) for the cover, but then there was all that stuff about that lot—they put out that album cover in Europe or something, with all the young ladies.

David King (art director, Track Records): We wanted to make it a kind of untouched cover. I asked David Montgomery to take the photos and make the women look like real people.

Eddie Kramer: I think Track Records, in their infinite wisdom, decided that an album cover of

Lee Michaels recorded with Hendrix on 27 October 1968, a couple of years before his US hit 'Do You Know What I Mean'

naked ladies would do well on *Electric Ladyland*. When Jimi saw it, he was furious, apparently. He thought it was definitely not in good taste.

Jimi Hendrix: I don't know anything about it. I didn't know it was going to be used.

Linda Eastman: I think everybody thought it was his idea. We did get something in the American cover, which had an open-out cover. All the photographs inside were black and white, which I took. They showed him as a human being, rather than a freak, you know?

6 November 1968: Hendrix works on producing an album for Cat Mother & The All-Night Newsboys at the Record Plant.
Jimi Hendrix: I like producing records by other groups. As long as I like what they are playing. I liked doing the Eire Apparent record, but it was never really finished, according to my standards. Then I produced Cat Mother. They're presentable enough, but not as good as I wanted them to be.

8 November 1968: Peter Goodman of *Beat Instrumental* interviews Jimi in New York.
Jimi Hendrix (to Peter Goodman):

> Sometimes news leaks back that we're being accused of losing contact with the fans in Britain, but I can assure everybody that we'll be back soon. Could even be by Christmas, but certainly in the New Year. It's just that when you've got a groovy scene going, it's kinda hard to bust it up before you have to.

9 November 1968: A Hendrix interview appears in *Melody Maker*.
Jimi Hendrix (in Melody Maker*):*

> Mitch and Noel want to get their own thing going—not a group: producing and managing other artists... so very soon, probably in the New Year, we'll be breaking the group, apart from selected dates... there are other scenes we want to get into.

10 November 1968: Hendrix's US TV debut, on the *Ed Sullivan Show*, is cancelled, allegedly because of a camera crew strike.
Bob Levine: Bob Precht, Ed Sullivan's son-in-law, produced the *Ed Sullivan Show*. Sullivan Productions really wanted to have Jimi on... so Sullivan Precht, Jeffery and I sat down to talk. Sullivan wanted to have the Vienna Ballet dance to his music, with Hendrix in front of a big orchestra, done on location in Europe.

Jeffery figured out the money he would need, and agreed to the concept verbally. He left the meeting to speak to somebody—I don't know who—and when, a day or so later, I told him he was supposed to follow-up with Bob Precht, he replied, 'We aren't going to do it.' I asked if he had spoken to Jimi and he said, 'No. I am not going to let Hendrix do that. I've got my reasons.' Jimi would have loved to have done it.

11 November 1968: Hendrix jams with Fleetwood Mac at The Scene.
Mick Fleetwood: On off-nights we'd hang out at the hip club of the day, Steve Paul's Scene. Jimi would come in to jam, turn Pete's guitar upside down, so he could play it left-handed, and off he'd go. It was unbelievable.

Peter Green: We were invited along to The Scene to play with Jimi, so me and Danny (Kirwan, guitarist Fleetwood Mac) went down. Hendrix wasn't playing a gig, the place was empty, but he was up on the stage, playing about with his guitar and he asked me if I would like to get up and play.

His playing wasn't good that night, not like it had been when I saw him in the early days. He was making a lot of wrong notes, sort of slowing them down and nothing was coming out. He seemed to be in a world of his own up there. He looked to me like he was on heroin, or something. I liked him as a person though. I remember he let me touch his frizzy hair and shook hands with me.

15 November 1968: Gig at the Cincinatti Gardens, Ohio.

16 November 1968: As *Electric Ladyland* hits the top of the US charts for the first of two weeks, the band plays at The Boston Garden, Boston, Massachusetts.

17 November 1968: Gig at Woolsey Hall, Yale University, New Haven, Connecticut.

18 November 1968: The sixth Experience single in the US, 'Crosstown Traffic', is released.

22 November 1968: Gig at the Jacksonville Coliseum, Florida.

23 November 1968: Gig at the Curtis Hixon Hall, Tampa, Florida; Chas Chandler interview appears in *Melody Maker.*

Chas Chandler (in Melody Maker*):*

> I wouldn't blame any group for giving up touring, but I can't see the trio splitting up. They've come too far to go back. What will probably happen is that Jimi will spend more time at home in America and, naturally, Noel and Mitch will want to come back to England. They may only get together for rare appearances and record sessions, but I'm sure they will go on.

24 November 1968: Gig at the Convention Hall, Miami, Florida.

25 November 1968: On their return to New York, the Experience find themselves barred from the Hilton, so move to the Penngarden Hotel.

27 November 1968: Gig at the Rhode Island Arena, Providence, Rhode Island, followed by a birthday party for Hendrix.

Kathy Eberth (Mike Jeffery employee): We baked a cake for Jimi and everything known to mankind went into it. The remains of the birthday cake were left on the desk of this very, very straight secretary. When we came back to the office, she was typing away and eating the cake and, though acting a little bit strange, was handling it very well. When Joe Head, the chauffeur, came in and said, 'Oh, you're having Jimi's cake! Is this your first trip?' she freaked out, running around the office covering her eyes, yelling, 'Kathy, I can't see! I'm blind!' Then she ran out of the office into the street, screaming up and down Park Avenue.

28 November 1968: An Electric Thanksgiving, The Philharmonic Hall, New York.

Mitch Mitchell: Lovely hall, very prestigious, no rock band had ever played there. Only one problem—a member of the band had to play in a symphonic context. Jimi and Noel flatly refused, so I thought, okay, what the hell, I'll do it. Would I mind having tea with Leonard Bernstein? Which I did. Charming chap. He suggested that I might like to play percussion with the New York Brass Ensemble. It was fine. I went on with them with a collar and tie on. We did some Bach and a little Mozart, great, after which the Experience played.

30 November 1968: Gig at the Cobo Hall, Detroit, Michigan.

Noel Redding: Mitch and I caught the plane and Jimi never showed.

Bob Levine: About 5pm, as far as I knew, he had left. Then in walked Gerry Stickells. I said, 'What are you doing here?' He replied, 'I've got a problem. Jimi's in the car.' 'What car? Didn't he leave at two o'clock?' Stickells said, 'I just couldn't get him to go.'

I sat Hendrix down in my office but, just as I said, 'Jimi' the phone rang. When the secretary said, 'Bob, it's a promoter from Detroit,' I knew immediately that it was Bob Bageris from Cobo Hall. Bageris said, 'Listen, I checked at the hotel, and the two boys are there with a road manager but there's no Hendrix.'

Jimi was sitting right in front of me but I assured Bageris that he had left for Detroit some time ago. I then spoke to Jimi. 'Jimi, I'll tell you why you have to do this. You don't have to do this for money. You have to do this because you are Jimi Hendrix and you have over 10,000 people in that hall waiting to see you. You owe it to them. You've got to be there, and you know it.'

Noel Redding: Jeffery then phoned. 'Jimi has freaked out,' he says, 'and is refusing to come.'

Bob Levine: After half an hour of cajoling, Jimi finally obliged, so I got straight on the phone to Butler Aviation. 'This is the Frank Sinatra office,' I said. 'Oh, yes sir,' came the response. 'We have a slight problem here. Mr Sinatra must be in Detroit via Lear Jet in the next hour or so.' 'Hold on sir, I don't know.' 'No,' I said. 'There are no ifs, ands or buts about it. If you are going to say no, you tell it to Mr Sinatra. Because I'm not.'

He came back on the line after a minute and gave us a number and a gate. I knew Stickells would have access to a bag of cash once he arrived in Detroit, so I sent them off in the limousine. Then the promoter called again. 'The first group has gone on and Hendrix isn't here.' I didn't tell him what was going on, but I promised him that Hendrix wouldn't let him down.

Noel Redding: In spite of it all, the show is a good one. Probably played well out of sheer relief.

WINTER 1968

1 December 1968: Final concert of this tour, at the Coliseum, Chicago, Illinois.

Early December 1968: Jam with Arthur Brown at The Scene club.
Arthur Brown: I lived in New York for a while, so I hung out a bit with Jimi. Chris Stamp brought him down to The Scene one night and we jammed together with a couple of other musicians, just totally improvised the whole thing, and it was great. I remember a lady came up to me afterwards and said, 'Aaaah, that was a festival of joy.' She'd obviously been transported by the music.

One day Jimi's road manager, Tony Garland, took me over to Jimi's hotel apartment and Jimi asked me if I would be interested in joining him. The idea was to have the three guys from the Experience plus me on vocals and my organist Vincent Crane. He said he felt he'd gone as far as he could with a three-piece and wanted to extend the music. He was also planning huge projection screens and backing tapes of music by Wagner, all kinds of things to open up the visual side and the spiritual side. My band was falling apart, but I really didn't want to just be part of someone else's group, so it never happened.

13 December 1968: Johnny Winter arrives in New York.
Johnny Winter: I met him at The Scene club that my manager Steve Paul had in 1968. Jimi was always at The Scene when he was in New York and we played many times together. He was just everywhere... no matter where he went he would go out and play with whoever was around and do a lot of recording with other people, just recording the jamming. They would be down at the club all night and then whoever was sober enough he would bring back to the studio at the end of the night—he really did like to play!

Tommy Shannon (bass, Johnny Winter Band: He sat in when we were playing at The Scene with Johnny Winter. And I still can't figure out how he did it. He just flipped my bass upside down and played it. He didn't sound like a guitar player playing bass—he sounded like a bass player playing bass, and there's a big difference.

14 December 1968: Al Kooper invites Jimi to join him for a Super Session at the Fillmore East, on a bill with Sam & Dave.
Al Kooper: Mike Bloomfield and I were scheduled to play at the Fillmore and Bill Graham's limo came to pick us up. As I got in the car, the driver told me he had just picked up Jimi from the airport and dropped him off, just five minutes previous... Impulsively, I had the driver stop at Jimi's flat. I went to the door and it was wide open. Providence. I remember thinking, 'This is meant to be.'

I walked in, hollering his name, and there he was. 'Wass goin' on?' he slurred at me. Uh-oh, bad timing. He had just gotten off a trans-Atlantic flight and he was toast. I persevered anyway. 'Remember how you said you wanted to play on one of those Super Sessions? Well, there's a car outside, and me and Bloomfield are playing at The Fillmore tonight with Sam & Dave on the bill. You game?'

He smiled weakly at me. 'Bad timing, Al, but we'll do it some other time soon. OK?' I apologized profusely and beat a hasty retreat, carefully pulling the door shut on my way out.

16 December 1968: A UK work permit, organized by Harold Davison Ltd and valid until 7 February 1969, is issued to Hendrix.

20 December 1968: Jimi jams with The James Cotton Blues Band at the Fillmore East.

21 December 1968: 'Crosstown Traffic' stalls at its US singles chart peak of Number 52.

24 December 1968: Hendrix attends an evening of poetry at St Marks Church, The Bowery, New York.

26 December 1968: In New York, Jimi falls in snow and injures his leg.

27 December 1968: A new roadie, John 'Upsey' Downing, joins the Experience crew.
John Downing: Hendrix was just like anybody else really, except that he got really hung up on whether people wanted to know him as a person or because of who he was. He used to say he only had five friends—the three roadies and Mitch and Noel.

One of the few photographs revealing the shy, sensitive side of Hendrix remembered by so many people who knew him

1969

1 January 1969: Record Plant, New York.

2 January 1969: The Experience fly into London. Jimi takes up residence with Kathy Etchingham at 23 Brook Street.

3 January 1969: UK music press interview at 23 Brook Street, London.
Kathy Etchingham: I used to have to hide in the bathroom when Jimi was giving any interviews.

4 January 1969: Recording the *Happening For Lulu* TV show, Studio 4, BBC TV Centre, Wood Lane, Shepherds Bush, London.
Billy Sloan (Lulu's brother): Lu was just 18, which was amazing for someone hosting their own prime time TV show. That night, as well as Jimi, she had The Iveys on, who later became Badfinger.

Chris Welch: Mitch and Noel had a little hash which they were trying to get together in the dressing room and they dropped it down the plug-hole in the sink. One of the roadies, with spanners and stuff, pulled the pipes off the wall trying to get this bit of hash out.

Noel Redding: We were doing 'Hey Joe' on Lulu's show, then Hendrix stopped and says, on a live BBC TV show, 'I'm sick of playing all this rubbish, we're gonna do this thing for the Cream.' And went straight into it.

Mike Gibbins (drummer, The Iveys): Here we were in suits as The Iveys, and Hendrix is on doing Cream songs—on fucking heroin.

Jimi Hendrix: It was the same old thing, with people telling us what to do. They wanted to make us play 'Hey Joe'. I was so uptight about it, so I caught Noel and Mitch's attention and we went into the other thing.

Lulu: Jimi was genuinely upset about the fact that Cream were splitting up so halfway through 'Hey Joe', he just decided to forget it and sing a tribute to Cream. He didn't consult anybody. Just did it. It was so exciting. The floor manager was going crazy, trying to wind Jimi up. I really didn't know what was happening.

Noel Redding: It was completely ad libbed. I remember shouting, 'Shit, I'm not sure!' but I guess they edited that bit out from the CD. The director, Stanley Dorfman, put his hands up to say, 'Stop! Stop!' but I just thought we couldn't stop because the show used to go out completely live. We only had about two minutes to go anyway, so we just carried on. As we came off air, I said to Hendrix that we'd get banned from the BBC. All he said was, 'Huh, yeah, man.'

Billy Sloan: I remember looking from Hendrix to Lu, who was watching from out of shot. She was just totally absorbed in the moment. It was fantastic, because people just didn't do things like that on live television.

Lulu: I remember walking past dressing room two, where Jimi was, and his door was open, and he said, 'Lu, I'm really sorry if I messed your show up.' And I said, 'Listen, don't even worry about it. It was fabulous television.'

Barrie Martin (BBC employee): I met him as he came out the door of Studio 4, and he said, 'Where's the bar, man?' So I took him up to the fourth floor and we sat in the corner with him drinking American whiskey. He didn't seem at all perturbed by what he'd just been through.

Noel Redding: Stanley Dorfman was in the bar afterwards and, despite all the trouble we seemed to have caused, he came up to us and said quietly, 'Lads, that was great. Fancy a pint?' There was just nothing they could do.

Lulu: After the show, my husband Maurice (Gibb, of The Bee Gees) and I went back to our place and watched the whole thing all over again on our reel to reel video recorder, an old Revox.

5 January 1969: Hendrix adds his guitar solo to 'Rock'n'Roll Band' by Eire Apparent at Polydor Studios, London.
Carlos Olms (engineer): Eire Apparent had come in around 6pm. We messed around trying to get the right sound until 10 or 11 o'clock before Jimi arrived in his very colorful dress. He sat very quietly in a corner. After he heard our work, he started to convert everything to his taste. He started with the drums, setting up each microphone to get the right sound, then the right equalisation. The boys had a hard time trying to please him with their sound, but I was impressed with his way of working.

We did about five or six complete versions but Jimi always found something which he felt was not correct, and we would do it again. It was 3am before he started to put his parts down on tape. He had to play the middle-eight part and the ending.

He asked me for a very insensitive microphone, because he said, 'I will play quite loud.' We turned the lights down so low in the studio that I could just see the shadow of his guitar and amplifiers. Every time he played his part, we thought it was fantastic. Only Jimi didn't think so. He always raised his hand and said, 'Again.' He was still playing his part at 5am, but was not satisfied.

6 January 1969: During an interview with the *Daily Mirror*, at 23 Brook St, Hendrix makes his relationship with Kathy Etchingham public.
Don Short (in the Daily Mirror):

> The attic of the house, which has become Hendrix's favourite room, contains an assortment of bric-a-brac and a bed with a Victorian shawl pinned to the ceiling as a canopy.
>
> At two in the afternoon, Hendrix is making the bed, neatly folding back the black sheets and straightening the colourful Persian bedspread. Then he grins and calls Kathy to open a bottle of wine.
>
> Kathy Etchingham is a 22-year-old redhead from the north who shares the flat. Jimi explains her presence: "My girlfriend, my past girlfriend and probably my next girlfriend. My mother and my sister and all that bit. My Yoko Ono from Chester.'

7 January 1969: Interview at 23 Brook Street, London for Canadian Broadcasting Corporation.

8 January 1969: Gig at the Lorensberg Cirkus, Gothenburg, Sweden.
Ingmar Glanzelius (fan): Hendrix played several of the old songs from his records, but in a completely different way. He transforms them into fragments, references and springboards. They are a platform from which he jumps into the world of total sound... The guitar rarely sounds like a guitar, but instead like an organ, a choir, an electronic apparatus or a cello. He played the strings with his hands, his stomach and his teeth.

Chas Chandler: It was a dire concert. You could just see there was trouble with the band. There was friction, it wasn't together, it just didn't work.

Gerry Stickells: Noel was getting frustrated because he wanted to play guitar. Since there were only a handful of us out on the road, he could only talk to so many people. It isn't like now, where you may have 30 guys travelling with you.

9 January 1969: Jimi interviewed by Lennart Wretlind for *Pop 69 Special* TV show, then two shows at the Konserthuset, Stockholm. Eva Sundqvist and her mother attend the first show. After the second show Jimi and Eva go to the Hotel Carlton. That night, James Daniel Sundqvist (Jimi Hendrix Jr) is conceived.
Ulla Lundstrom (journalist, Vi I Tonaren*):* The concert advertizements stated, 'Last chance to see Jimi Hendrix'—in other words, the group will dissolve. Many people emptied their January-thin wallets to hear Jimi for the last time. They didn't know that it was a ruthless PR trick, invented by clever PR men with cash-hungry brains.

Jimi was completely at the mercy of the pop managers. A human goldmine in which they have invested their money. Of course, they expect to get their share of the profit. Big shares. To them, Jimi is just a bundle of dollar bills.

Jimi's visit to Sweden was stress, journalists, PR men, impersonal hotel rooms. The plane landed at 14.25 hours. The press conference began at 16.00. No time to relax. A nice room at the Carlton Hotel, white table cloths, golden mirrors. Fussy PR people. And journalists and more

Lulu with her then-husband Maurice Gibb: Hendrix' departure from the script on her live TV show has become legendary

journalists. Photographers. All ready to throw themselves on Jimi when he entered the room.

Ian Anderson (Jethro Tull): This was the first time we had supported Hendrix. Although the press conference was for him, our manager Terry Ellis hustled us into the room hoping to get us some exposure. Noel and Mitch were chatting to the journalists but Jimi was nowhere to be seen. After about half-an-hour of rather drab sandwiches, I decided I'd had enough and went out into the hall. I was lighting up a Rothman's in this dimly lit corridor when a voice came out of the gloom. 'Hey man, good to meet you.' It was Jimi. He was lurking in the shadows. I said, 'Why aren't you in there?' He replied that he just couldn't face it. He'd been waiting out here all that time and was obviously trying to pluck up the courage to go in.

Ulla Lundstrom: Jimi came dressed up in bracelets, rings, his hair a big frizzle. He was practically helped in, placed on a sofa. Answered politely ten times the same questions, friendly but without enthusiasm. Politely but with tormented undertones. His mouth formed answers.
His eyes were depressed.

Jimi Hendrix (on radio in Stockholm): I can't play guitar any more the way I want to. I get very frustrated on stage when we play... Every time we come into town, everybody always looks towards us for some kind of answer, for what's happening to them and... which is a good feeling... but it's very hard.

10 January 1969: Danish radio interview by Niels Olaf Gudme, then two shows at the

Falkoner Theater, Falkoner Center, Copenhagen, Denmark, supported by Jethro Tull.
Ulla Lundstrom: Ten o'clock in the morning the day after the concerts, Jimi was on his way. To a new hotel room. A new stage. A new press conference.

Ian Anderson: Watching from the wings, what intrigued me was that when Hendrix was on form, he was absolutely brilliant, but when things went wrong, he completely crumbled. He was playing a white Gibson SG and having trouble keeping it in tune, which made the audience a bit restless, and he really went to pieces. He seemed to be either all the way up or all the way down.

Offstage though, he was very considerate and approachable, always with a big grin. I learned much later that we subsequently got a tour in Germany because Jimi had personally gone to the trouble to tell the top German promoter Fritz Rau that we were a great band and that he should book us.

11 January 1969: Gigs at the Musikhalle, Hamburg, Germany.
Gerry Stickells: It wasn't as if you planned to tour in support of your album. You just strung together dates to maintain your cash flow. They obviously wanted him to work all the time. Remember, record deals weren't what they are today. Percentages were very small.

12 January 1969: Gigs at the Rheinehalle, Düsseldorf, Germany. At the Park Hotel, Jimi meets Monika Danneman, with whom he will spend his final hours.
Monika Danneman: I went in and we sat down at the bar, and then Jimi came in. He just sits next to me. He talked to me for two hours and, through that, I noticed that the picture I had of him was completely wrong. He was really very kind, intelligent, and he really fascinated me.

He first asks everything about me, and in ten minutes he asked me if I had a boyfriend, which I did not. He didn't believe me. Anyway, within half-an-hour he asked me if I would become his girlfriend. I thought he was joking. And if I would come to England and live with him and everything. And he kept on saying these things. He really tried to push me. I was trying every way to get around and change the subject, because it was too quick for me.

He took me backstage and made me promise I wouldn't vanish while he was playing.

He was just standing (during the concert), not moving. I couldn't believe how quickly he moved his fingers. It was fantastic, the music that came out of the guitar. I felt that his music was spiritual.

I said I'd only stay with him that night if nothing happened, because I'd saved myself for the one I loved. Later he said that really impressed him. We talked until 5am and he told me all about his childhood. He kissed me, but that was all.

13 January 1969: Monika Danneman joins Hendrix in Cologne, Germany, where he is interviewed for the *Beat Club* TV show.

14 January 1969: Gig at the Halle Munsterland, Munster, Germany.

16 January 1969: Gigs at the Meistersingerhalle, Nuremberg, Germany.

17 January 1969: Gigs at the Jahrhunderthalle, Frankfurt, Germany, where the audience calls out repeatedly for 'All Along The Watchtower'.
Jimi Hendrix: There is something we would like to tell you about that 'Watchtower' scene...

We recorded that a year ago and, if you've heard it, we are very glad. But tonight, we're trying to do a musical thing, OK? That's a single, and we released it as a single, thank you very much for thinking about it, but I forgot the words. That's what I'm trying to say.

19 January 1969: Gig at the Liederhalle, Stuttgart, Germany.
Monika Danneman: I never liked it, because you never have any private life. No matter where you go, if it's a restaurant or a café, even in the hall of a hotel, you meet other people and they want to go out or just to talk with you. After a certain time I realized that there were a lot of people wanting to be near Jimi, not because of him but only because he was famous. And they took a lot of liberties. For example, when we were in a restaurant, they would just come and sit at the table without asking... order drinks and food and never pay. Jimi was far too gentle and quiet. He didn't like it, but he could not say anything

against them. He knew what kind of people they were and he just didn't want any trouble.

20 January 1969: Jimi and Noel write songs in Jimi's hotel room, before flying on to Strasbourg.

21 January 1969: Gig at the Wacken Halle 16, Strasbourg, France.

22 January 1969: Gigs at the Konzerthaus, Vienna, Austria.

23 January 1969: Concert at the Sport Palast, Berlin, Germany.
Noel Redding: There were about 20,000 people, and we were told before we went on that there was going to be a riot.

Gerry Stickells: We were told that if there was any trouble, there would be no more rock concerts. Frank Zappa, among others, had seen his gear smashed, and people that night were trying to do the same to us.

Abe Jacob (road sound engineer): We were escorted by armed police with dobermans to the stage from the dressing room.

Noel Redding: I walked on stage and the first thing I saw, virtually, was someone being beaten up in the audience. The police had to surround the stage in the end.

24 January 1969: Flight back to London.

29 January 1969: A new music publishing company, Bella Godiva Music, is set up for Hendrix in the US; Hendrix and Pete Townshend perform a memorial gig at The Marquee, London, in remembrance of Brian Epstein.

30 January 1969: Jimi flies to New York for meetings with Eddie Kramer and architect John Storyk (designer of hip New York club Cerebrum) about the conversion of the Generation Club.
Eddie Kramer: In 1969 I became a sort of independent engineer. Michael Jeffery and the rest of the gang called me up and told me they'd bought a club downtown, and Jimi wanted to put a small studio in it. So I went down and said to them, 'You must be out of your minds.' They had this small little studio that they had designed for the corner of the club—like an 8ft by 8ft area.

John Storyk: I think Michael Jeffery was really building the club with very little input from Jimi. If Hendrix cared about any of this stuff, he really didn't say it to too many people.

31 January 1969: Jimi rings the London office to tell them he will be back on 3 February.

1 February 1969: ROLLING STONE votes Jimi Performer of the Year.

2 February 1969: Noel Redding rehearses with his new band Fat Mattress.

3 February 1969: Jimi flies to London.

4 February 1969: Noel Redding rehearses with Fat Mattress.

5 February 1969: Jimi is busy organising details of the upcoming Royal Albert Hall shows, and the conversion of the Generation Club.

6 February 1969: Redding is interviewed for the US and Canada about Fat Mattress.

7 February 1969: Jimi is interviewed at Brook Street by the *Sunday Mirror.*

8 February 1969: Fat Mattress record their album at Pye Studios for a total cost of £31; Jimi goes to see John Lee Hooker at The Speakeasy.

9 February 1969: More Fat Mattress rehearsals.

10 February 1969: Jimi buys records at One Stop in South Molton St, then flies to New York.

11 February 1969: Hendrix acts as producer on the Buddy Miles Express album, *Electric Church,* at the Record Plant, New York. The tracks are 'Destructive Love', 'It's Too Bad', '69 Freedom Special' and 'World Traveller'.
Billy Rich (bassist, Buddy Miles Express): A lot of energy was put into that session. It was so much fun that it was like a dream. I'm just sorry that ('69 Freedom Special') was edited down before it was put on the album, because there are a few more great solos recorded on that track.

Buddy Miles: Hendrix was always there for me. On two or three occasions he gave me $5,000 cash to help keep the Buddy Miles Express going.

12 February 1969: Hendrix flies to London.

13 February 1969: Jimi, along with Paul McCartney and Donovan, attends the launch party for Mary Hopkin's album *Postcard,* in the Post Office Tower restaurant, London.

14 February 1969: Jimi tries out 'Roomful Of Mirrors' at Olympic Studios. At the Seymour Hall, Jimi is presented with *Disc's* award for World's Best Musician, by Bee Gee Maurice Gibb.

15 February 1969: Work at Olympic Studios.
George Chkiantz (engineer): We did those sessions in Studio B and I thought they were terrible. Hendrix was in a bad mood, but he wanted to come in and do something.

Noel Redding: We argued. There seemed no way to get working.

George Chkiantz: Studio B was the wrong place for Hendrix to record anyway, because there wasn't room for his sound to properly expand. Hendrix's response was to double his amplifiers, which made it nearly impossible to hear anything in the control room... He seemed really lost, and the whole thing was very sad.

16 February 1969: More attempts at recording, Olympic Studios.
Noel Redding: Mitch was late. I suppose it was partly because we didn't want to get it together.

The pressure from the public to create something even more brilliant each time, while basically expecting us to stay the same, was crushing.

17 February 1969: Hendrix telephones Chas Chandler.
Chas Chandler: I had already parted company and come back to England when they came over for the Albert Hall concerts. I was going there to say hello, but Jimi rang me up the night before and asked if I would come down, as he was thoroughly aggravated with the whole affair.

18 February 1969: Concert at the Royal Albert Hall, London.
Noel Redding: We went there in the afternoon to see if the amps worked. That was our first proper rehearsal... and our last English gig.

Chas Chandler: When I arrived for rehearsals and sound checks, Hendrix was having trouble with feedback through his amplifiers...

Abe Jacob (sound engineer): We used a Charlie Wadkins/WEM sound system in there, because we hadn't taken our stuff over to England. We used a wall of sand-filled speaker cabinets, large columns filled with sand for damping.

Chas Chandler: ...and there was also interference in the recording equipment. It was a shambles. I ended up running both shows for him, trying to get everything right. I hadn't been hired. I was there to help out friends.

Chris Welch: When he broke into 'Purple Haze', feet pounded the hallowed floors, and whistles pierced the Victorian dome. The Hendrix electricity was still working.

He even managed to get away with avoiding 'Hey Joe' without any audible protest... yet those in a position to compare past Hendrix performances might have been critical... the lengthy performances stretched his improvisational powers to the limit. He made brilliant use of wah-wah pedal, string scraping, and probing, producing amusing and surprising sound effects, but The Experience lacked rehearsal.

On several occasions they failed to swing or rock, and seemed to be dragging the beat. Drummer Mitch was in subdued form.

Chas Chandler: That was a lousy show. Among the worst I had ever seen Jimi play. And it wasn't his fault, it was Mitch and Noel's.

They were lifeless. Mitchell's timing seemed totally off. He was coming in late so often it seemed like he was out of his brain, and Redding was just trying to show how awkward he could be.

Mitch Mitchell: One of those shows where you wish you could go back and put it right.

Chas Chandler: Up until that point I had been a supporter of the group, because I thought that they made for a good unit. Now I felt it was time they got thrown out. If I had still been in charge, they would have been sacked the next day.

19 February 1969: Hendrix is interviewed by NME's Richard Green.

20 February 1969: Jimi goes to Olympic to watch a recording session by Glass Menagerie, who are being produced by Chas Chandler.

21-22 February 1969: Noel Redding rehearses with Fat Mattress.

23 February 1969: Hendrix jams at The Speakeasy with Dave Mason and Jim Capaldi; in New York, architect John Storyk gets a phone call from Jim Marron, president of Electric Lady Inc.

John Storyk: Marron said, 'No club. It's not going to be a club.' I was heartbroken. I thought my whole career was gone.

Jim Marron: With Jimi being black, he couldn't go into the nightclub business on 8th Street, because it was Mob-governed and there were four Italian clubs already there.

Eddie Kramer: I convinced them that we should just build a recording studio instead. Of course, this pissed off John Storyk because he had already designed the whole nightclub and he had to scrap all the plans and start again. It cost like, a million dollars, a lot of money for 1970.

It took a year to construct because Jimi kept running out of money, and he had to go on the road to get money to pour into the studio. We started with a $400,000 budget which we eventually more than doubled.

24 February 1969: Concert at the Royal Albert Hall, London.
Phil Ceney (fan club member): I bought the most expensive ticket, at 21 shillings, and the train from Birmingham was £2 4s. My neighbour, Bryan Badhams (later in Steve Gibbons Band), KK Downing (later in Judas Priest) and two other friends were with me on the train.

We left at nine in the morning, in the hope of catching Jimi at the stage door and maybe talking our way into the soundcheck. We walked around the hall until we found the stage door and then just hung around. Road crew came and went, then Mitch and Noel arrived. They were quite happy to stop, talk and sign autographs.

He (Jimi) was wearing bright green velvety cords, moccasin suede boots, mauve silk shirt, jacket with fringes, and a black hat with floral bandana.

He seemed genuinely surprised that we had taken such time and trouble to catch him... There was the usual chat, then we asked if he could get us into the soundcheck. Jimi's reply was that he could not take us in personally but there would be a door open somewhere and we should go in.

We looked around and saw a mobile recording truck with a cable as thick as your arm going in a door that consequently could not be closed. Slipping into a maze of corridors, we found our way down to the hall and sat as inconspicuously as possible about three rows back. It didn't take long until the gear was ready and Mitch, Noel and Jimi came out.

Jimi and co. proceeded to do endless takes of 'Hound Dog' for the sound check. The film crew asked Jimi to take his hat off so that his face would show in the film. At one point, Jimi looked at us and said, 'You guys made it then?' Amazingly, no one took any notice of us and we stayed until the end.

We went back again to catch Jimi leaving the stage door, then hung around 'til the evening when he came through again for the show.

I remember Jimi used a black Strat and a white one. My most vivid recall is 'Little Wing', because I was amazed that he played it. I thought it would stay just an album track. It was such a contrast to the other violent stuff. I can see the little red circle that was his 'fuzz-face' by his feet. The sound was great, clear as a bell.

Jimi did smash a guitar, but you could see he was tired of it. Bits of the guitar were thrown into the audience, the roadies fought to get the body back, but someone did get away with the neck.

Mitch Mitchell: It was on that one that Dave Mason and Chris Wood came up and joined us at the end for a jam. Yeah, good show.

Dave Mason: I was with Mason, Capaldi, Wood & Frog, opening the show for Hendrix. We jammed. It was fun. I made no pretence of keeping up. I just played rhythm.

Margaret Redding (Noel's mother): Jimi was sitting (afterwards, in the dressing room) right against the wall at the end with his eyes shut. I took out my handkerchief and wiped his forehead. He opened his eyes, looked up and said, 'Oh, it's you. Could you check on my white guitar?'

25 February 1969: The Experience have a business meeting with Chas Chandler; Jimi is interviewed by Bob Dawbarn of *Melody Maker*.
Jimi Hendrix (to Bob Dawbarn):

> The word church is too identified with religion, and music is my religion. Jesus shouldn't have died so early,and then he could have got twice as much across. They killed him and then twisted so many of the best things he said. Human hands started messing it all up and now so much of religion is hogwash.

26 February 1969: More business meetings with Chandler; Kathy Etchingham attends recording session at Olympic.

27 February 1969: Recording continues at Olympic; Kathy Etchingham is again present.

28 February 1969: Mitch Mitchell fails to turn up for further meetings with Chandler; Hendrix jams at The Speakeasy with Kwasi 'Rocky' Dzidzournu.

Dave Mason, lately of Traffic, admits he couldn't keep up with Hendrix in their jams—wisely he stuck to rhythm parts

MARCH 1969:

Monika Danneman: We were somewhere in London, and he went into a jewellery shop and he bought two rings, snake rings. And in the evening we went to The Speakeasy, and there he declared to everybody that we were engaged. And he went everywhere around with me, all over the place, showing everybody that we were wearing the rings.

1 March 1969: Kathy and Jimi pass the evening at The Speakeasy.

3 March 1969: Hendrix has a *Daily Telegraph* photo session at Brook Street, then spends the evening at The Speakeasy with Kathy.

5 March 1969: Valerie Mabbs of *Record Mirror* interviews Jimi.

6 March 1969: John Grant of NME interviews Jimi; jam at The Speakeasy with Billy Preston.

7 March 1969: Jimi attends a Fat Mattress recording session at Olympic, then sees Roland Kirk at Ronnie Scott's club.

8 March 1969: Jimi jams with Roland Kirk at Ronnie Scott's.

9 March 1969: Jimi again jams with Roland Kirk at Ronnie Scott's, and the pair continue at Brook Street.

10 March 1969: Jimi jams with UK rock band The Gods at The Speakeasy.

11 March 1969: Jimi is interviewed by Jane de Mendelssohn of *International Times.*
Jane de Mendelssohn: I was very surprised that, when I got to his flat in Mayfair, he opened the door in the nude. I followed his naked torso up the stairs to the first floor. As soon as he got into the room, he got into bed. Quite a strange way to start an interview with a famous pop star—or anyone else come to that.

Most of the interview was conducted with Jimi in bed and me sitting on the side of the bed. And on his bedside table was the biggest collection of alcohol and drugs. I mean, there were three different types of hash, grass, amyl nitrates, pills and lots of different kinds of bourbon and whisky. We just helped ourselves.

He was constantly smoking joints and we were both drinking... at one point he offered me some amyl nitrate and we both went out of our skulls.

I get the feeling he was quite insecure. When I asked him about his family, he didn't want to talk about it. All the alcohol and drugs were some kind of compensation. Also, it was quite clear all along that if I wanted to go to bed with him, I could have just got inside. He never touched me, but it was 'understood', free and easy. But I didn't—it was a question of pride. I didn't want to be seen as a groupie... I came away feeling I'd met somebody.

12 March 1969: Jimi moves out of Brook Street.

13 March 1969: Jimi returns to New York and books in at the Pierre Hotel, 5th Avenue.

15 March 1969: Mercury Sound Studios, New York, working on 'Blue Window' and 'Message To Love' with Buddy Miles Express.
Albert Allen (friend): Jimi loved to party and get laid. We would go to after-hours clubs, night spots uptown, parties at hotels or just spend money shopping. He loved to do that.

18 March 1969: Working on 'Star Spangled Banner' and 'Hey Gypsy Boy' at Record Plant.
Eddie Kramer: I thought it ('Star Spangled Banner') was a pretty unique rendition of the song. I was intrigued by the fact that Jimi was able to make the guitar sound like an early synthesiser, pre-dating the guitar synthesizers which came in later.

19 March 1969: Kathy Etchingham joins Jimi at the Pierre Hotel.
Kathy Etchingham: One day, while I was at the Pierre Hotel, this guy comes along—he looked like Columbo—he sort of limped in and he sat down and he put this bag down at the side of the chair and it gaped open at the top and the bag was absolutely full of packets of white powder, big packets, and on the top was a gun. I'd never even seen a gun before but I knew it was a real one, a big, heavy gun.

Seeing that gun was the turning point. I thought, Wow! I was frightened and it was at that point that I decided I'd had enough and I wanted to get back to England where I felt safe.

21 March 1969: Eire Apparent release 'Rock'n'Roll Band' as a single in the UK.

25 March 1969: Jimi signs a new agreement with Yameta; works with John McLaughlin on 'Drivin' South' and 'Everything's Gonna Be Alright' at the Record Plant; jam with Jim McCarty, guitarist in Mitch Ryder's band.
John McLaughlin: I first met Jimi in New York, through Mitch Mitchell, who had been with Georgie Fame & The Blue Flames. I used to play with Georgie years and years ago but, at the time, I was with Tony Williams' Lifetime. Mitch was really nutty about Lifetime. He came over and said, 'You better come down to the Record Plant because we're recording tonight, just come on down.'

When I got there, Mitch wasn't actually there at all. There was a guy called Buddy Miles playing drums. I didn't know Buddy at the time; I just saw this guy who was playing some boogaloo. So I played, and then Jimi came and joined in. Dave Holland (Miles Davis' bassist) was there, and we played all night—it was really nice.

Jimi used Marshall amps and would vary between a white custom Gibson Les Paul and a Fender Stratocaster. I was using a flat-top Gibson with a pick-up on it. We worked some chords out, but nothing complicated. We were just jamming. I just saw Jimi about two or three times after that jam at the Record Plant, but we didn't play together then. Every time we met we were in a rehearsal studio, and it just happened.

Jimi was a beautiful guitar player. He wasn't very schooled; he had a limited knowledge as far as musical harmony is concerned. But he had such an imagination that he made up for it. He wasn't pretentious or anything. He was just a guitar player; that's all he ever wanted to be. I mean, he got spaced, you know, but we were all spaced in our own way. But he was still into the blues.

Jim McCarty: It was one of those nights where Jimi had been jamming at a number of clubs. We ended up at Ungano's and, after it closed, we went down to the Record Plant. It was four or five in the morning and we were just playing. It wasn't a question of Jimi saying, 'OK, we're going to try this.' It was just people playing...

On Mitch's floor tom was a substantial pile of Peruvian Flake and so, when somebody wanted some, they'd do a little bump. The size of that pile is something that I won't ever forget... when we were finished playing, the sun was out.

29 March 1969: Jimi flies to Los Angeles to collect his new Corvette Stingray.

30 March 1969: Jams with Delaney & Bonnie at the Pop Expo/Teenage Fair, Hollywood Palladium, California.
Delaney Bramlett: My guitarist at the time, Jerry McGee, was drafted out to tour with Kris Kristofferson, and we were performing in Los Angeles at the Palladium. I was backstage in the dressing room, feelin' down because I didn't have a replacement, and my songs call for two guitarists. And all of a sudden this shadow comes across the room, of this guy holdin' a guitar over his shoulder. It was so dark down there, I couldn't see anything. I thought, Who in the hell is that? Then I finally saw who it was, and I said, 'Jimi, is that you?' And it was him. And he said, 'Can I play with you tonight?' And I went, 'You bet your sweet bippy!'

When we'd go up onstage, of course, he didn't play any of that feedback stuff or any of that craziness. He just played straight, blues and rock'n'roll. He played so damn tasty, it was ridiculous. He'd do whole shows with us, but he wasn't hired. We didn't pay him a dime. He was just hanging out and pickin'.

31 March 1969: Hendrix flies back to New York.

Spring 69: Michael Jeffery, lawyer Steve Weiss and booking agent Ron Terry devise a new company, Concerts East, to be run by Vanilla Fudge manager Phil Basile.
Ron Terry: Concerts West (tour promotion company) sounded too much like California. What I had to do was make it sound bigger. So I went back to Les Smith (investor) and said, 'Les, we're going to branch out, start a second company and make the network bigger. We're going to form a company called Concerts East.'

Tom Hulett: We (Concerts West) had put this tour on sale... LA Forum, Oakland Coliseum, Dallas, Houston and a bunch of other dates, then I got a phone call from Steve Weiss. He said, 'Tom, we've got a problem.' Weiss told me that Michael Jeffery had not approved the dates. Meanwhile, in good faith, we had put up money for deposits. I think I already had 8,000 seats sold at the Forum, and the Oakland Coliseum was already half sold.

So I got on a plane and went to New York without announcing myself, and I called Steve Weiss's office and told him I wanted to meet him. I walked in this room and there with Steve were Phil Basile, Jeffery, Bob Levine and Ron Terry. The problem, I was told, was that other promoters had the cities and dates we had.

Even though Concerts West had gone on sale with some of the dates, I told them that I was prepared to refund all of the money to the public and that they could do as they want. I went back to the New York Hilton and, by the time I got there, there was a page for me. It was them, so I went back and we sat down and had a better meeting. At that point I think I got some respect, which I didn't have before.

Phil Basile started calling his company Concerts East, and he was going to get Boston, New York and that area of the country.

1 April 1969: Recording 'Ramblin'' at Olmstead Studio Sound, New York.
Eddie Kramer: I went over to Olmstead only to help Jimi out. I wasn't being paid, but I hadn't worked with Jimi for some time and wanted to hear what he was doing... The sessions didn't go very well, as things were pretty crazy. There was a lot of partying going on.

2 April 1969: Recording 'Hear My Train A Comin'' and various outtakes at Olmstead Studio Sound, New York.

3 April 1969: Recording 'Midnight Lightning' at Olmstead Studio Sound, New York; 'Crosstown Traffic' released as a single in the UK.

4 April 1969: The final session at Olmstead Studio Sound, New York, recording 'Trash Man'.

5 April 1969: Hendrix returns to the Record Plant, New York.

6 April 1969: Work on 'Ships Passing In The Night' at the Record Plant.

7 April 1969: Work on 'Stone Free' and "Earth Blues' (aka 'Lullaby For The Summer').
Doc Storch (Zygote magazine journalist): Jimi turns up with a small army of women in tow, including Devon. In a typical piece of groupie power-play she heads straight for the control room to claim a seat next to the engineer, Gary Kellgren. A guy named Mark appears, claiming to be Jimi's 'dealer' and proceeds to lay out the evening's supply of grass and cocaine.

8 April 1969: Work at the Record Plant, New York, with Roger Chapman of UK rock group Family helping out on vocals for 'Stone Free'.

9 April 1969: Still working on 'Stone Free' and "Hear My Train A'Comin" at the Record Plant.
Jeff Beck: 'Stone Free' has got bits of Buddy Guy; it sounds like Les Paul in places. Jimi does every trick in the book and nails it all together so tight that you can't even see the joints.

10 April 1969: Hendrix goes to the Fillmore East to see Ten Years After and The Nice.

11 April 1969: US tour opens at Dorton Arena, Raleigh, North Carolina. Fat Mattress support.
Mitch Mitchell: Noel was getting more involved with his own band, Fat Mattress. He had insisted they open for us in Europe and they were doing so on this tour as well. I always thought that was strange, him doing that, and Jimi resented it. Fat Mattress were essentially a pretty lightweight band. Hendrix used to call them Thin Pillow.

Michael Hecht (accountant): We sent Arthur Johnson (accountant) on the road with them. He would take each concert's receipts, buy a bank check the next day and then send the bank check back. Stickells had said that he didn't want the sole responsibility of carrying so much cash while handling all of his other duties, and I don't blame him. The people on the road were crazy and had crazy demands.

12 April 1969: Gig at the Spectrum, Philadelphia, Pennsylvania.
Frank Moriarty (13-year-old fan): I watched Noel Redding take the stage at the helm of Fat Mattress, and the band ran through material

from their yet-to-be-released debut album. The crowd received them well, although it was clear from the excitement that the Fat Mattress set was simply a precursor to the night's main event.

As the stage was being set up for the Experience performance, an MC took to the stage to talk to the crowd about the police harassment that was common at the Electric Factory. Police Commissioner Rizzo had gone so far as to hold a press conference in front of the Electric Factory, vowing to 'turn this joint into a parking lot'.

With each new reference to 'the man hassling us', the crowd's intensity went up a pitch, and the spiel ended with huge cheers as everyone optimistically vowed that the police would never succeed in closing the Electric Factory.

Soon the lights went down to a roar from the crowd as everyone scrambled on top of their seats to get a better view. I had abandoned my seat in the rafters, taking advantage of the fact that I was just a kid to work my way past security and toward the stage. I reached the sixth row, where a kindly girl let me stand on her seat so I could see.

Beneath the Spectrum seating, Jimi emerged from the Philadelphia Flyers' locker room, carrying his white Stratocaster with maple neck. Escorted by police and security, Hendrix walked through the tunnel toward the arena and ran the gauntlet to the stage.

As at most of the concerts presented at the Spectrum in its first years of operation, the stage this was located in the middle of the arena floor. The circular platform would slowly revolve throughout the concert, giving everyone a constantly shifting point of view. To a tremendous roar Jimi mounted the steps and walked onto the stage.

Walter F. Naedele (Philadelphia Evening Bulletin): Jimi came on, blue silk headband flowing to his legs, scarves knotted at elbow and knee, a soft-spoken young man and his bad-mouth electric guitar.

Frank Moriarty: The band launched into 'Fire', Hendrix working his effects and pushing his amps as he fed off of the crowd's energy. Jimi capped off the solo with some quick guitar gymnastics, finishing the song with the inevitable pitch bends and clouds of feedback. The huge sound of the Experience was rivalled only by the cheers of the audience.

Walter F. Naedele: Different from BB King's Lucille, the guitar became a woman Hendrix was love-fighting all night. To his wailing, she would shimmer back her own sass. As she built toward her screams, Hendrix would stagger back from the effort to get that much fight out of her. Sinking to his knees, holding her at arm's length while she ran off at him, he would at last draw her around him, fondling her, kissing her into submission. All that, in ten minutes of 'Red House'.

Frank Moriarty: Hendrix put extra emphasis on the 'Wait a minute, something's wrong' line and repeated it to dramatic effect before grabbing high, wailing bent notes as he worked the upper reaches of the guitar neck during the long solo.

The entire performance at the Spectrum was characterized by lengthy versions of Jimi's songs. While the set list may have been shorter than at other shows on the 1969 tour, the Experience had more than made up for it by stretching out instrumentally to an even greater degree than usual.

Jimi left the stage and, surrounded by police once again, rushed through the barricades protecting him from the crowd as he fled towards the dressing rooms. I made my way out to the bus, with ringing ears and awed by what I had seen. Some of the others on the bus didn't seem to get it—but I had definitely been experienced.

"JIMI WAS STANDING RIGHT NEXT TO ME BUT THIS GUY DIDN'T ADDRESS HIM IN ANY WAY. 'YOU TELL THAT FUCKIN' NIGGER THAT IF HE PLAYS "STAR SPANGLED BANNER" IN THIS HALL HE WON'T LIVE TO GET OUT OF THE BUILDING. NO ONE DOES THAT IN DALLAS, TEXAS AND LIVES TO TELL ABOUT IT'"

TO GET OUT OF THE BUILDING. NO ONE DOES THAT IN DALLAS, TEXAS AND LIVES TO TELL ABOUT IT'"

14 April 1969: More work on 'Ships Passing In The Night' at the Record Plant, New York.

16 April 1969: The Experience rehearse at The Scene club.

17 April 1969: Jimi sends a memo to Mike Jeffery requesting account balances for all Hendrix-related companies; recording 'Keep On Groovin'" at the Record Plant.
Bob Levine: I never saw a problem for Jimi to get money within reason. If he had it in the bank, Michael Hecht would give it to him. He just had to ask for it and sign a receipt. These were required because Jimi wanted to know exactly where his money was and where it went.

MID-APRIL 1969:

Bob Levine: Ron Ziegler, press secretary for the White House, called us up personally. He wanted to ask Jimi if he would come to the White House, not to perform but to meet with President Nixon for a fireside chat. Ziegler told me that the President wanted to hold a youth conference and felt that Hendrix would give him a better grip on the counter-culture. Jeffery flatly turned him down. He didn't even tell Jimi about it.

Kathy Eberth (Mike Jeffery staff): I told Jimi. He wanted to go have dinner at the White House. The conference didn't mean much to him, but he did want to go to the White House and see how it looked.

18 April 1969: The Experience arrives late for gig at North Hall, Ellis Auditorium Amphitheater, Memphis, Tennessee. Hendrix meets Billy Cox privately to discuss working with him again.
Jimi Hendrix: I liked Billy's solid style of playing bass. He could really keep a nice groove going. Even though he wasn't what you call a spectacular bass player, he kept things nicely together.

Billy Cox: He looked good but he had changed since I had last seen him. He wasn't the tall chubby guy I knew. It looked as if he had dropped about 25lbs...

He told me that he wanted me to be his bass player. He said that things weren't the way he wanted them and would I come as a friend and help him out. He said he'd take care of me and everything would be okay. I gladly accepted. I went back to Nashville, closed my music publishing company, dropped everything else and left for New York.

19 April 1969: Concert at the Sam Houston Coliseum, Houston, Texas.
Ron Terry: Jimi used to do 'Star Spangled Banner' near the end of every show but, when we did it in Houston, a few minutes past our 11pm curfew, the cops got weird. As he was playing the anthem, a cop came over and pushed me up against a wall, telling me to instruct them to stop. I said, 'Hey, he can't stop right in the middle of a song! Don't worry about it...' We got through that night but the vibes backstage after the show were terrible. We didn't know if we were going to get out of there.

20 April 1969: Hendrix finds five thugs blocking the entrance to his dressing room at the Memorial Auditorium, Dallas, Texas.
Ron Terry: The leader got up in my face and said, 'You running this thing?' Jimi was standing right next to me but this guy didn't address him in any way. He just asked me again and I said, 'I guess... I don't know.' He said, 'Well, you tell that fuckin' nigger if he plays 'Star Spangled Banner' in this hall tonight he won't live to get out of the building. I was stunned, replying, 'Come on, get serious.' 'Did you hear what I said? No one does that in Dallas, Texas and lives to tell about it. We'll start a riot and, if he don't make it out of the building, that's just the way it fucking goes.'

The Experience do play 'Star Spangled Banner' that night and emerge unscathed.

21 April 1969: Hendrix returns to work on 'Room Full Of Mirrors' at the Record Plant in New York; Mitch and Noel fly to Los Angeles.
Kathy Eberth: That song took forever. Hendrix didn't feel the lyrics equalled the music. He tinkered with that song for more than a year. Later, when Electric Lady Studios opened, he was struggling to try and finish the lyrics so it could be included as part of his next album.

22 April 1969: Hendrix countersigns a memo from Jim Marron (president of Electric Lady), authorizing the purchase of Ampex tape machines at a cost of $84,000 for Electric Lady Studios; records 'Mannish Boy' at the Record Plant.

24 April 1969: Recording 'Crash Landing', 'Bleeding Heart', 'Hey Country Boy', 'Night Messenger' and 'Drone Blues' (with Stephen Stills on bass, Dallas Taylor on drums) at Record Plant.

25 April 1969: Hendrix flies to Los Angeles, books in to the Beverly Rodeo Hotel and attends at party for Donovan at The Factory.

26 April 1969: The Experience play a concert at The Forum, Los Angeles, supported by Cat Mother and Chicago Transit Authority.
Pete Johnson (in the LA Times):

> If Jimi Hendrix has anything serious to say, he is starting late and badly. If he has anything serious left to play, he hid it well.

27 April 1969: Concert at the Oakland Coliseum, Oakland, supported by Cat Mother and Chicago Transit Authority. Jack Casady of Jefferson Airplane joins in on bass for a jam.
Bob Levine: Concerts West knew where their bread was buttered. They took care of Jimi and made sure his needs were met. Remember, those gigs were self-promoted, so Jimi usually came out with 85 per cent of the money.

29 April 1969: Dressed as Hell's Angels and cowboys, the Experience are photographed by Ed Thrasher for the US cover of *Smash Hits*.
Ed Thrasher (art director, Warner Bros): I brought them out to the Warner Films backlot for a full-day photo session. I wanted to shoot a take-off on the television show *Gunsmoke*... They were having fun with the horses, drawing on each other with the guns, just having a great time.

May 1969: Hendrix meets guitarist Harvey Mandel again. Mandel has moved to California.
Harvey Mandel: It took place at a crowded club in Los Angeles. Jimi arrived unexpectedly and sat down in the crowd. I recognized him and wondered if he remembered our first meeting.

Then I saw him heading towards me. He greeted me as if I were one of his closest friends, and we spent the next half hour in the back room discussing the music scene. Neither fame nor glory could build a wall between Jimi and his love of music or his fellow musicians.

1 May 1969: Hendrix is interviewed at the Beverly Rodeo Hotel by Sharon Lawrence.
Sharon Lawrence (US journalist/friend): He told me, 'I've seen my father twice in six years and the only time I hear from him is when he'd like me to send him a cheque.' I said, 'I read in the papers your father has another wife,' and Jimi said, 'He lives with a woman who has two daughters.' I said, 'Do you like them?' and he said, 'I've met them twice for a few minutes.'

2 May 1969: Concert at the Cobo Arena, Detroit.
Dave Atchison (fan): I met and spoke with Jimi for quite a while before his last show in Detroit. It was really quite easy to get to him. Such a nice guy.

My friend Frank Osako and I had our tickets, and Frank had been calling downtown Detroit hotels that afternoon, trying to find Jimi. Frank told me that he had found Jimi at the Pontchartrain Hotel, had been put through to his suite with no questions asked, and had spoken with Jimi on the phone. And, incredibly, Jimi had asked Frank to stop by his hotel room if he had some free time before the concert.

Frank and I went to the hotel room and knocked on the door. The door opened, and there was Jimi. I was 15 years old... and here he was a few feet away, inviting us into his privacy with a smile on his face and interested in spending time with us before his concert.

Sitting on the couch was a blonde-haired young woman, watching a Detroit Tigers game on TV. It was so mundane, like walking through the front door of a neighborhood friend's house.

We stood there, just inside the door, and spoke to Jimi, asked him questions. We laughed together. He was soft-spoken, self-effacing, curious about us—a warm and generous person.

We spoke like this for what must have been 30 minutes, then... Jimi came out into the hall. We talked some more and he shook our hands. I remember gripping that incredible right hand. His fingers were long and thin, his grip was cool and soft.

Ron Terry: There were a few moments of brilliance (in the performance) otherwise it was terrible. But the people didn't care. They were all fucked up and they clapped and jumped up and down. It didn't make any difference.

Mitch Mitchell: We were in the Cobo Hall and the word came through the grapevine that there were going to be problems in Toronto. The roadies came round and said, 'Just check all your baggage and make sure that there's nothing that could possibly be planted.'

3 May 1969: Hendrix's bag is searched by Officer Marvin Wilson as he comes through Customs at Toronto. Hendrix is arrested but freed on $10,000 bail, allowing him to play a gig at Maple Leaf Gardens.
Noel Redding: I was standing beside him, actually, and they opened up his airline case...

Tony Ruffino (promoter): The Customs guy said to me, 'If that's not yours, keep your hands off it.' I said, 'Well, I work for him.' He insisted, 'Keep your hands off the bag.' Looking at Jimi the officer asked, 'Is that your bag?' Hendrix said, 'Yes.' He opened it up and inside were these small packets of heroin. He said to Jimi, 'What's that?' Hendrix said, 'I don't know.' That's when I knew we were in trouble.

Mitch Mitchell: I made a point of wearing a suede suit with no pockets and no underwear. There was no way they could plant anything on me. So, as far as I was concerned, it was a plant. By whom, and on whose authority, I don't know.

Louis Goldblatt (chauffeur): He was genuinely dumbfounded by the whole affair.

Douglas Pringle (Arts Canada): Jimi Hendrix swung out on stage (at the Maple Leaf Gardens), took up that incredible curved stance, knees bent, pelvis up; he made an unfelt effort at his usual rap on chicks and The Experience, but stopped at the bitter taste of it.

*Ritchie Yorke (*Rolling Stone*):* He walked on stage and said, 'I want you to forget what happened yesterday and tomorrow and today. Tonight we're going to create a whole new world.' This may be part of his usual rap, but the arrest gave it special impact.

Unfortunately—understandably—however, it was not one of Hendrix's best evenings. He played well, but it never quite got off the ground. The effect was rather like watching a bullfighter who's so good that no bull really challenges him, and therefore there is no danger, and no suspense. Hendrix was just too cool.

Douglas Pringle: He called three songs, none appeared, then laid into the fourth, mostly guitar, words from the past that caught in his throat... so hard to smile.... His hair is so much shorter now, and tied back with a scarf, and the next record is dedicated to the Panthers.

Early May 1969: Billy Cox arrives in New York to work with Hendrix.
Billy Cox: Jimi had told me all of these fabulous stories about how a limousine would pick me up at the airport, and I believed all this, of course. Nobody from the office, however, was there to pick me up. That's when I started to realize that Jimi wanted me here, but the office didn't seem so sure. At that point, I knew it was going to be a battle from there on.

When I arrived in New York, Jimi sat me down and admitted that his creativity had run dry. He just felt that he couldn't think of anything new.

Noel Redding: I found out through somebody in the office that I'd been asking too many questions about money and so on, and Hendrix had been 'advised' to get somebody else and just employ them. That was Billy Cox.

Billy Cox: Jimi still had obligations with the Experience to fulfil. He told me, 'Look, we'll just work together and come up with some great songs.'

At that point he didn't have an apartment in New York and was staying in a hotel. He had a little amp there and we would work day in and day out with little patterns, trying to put together some good music.

4 May 1969: Concert at the Memorial Auditorium, Syracuse, New York.
Larry Vaughan (Concerts East staff): It was right around the time when black students were protesting and rioting at Cornell University. Before the band went on, the house played a recording of 'Star Spangled Banner' over the public address system. When the lights went

down, a white kid in the front row screamed at the top of his lungs, 'I love you!' Hendrix paused to look at him, and then the audience, and said, 'The feeling's mutual, man, but let's do something about those guns. It's getting frightening.'

Ben Fong-Torres (Rolling Stone *):* Hendrix improvised a verse or two of new lyrics for a new song. The words came out something like '...and I was in this room full of light and a thousand mirrors.' Those hours of interrogation by The Mounties had apparently taken their toll.

Ron Terry: We decided that we were not going to think about it (the drug bust) any more, so we just partied. He and I got adjoining suites at the end of a hall and partied all night with three stewardesses we had met on the flight to Syracuse.

5 May 1969: Hendrix flies back to Toronto and appears before Judge Fred Hayes, who sets a preliminary hearing for 19 June.

6 May 1969: Hendrix returns to New York; recording 'The Things That I Used To Do' at the Record Plant, with Johnny Winter on slide and a somewhat drunken Stephen Stills on bass.
Johnny Winter: I first met Jimi at The Scene. We jammed together there a good bit. What we would often do after the club closed is go over to a studio where he had recording time booked regularly, and play around with things, maybe play for several hours and then, some other day, listen to the tapes to pick out the good parts for ideas to work into songs.

About that time, Jimi was real fascinated with the old bottleneck blues style. So we both went into the Record Plant studios... got the engineer to roll the tapes and we just jammed together. You couldn't show that man anything new. It was a case of Jimi watching how I used a bottleneck when playing. I guess Jimi and I must have played together for at least two or three hours on that day.

Stephen Stills: I could barely see. After a while, Jimi leaned over and nudged me with his guitar. Then he literally moved my hand on the bass. I was a fret off... I nearly died of embarrassment.

7 May 1969: Concert at the Memorial Coliseum, Tuscaloosa, Alabama.

Tony Ruffino: We had trouble checking in at the Ramada Inn. The police did not appreciate all of the white girls crowding the lobby being so crazy about him. Nothing was going on, just some kids screaming, excited about seeing him. He had just broken through in the South and people were beginning to recognize him.

9 May 1969: Concert at the Charlotte Coliseum, North Carolina.
Ron Terry: I called Jimi 'The Bat' and he called me 'Sun God'. He never opened the drapes until the sun went down, always had room service and never went to restaurants.

To show you what his sense of humor was, once when we were in Charlotte, I was sitting by the pool and he came running down from his room, in his bathrobe, with the hood on so that the sun couldn't get to him, and gave me an issue of the *National Enquirer.*

On the front cover was a picture of a lady whose face had been decayed by the sun. He said, 'This is what's going to happen to you, you silly ass.' And ran back to his room. While I was reading it, I looked up at his window and he was peeking through the drapes to see what I was doing. It was silly, but it was just his way of showing he was really aware of what was going down all the time.

10 May 1969: Concert at the Civic Center, Charleston, West Virginia.
Noel Redding: We got through that last tour by constantly telling ourselves, 'This is our last American tour. We can do it. We'll survive, we'll survive, we'll survive' when we felt like death warmed up.

11 May 1969: Concert at Fieldhouse, State Fairgrounds Coliseum, Indianapolis, Indiana.
David Bruce (fan): Compared to when I'd seen him in Muncie a year or so earlier, the humor was gone, so the stunts had pretty much been dropped.

Hendrix now had shorter hair and the silk headband, much like his appearance in the Woodstock film. He seemed moody and untalkative. He was quite unhappy with the building's sound system—vocals at the time were still usually routed through a standard PA system. He mumbled derogatory remarks about this.

Hendrix played the older songs with a perfunctory delivery and made almost insulting remarks to fans calling out for the old favourites.

12 May 1969: The band return to New York.
Jimi Hendrix: I had friends with me in Harlem. Even in my own section, we would be walking down the street and girls, old ladies, anybody, would say, 'Look at that. What is this, a circus or something?'

Arthur Allen: The black community was very conservative at that time. Jimi was totally different to anyone in the community. He would wear blues hats like the old masters, blues-master hats we used to call them. Then he would put buttons on them to make them his style. He wore pins. My brother and I began wearing bell-bottom pants because of him. Most blacks associated bell-bottom pants with clowns.

13 May 1969: Recording at the Record Plant, with Sharon Lane on keyboards and Juma Sultan on percussion; jam at The Scene Club with Stephen Stills and Johnny Winter.

Billy Cox: Jimi wanted to try and take his music in a number of different directions. He asked if I knew of any organ players. I told him that I knew a pretty nice one in Nashville. He said, 'Get him up here.' I said, 'Hey, it's a girl.' He shot me a look, but told me to bring her up anyway. She did two nights in the studio but it didn't work out too well.

Tony Bramwell: I was in New York because James Taylor, another of our artists, was playing his first gigs at The Bottom Line. So I dropped into The Scene, and there was Judy Collins singing 'Both Sides Now', followed by Steve Stills doing 'Suite: Judy Blue Eyes', and eventually Johnny Winter got up and Jimi got up and it turned into a massive long jam, everybody trading licks furiously.

14 May 1969: Recording 'Villanova Junction', 'Hallaluya' and 'Ships Passing In The Night" at the Record Plant.

15 May 1969: Recording 'Power Of Soul' at the Record Plant.

Billy Cox: Jimi wanted to experiment with having three or four horns. The horn players from the Buddy Miles Express had said that they would help. I thought the move would have brought his music too far back to R&B.

'Power Of Soul' came together when Jimi heard me playing a riff from 'Mary Ann', an old song Ray Charles used to do. I hadn't meant anything by playing it. I was just goofing around, but that was all he needed to get started.

16 May 1969: Concert at the Civic Centre, Baltimore, Maryland.

17 May 1969: Concert at the Rhode Island Arena, Providence, Rhode Island.

Jimi Hendrix: What I want to do is rest completely for one year. Completely. I'll have to. Maybe something'll happen and I'll break my own rules, but I'll have to try. It's the physical and emotional toll I have to think of.

For three years we've been working non-stop. That is a lot of physical and emotional strain. You go somewhere, and the show is a bit under what it should be and you are told you are slipping, but it's the strain... of the moral obligation to keep going even when you don't feel that you can manage even one more show. I'm thinking about it most of the time now, and that doesn't help create the right mood.

18 May 1969: Gig at Madison Square Garden, New York. Jimi finds time to catch The Who performing 'Tommy' at the Fillmore East.

"THE BLACK COMMUNITY WAS VERY CONSERVATIVE AT THAT TIME. JIMI WAS TOTALLY DIFFERENT. HE WOULD WEAR BLUES HATS LIKE THE OLD MASTERS, THEN HE'D PUT BUTTONS ON THEM TO MAKE THEM HIS STYLE. HE WORE PINS... MOST BLACKS ASSOCIATED BELL-BOTTOM PANTS WITH CLOWNS"

19 May 1969: Paul Zimmerman of *Newsweek* interviews Hendrix.

20 May 1969: Jimi dines with Timothy Leary, Devon Wilson and Jann Wenner of *Rolling Stone* in Greenwich Village; later he records 'Live And Let Live' at the Record Plant.

Mid-May 1969: Hendrix meets percussionist Jerry Velez at The Scene.
Jerry Velez: I had just finished jamming with The McCoys and, when I walked over to my table, Jimi and his entourage were sitting behind me... he leaned over and said, 'Listen, I'm recording this jam over at the studio tonight. We'll be starting around four, after this thing ends tonight. Do you want to come down and jam?' I said, 'Sure.' I went over that night and jammed with Jimi and Buddy Miles, and we seemed to hit it off.

Jeffery said, 'Who the fuck is this kid, Jerry Velez? I've never even heard of him.' Jimi explained that he liked playing with me and wanted me in the band. Then Jimi decided to have two percussionists, with Juma and I providing both an African and Latin flavour.

Billy Cox: Jimi's intentions were good, but it just didn't work when you had congas and timbales competing with what Mitch was trying to play.

21 May 1969: Jimi's guitar is stolen from his Corvette while he is in a clothes store on East 9th St; recording 'Valleys Of Neptune', 'Hear My Train A'Comin'', Bleeding Heart, 'Villanova Junction and 'Earth Blues' at the Record Plant.
Dave Ragno (engineer): The party atmosphere seemed to be a deterrent to what Jimi was trying to accomplish. If Devon wasn't trying to drive him crazy, then someone else would come into the control room chugging a bottle of tequila and portioning out cocaine to anybody who wanted it.

22 May 1969: Recording 'Message From Nine To The Universe' at the Record Plant.

23 May 1969: Concert at the The Coliseum, Seattle, supported by Fat Mattress.
Ann Wilson (fan, later of Heart): The striking thing about it was the noise. I think the other bands included The Ike & Tina Turner Revue, but when Jimi came onstage the crew backed off, and the whole audience—which must have been 20 or 30,000—backed away from the stage, just from the sheer volume of his performance. The noise was huge. It was great.

Jimmy Leverton (bass player, Fat Mattress): The stadium had a glass dome and a revolving stage in the middle. He was playing his white Stratocaster, playing really blistering guitar. Lightning flashed overhead. The whole place... it was a great effect. Steven Spielberg on lights. An awesome experience.

Janie Gressel (Seattle Post-Intelligencer): Hendrix's guitar seemed to be an extension of his body; the peculiar positions from which he sometimes played seemed a result of emotion—as if just to hold the guitar could not express his erupting feelings.The impression was that if Hendrix were to have to put down his guitar, the music would have to come from his body—that the instrument was entirely superfluous.

24 May 1969: Concert at the International Sports Arena, San Diego, California.
Jim Brodey (San Diego Free Press): Top 40 radio station KCBQ had sponsored a contest in which entrants who had made the 'grooviest love medallion' would win a free ticket to the concert and present their love beads to Hendrix in person. Jimi, who knew nothing of the contest, refused to save face for the bumbling KCBQ, and wouldn't see the winners.

25 May 1969: The Experience play the San Jose Pop Festival, Santa Clara, California, with Taj Mahal and Eric Burdon.
Carlos Santana: I think that was the best concert I ever heard him play. He had supreme confidence that day. There was nothing in his mind about business or chicks or anything that I could tell, because he just came out like Michael Tyson, when Michael Tyson would knock guys out in three seconds. There's a certain 'stance'. That's what Miles Davis said: 'I can tell whether a person can play just by the way he stands, you know.' He had a certain stance, man. He was all over that Strat and had supreme confidence, that's all I can say.

26 May 1969: The Experience fly to Hawaii.
Jimmy Leverton: Mike Jeffery and the tour promoters weren't going to take Fat Mattress to

Hawaii... it was Hendrix who said, 'Come on, they've done the graft, they deserve the perk.' That was really nice of him. That was great.

27-29 May 1969: During three days off, at the Diamond Head mansion in Honolulu, the local chapter of the Black Panthers come knocking on Hendrix's door.
Kathy Eberth: I answered it and said I was the maid. I heard this muffled laugh from the next room. They heard it as well and came in. They were talking to him about money and the fact that he, like them, was a 'brother'. They were putting the guilt thing on him. He tried to quell them by telling them that 'the only colors I see are in my music.'

30 May 1969: During the concert at the Waikiki Shell, Honolulu, Hendrix is plagued by buzzing amplifiers.
Tom Hulett (Concerts West): The audience was dead. They seemed stoned and gave no reaction. Jimi spoke to the crowd and excused himself, saying that he had to have this problem fixed. He went and got into his limousine. Eric Barrett and Gerry Stickells ran around trying to fix the problem. I was getting nervous. We were sold out and all of a sudden nothing was happening. Then Stickells came up to me and said that Jimi didn't want to go back on.

I told Stickells to keep people playing with the wires while I went out to the car and spoke with Jimi. Stickells and I must have tried for about half-an-hour but he was not going back on. Jimi said to tell everybody to come back tomorrow night. He would more than make up for it then.

I tried to explain that they were all here now and we had already torn their tickets in half, but I knew him too well. He wasn't going back on. Knowing this, we got hold of the building manager, ran down to the old Honolulu Arena used for wrestling matches, and picked up rolls of tickets. We made an announcement that the sound system couldn't be repaired and Jimi

The Black Panthers tried unsuccessfully to co-opt Hendrix, who insisted that the only colors he saw were in his music

Hendrix wouldn't want to perform with substandard equipment—all of which was bullshit—and that if they all left quietly and picked up a ticket stub, they would be admitted to the next night's concert.

Everybody was pissed off. These people were all fucked up on drugs and little more than 1,000 picked up their stubs. The rest were yelling, 'Fuck you!'

31 May 1969: Second concert at the Waikiki Shell, Honolulu.
Tom Hulett: The next night, the venue was overfilled, which is why, in my opinion, there are no more rock shows at the Waikiki Shell. We were paranoid, security was paranoid—because everybody had heard what had happened, came to the gate and said that they had lost their ticket stub—so we let everybody in. The crowd spilled over into the park behind the shell. Jimi said to let them all in free and he was brilliant on stage that night.

1 June 1969: Third concert at the Waikiki Shell, Honolulu.

2 June 1969: Building work starts to convert the Generation club into Electric Lady Studio; Jimi begins a 'working holiday' at the Beverley Rodeo Hotel, Los Angeles.
Mitch Mitchell: If any money was made, it was spent very quickly in a studio anywhere in the world. That was probably Hendrix's major luxury in life. That's why he built Electric Lady studio.

John Storyk (designer): None of us knew what we were doing because no one had ever done it before.

Jim Marron: It was funded hand-to-mouth as the earnings came in... Jimi would go out and do a Coliseum date, in San Diego, say, and come back with $100,000 in his pocket. So he'd peel off $50,000, hand it to me and say, 'OK, start it up again.' And so I'd get the crews back in—we had to use ponytail carpenters to get it done, because of the way construction would start and stop—and we'd go until the money ran out again.

Eddie Kramer: We built Electric Lady completely with Jimi in mind. It was a very warm environment; the walls were carpeted white and we had colored lights that could then be projected onto the walls—greens, blues, reds, yellows, purples. Through an instrument panel, Jimi could control the lights to suit his mood. Jimi loved that studio. It was his baby, it was the womb in which he was going to create.

7 June 1969: At the Beverly Rodeo Hotel, Hendrix writes 'Valleys Of Neptune... Arising'.
Sharon Lawrence: Jimi and I went to see Henry Steingarten when he came to Los Angeles and we told him that Jimi wanted to withdraw from Mike Jeffery as a manager, and also to withdraw from the studio

Jimi found it very hard to say all this because he found it very emotional. He was afraid the group was going to break up and Jeffery and Stickells would tell him he would be nowhere if it broke up.

He told him he wanted to be bought out of the studio if Jeffery would reimburse him for his investment, and Steingarten said he would take it up with Jeffery. If Jimi felt that strongly, then, yes, they should do it, and Jimi then told him that to get out of the contract, if he didn't work again until it ran out, he was willing to do that to get away from Mike.

Steingarten asked Jimi and me to gather as much evidence as we could in ways that Mike had been crooked, or had not Jimi's or the Experience's best interests at heart, and he asked us to find documents, to make notes, to tape anything and to talk to Gerry Stickells and see how helpful he would be.

8 June 1969: Hendrix is interviewed by Jerry Hopkins for *Rolling Stone*, at the Beverly Rodeo Hotel.
Jimi Hendrix (to Jerry Hopkins):

> We're going to play mostly outside, places that hold a lot of people, y'know. It'll be like a sky church sort of thing. You can get all your answers through music anyway, and the best way is through open air. We're going to play a lot of places, like in the ghettos, in Harlem and so forth...

9 June 1969: Cat Mother's album *The Street Giveth... And The Street Taketh Away*, produced by Hendrix, is released in the UK. Jimi has also played rhythm guitar on it.

10 June 1969: Eddie Kramer completes three days of work at Wally Heider Recording, Los Angeles, during which he has reviewed and mixed various Hendrix concert recordings, intended for a live album.

15 June 1969: Jimi is interviewed by Nancy Carter at Beverly Rodeo Hyatt House, Beverly Hills; the tapes Eddie Kramer prepared at Wally Heider Recording are scrapped.

Mid-June 1969: Jam at Stephen Stills' house in Studio City, with Buddy Miles and Rick James.
Dallas Taylor (drummer): The music room at Stephen's smelled like a mixture of locker room, incense, pot and booze. We'd nailed old Persian rugs to the walls to muffle the noise and the room was forever dank and muggy. As we walked in, I saw Hendrix sitting on one of Stephen's amps, playing his ass off, while Buddy Miles was literally pounding the shit out of my drums. It was very loud and hurt my ears.

I don't think Hendrix liked me very much, because of Denise (a shared girlfriend).
In general, he struck me as an extremely unhappy person, kind of scared. He always had a guitar in his hands unless he was getting high or getting laid.

Jimi stopped playing when we walked in. There was a big pile of cocaine on a mirror sitting on top of the B3 organ, and we all gathered around and took turns snorting from it. 'So, you guys gigging yet?' Jimi asked Stephen.

'Nah, we can't find a bass player,' Stephen said.

'Yeah,' said Jimi. 'That's the story of my life. There's a definite shortage of bass players.'

We played off and on that night. Mostly we attended to the coke, but I do have tapes.

19 June 1969: At the Court House, Toronto, Canada, Judge Robert Taylor sets Jimi's trial for 8 December 1969. Hendrix' publicist Michael Goldstein endeavours to kill the story.
Michael Goldstein (publicist): I never minded stories like that being in *Rolling Stone* or in our own (underground) newspapers. Where it would hurt you was not there, it was in the daily papers across the country, which would make large concert hall promoters close down all your concert dates. I knew that a million dollars was riding on that story not getting on UPI and the AP wire… It didn't get on the national wire. It got lost. That's what you pay a press agent for.

A press agent with an act like Jimi ought to have $500 in his pocket of the company's money to do whatever he has to do—to pay guards, to pay police, whatever. By his nature, a press agent is unscrupulous in defense of his act.

20 June 1969: Outdoor gig at Newport 69 Pop Festival, Devonshire Downs, San Fernando Valley State College, California. Hendrix collects $125,000, said to be the largest concert fee for a single artist up to this date.
Jimmy Leverton: The Black Panthers were moving in for money. I wasn't allowed near it, but backstage it was real heavy.

Noel Redding: It was a big gig. We had one of these caravans backstage. I wandered into the caravan, there were all these Black Panther type people—in my mind anyway—about six or seven of them sitting around Hendrix, and Hendrix was looking white. I said to these guys, 'Hey, what are you doing in our dressing room?' And I got them thrown out. And Hendrix said, Thanks, man.'

Mitch Mitchell: I think someone spiked Jimi, or maybe he'd taken something of his own and then someone had spiked him on top of that. It was a disaster. I kept thinking, This is weird—all this money… One of the worst gigs we ever played.

"A PRESS AGENT WITH AN ACT LIKE JIMI OUGHT TO HAVE $500 OF THE COMPANY'S MONEY IN HIS POCKET TO DO WHATEVER HE HAS TO DO — TO PAY GUARDS, TO PAY POLICE, WHATEVER. BY HIS NATURE, A PRESS AGENT IS UNSCRUPULOUS IN DEFENSE OF HIS ACT"

22 June 1969: Hendrix returns for an unannounced jam at Newport 69, this time including Eric Burdon on vocals and Buddy Miles on drums.
Mitch Mitchell: Jimi decided to go back, bless his heart, to play again. Not for any money or anything, just because he felt he wanted to make up for it... He did the right thing as a musician. I wish I'd done it as well.

28 June 1969: Hendrix announces publicly that, in future, his bassist will be former army buddy Billy Cox, but Noel Redding and Mitch Mitchell are not necessarily out of the band.
Arthur Allen: Billy Cox was way, way laid back, from a completely different side of Jimi Hendrix. Musically, Billy could stay in the pocket and never created stress for Jimi. Hendrix needed that more than anything.

Noel Redding: It was in mid-'69 when Jimi and I had discussions about writing together properly. I noted it in my diary—'It's important that the band involves everyone.' It didn't happen.

29 June 1969: Final gig of the US tour, at Mile High Stadium, Denver Pop Festival. It will be the last gig by the Experience.

Noel Redding: A journalist came up to me in the hotel before the gig and said, 'What do you think about Jimi announcing he's expanding the band?' I was like, 'What you talking about?' because he'd said nothing to me. I decided on the spot to leave because, if you're in a band, everyone should know what's going on.

We did the gig in front of 30,000 people who basically tried to get on stage with us.

Jimmy Greenspoon (vocalist, Three Dog Night): I don't know exactly who started it, but I think it was Hendrix, because someone on stage said, 'Come on and break the barriers down!' With that, the whole crowd came running toward the stage en masse.

The cops came out with their riot gear, complete with tear gas, and lobbed it into the audience. It turned into a real ugly scene.

Noel Redding: The police used tear gas but the wind was coming towards the stage and we had to stop. We got off and there was no cars, so they put us in a van and locked us in but all these fans started climbing over it.

Jimmy Greenspoon: The cops got way too rough with their clubs and... a lot of the kids did get hurt.

Mitch Mitchell: We were ushered off stage through the tear gas. Gerry Stickells found us a U-Haul rent-a-truck, one of those two-ton jobs with aluminium sides and top. The band got into the back...

Herbert Worthington (acquaintance of Hendrix): I looked over to my right and there was a truck backed up, and Noel and Mitch were already in there, and Jimi shouted, 'Come on! Come on!' And I ran and got in this truck. There were kids climbing on top, yelling, 'We love you!'

Noel Redding: You could hear the roof buckling as we drove back to the hotel... I went up to Jimi that night, said goodbye and caught the next plane to London. I don't think Jimi believed I'd do it.

John Downing (roadie): I don't think he ever got over Noel leaving.

30 June 1969: Noel Redding flies to London.
Herbert Worthington: I didn't know it at the time, that Noel had quit, but I could tell Jimi was very concerned. He was very nervous about it.

Mitch Mitchell: The band never split up for me. Jimi and I always played together, and it was fun. Even while the Band Of Gypsys was going on, we carried on working in the studio together.

Arthur Allen: Mitch was like part of the family. I loved Mitch and so did Hendrix. He and Jimi were very close and his personality superceded the racial thing.

Noel Redding: We can't find out the exact figures but, by counting the number of multi-platinum records that the Jimi Hendrix Experience sold, it seems we're talking about at least $30m to $40m. It would be nice to know what they did with the money. No one knows where it went.

Summer 1969: Hendrix meets Alan Douglas.
Alan Douglas: Someone brought him to my house, then he moved right around the corner, so

he was in my place every day… So we were friends before we ever started working together.

Summer 1969: Hendrix jams with jazz musicians at Juggy Sound, New York.
Alan Douglas: I wanted to push Hendrix into a jazz bag just to see what happened, because jazz players were constantly trying to figure him out.

Stefan Bright (engineer, Douglas Records): To hear how Hendrix would sound we organized an informal session over at Juggy Sound with Dave Holland on bass and Mother Hen on keyboards. We had been rehearsing for about 45 minutes when someone walked in with a pipe. Without knowing it, Hendrix and I were smoking what turned out to be angel dust. We had just smoked a little bit, but neither Jimi nor I knew what was going on. The session had to be stopped.

Bob Levine: The angel dust incident was all Jeffery had to hear. He was incensed.

Summer 1969: A session is booked at Hit Factory, New York to enable Miles Davis and Tony Williams to play with Hendrix.
Alan Douglas: The idea came from Miles. Every Saturday afternoon it'd be a big hang-out down at my wife's store—Miles, Jimi, me, whoever else was in town and, every Saturday, Miles would be saying, 'Let's make a record.'
Miles Davis: I first met Jimi when his manager called up and wanted me to introduce him to the way I was playing

Alan Douglas: The session was scheduled to start at eight and Hendrix and I were in my office getting ready. At seven-thirty, the phone rang and it was Jack Whittemore, who doubled as Miles' promoter and manager. He said, 'Alan, I hate to tell you this, but Miles wants $50,000 before he goes to the studio.'

I looked at Hendrix in disbelief and said, 'Did you hear that?' I then put Jimi on the phone with him, but it was to no avail.

Right after he hung up, I called Miles' house. His wife Betty answered and told me he wasn't home. I insisted, 'Betty, that's bullshit. Let me talk to him. When Miles came on the phone, I said, 'Is what I just heard from Jack true?' He said, 'Yeah. C'mon man, you got it.' I cursed him and slammed the phone down. I had gone through this entire process for Miles, because he had wanted to record with Hendrix so badly.

Hendrix shrugged and said, 'Fuck it. I'm almost relieved that it didn't come off anyway.' Just before we decided to go out and eat, the phone rang again and it was Tony Williams. He said, 'I hear you're giving Miles $50,000. Well, I want $50,000 too.' I laughed and said, 'Tony, the session's cancelled.'

July 1969: Mike Jeffery instructs his associate Jerry Morrison to acquire a house for Hendrix.
Jerry Morrison: Mike believed that Jimi couldn't get his trip together in the city because of all the leeches. He wanted me to find a house that was isolated and insulated.

1 July 1969: Mitch Mitchell flies to London; Hendrix books into the Hotel Navarro, New York.

2 July 1969: Hendrix's friend Brian Jones of The Rolling Stones dies at his home in Sussex.
Mitch Mitchell: Brian Jones' death hit Jimi very hard.

5 July 1969: *NME* reports that Noel Redding has quit The Jimi Hendrix Experience, and that Mitch Mitchell is also thinking of leaving.

7 July 1969: Hendrix is a guest on *The Dick Cavett Show*, ABC TV studios, New York. He performs 'Hear My Train A'Comin" backed by the Jack Rosenbaum Orchestra.
Jimi Hendrix (on The Dick Cavett Show*):* The belief comes… through electricity to the people. That's why we play so loud. Because it doesn't actually hit through the ear drums like most groups… They got this real shrill sound, you know, and it's really hard. We plan for our sound to go into the soul of the person… actually see if they can awaken some kind of thing in their minds, 'cause there's so many sleeping people.

10 July 1969: Jimi invites old friend Larry Lee to come from Memphis and join his band; later Jimi is interviewed by Flip Wilson on *Johnny Carson's Tonight Show,* NBC TV, New York.
Billy Cox: Jimi had played both the rhythm and the lead with The Experience. He thought it might free him up to concentrate on his lead

playing if he had someone else playing rhythm. Larry Lee was the first and only guy considered.

Ed Shaughnessy (house drummer, Johnny Carson Show): About noon, at home, the phone rang. It was the NBC music department telling me that Jimi had requested I play with him later that day. Needless to say, I was surprised (and pleased) at the news, and resolved to get to work early.

Jimi was there setting up when I arrived, and he gave me a warm greeting and told me that Mitch Mitchell was ill. I, of course, responded at how glad I'd be to play, and hoped I could please him.

His response thrilled me. 'Man, I heard you with Charlie Mingus the other night, and know you'll be great with us.' Naturally, my anxiety went away (mostly) and we rehearsed 'Voodoo Chile (Slight Return)' and a high energy piece called 'Fire'.

Jimi's only advice was, 'Ed, play loud as hell, and give me plenty of cymbals.' The rehearsal went fine. They cautioned Jimi not to hit his monster effects pedal 'cause it might blow a TV line in the studio. During the show, Jimi got wound up and, while absolutely burning a solo, stepped on the monster and blew a line out. We had to wait for re-wiring and do the tune again.

12 July 1969: Jimi buys equipment at Manny's Musical Instruments shop, New York.
Henry Goldrich: Any kind of new toy or sound effect, he bought immediately. Whenever he walked in he was good for $1,500 to $2,000.

Roland Robinson: He bought things in tens. He'd go to Manny's and say, 'What do you have new? Four Sunburst Strats and two white ones? I'll take 'em. Then he'd just pull them out of the box, re-string them, play them until the strings broke, and then pick up another one.

14 July 1969: Larry Lee arrives in New York.
Larry Lee: I was scared, man. I just got out of Vietnam. I just wasn't ready for a lot of things. I went up there and him and Buddy Miles met me in a limo… that was my first time meeting Buddy, that's how it got started.

17 July 1969: Hendrix signs a contract to play at Woodstock Festival.
Michael Lang (producer, Woodstock Festival): We set a limit of what we'd pay an act, which was $15,000, and stuck to it. The only one that negotiated beyond it was Jimi Hendrix. He had a booking a week before for $150,000 in California, and I still wouldn't pay him more than $15,000, but he insisted on it being thirty. And I said, 'Fine. We'll pay you thirty if you'll play twice—the first day and the last day.'

Ron Terry: I got with the guys from Woodstock Ventures and instructed them to give me $18,000 immediately and place the rest in escrow. When they did, Michael Goldstein was instructed to issue a press release saying that Hendrix would perform at the festival. Weiss, Jeffery and I had a meeting with Hendrix and told him we were getting more money than anyone else and that this was an important gig to play. Hendrix said, 'If you feel it's that important, let's do it.'

19 July 1969: At the Navarro Hotel, Hendrix writes two songs, 'Let It Grow' and 'Ball And Chain'.

23 July 1969: Hendrix authorizes $660 of payments for two staff in an eight-bedroomed house he has rented at Traver Hollow Road, Shokan, New York, at $3,000 per month.
Jerry Morrison: The house was rented in my name. I'd known the owner and I told him I wanted the house for some clients. When he came up there and saw all those black musicians, he got uptight. But he was a nice man and backed off.

Claire Moriece (cook): I was living in the house for about three days before Jimi came in. My instant impression was what a sweet, humble, funny guy. I don't think that image of him has ever been projected. He felt like he was really lucky and he just expressed gratitude. I baked blackberry pies and I made lots of different soups. Jimi loved soup and chocolate-chip cookies and corn cakes.

28 July 1969: Hendrix is given $2,100 by Bob Levine.
Billy Cox: Finally, Jimi had completed most of the obligations he had with the Experience and we wound up with a place in upstate New York outside of Woodstock where we had a lot of time to rehearse. It was spent creating.

The whole problem started as soon as we got to the house in Woodstock. There were people who just did not want this band to succeed. It was one thing after another.

There was the shootout down at the front gate of the Shokan house, the infiltration of people into the house, drugs being put into people's food—just a lot of unnecessary, underhanded things being done for no reason. I didn't have time to try and figure out who was behind all this and why they were doing so.

Jimi had gone down into this well. He said, 'Man, I just can't get it together. I've gotta rest my head.' He told me that if he could, he was thinking of going off to Africa...

29 July 1969: Hendrix authorizes payments for his accompanying musicians at Woodstock.

30 July 1969: *Smash Hits* compilation is released in the US; Hendrix flies to Paris, en route to Essaouira, Mogador, Morocco with Alan Douglas, Stella Douglas and her sister, clothes designer Colette Mimram.
Juma Sultan: There was some mysterious circumstances behind that whole situation. I think Jimi going wasn't totally by choice.

Claire Moriece: Jimi went to Morocco on a vacation. Alan Douglas's wife's sister, Colette, was having an affair with Jimi at the time.

Faye Pridgeon: Jimi was kind of smitten with Colette. If there was anybody I thought he might be in love with, it was her.

Stefan Bright: Stella and Colette... were so sensual. The attraction was mutual, they were both beautiful but, at the same time, very sad people. Their relationship with Hendrix was intimate. It wasn't just 'Let's go down to The Scene and listen to Jimi.' It went way beyond the club scene. Stella and Colette were more emotionally stable than Devon, who was in and out with Jimi so many times it was unbelievable, but in the end he always came back to the three girls.

31 July 1969: The first day of the six-day 'holiday' in Morocco.
Colette Mimram: It was probably the only vacation he ever had. It was very relaxed and very peaceful and very wonderful. There was no hassle, it was really a lot of fun.

Claire Moriece: Something happened with some sabres... the details of the story I never quite got, but I know that he was frightened while he was there.

6 August 1969: Hendrix returns from Morocco to New York.
Claire Moriece: He came back and I think that he felt that his life wasn't in his own hands any more, that kind of thing.

7 August 1969: Bob Levine gives Hendrix $200.

8 August 1969: Rehearsal at Jimi's house, Shokan, New York.
Billy Cox: I think Jimi basically wanted to get away from the city and the hangers-on and concentrate, because he knew that the stuff we were doing was really serious. We worked hard at trying to put together new music. I also think they were pushing him to put another album out because the only thing that they had left was *Smash Hits*, so he needed some new, fresh material and the only way to do that was to just buckle down and get it done. Woodstock became the place, since the house was out in the country and we weren't distracted. We had everything we needed and were very productive in that house.

Juma Sultan (percussionist): 'Why don't you come up to the house and jam?' said Jimi. And so I did, and he asked me to play with his group.

Jerry Velez: We would set up a circle in the round and play a lot. Upstairs, across from these

"THERE WERE PEOPLE WHO DID NOT WANT THE BAND OF GYPSYS TO SUCCEED. THERE WAS THE SHOOT-OUT DOWN AT THE FRONT GATE OF THE HOUSE, THE INFILTRATION OF PEOPLE INTO THE HOUSE, DRUGS BEING PUT IN PEOPLE'S FOOD — JUST A LOT OF UNNECESSARY, UNDERHANDED THINGS BEING DONE"

1969

two bedrooms, was a large living room, where we did a lot of acoustic jamming. Then downstairs, we had all of our heavy gear in a big room.

There was a lot of pressure from the management: 'Jimi, don't get rid of the Experience.' But Jimi wanted to stretch out and that's where I got involved. He brought up Larry Lee, Billy Cox and Juma Sultan. Juma looked like an African prince—he was introducing Jimi to a lot of avant-garde music.

Billy Cox: I preached to Larry about getting a different guitar but he preferred to play that (Gibson) 335 which was not compatible with where we were at musically. Consequently it did not blend properly. I would tell him that he needed a Stratocaster, but he just didn't listen.

9 August 1969: Rehearsal at Jimi's house.
Gerry Stickells: Rehearsals, as I remember they called them, consisted of getting stoned and talking about how great it was going to be. The fact that they kept adding people to the line-up proved to me that it wasn't together. They went along because someone else was paying the bills.

Jerry Velez: He was the world's worst horseman. In the morning I'd go out and get the horses and go riding. The first time I brought Jimi out he was scared to death. All of a sudden, the horse knew it and started to take off. Jimi's going, 'Jerry, Jerry, come here!' I was laughing all the time because he looked so ridiculous. There he was in this great outfit he always had on and the saddle just slipped and fell down in the shit and knocked the wind out of him. I was laughing so hard, I couldn't help him. That was the last time I could get him on a horse.

Jerry Morrison: We tried to keep the groupies away from the place but Jimi went into Woodstock and brought a few girls back. That let it out and, after that, they were always infiltrating. One night he called me at my house in Phoenicia Valley and said, 'Come right over'... Jimi had a huge bed and there he was in the middle of it, covered by six or seven girls who were sucking on every orifice and protuberance.

Larry Lee: We rehearsed as we could. We didn't have a band. I mean, we had some cats from the Paul Butterfield band... we were waiting on Mitch, we were waiting on Buddy. Jimi said he was going into town and, some way, we didn't see him no more. So we called the office in New York and they told us Jimi was in France or somewhere. So we spent a lot of time up there doing nothing.

Jimi said we gonna have the Woodstock festival coming up, and that was gonna be our first gig... we had about two weeks to get everything together.

10 August 1969: Jam session at the Tinker Street Cinema, Woodstock. Jimi first uses the Uni-Vibe effects unit.
Artie Traum (local musician): Back then, any schlub musician could live here (Woodstock) and make $50 to $75 a night, playing backup in a club or doing a recording session. It was a true renaissance.

Jim Weider (local musician): Everybody from Janis Joplin to all the great musicians who backed them lived around town and they'd go and jam locally. You never knew who was gonna come in, whether it was Rick Danko or Jimi Hendrix.

Artie Traum: You'd see Joplin, Hendrix, Morrison in the street, playing in the clubs. The combination of old-school Republican farmers and drug-crazed hippies certainly produced an interesting atmosphere.

11 August 1969: Rehearsal at Jimi's house.
Jerry Velez: Mitch was always hard to get. We didn't know whether Mitch was gonna do the gig and you would hear that Buddy was going to come back... we were having problems with Mitch.

Juma Sultan: A lot of people knew that if they got him to yield to certain drugs they would have a certain influence in his life.

Jerry Velez: ...on the coffee table downstairs, there would be every drug imaginable available. Every major drug-dealer would come up to Jimi and say, 'Hey, man, I just got this great stuff from Nepal.' Or 'I just brought this from Marseilles.' These people all kept coming, wanting to get in with him.

Claire Moriece: Everybody did a lot of drugs then, there's no question about that. There wasn't too much heroin around then, but there was enough coke and psychedelics. We took mescalin up at the house, but those days were different—people took drugs to get spiritual and Jimi was really a deeply spiritual and wonderful guy.

Leslie Aday (friend): He was sure that he would go to jail (because of the Toronto drug bust) and be made an example of. I said, 'No, no, you'll have the best lawyers and all your fans behind you.' But he shrugged and replied, 'This is international. There are a lot of people who would like nothing better than to point at me in jail as a bad example.'

Mid-August 1969: Rehearsal at Jimi's house.
Billy Cox: Early one morning at the Woodstock house, I was sitting outside on the patio. Someone had set up the amplifiers the day before, and we had let them stay outside all night.

I don't know why, but I was thinking of Big Ben in England, so I grabbed my bass and started playing, da-doo da-doo, da-doo da-doo. Jimi came to the window in his shorts and started hollering, 'Hey man, keep playing that! Don't stop!' He came running down, grabbed his guitar and said, 'How about this?'

He had the first line almost together. Then I came up with some different notes to act as a close. 'Dolly Dagger' was born in that instant. That was how we complemented each other.
Leslie Aday: They would rehearse these great free-form fusion work-outs but, on stage, they would never have that kind of time to get to the groove. It sounded great in the house but before an audience...

15 August 1969: Eddie Kramer arrives at Woodstock Festival site to begin setting up.
Eddie Kramer: It was a complete fucking disaster. I mean, a clusterfuck of the most immense proportions. Imagine going in at 6am on the Friday morning, expecting to see everything working and the stage wasn't even built yet—they were in the process of building the stage. The PA system was under construction as well. There were soldering irons and wires flying everywhere—it was a zoo. It was supposed to start at 11 and it didn't until one or two in the afternoon. I was amazed that sound actually came out of the bloody microphones.

The console was noisy, switches were bad, microphones would break on stage and cables would get trampled on. It was amazing that we got anything on tape at all.

16 August 1969: The Fat Mattress album is reviewed in *NME*.

17 August 1969: Hendrix arrives at Woodstock in Claire Moriece's Dodge. He books in to a Holiday Inn near the site.
Mitch Mitchell: It was a shambles for us... It took us hours to drive up there in a couple of estate cars (station wagons). There were no facilities for dressing rooms or anything. In the end, we finished up trekking across this muddy field for half-a-mile to this little cottage with no heating, nothing.

Eddie Kramer: Michael Jeffery and Albert Grossman (manager of Bob Dylan, Janis Joplin) arrived (on site) well before Jimi, and one of my most vivid memories of the festival was seeing the two of them, in a heavy rainstorm, trying to push a jeep stuck in deep mud.

Jerry Velez: Woodstock was my first professional gig. At that time, Jimi didn't know that. They were ten hours behind schedule. There was a problem with the helicopter so we went in cars and vans. We were pretty much spinning by that time. We didn't know whether Mitch was gonna do the gig, and you'd hear that Buddy Miles was gonna come. I guess all Mitch wanted was the Experience to continue.

Eddie Kramer: The stage was set up on wheels so that it could turn. The idea was that while one band was playing on half of the stage, the next band could set up on the other half. Then they could just turn it round and continue the show. Well, after the first band, they tried turning it and all the wheels collapsed. They abandoned that brilliant idea.

Elliot Roberts (manager, CSN&Y): I went with Neil (Young) and Jimi Hendrix in this stolen pick-up. Neil hot-wired it, then drove the truck with Hendrix on the hood. Jimi Hendrix was the hood ornament! And we were all tripping on mescaline or something. It was just insane.

Neil Young: Stealing a pick-up truck with Jimi at Woodstock is one of the high points of my life.

He was at one with his instrument. No one else had brought the electric guitar to that level; no one has since. It was like handstands above everyone else, so liquid. Absolutely the best guitar player that ever lived.

Leslie Aday: Hendrix was in a farm shack, but he was the only artist who didn't have to crowd into the tents backstage. I could see that Hendrix was ill, dosed (with LSD), I'm afraid, by drinking the water backstage. He seemed really sick, or really high, and was sweating bullets. I was feeding him vitamin C, fruit, and having him suck on lemon slices. As we sat there, he seemed very nervous and didn't think he could pull it off. He didn't feel the band knew the songs well enough or had enough rehearsal. He was stressed out.

Jerry Morrison: There was an argument between me and Mike Jeffery over whether or not Jimi should play 'The Star-Spangled Banner'. Mike said no—it'd caused a riot in Dallas, and he thought things were bad enough here already without making them worse. I disagreed. Because Jimi was going on as the final act, I thought he had to play the national anthem. It didn't matter. When Mike left the house, I told Jimi to go for it.

Eddie Kramer: No one knew if he would get to go on because the circular stage had broken and band change-overs had been taking too long.

18 August 1969: As the sun rises, Hendrix, under the banner of Gypsys Suns And Rainbows, finally performs at Woodstock.
Jimi Hendrix: They didn't give a damn about the sound equipment. The people way out there that couldn't hear nothing.

Larry Lee: It was more punishment than fun. We were the last act to go on, so we didn't really have to endure a lot of stuff. People wanting to sit on the front row seats at the first show, man, them cats were lying out there asleep in the mud. It looked they were dead and rained on... I felt sorry for a lot of those folks lying out there. I didn't think people should like music that well.

Jerry Velez: At Woodstock, the miking situation for me and Juma was terrible. I had these sensitive pick-ups on the head of my congas and I said, 'Please be careful' and they dropped it. Juma and I were gonna have a confrontation about what they were doing. Jimi tried to cool it all out, but he was caught in the middle and we didn't want to lay it on him.

Billy Cox: I think even Jimi was shook up when they carried our stuff up on the stage and we looked out at that crowd. I looked at Jimi and Jimi looked at me. Mitch looked at us and said, 'God, look at those people.' God bless Blue Nun wine. That's how we made that gig.

Carlos Santana: By the time Jimi Hendrix went on, it was too late. He paid the price for being the big thing and closing the show.

Mitch Mitchell: Playing-wise, you couldn't hear a bloody thing.

Juma Sultan: I walked out there, the sun was coming up and there was a sea of people, all this good energy, they were coming with the sun and the light. It was overpowering. We could have played for hours more.

We did not have a plan. We didn't know what he was gonna play. My position was that, if he came out with something I hadn't played before, if I could add my ingredient with continuity, I would play. If I couldn't, then I wouldn't.

Larry Lee: I was getting electrocuted most of the gig. I had bought a pair of moccasins and it had rained on stage. We had a little rug that didn't extend too far from my amplifier. Every time I wanted to solo, I had to step away from the rug

"I WENT WITH NEIL YOUNG AND JIMI HENDRIX IN THIS STOLEN PICK-UP. NEIL HOT-WIRED IT, THEN DROVE THE TRUCK WITH HENDRIX ON THE HOOD. JIMI HENDRIX WAS THE HOOD ORNAMENT! AND WE WERE ALL TRIPPING ON MESCALINE OR SOMETHING. IT WAS JUST INSANE"

"I WENT WITH NEIL YOUNG AND JIMI HENDRIX IN THIS STOLEN PICK-UP. NEIL HOT-WIRED IT, THEN DROVE THE TRUCK WITH HENDRIX ON THE HOOD. JIMI HENDRIX WAS THE HOOD ORNAMENT! AND WE WERE ALL TRIPPING ON MESCALINE OR SOMETHING. IT WAS JUST INSANE"

to keep the feedback off. So on a lot of my solos there's some feedback, and when it ain't feeding back, I was actually getting electrocuted.

Eddie Kramer: I was in the back of a trailer with two eight-track machines, of which one was in an orange crate. Communication between the stage and the truck might as well have been on a piece of wire. It was really funny. I remember during a break, standing on stage next to Bill Graham and we were looking out on a sea of people, a half-million or so, and he looked at me and said, 'You know, if there's a riot, we'd be dead.' I said, 'Thanks a lot. I think I'll go back to my truck.'

Chip Monck (lighting director): Hendrix's 'Star Spangled Banner' was exquisite. I was always amazed at that group because there were so few of them, which was always a great pleasure from a lighting point of view.

Tom Law (Woodstock staff): When he did the national anthem, that was a quintessential piece of art because he hooked us up with Vietnam, with the devastation and the sin and the brutality and the insanity of that end of the world. So the festival became a symbol of intelligence and humanity, co-operation and love and affection.

Jimi Hendrix: When it ('Star Spangled Banner') was written, it was played in a very beautiful state, you know? Nice and inspiring, you know? Your heart throbs and you say 'Great, I'm American' but nowadays, we play it the way the air is in America today. The air is slightly static, isn't it? You know what I mean?

Eddie Kramer: The whole thing was a mess but it was an amazing event. I was up for three days and nights and the only thing that kept us going was the vitamin B-12 shots in the bum. It was pretty wild. We slept on the floor and just carried on.

Jimi Hendrix: Woodstock was groovy and all that, but anybody can get a field and put a lot of kids in there and put band after band on. I don't particularly like the idea of groups after groups. It all starts merging together.

Bob Levine: The idea was to bring Hendrix down (to appear on *The Dick Cavett Show)* as soon as Woodstock finished, so that viewers could get a first-hand description of the festival. But Jimi went missing...

Leslie Aday: We left by helicopter. Jimi was tired, cold and hungry. We had adjoining rooms at the hotel and, as soon as we'd checked in, I volunteered to find some food. He was unhappy with his performance and just wanted to get away where no one could find him. The hotel was filled with people who had come over from the festival and, when I came back, I heard a great deal of commotion in his room and peeked through the door. There were a number of people getting high who were not there in Jimi's best interests.

Larry Lee: It (LSD) was in some fruit punch and I said, 'Let's have a jam.' Jimi picked up a bass and I picked up a guitar and we started to play some of the old numbers we used to play in Nashville and we were laughing. He stopped laughing but I couldn't... I laughed for nine-and-a-half hours.

Leslie Aday: After they left, I went back to check on him,and he had passed out on the bed with a cigarette going. It had burned a large hole through his sheet before going out. He was fortunate he hadn't been killed.

Bob Levine: Gerry Stickells and I had no way of reaching him. Cavett's show was live in those days, and he kept saying, 'Hendrix should be here anytime now...' After an hour-and-a-half Hendrix didn't show and, though we vowed to make it up to him, Cavett never forgave us.

Autumn 1969: Mike Jeffery encounters financial problems.
Jim Marron: Jeffery had burned a lot of bridges in London. He didn't pay anyone. He owed one 'investor' $20,000 and, in an effort to retrieve the sum, they sent a guy over to kill him if he didn't pay... Jeffery gave the guy $20,000 he had borrowed and sent him back to England.

21 August 1969: Rehearsal at Jimi's house.
Billy Cox: The telephone never stopped ringing. It was always, 'Hurry up and do this. Get this thing done, get that thing going.' They never let him have any peace.

22 August 1969: Rehearsal at Jimi's house.
Leslie Aday (friend): Jimi used to drive through

Hendrix at Woodstock Festival: a defining moment for hippy culture and, against the odds, he rose to the occasion

town in his Corvette. He'd have the top down and be dressed in all of his glory. Nobody in Woodstock had a red Corvette. These people were into growing organic vegetables and making their own clothes.

23 August 1969: Rehearsal at Jimi's house.
Claire Moriece: Jimi had a girl with him who was from Texas. I recall her father was wealthy, and she phoned home bragging that she was with a big rock star and he sent the cops! I had to pretend Jimi wasn't home.

There were some real bona-fide nut jobs. I mean, the dregs of the earth came to seek him out. At the same time, Jimi would pick up hitch-hikers in his flashy silver Corvette car. At one time, he picked up a group of people and then went to Woodstock and bought a whole huge bag of art supplies. We started a fire and, after dinner, everyone sat round and drew. He did a lot of drawings back then.

24 August 1969: Rehearsal at Jimi's house.
Jerry Velez: We would drive around, but Jimi had a car and no license. He was one of the world's worst drivers. He had a big trunk filled with records from black comedians, and everything was X-rated—every other word was fuck. Although Jimi wasn't really a member of the black community, he desperately wanted to get a little bit more involvement.

25 August 1969: Rehearsal at Jimi's house.
Michael Hecht (accountant): I paid the bills for the house they trashed up there. They had gouged out the floor moving their equipment about and ruined artwork by painting on it.

26 August 1969: In a black limousine, Mike Jeffery pays a visit to Jimi to convince him to play a gig at the gangster-controlled Salvation Club.
Juma Sultan: You could see that the two men that were flanking Mike Jeffery, plus the driver, were armed. It was visible. They were carrying guns.

They went upstairs with Jimi, and then the driver comes up and put a target up about 25 yards away, near a tree, pulls out his .38 and POW! POW!—bullseyes every time—while the conversation with Jimi is going on.

It was obvious that it was meant to send a message. 'Milk the cow until it dies,' would be my phrase.

Billy Cox: When you get down to people fighting with guns out in front of the house, there is something seriously wrong. All I knew was that I was going to do the Woodstock gig, help out my buddy, and carry my ass back to Nashville. That was my focus.

27 August 1969: Hendrix books into the Hotel Navarro, New York.

28 August 1969: Working on 'Message To Love' (aka 'Message To The Universe'), 'Easy Blues', 'Izabella' and 'Beginning' at Hit Factory.
Billy Cox: Jimi had the opening guitar riff (of 'Message To The Universe') on a little tape he had made at home. When he played it to me, I suggested some changes to the riff he was playing, and that made one complete pattern. The next pattern was repeated twice before the melody came back to the top. That's all it was.

Jerry Velez: You couldn't slow Jimi down when he got going. Once I brought half-a-dozen girls, champagne, food, crashed into the studio. Jimi said, 'Hey man, you can't do this. You're interrupting the session.' That was my first slap-down. Jimi knew what he wanted. We stayed away from the control room but Jimi was involved in every aspect. He had his sound ideas, he had mixing ideas, he had concepts.

29 August 1969: Work on 'Message To Love', 'Izabella' and 'Machine Gun' at Hit Factory.
Mike McCready (Pearl Jam): There's a feeling you get, sometimes, playing leads. It's like you're out of your mind, you're in a state of Nirvana. It sounds silly, but it's spiritual. I get that when I hear 'Machine Gun'—he's playing that one fucking note and it brings you to tears.

30 August 1969: Working on 'Stepping Stone' (aka 'Sky Blues Today'/'I'm A Man' and 'Mastermind' at Hit Factory.

Autumn 1969

3 September 1969: Press conference for the upcoming United Block Association Benefit at Frank's Restaurant, Harlem.
Jimi Hendrix: This whole thing is done in the benefit of the UBA. And we hope to do some more gigs, for it, you know, some more benefits. Matter of fact we're trying to stress also that music should be done outside in a festival type of way. Just like they do it anywhere else. And like, if they can, uh, have more gigs like this in Harlem where you play outside, for instance, three days, and the fourth day you play half the day outside, for instance, and maybe the other time in the Apollo, four shows or whatever, you know?

'Cause a lot of kids in the ghetto, or whatever you want to call it, you know, don't have the money to travel across country, to see these different festivals, what they call festivals. I mean, $7 is a lot of money. So, ah, I think, more groups that are supposed to be considered heavy groups should contribute more to this cause.

4 September 1969: Hendrix authorizes a personal loan of $1,500 to Larry Lee; later he works on 'Mastermind' at Hit Factory.

5 September 1969: UBA benefit gig, Harlem; recording 'Burning Desire' at Hit Factory.
Eddie O'Jay (DJ, WWRL Radio): Jimi and his group arrived in a van with their instruments. The makeshift stage had been placed on the street. The kids were all gathered around waiting for the entertainment to start.

Gerry Stickells: When we arrived, there was pressure from the Black Panthers. All of the white guys had to hide in a burned-out, defunct laundry until it was time to go on. We had to put the gear up quickly because people were throwing stuff and spitting on us.

Jimi Hendrix: Sometimes when I come up here, people say, 'He plays white rock, for white people. What's he doin' here?' Well, I want to show them that music is universal—there is no white rock or black rock.

Arthur Allen: Jimi started playing, but he came out with too much noise. He wasn't projecting like he should have. Nobody knew him. 'Get off, so we can hear Big Maybelle.' 'Who is this Jimi Hendrix?' 'Jimmy who?' 'Jimmy Witherspoon?'. He started making some kind of distortion out of his guitar, feeling the public, like throwing something at them. And the audience replied with an egg, someone threw an egg out of a window and it really freaked him out. He started playing like he'd never played before and blew everyone's mind, had everyone on their toes. And that was his first communication with black people and they dug him.

6 September 1969: Working on 'Lover Man', 'Valleys Of Neptune', 'Lord I Sing The Blues' and 'Stepping Stone' at Hit Factory.

8 September 1969: Jimi is interviewed and plays 'Izabella' and 'Machine Gun' on *The Dick Cavett Show,* ABC TV, New York.
Juma Sultan: They were trying to extricate me at that time. Jimi said, 'Show up, and I'll pay you for the gig.' So I show up for *The Dick Cavett Show* and they left my drums at the house. So I went round the corner and got a conga from a friend.

Larry Lee: They didn't let me play on *The Dick Cavett Show* 'cause they wanted to keep the image steady. Juma sneaked down and played… he wasn't supposed to play. It was supposed to be Mitch, Jimi and Billy, so that our group wouldn't be publicized. After seeing that go on, I told Jimi as a friend, 'It might do you more good if I went home. This is turning into a disaster.'

Steve Stevens (guitarist for Billy Idol): I remember seeing him on *The Dick Cavett Show* when I was a kid. He didn't actually play. They played a bit of footage, and he came out and spoke. Cavett brought up the fact that Hendrix was in the 101st Airborne, and brought up 'The Star Spangled Banner', because people were up in arms about it. Hendrix just tried to clarify that he thought it was a real compliment the way he did it, not derogatory.

9 September 1969: At a meeting with Henry Steingarten and Steve Weiss, Hendrix instructs them to cancel an upcoming ten-date tour; later that night, he jams with Mountain at Ungano's in New York.
Ron Terry: There was no real purpose for dates at that point, except that Jeffery was over-extended and needed money. A lot of weird shit was going down. Jeffery was trying to get deposits sent to him personally instead of to Hecht or Weiss.That worsened the paranoia between him and Hendrix.

Bob Levine: Michael's biggest problem with Jimi was that he couldn't communicate with him. He tried drugs, mysticism, intimidation and CIA-MI5 tactics, but he was unable to do it.

Leslie West (Mountain): We jammed together over at Ungano's on 71st Street. He came in there late one night and I said hello to him, and I asked him if he wanted to play and he said yeah, but he didn't have any equipment. So we went in his limo down to our loft on 36th Street and picked up some equipment. I remember my road manager was sleeping. There we were, me and Jimi Hendrix, standing right over him when I woke him up from a deep sleep. He nearly shit. We put some amps into the limo and went back to the club and jammed.

Bud Prager (partner of Mountain's bass player and producer Felix Pappalardi): One night in Greenwich Village I sat with Eric Clapton who said, 'As long as Cream exists, Felix Pappalardi will be the producer.' When Eric left, I sat with Jimi Hendrix who said, 'I wish Felix would produce one of my albums.' I said, 'Why? You have two albums in the Top 10. How much better can it get?' He said, 'Felix knows things I don't. He could help me make better records.' At the time I really didn't understand…'

10 September 1969: Hendrix plays at The Salvation Club, New York. The show is allegedly organized by Mike Jeffery, under pressure from the gangster connections of the club's cocaine-dealing owner Bobby Woods.
Roland Robinson (former bassist, Buddy Miles Express): Jimi called me to ask if I had received my ticket. I said, 'What?' He told me to come on up and try things with the band. When I got there, it was really screwed up, because I had quit the Express on bad terms. Billy Cox was there and he was really quiet. So I'm there feeling weird, and it occurred to me that Jimi hadn't told these guys that they weren't in the band any more. We had two bands there. You had two bass players, two drummers, and a lot of real hostility in the air.

Leslie West of Mountain, who jammed with Hendrix on several occasions. Jimi loved their big song 'Mississippi Queen'

Richie Rivera (barman): There were a couple of cops at the top of the stairs leading down into the club, and Bobby was at the door grabbing the money as people came in and stashing it away. He kept coming to the bar and taking receipts.

Roland Robinson: Jimi's management was there, freaking out over all the people he was trying. Jimi started yelling, 'Just leave me the fuck alone! Let me play with the people I want to play with and I'll make you all the goddam money you want.'

We then got into this one jam, and Billy Cox was sitting in front of me with his arms folded, and Buddy was playing half-assed and scowling at me from behind the drums. Afterwards, Buddy started to get pissed off, and he told Jimi that if I was in the band, I'd be trying to take it over. So that set me off, and I'm shouting at Buddy that I'm going to kill him. It all got really funky, and I just said, 'Forget it.' It just wasn't going to fly.

Velvert Turner (friend): Jimi was wiped out. He grabbed me at The Salvation and whispered, 'Don't you ever fuck up your life like I have.' He seemed tortured.

Bob Levine: He spent the night with Bobby Woods. He didn't really know who he was. To Jimi he was just a nice guy who sold cocaine.
Jim Marron: Hendrix was very scattered. Drugs had become the vehicle to escape his problems. He was using marijuana, hashish, cocaine—anything he could get his hands on, three to five times a week. Drugs were fast becoming a way of life.

Bob Levine: The next night, Woods was found murdered gangland-style. The 'boys' knew Hendrix had spent the night with Woods and wanted to know what he had heard from him. Hendrix hadn't heard anything about their business, but they had to make sure.

Mid-September 1969: Hendrix is kidnapped.
Trixie Sullivan: The music business in those days was like the Wild West. What it was, the 'junior' Mafia was always trying to move into the music business. The older Mafia wasn't really interested. And Jimi was kidnapped by some guys that were holding him for ransom to get his contract.

Jimi Hendrix: Before I realized what had happened, I found myself forcibly abducted by four men. I was blindfolded and gagged and shoved rudely into the back of a car. I couldn't understand what the fuck was going on as I lay there sweating with someone's knee in my back.

I was taken to some deserted building and made to believe that they really intended to hurt me. They never did tell me why they abducted me. The whole thing seemed very mysterious because, after a while, I realized that if they really had intended to hurt me, they would have already done it by this time.

Jerry Morrison: It was serious. When Jimi called, he told Bob (Levine) that he was being held by guys who wanted Jimi's management contract. Jimi said that if Mike didn't turn it over, the guys were going to kill him.

Bob Levine: It wasn't a hostile kidnapping. It was a 'house arrest'. Jimi was missing and we couldn't find him. Fortunately, this happened during a lull, when we didn't have any dates scheduled. The 'boys' sent word down that he was being treated comfortably and would be released in a couple of days.

Jim Marron: Jeffery was incensed that someone would actually steal his artist and question his power. It was a show of force against him. Though the entire affair was really about Bobby Woods and cocaine, Jeffery was determined to back them down rather than accept any of their terms.

Trixie Sullivan: Mike had his contacts in the music business, which could be quite heavy too. Mike found, or was given an introduction to, people who would go with him to sort it out.

Jim Marron: He'd developed his own connections, and his were much more powerful than theirs. It cost Jeffery a favour but, once his brutes arrived, the people who had been keeping Jimi under house arrest put their guns away and left.

Trixie Sullivan: Mike was teamed up with these guys in limousines, they were taken to where Jimi was being held. When they realized who Mike was with, they let him go.

Jimi Hendrix: The whole thing seemed even more mysterious when I was rescued by three men supposedly sent by the management. They really effected a story-book rescue.

Claire Moriece: He told me about how he was kidnapped in some place in New York and then his management came and mysteriously found him, and it made him very paranoid.

Monika Danneman: What Jimi told me was that Mike Jeffery, his manager, told him if they hadn't rescued him, he would be dead and he should be grateful, but Jimi started to think, and he thought the whole thing was strange, how they just came in and freed him. He figured out that the whole thing was a set-up by his management.

Stefan Bright: Hendrix was so totally fucked up by that time that I think it put a damper on his creativity. He seemed consumed by insecurity and paranoia, not knowing what Jeffery was doing for him or to him.

Bob Levine: Jeffery had backed them down, but Jimi saw right through that. Though Jeffery had flexed his muscles and proved his own power, he had no control over Hendrix.

Kathy Eberth: By this time, if Jeffery wanted something from Hendrix he would come to me and say, 'See if he will do this.' ... Jimi and I used to laugh about it.
Jim Marron: She was like the mouthpiece between Jeffery and Hendrix during that time. Jeffery could not get a straight answer out of Hendrix but was still desperate to know what he was thinking.

15 September 1969: 'Stone Free' is released as single in US; Hendrix records 'Stepping Stone' at Record Plant.

Mid-September 1969: Larry Lee quits the band.
Billy Cox: Larry just said, 'I think I'm probably in the way', and took it upon himself to leave on good terms. There was just too much bullshit around him to handle. He just decided that he had had enough.

16 September 1969: Hendrix buys equipment at Manny's.
Henry Goldrich: Jimi used to buy three or four guitars every other week, but he lost them or gave them away. I'd see kids come in the store with guitars I'd sold Jimi the week before. If he liked a kid, he gave him his guitar, brand new.

17 September 1969: June Harris of *NME* interviews Mitch Mitchell in New York.

19 September 1969: Jam with Juma Sultan and Mike Euphron at Jimi's house.
Billy Cox: It wasn't quite hitting it on the nose. When you get down to business, that group (Gypsys Suns & Rainbows) was disbanded as I don't think Jimi had 100 per cent control of that anyway... There was a lot of things going on that I just wasn't happy with and I left.

20 September 1969: *Rolling Stone* reporter Sheila Weller drives up to Hendrix's house at Shokan, near Woodstock.
Jimi Hendrix (to Sheila Weller):

> I don't want to be a clown any more. I don't want to be a rock'n'roll star.

21 September 1969: Hendrix, Sheila Weller and Juma Sultan go for an early morning drive.
Sheila Weller (in Rolling Stone*):*

> We crowd into Jimi's metal-flecked silver Stingray for a sunrise drive to the waterfalls. The talk is of puppies, daybreak, other innocentia... back at the house, he pads around, emptying ashtrays, putting things in order... it's 7am and he has to be at the recording studio in Manhattan at four in the afternoon. Everyone's exhausted.

22 September 1969: At Record Plant.
Gerry Stickells: He truly was frustrated, and he was going through a period where he felt he couldn't write anything. Everything sounded the same as before. He was bored and directionless.

Kathy Eberth: He was hearing music in his head and seeing it in colors, but he just couldn't reproduce the notes. One night, after he kept playing the same song over and over, I watched him throw one of his favorite guitars across the room.

23 September 1969: Jerry Velez quits the group; Hendrix asks Billy Cox to rejoin. Jimi works on 'Drinking Wine', 'Message To Love' and 'Beginnings' at Record Plant.

Jerry Velez: There was definitely friction but I saw more of that from management and road guys. They would take our instruments and throw them around. The vibe was like 'What's Jimi doing with all these niggers?' They didn't want any blacks or Puerto Ricans, they wanted us out. There was a lot of that hostility.

Billy Cox: I received a telephone call from Jimi and Michael Jeffery to come back. So I made some demands and they adhered to those demands and I came back.

When I agreed to come back, Jimi sat me down in his apartment and explained what was going on. My thought was just to give them (PPX and Capitol) something. Over the next couple of days, he came up with the concept that we would try something outside of The Experience. I asked whether he had talked to Mitch, but he only mumbled something I couldn't hear and wouldn't go any further with it. Buddy Miles called me, and I told him of the situation. He said, 'Well, I'll get help. Let's get him out and jam.'

24 September 1969: Working on 'Stepping Stone' and 'Power Of Soul' (aka 'Jimi's Tune' at Record Plant.
Alan Douglas: I was lying in my bedroom, because I was whipped. There was a dinner thing going on in the front room and the gang was there—Jimi, Devon, Stella, Colette, Pete Cameron and some other friends. I was just about to fall asleep when Hendrix came in and sat on the edge of the bed. He asked if I wanted to come down to the studio tonight. I was exhausted and said, 'Well, not really,' but he wasn't about to let me go to sleep. It was close to midnight when we left for the Record Plant. Everyone else showed up about two hours later. I never saw such disorganisation in all my life. No one, in either the control room or the studio, was taking care of business for him. The engineer just kept putting rolls of tape on the machine and pressing the record button. I was sitting there thinking, What the fuck is this? I had no idea what was going on. I had never recorded with him in a studio before and had no idea what was in his head.

Billy Cox and Buddy Miles were there and the three of them jammed all night long. I sat there for four or five hours until I went out and told him I was beat and had to go. On the way home, I wondered why he had asked me to come.

25 September 1969: Frustrated by the situation, Mitch Mitchell returns to the UK; Jimi works on 'Stepping Stone' and 'Room Full Of Mirrors' and various jams at Record Plant.
Alan Douglas: The next day, he came over for dinner and I asked him to explain what he wanted me to do. He said, 'Somebody has got to organize things for me.' I was very, very busy with my own projects and I needed to know how much time he needed from me—I wasn't getting paid—but he said, 'Just come down.'

So I went back the next night and saw pretty much the same thing. It took me a while, but I started figuring out what Hendrix was doing. He was jamming, but he was trying to create a rhythm pattern for Miles and Cox to follow. Once those two were in the groove, Hendrix would break into a tune. I said, OK, so this is how you get tracks out of the guy.

I was doing this for a friend, nobody was paying me at all. I felt that the way I could help was to make sure there was efficiency in the control room and that they were not wasting tape.

30 September 1969: Record Plant, New York, working on 'Live And Let Live'.
Juma Sultan: Jimi wanted to work with Alan but they had artistic clashes. I was in the studio when Alan called Miles and asked him to come in. But Jimi wanted to do it his way, and it wasn't about Alan's way, and that's where the conflict came in.

"HE WAS HEARING MUSIC IN HIS HEAD AND SEEING IT IN COLORS, BUT HE JUST COULDN'T REPRODUCE THE NOTES. ONE NIGHT, AFTER HE KEPT PLAYING THE SAME SONG OVER AND OVER, I WATCHED HIM THROW ONE OF HIS FAVORITE GUITARS ACROSS THE ROOM"

Jeffery hated Douglas, because Jeffery knew he and Alan were both from the same mould.

Alan Douglas: I became a kind of consultant to Jimi on a business basis. Mike's jealousy with me was on that basis. It was constantly, 'There's not enough to deal with what you want' which was not really true, but he fell for it always.

Late September 1969: Billy Cox quits.
Billy Cox: After Woodstock, I hung around as long as I could, but there was just too much bullshit going down all around him.

October 1969:
Alan Douglas: When Jeffery first called me and told me he was Jimi's manager, I said, 'Oh, really?' I just loved the guy's records. You've got to understand, my business was cooking. We had books and records coming out and I had just started the film *El Topo*. Jimi was just a friend in a confused state who seemed lost and had nobody to help him. I was just saying, 'I'll meet you down at the Record Plant at midnight.'

Never thinking about money. It was Hendrix who was telling people to talk to me instead of Jeffery. I know that really pissed Jeffery off, but Hendrix was doing this simply out of frustration.

Gerry Stickells: Douglas was obviously trying to hoist the management away as well as trying to be his producer. In my opinion, for him to say he was his producer or whatever is essentially not true.

3 October 1969: *Life* magazine runs a feature on Hendrix.

5 October 1969: Jimi's son, James Henrik Daniel Sundquist, is born in Stockholm to Jimi's former girlfriend Eva Sundquist.
Eva Sundquist: I wrote his (Jimi's) name on a piece of paper and put it in an envelope, which only was permitted to be opened in case something happened to me. I didn't want Jimi to have the trouble a fatherhood would bring. Welfare officers… demanded finally that I should tell them who the father was. Otherwise I would not get any advance maintenance payment.

James Henrik Daniel Sundquist: My mother talked about it a lot, almost all the time. She showed me records, played tapes, showed me pictures, everything. I started to get tired of my father at an early age, because I heard about him all the time. She kept going on about him… In the end, instead of talking it over with her, I turned inwards, into myself. I said, 'Don't tell me any more, I don't want to know about my father.'

9 October 1969: Gerry Stickells gives $2,300 in cash to Hendrix.

17 October 1969: New roadie Eugene McFadden joins Hendrix crew; recording at Record Plant.

Mid-October 1969: The Band Of Gypsys is formed.
Noel Redding: The Band Of Gypsys was done for legal reasons. There was a guy called Ed Chalpin from PPX Enterprises in New York who had signed up Hendrix for a dollar or something. He sued us and, basically, he started to get royalty points off the albums. Annoying, considering that I never got a cent. To get out of it, Hendrix had to cut an album for Capitol Records for the guy.

Gerry Stickells: He drifted into it. He felt a little bit pressured about it as well, as if it was something he should be doing. It was the same thing with Douglas and Stefan Bright. They were a joke, not even in the same league as Hendrix.

Buddy Miles: Douglas was only involved with the Band Of Gypsys because Hendrix was feuding with Jeffery. It was a very strange time. Hendrix couldn't communicate with Jeffery so he made Douglas his 'spokesman'. The Band Of Gypsys were put together in his office.

Arthur Allen: Jeffery did not like the idea of the Band Of Gypsys coming together and he expressed that. Jimi was deeply offended that Jeffery would interfere with a creative decision. That's when he first expressed a serious desire to break away from him.

20 October 1969: Recording at Record Plant with Stephen Stills, John Sebastian and Buddy Miles. This is the first session to feature Alan Douglas as producer.
Stefan Bright (engineer, Douglas Records): We had set up a jam session at the Record Plant with Buddy Miles, Duane Hitchings (Miles' keyboard player), John Sebastian and Stephen Stills.

When we arrived at the studio, Hendrix was there. He wanted to know who was coming to the session.

When he heard that Steve Stills was expected, he didn't want to play lead guitar. We thought that was strange, but he did volunteer to play bass. There wasn't a left-handed bass in the studio, only a right-handed model, so he just turned it upside-down and played some of the most fantastic bass guitar I've ever heard.

Stills was the last musician to arrive and, when he did, he burst into the studio saying, '(Joni Mitchell) just wrote this song and I'd like to try and jam on it.' It was Woodstock... Stills led the guys through a 25-minute jam based on that song.

Mid-October 1969: Band Of Gypsys rehearse at Juggy Sound, New York, with Stefan Bright and Alan Douglas co-producing.
Billy Cox: We were just goofing around during those sessions at Juggy. It was a lousy deal with a lot of bad vibes around. There was a spiritual side to the music we were creating, and the atmosphere at Juggy didn't allow Jimi to create. He sensed it, and nothing we did there ever worked out.

Bright and Douglas knew that I didn't think they were necessary. I wasn't in their corner because I didn't think they were on Jimi's level. They weren't needed for the production of the music. Jimi was well equipped to do that.
Bright would do things like tell Jimi and Buddy that they didn't need me, but Jimi was determined to have me play with him.

Late October 1969

Bob Levine: Douglas became the 'enemy' because Jeffery made him so. He was essentially harmless, but Douglas did have a relationship with Jimi, and that bothered him.

Jim Marron: Douglas was labelled by Jeffery as the enemy... to me he seemed like a bearded Village hippy who got high with Hendrix. Jeffery described him as this guy who fed off dead artists. He told me about the Lenny Bruce thing (a posthumous album by the comedian which Douglas had produced) and that his speciality was resurrecting dead artists and making money off new projects.

Jeffery had just put down a Mafia takeover of Hendrix a couple months earlier and now was paranoid that Douglas was trying to steal his artist.

November 1969: Hendrix moves to 59 West 12th Street, New York.
Alan Douglas: He used to hide in my house or at my office so that Jeffery couldn't find him. I put aside a soundproof rehearsal room for him on the first floor so he could practice because everyone in his apartment building was screaming at him for playing too loud.

Alvenia Bridges (friend): He'd call in the middle of the night. He'd come over to sleep. There were too many people at his apartment. We'd go to Colony Records or go for a ride in a carriage in Central Park. He called one night when I was living on the West Side and he came over and he slept for 18 hours straight.

Alan Douglas: I had no authority to make any deals for him but Jimi was telling people to come to me. I remember Bill Graham coming to my office to talk about two Fillmore East contracts. I said, 'I'm not his agent or manager. What do you want to talk to me for?' I was even getting calls from Mo Ostin, asking how Jimi's next record was coming and when would it be finished.

November 1969: Kathy Etchingham marries Ray Mayer, an employee of Eric Clapton's.
Kathy Etchingham: I really feel guilty that I had deceived Jimi. He wasn't planning on anything like that. He was devastated. I allowed myself more freedom than he was expecting.

November 1969: At the Record Plant, Hendrix provides musical backing for proto-rap pioneers The Last Poets.
Alan Douglas: Jalal from The Last Poets was in my office just hanging out. We walked down to the Record Plant and Buddy Miles was there waiting for Hendrix. I said to Jalal, 'Why don't you do one of your poems for Buddy?'

During the middle of it, Jimi arrived and got all excited about what was happening. When they finished, I went out into the studio and told Jalal to do 'Doriella Du Fontaine'... We did one take, 13 minutes straight. When it was over, everybody was amazed that it came off non-stop. Jimi was on guitar and Buddy on drums. We then overdubbed Jimi playing bass and Buddy on the organ.

Buddy Miles: I wasn't no great organist or nothing but I was the only thing Alan could get his hands on.

2 November 1969: Work starts on the Band Of Gypsys album at Record Plant, with Alan Douglas as producer.
Alan Douglas: I didn't even know where Hendrix was going. He was talking about an album, but I couldn't see it anywhere. I was just going to do some songs with him... Hendrix himself didn't know where he was going.

Stefan Bright: There was a real adjustment period that went on with that band because, when they first started, they weren't that good. Hendrix was looking for something that I don't think he found. There was just too much pressure on him to make the next big step forward.

3 November 1969: Gerry Stickells gives Hendrix $3,500 in cash.

6 November 1969: When Noel Redding marries Susan Fowsby in Kent, Mitch Mitchell attends the wedding.

7 November 1969: At Manny's music store, Hendrix spends $1,756.30 on an Epiphone Casino guitar, an Echoplex and Ernie Ball strings; works on 'Izabella', 'Ezy Rider', 'Shame Shame Shame' and 'Room Full Of Mirrors' at Record Plant.
Tom Erdelyi (second engineer): Douglas and Bright just sort of came in and took over. They were running the show. I was surprised, because I was a fan of The Jimi Hendrix Experience, and no one seemed to understand what Jimi was trying to accomplish. Jimi was such a perfectionist. It seemed as if he was just taking his time, because no tracks were being completed. We just thought that Douglas was being patient.

Stefan Bright: We specifically brought in Tony Bongiovi to engineer 'Izabella'. Jimi would say things about Tony like, 'What the fuck is this kid doing in the studio?' because Tony, at that time, looked very young.

Tony Bongiovi: 'Izabella' was the last full session I did with Hendrix. We recorded that song from start to finish, with (bassist) Billy Rich and Buddy Miles backing him. We even mixed the song at the end of the session.

Stefan Bright: Tony gave Jimi's sound a groove which, we felt, hadn't been done before. With 'Izabella', the sound of the bass and drums was so funky. Tony had worked at Motown, and he went for that element in his sound.

Arthur Allen: Mountain were recording in Studio B. Leslie West was recording 'Mississippi Queen' and Hendrix was so knocked out by the riff that he invited him over for a jam.

Leslie West: Felix (Pappalardi) finished mixing my record and I went out in the hallway and got Jimi to come in and listen. So he listened to 'Never In My Life' and he was really taken with it. It made me feel real good that Hendrix was sittin' in the control room listening to my stuff.

10 November 1969: Hendrix fails to turn up for a meeting with Henry Steingarten to discuss the upcoming Toronto case, the PPX matter, damage to the Shokan house and other matters. Works on 'Lonely Avenue' at Record Plant.
Buddy Miles: Jimi was not happy. He felt powerless. He couldn't do what he wanted to do. So he missed meetings, he missed gigs. He could be a real bastard. Sometimes, when he didn't want to rehearse, one of the things he'd do was to get real stoned, really high; didn't want to talk to anyone. He used the drugs to put a barrier, partly.

11 November 1969: Henry Steingarten writes to Hendrix about various worrying legal matters, including the recent cancellation of various live dates.

> Your failure to keep the Boston date, as well as the dates agreed to by you on which Concerts West began work, is costing you approximately $25,000 in re-imbursement of expenses. This was a very unwise move on your part, and one for which you alone are responsible.

12 November 1969: Working on 'Look Over Yonder' at Record Plant.
Billy Cox: At the time, I was there, and I think Mitch was in England. He was asked to do it, but I think he wanted to stay in England. Buddy was easily

available. So me, Buddy and Jimi rehearsed for a couple of weeks and that was The Band Of Gypsys. Mitch was cool. He didn't even talk about the Band Of Gypsys. He just went about his business... There was a real respect between Mitch and Jimi. We just got down to playing.

14 November 1969: 'Fire' is released as a single in the UK; in New York work proceeds on 'Power Of Soul' 'Burning Desire', 'Cherokee Mist', 'Stepping Stone' 'Further On Up The Road', 'Villanova Junction' 'Ezy Rider' 'South Saturn Delta', 'Izabella' and other tracks.
Chas Chandler: It was around this time that I found myself in New York. I attempted to contact Jimi about his transition from the Experience into the Band Of Gypsys with Buddy Miles. He had been virtually a recluse in his New York flat for almost a year, and only ventured out in the early hours of the morning to do recording.

17 November 1969: Work on 'Room Full Of Mirrors', 'Lonely Avenue' and 'Look Over Yonder' at Record Plant.
Carlos Santana: This was a real shocker to me. He said, 'OK, roll it', and started recording and it was incredible. But, within 15 or 20 seconds into the song, he just went out. All of a sudden, the music that was coming out of the speakers was way beyond the song, like he was freaking out, having a gigantic battle in the sky with somebody. It just didn't make sense with the song any more, so the roadies looked at each other, the producer looked at him and they said, 'Go get him.' I'm not making this up. They separated him from the amplifier and the guitar and it was like he was having an epileptic attack. I said, 'Do I have to go through these changes just to play my guitar? I'm just a kid.' When they separated him, his eyes were red... he was gone.

To me, it was a combination of the lifestyle—staying up all night, chicks, too much drugs, all kinds of stuff. It was a combination of all the intensities he felt, along with a lack of discipline.

20 November 1969: Working on 'Burning Desire', 'Hear My Train A-Comin'', 'Lover Man', 'New Tune' and 'Them Changes' at Record Plant.
Billy Cox: That ('Hear My Tain A Comin") was a song Jimi had done with the original Experience. It was a simple blues song in the key of B, but he felt comfortable doing it because it was Jimi's kind of blues. I think the lyrics he had for the song, about coming back to buy the town and put it all in his shoe, was his way of talking back to the establishment. That was Jimi's way of singing the blues. People weren't going to be able to push him out of the way, because he was going to get rich and buy the town out from under them.

21 November 1969: Working on 'Izabella', 'Machine Gun', 'Burning Desire' and 'Power Of Soul' (aka 'Paper Aeroplanes'/'With The Power').
Billy Cox: We decided that we couldn't do any songs that had already been released. We wanted to give them something different. So we went at the project in a joyous, creative posture and ultimately developed the repertoire of the Band Of Gypsys.

Alan Douglas: We finished 'Room Full Of Mirrors' in the studio. Yes, there were some flaws, but those could have been fixed easily later on. 'Izabella' finally sounded as if Hendrix was off into a new place. Those tracks were working for me and were saying something different than what he had done before. Both the songs and concepts were good.

23 November 1969: Hendrix gets $2,500 cash from Gerry Stickells.

27 November 1969: On his 27th birthday, Hendrix attends a Rolling Stones gig at Madison Square Garden, New York. Later, there is a party at producer Monte Kay's apartment, attended by the Rolling Stones.
Stanley Booth (journalist): Mick Taylor and I sat on a bench (in the Stones dressing room) with Hendrix, who seemed subdued but pleasant. I told him about seeing Little Richard and he said, smiling as if it cheered him up to think about it, that once when he was with Richard, he and the bass player bought ruffled shirts to wear onstage, and Richard made them change.

Mick Taylor handed his guitar to Hendrix and asked him to play. 'Oh I can't,' he said. 'I have to string it different.' Hendrix was left-handed but he went ahead and played the guitar upside down, a wizard he was.

End November 1969: Michael Jeffery refuses to pay for the Alan Douglas sessions at Record

Plant, and forwards the bill to Warner Brothers.
Bob Levine: Michael Hecht called and told me he was having trouble with Warner Brothers over a recent bill we had submitted. They wanted to know what exactly 'Room Full Of Mirrors' was.

We had submitted Hendrix's $36,000 charge from the Record Plant and Hecht wanted to know if it represented the total costs for the album due Capitol Records. I said, 'No, that song will be a single when it's finished.' Hecht said, 'What? Do you mean it hasn't been finished yet?' I said, 'No, Hendrix is still working on it.'

December 1969

John Phillips (THE MAMAS & THE PAPAS): We often went to Hippopotamus in the Village and sat in a dark back booth. We talked about fame, how quickly it can come and go through your life. We talked about the hangers-on, the rip-off artists who come out of the woodwork once you've struggled to the top.

I remember Jimi looking up behind him at a tiger skin nailed to the wall. 'That's where they want me, man,' he mumbled, 'on the wall like a trophy.'

3 December 1969: Fat Mattress begins a promotional tour of the US.

4 December 1969: Hendrix signs a contract with Bill Graham for two shows at the Fillmore East, with a fee of $12,500.

5 December 1969: Hendrix receives a letter from Alan Douglas stating that he can no longer continue as producer.

6 December 1969: Hendrix is stunned by the news of the Hell's Angels/Meredith Hunter disaster at the Altamont Festival.

7 December 1969: Hendrix flies to Toronto with Bob Levine and witness Sharon Lawrence and Jeanette Jacobs.
Bob Levine: Hendrix had a limousine pick me up at the office on 37th Street. On the way to the airport, I couldn't help but notice that he was putting a bunch of things into his guitar case. I didn't know what they were but I had to ask. I said, 'Jimi, we *are* going to be going through Customs.' 'Don't worry, Bob,' he promised, 'we're cool.' He kept saying, 'Trust me, Bob, no one is going to recognize me.'

When we arrived in Toronto, he passed through Customs and promptly got arrested. I had to call Henry Steingarten from a pay-phone at the airport. Steingarten thought I was calling to let him know that we had arrived safely, but I cut him off with, 'Henry, sit down, you are not going to believe this. We are still at the airport and Hendrix has been busted again.' Steingarten went berserk.

8 December 1969: After spending the night in jail, Hendrix goes on trial in Toronto before Judge Joseph Kelly.
Bob Levine: I took him to a number of stores that specialized in tailored suits. We found a conservative suit that looked great on him. It was hilarious. He was like a hick, awkwardly fidgetting around and trying to loosen his tie. I didn't care how uncomfortable he was, the suit was perfect.

9 December 1969: Hendrix gives evidence in Toronto, admitting that he had often used drugs but denying this specific incident.
Bob Levine: He dictated this shopping list of illegal substances that he had experimented with throughout his life—from acid to Valium—for what seemed like an eternity. He admitted that he had a problem, but assured the judge and jury that someone had placed the heroin in his bag without his knowledge. I could see that his frank, honest approach impressed them. The jury expected him to be flashy and confrontational, but he was humble, and that won them over.

10 December 1969: After eight hours of deliberation by the jury, Hendrix is found not guilty on all charges.

11 December 1969: Bob Dawbarn of *Melody Maker* interviews Hendrix by telephone.

14 December 1969: Noel Redding is unable to appear with Fat Mattress in Chicago. The group splits up soon afterwards.

15 December 1969: Working on 'Message To Love', 'Them Changes', 'Burning Desire', 'Here Comes Your Lover Man', 'Born Under A Bad

Bill Graham, America's greatest rock promoter, was one of the few music business moguls who was trusted by Hendrix

Sign', 'Power Of Soul', 'Izabella' and 'Earth Blues' at Record Plant.

16 December 1969: Bob Levine gives Hendrix $1,000 cash.

18 December 1969: Rehearsing at Baggies, New York; working on 'Message To Love', 'Ezy Ryder' and 'Bleeding Heart' at Record Plant.
Billy Cox: With the Fillmore shows coming up, the studio was laid aside and we rehearsed at a place called Baggies in New York. We realized that we had to do four shows and were working up a set of the songs we were going to perform for the concerts.

19 December 1969: Working on 'Earth Blues' and 'Message To Love' at Record Plant.
Billy Cox: We toyed with the tempo on that song ('Message To Love'). Buddy wanted to slow it down, but Jimi wanted it more upbeat. Jimi would say, 'If you can't see little kids skippin' on your fast songs, you got nothing.'

20 December 1969: Hendrix is at Baggies, New York, working on various tracks. Noel Redding flies back to England.

21 December 1969: Work proceeds on various tracks at Baggies.

22 December 1969: Work continues on various tracks at Baggies.

23 December 1969: Hendrix instructs Henry Steingarten to re-establish him as half-owner in Electric Lady recording studio; later, at Record Plant, he records 'Honeybed' and 'Night Bird Flying'.
Bob Dylan: The last time I saw him was a couple of months before he died. He was in that band with Buddy Miles. It was an eerie scene. He was slouched down in the back of a limousine. I was riding by on a bicycle. I remember saying something about a song 'The Wind Cries Mary'—it was a long way from playing behind John Hammond... It was strange, both of us were a little lost for words. He'd gone through like a fireball without knowing it; I'd done the same thing like being shot out of a cannon.

Buddy Miles: To some degree, Hendrix suffered from the drugs he was taking, because he was doing heroin and after a while that will hurt anybody.

24 December 1969: Henry Steingarten writes to Hendrix about his investment as part-owner of Electric Lady Studios.

> The amount of money you are committing yourself to invest is very sizeable, particularly if you have to pay taxes on it, and it is important for you to realize that you must continue to produce albums and to make personal appearances...
>
> If you do not take this commitment seriously, your entire career can be seriously hurt, if not destroyed.
>
> The answer lies entirely in your hands. You must stop wasteful spending and sacrifice unnecessary things for the long-term benefit which the studio represents.

Alan Douglas: Jeffery couldn't stand Buddy Miles. He was caught up in the success syndrome and thought Hendrix was fucking it up.

I was recording Hendrix playing with his buddies and Jeffery felt that that was holding up the works. Hendrix wasn't touring, hadn't finished a record, wasn't making any money and Jeffery was feeling the pressure.

He was doing everything he could to turn Jimi against Buddy.

Buddy Miles: Jeffery was scared of me because of my relationship with Jimi. I never tried to take advantage of Hendrix, but Jeffery still tried to victimize me as a hanger-on... Douglas was no better than Jeffery. He used Devon and me as scapegoats to get to Jimi.

25-30 December 1969: Rehearsals for the Fillmore East shows.
Alan Arkush (Fillmore East staff): They let him rehearse during the afternoon all through the Christmas shows, so I saw them jam every day and play all kinds of great blues things.

Jimi Hendrix: We spent 12 to 18 hours a day practicing this whole last week, straight ahead, and then we went into a funky little club and jammed down there to test it out.

31 December 1969: The Band Of Gypsys play two concerts at the Fillmore East, New York, which are recorded for a live album. The shows are followed by a jam with the James Cotton Blues Band at Café A Go Go. Future rapper Ice T is in the Fillmore audience; it is the first concert he has attended.

Billy Cox: We had two shows New Year's Eve, and two shows New Year's Day. We didn't know what to expect from the audience and the audience didn't know what to expect from us, but from the time we hit that first note, they were in awe. You had Jimi Hendrix, a drummer who had been with the Electric Flag and Wilson Pickett, and I was the new kid on the block.

Alan Arkush: This guy came to the stage entrance and said, 'I got a package for Jimi.' The word was that nobody came backstage to see Jimi. I mean, no one could give him anything. But this guy begged and begged. So I said, 'Well, I can't let you backstage. But I can give it to him, if you want.'

I brought it back and Jimi opened the box and it was full of cocaine. The cocaine was glistening. It had sparkles on it.

Jimi did some of it and passed it on... it was so strong. Jimi said, 'Thank the man. Thank the man.' I went back down there and the guy was gone.

Bill Graham: I introduced the band and I walked to the side of the stage and watched a little bit from there. Then I went to the back of the house and watched a little bit more, and I was going to go into the office, but I said, 'Jesus, I can't believe this is happening!'

He never really played... He did every one of his moves. Side. Up. Under. Piercing. Throwing. Kissing. Fire. Fucking. Humping. He did it all. Picking with his teeth... they thought he was the greatest, and he was, but not during that set.

Billy Cox: At the Fillmore East he used a Fuzz Face, wah-wah pedal, Uni-Vibe and Octavia and it was incredible. In fact, you could hear all of it kicking in on 'Machine Gun'. There were people in the audience with their mouths open.

Bill Graham: Just before we opened for the second show, I was sitting in the back office when Jimi came in... Hendrix was a very quiet man, very shy. Jimi never asks, but he says, 'What'd you think, Bill?' And I didn't want to answer him, so I ask the others to leave the office. And I said, 'Jimi, you're the best guitar player I know, and tonight, for an hour-and-a-half you were a shuck. You were a disgrace to what you are.'

And the guy's face just came down. He said, 'Didn't you hear that audience? They went crazy.'

I said, 'I know. You know what you did? You made the same mistake too many of the other great ones make. You subconsciously play what they want. You sock it to them. You did an hour-and-a-half of shuck and grind and bullshit that you can do with your eyes closed lying down somewhere. But you forgot one thing. You forgot to play. And it's tragic for you, because you can play better than anyone I know.'

Well, the guy fell apart. 'Why are you telling me that?' BECAUSE YOU ASKED ME! And we had a bad scene, pushing the furniture around, yelling. And Jimi's a quiet guy.

What followed (on the next show) with respect to Carlos and Eric and all those others, was the most brilliant, emotional display of virtuoso electric-guitar playing I have ever heard. I don't expect to hear such sustained brilliance in an hour and 15 minutes. He just stood there, did nothing, just played and played and played.

Mike Jahn (in the New York Times*):*

> His playing is so loud, so fluid and so rife with electronic distortions that it resembles that of no other currently popular performer.

Bill Graham: He comes off the stage afterwards, a wet rag, and says to me... 'All right?' I said, 'Jimi, it was great.' And I hugged him and got all wet, and I asked him if he would do an encore. 'Yeah.' He goes out and does every conceivable corny bullshit thing he can do.

Ice-T: Jimi's music is definitely a motivating force for us black rock'n'roll musicians. He was at least 20 or 30 years ahead of his time. Nobody knows where his music would have been today. The stuff he did back then still sounds current.

Hendrix is transformed into an electric Medusa in this poster for a concert in Stuttgart, Germany, in January 1969

Keith Emerson fronting ELP. In their formative stages, Mitch Mitchell thought he could interest Hendrix in joining them

1970

1 January 1970: Mike Jeffery rings Noel Redding and offers Fat Mattress a tour with Jimi. In the evening, Band Of Gypsys have another gig and live recording at the Fillmore East.
Buddy Miles: Jeffery was putting pressure on Hendrix like a motherfucker... he simply did not want the Band Of Gypsys to exist.

Alan Douglas: Jeffery felt that Miles was holding up the works. He wanted to see Mitch Mitchell return and pull the Experience feel back together.

Buddy Miles: I'll never forget our first set. He (Jimi) tried to come out and be real modest, but when we jammed for about three or four hours, you could see this whole thing building up and, when we hit 'Wild Thing', all hell broke loose.

Jimi started bending and squatting, and picking his guitar with his teeth, and the audience went nuts. Jimi was a good showman and I think he enjoyed doing all the pyrotechnics, because when he did that, it meant that he felt good and was really into it. That particular set, when he just stood there, was incredible. A lot of the time I was just watching him. I was getting off on what he was doing, just like a paying customer.

Eric Bibb (fan; later contemporary blues artist): Hendrix had changed a lot since I'd seen him at Hunter College in 1968. He was a lot funkier and bluesier, as if Buddy's style, especially his singing, had influenced Jimi. It was a very exciting night.

Alfred Aronowitz (journalist, in the New York Post*):*

> By the time the second set ended, at 8.00 this morning, the audience was on its feet, clapping to the music and singing along... After it was all over, Bill Graham had to come up to the dressing room and tell him that it was probably the best set ever played on the stage of the Fillmore East.

Billy Cox: Jimi was quite relieved. He was getting this whole situation off his back.

6 January 1970: Work in New York.
Buddy Miles: After the Fillmore gigs, we were splitting time at Baggy's and the Record Plant, and I would personally go and get Hendrix every day at his apartment. Jeffery had him so petrified, he'd be spaced out.

7 January 1970: Working on 'Cherokee Mist' and 'Stepping Stone' at Record Plant.

10 January 1970: Mitch Mitchell meets with Keith Emerson and Greg Lake.
Keith Emerson: In the early part of January 1970, I was starting to get together the group that eventually became Emerson Lake & Palmer. But before I got Carl Palmer on board, Mitch Mitchell came around to Greg's place in London. Mitch was a great drummer, and obviously worth considering. He said he'd like to be involved in what we were planning, and even went so far as to say he thought he could get Hendrix interested in joining us too. Of course, it never happened. I think Greg was quite relieved, because Mitch had been talking about security and bodyguards, which sounded a bit paranoid to us.

Jimi Hendrix (in Record Mirror*):*

> I just would rather play. I never sang before we formed The Experience—it was just something they made me do in England. Anyway, Buddy has the right kind of voice for what we want to do, so let him do it.

16 January 1970: Working on 'Send My Love To Linda', 'Power Of Soul', 'and 'Burning Desire' at Record Plant.
Eddie Kramer: After the recording (of the Fillmore shows) Jimi and I sat down and rough-mixed all the songs from the four shows, at Juggy Sound... I remember very clearly a lot of whining on Jimi's part when it came time for Buddy's solo stuff, which went on ad infinitum. Jimi would say, 'Oh Christ, Buddy, would you shut up?' We had to do a lot of editing to make it right. I mean, he loved playing with Buddy. Don't get me wrong. It's just that, at

times, Buddy could be a bit excessive and Jimi felt it was appropriate to do some judicious editing.

Gerry Stickells: Buddy was a solid, lay-down-the-beat, rock'n'roll drummer. Mitch had a certain bit of jazz background there that allowed him to move around a bit, around what Jimi was doing.

17-23 January 1970: Further working on various tracks at Record Plant.
Dave Ragno (engineer): You really could see that Jimi had turned the corner. Jimi cut back on the party crowd and was trying to focus on his work. He came in alone on a lot of nights, just wanting to do guitar overdubs or experiment with some mix ideas he had. His creativity was on the upswing because he didn't have all of these people around him. His own drug use, just by what we could see, had also diminished. It was a healthier situation.

Late January 1970: Mike Jeffery tells Hendrix to fire Buddy Miles and re-form The Experience.
Bob Levine: There was rage in Jeffery's eyes. He faced Hendrix down and thrust his management contract at him, imploring Hendrix to tear it up. This wasn't the first time he had threatened to walk. For all of Hendrix's talk of changing management, he never took Jeffery up on his offer. Privately, he would say, 'The devil you know is better than the devil you don't.'

26 January 1970: Noel Redding flies to New York to discuss re-forming the Experience.
Noel Redding: I was at home when Jeffery called and asked if I wanted to make some money playing with Hendrix. I jumped at the chance.

28 January 1970: After the Winter Festival For Peace, Madison Square Garden,New York, Mike Jeffery fires Buddy Miles.
Noel Redding: I remember going to see him at Madison Square Garden where he was playing with Buddy Miles and Billy Cox. Somebody gave him a tab of acid just before the show. He was completely freaked.

Johnny Winter: When I saw him, it gave me the chills. It was the most horrible thing I'd ever seen. He came in with this entourage of people and it was like he was already dead. He just walked in and, even though Jimi and I weren't the greatest of friends, we always talked. Always. And he came in with his head down, sat on the couch alone and put his head in his hands.

Mati Klarwein (artist): We all got very stoned with him in his dressing room before he went on.

Billy Cox: Buddy and I walked over to Madison Square Garden, went into the dressing room, and there was Jimi. He was not in the best shape. Jimi was sitting next to Jeffery, and we knew it wasn't going to work.

Johnny Winter: He didn't say a word to anybody and no one spoke to him. He didn't move until it was time for the show.

Gerry Stickells: He didn't want to do the show. I had to convince him to perform.

Billy Cox: We thought about not going out there, because someone was trying to make assholes out of us, but we did. We thought Jimi might be able to make it...

Bob Levine: He was at his worst. He was out of it so badly... he never should have done the show in the condition he was in.

Buddy Miles: Jeffery slipped him two half-tabs of acid on stage as he went on. He just freaked out. I was pissed off.

Noel Redding: He freaked the audience and made a bad name for himself. He was rude to a girl in the audience and used bad language on stage. But he was tripping—spaced out. Very sad that was.

Steve Bloom (fan): It was a weird show. They played for about 10 minutes and stopped. Fans were yelling 'Foxy Lady!' and 'Purple Haze!', but Jimi had steered in a new, more soulful direction, leaving the psychedelic style of his much-beloved Experience behind.

Johnny Winter: Right in the middle of a song, he just took his guitar off, sat on the stage—the band was still playing—and told the audience, 'I'm sorry, we just can't get it together.' One of his people said he was sick and led him off the stage.

Jimi Hendrix: I was very tired. Sometimes, there's a lot of things that add up in your head... and they might hit you at a very peculiar time, which happened to be at the Peace Rally... I'd been fighting the biggest war I ever fought. In my life. Inside, you know? And, like, that wasn't the best place to do it.

Steve Bloom: Hendrix and his Band of Gypsys never returned to the stage that night. Or any other stage for that matter. It was the last performance by the Gypsys.

Alan Douglas: When he came off the stage, he actually fell off the apron. At first I thought he was hurt, but he wasn't.

Buddy Miles: The audience didn't get their money back. I told Jeffery he was an out-and-out complete idiot and a fucking asshole to boot. And he was. One of the biggest reasons why Jimi is dead is because of that guy.

Mike Jeffery: Musically it wasn't going down well between Jimi and Buddy... so I had the difficult position of getting rid of, removing Buddy from Jimi. Jimi felt it, but Jimi could never say no. Buddy was a friend of his in a non-musical sense. I told Buddy the trip was over. I did get the feeling that he took it very personally to me. We argued a bit and we shouted a bit. I think at that time, he felt he wasn't getting his share from the group. He felt that he was a star too, and I regarded him as essentially a supporting man for Jimi.

29 January 1970: Having quit the band, Billy Cox returns to Nashville.
Billy Cox: Buddy and I thought that because they had successfully marketed The Jimi Hendrix Experience as being these two white guys with Jimi in the middle, they didn't want to change horses mid-stream and go with three black guys up there. Who knows? I saw that I wasn't wanted, so I came back to Nashville and decided to do something else.

Late January 1970: Mike Jeffery begins planning a Hendrix film with producer Barry DePrendergast and director Chuck Wein.
Bob Levine: Jeffery was getting older, and that thought bothered him tremendously. His vanity was taking over. This was how Chuck Wein and Barry DePrendergast came into the picture. He was terrified of growing older and wanted nothing but youth surrounding him, hoping to be part of the New Age, non-materialistic generation that was coming in... It didn't take them long to know that if you manipulated his vanity, you could get anything you wanted from him.

Chuck Wein: I had known Jimi from The Scene, and I was living with Pat Hartley and Devon. I was into reading tarot cards, and I read the cards for Jimi and Mitch Mitchell and Billy Cox. Jimi started to tell me about being from an asteroid belt off the coast of Mars, so I said, 'Stop and I'll tell you about it, because it's a place I've seen three or four times, clear as a bell.' And that's the point that the deal got on, which was that there was something manifesting that had to be worked out. And that something eventually became *Rainbow Bridge.*

Early February 1970: Work on Electric Lady Studios is halted because of lack of funds.
Jim Marron: That was a sad day for me. I went to Jeffery's 37th Street office to discuss our options... The prices for all the work done by tradesmen kept escalating because every time the plumbers, electricians or air-conditioning men started working, we would invariably run short of cash, forcing me to shut the project down.

I sat with Jeffery and Steve Weiss to try and figure out how we could save the studio. Jeffery wanted to know one thing: how much money was needed to finish the project. My answer was a figure between $350,000 and $500,000. Steve Weiss felt he could secure a $300,000 direct loan from Warner Brothers, with payments of $50,000 every six months after the studio opened. This would be guaranteed against Hendrix's publishing and Jeffery's share of the same.

3 February 1970: Recording 'Power Of Love' at Record Plant.

4 February 1970: During interview by John Burks of *Rolling Stone* at Mike Jeffery's apartment in New York, Hendrix states that The Experience is re-forming.
Jimi Hendrix (to John Burks):

> We're in the process of getting our own thing together now again. We'll have time scheduled in a way so there'll be time on the side to play with your friends... I'll be jamming with Billy and Buddy and probably recording too, on the side.

> We're going to go out somewhere into the hills and woodshed or whatever you call it, to get some new songs and arrangements and stuff together. So we'll have something new to offer, whether it's different or not.

Mitch Mitchell: After the interview, Jimi went back to his apartment and I went back to my hotel and, within a few hours, I'd got a call from him... it came down to 'What do you think?' I knew that he meant Noel. It was very tricky. Jimi and I had great affection for Noel as a player and for his humor, but something didn't feel right... In the end, it came out in Billy Cox's favour.

Buddy Miles: The reason the band (Band Of Gypsys) folded up so quickly was because Jimi's manager, Mike Jeffery, did not want him playing in an all-black band. He was very obviously prejudiced, but Jimi was signed up to him to the point where he couldn't get out.

Early February 1970: Despite having announced the reformation of the original Experience, Hendrix asks Billy Cox to return.
Billy Cox: After the business at Madison Square Garden, I was real suspect. I agreed to come back in February, but that fell apart as well. I didn't hear from Jimi for about a month.

11 February 1970: At a meeting with Warner Brothers to finalize their loan, Mike Jeffery offers them a soundtrack album.
Jim Marron: Steve Weiss had just finished the deal to secure the loan for the studio. Jeffery thanked everyone for helping out and remarked, 'Now we're going to the studio to continue working.' One of the executives said, 'Finally, some product.' Jeffery turned to him and said, 'Yes, we're doing a soundtrack album. Would you like to buy it?' They exploded. 'What?!?'

Jeffery said, 'Yes, if you read your contract with my artist, it excludes soundtrack recordings.' They were pissed, and that's when I started worrying about Jeffery. You just don't do that to Big Brother and get away with it. But he did.

When one of them called him a shrewd bastard, he sat right down and said, 'Do you want a soundtrack? Let's negotiate. We are making a film.' I admired him for that, because that was what good negotiating was all about.

Bob Levine: He had to show Warner Brothers that he wasn't intimidated by their loan for the studio. He had to show that the relationship would remain business as usual.

12, 15, 16 February 1970: Working on various tracks at Record Plant.

25 February 1970: Michael Jeffery delivers the finished masters of the Band Of Gypsys album to Capitol Records in Los Angeles.
Ed Chalpin: That was a breach of contract. If you read the settlement agreement, PPX was supposed to receive a Jimi Hendrix Experience album, and I was supposed to be the producer. I did not accept the album, because it was not The Experience.

6 March 1970: Noel Redding flies to New York to begin rehearsals with Hendrix, unaware that he has been replaced by Billy Cox.
Billy Cox: I got a phone call from Jimi. He promised and promised that I would have no hassles so, like a fool, I came back for the third time.

Mitch Mitchell: Noel wasn't told until he came back to America, expecting to rehearse for the tour. Basically, no one had the balls to do it.

9 March 1970: Hendrix phones Kathy Etchingham.
Kathy Etchingham: He phoned me in early 1970 and said he had to get out of New York and I knew there was something wrong. He flew into Heathrow the next day.

"THE REASON BAND OF GYPSYS FOLDED UP SO QUICKLY WAS THAT JIMI'S MANAGER, MIKE JEFFERY, DID NOT WANT HIM PLAYING IN ALL-BLACK BAND. HE WAS VERY OBVIOUSLY PREJUDICED, BUT JIMI WAS SIGNED UP TO HIM TO THE POINT WHERE HE COULD NOT GET OUT"

1970

10 March 1970: Hendrix flies to London, moves into the Londonderry Hotel,and tries to convince Kathy Etchingham to leave her husband and return to him.
Kathy Etchingham: I met him and we had a long conversation. He told me things weren't working out with this and that, just ranting on and on about things. It was hard to figure out what he was going on about, but he seemed to be slightly paranoid. He said he didn't want to prance around and be a performer, he just wanted to play music. But I know what he meant really was that he just wanted to sit down and play the blues.

15 March 1970: Recording with Stephen Stills at Island Studios.
Stephen Stills: When he did the session with me for 'Old Times, Good Times', Jimi and I had been sort of farting around all over London, checking out different nightclubs and alternately playing either really magnificent or stinking up the joint. I had this solo album going, so I said, 'Why don't you come down?' I had the song and he did an overdub. It didn't really take long. When Jimi came up with that solo, we just wandered around the studio, plugging into different amplifiers and boxes, trying to find something groovy. It was his suggestion that we do something jazzy with that solo. He ended up playing right through the console, using a Fairchild limiter. He said that if the guitar sound got too big, it would cover up the organ part. He was right.

16 March 1970: Jimi has talks with Emerson Lake & Palmer about a possible joint tour; at The Speakeasy he is interviewed by Keith Altham.
Keith Altham (in Petticoat*):*

> Down the Speakeasy club, I spoke to an incommunicado Jimi Hendrix on a recent visit to try and get The Experience together one more time.

17 March 1970: Recording 'The Everlasting First', 'Ezy Ryder' and jam with Arthur Lee of Love at Olympic Studios.
Arthur Lee: In England, we'd hang around together, going to different places, riding up and down the countryside in England, having a good time. Plus, we both mysteriously had the same girlfriend. Devon Wilson was my girlfriend first... anyway, when I was in London, we were at The Speakeasy, and I told him, 'Neither one of us gonna be around very long, so while we are here we might as well do something together.' He fell for that. So we got together.

I tried to book something (at Island Studios), but Stephen Stills had booked all the studio time... so I got that Olympic Studio. Jimi and Remi Kabaka and these other two Africans, they're playing tabla.

Anne Bjorndal (journalist): They were in a very good mood together, making a lot of jokes.

Arthur Lee: We never got a chance to play (again as) he died. We were gonna start a band together... he said he wanted to try and get Steve Winwood, Remi Kabaka and myself. But it never materialised.

19 March 1970: Hendrix flies back to New York.

20 March 1970: Noel Redding starts work on his solo album, *Nervous Breakdown*, at Sound Center, New York.
Noel Redding: I went ahead and produced an LP in the States with Lee Michaels and Roger Chapman (vocalist of UK rock band Family) and a 15-year-old drummer. I paid for it all myself. They didn't release it. All it got us was a bad financial situation. I started drinking, and I got busted. Then I got sued for maintenance.

23 March 1970: Hendrix records 'Midnight Lightnin'' with Mitch Mitchell and Billy Cox at Record Plant.

24 March 1970: Recording 'Bleeding Heart' and 'Midnight Lightning' at Record Plant.

25 March 1970: *Band Of Gypsys* album is released in the US.
Billy Cox: When *Band Of Gypsys* came out, we both wished we had done it in the studio. We would have loved to have done some overdubs and correct some of the mistakes.

Jimi Hendrix: If it had been up to me, I never would have put it out. From a musician's point of view, it was not a good recording and I was out of tune on a few things... The thing was, we owed the record company an album and they were pushing us, so here it is.

Early April 1970: Arthur Allen introduces Hendrix to Harlem legal team Kenny Haygood and Ed Howard, to discuss leaving Mike Jeffery.

Ed Howard (lawyer): We met Jimi down at the apartment he had in the Village and he outlined for us a lot of the problems he felt he had in his business relationships, and with the people around him, and he advised us that he wanted us to become his new counsel. I told him that I needed to review his contracts relating to his management and music publishing, his songwriter agreement, and his recording contracts and all of the kinds of contracts that a musician like Jimi had. He didn't have any of them. Not one contract at all.

Arthur Allen: They told Jimi that they didn't want to make any moves until they spoke with Michael Jeffery. Hendrix was getting pissed off because they kept telling him they had no choice but to consult Jeffery. He finally exploded. 'What are these niggers talking about?' he screamed.

Ed Howard: He told me he would try to get these papers from the various people that had them and that he would make them available to me for my review and blah blah blah, so that I could get a background in terms of what his rights, exposures and so forth might be. That was the last we heard from him for a little while.

13 April 1970: 'Stepping Stone' is released as a US single by Band Of Gypsys. It is withdrawn soon after; it hadn't been mixed properly.

14 April 1970: Hendrix is stopped and summonsed for driving without a license by New York State Police.

15 April 1970: Hendrix is interviewed at his apartment, by Keith Altham for *Melody Maker*.
Jimi Hendrix (in Melody Maker*):*

> The Experience is dead. That's like pages in an old diary… It's nothing personal against Noel but we finished what we were doing with the Experience and Billy's style of playing suits the new group better. The Experience got into a cul-de-sac: we played for three years and had reached the stage where we were just repeating ourselves.

Keith Altham: Jimi proved to be much the same as when I last saw him—still sleeping in the day and grooving at night—surrounded by amplifiers, mattress on the floor and albums scattered about the room… His health was deteriorating and I think the drugs had got a hold.

18 April 1970: Hendrix flies to Los Angeles to prepare for the start of a new tour with Mitch Mitchell and Billy Cox.

25 April 1970: Twenty thousand fans see the Cry Of Love tour start at The Forum, LA.
Mitch Mitchell: For The Forum gig we were staying at Rodeo Drive again, at the hotel. I had a suite there, Jimmy had one with his own private elevator. Talk about hangers-on. I went up to see him once during the week we were there and stayed about two minutes. I thought, I don't want anything to do with this. He didn't want all these people around but he didn't know how to say 'No'.

Luther Rabb (leader, Ballin' Jack): After I moved to LA, I hooked up with Jimi again in Beverly Hills. His management had some other guy they wanted to have back the show but Jimi, he said, 'Hey, no, let's have Luther.' Ballin' Jack's first gig in Los Angeles was with Jimi Hendrix and Buddy Miles. We were the opening act at The Forum.

Judy Sims (reviewer, in Disc & Music Echo*):*

> About 20,000 people crammed in to see Jimi Hendrix in his first appearance here in almost a year. He was preceded by Buddy Miles and his new group… the spaced-out worshippers leaped from their seats for Buddy, but they weren't inspired to rush the stage… the crowd wasn't going to waste its energies for Buddy, they wanted Jimi.
>
> For a while, I thought Jimi was going to thwart them. He was relaxed, cool as ever, and did an almost casual set. He teased us with a few erotic movements during 'Foxy Lady' but, after that, he just stood there and played that guitar—mostly new songs from his Band Of Gypsys album.
>
> At the end of the set Jimi broke into our national anthem and ordered us to stand up, which we did.
>
> The aisles filled but still the space down front remained miraculously clear. Kids started leaping over seats so they could stand on chairs in the first two or three rows, and people from the aisles crowded into the rows. The ushers massed in front of the stage. Then Jimi went right into 'Purple Haze' and all hell broke loose.

JIMI PLAYS BERKELEY
A new film—
Hendrix at his peak.
The historic
Berkeley concert,
Memorial Day 1970.
With Mitch Mitchell
and Billy Cox.
Fly High.
PLUS "LOVE IS HARD TO GET", a hilarious new spoof on samurai flicks
30's serials with Peter Bergman, star of Firesign Theatre as love-crazed gorilla, Nasi Goreng.

By the time Hendrix played at Berkeley on 30 May, 1970, the Experience had disintegrated and his affairs were in disarray

There was an incomprehensible (and terrifying) backward thrust. Everyone up front was somehow invisibly thrown back with sledge-hammer force. Chairs went over, people went down. Like a fool, I'd been standing on my chair trying to see Jimi through the crowd, so I went over the back of the chair, suspended like a trapeze artist.

Craig Chaquico (stagehand for the next day's Sacramento gig; later of Jefferson Starship): I was like, 14 or 15 years old. Part of my payment was supposed to be free tickets. We stayed up all night painting this backdrop and the American flag goes pretty well. The Peace Sign went pretty smooth. It's three in the morning. 'OK, let's do the English flag. What does it look like? Red with some crosses on it?' No one knows what the English flag looks like. Logic is maybe not our best asset at that point. Someone says, 'Let's draw the Vietcong flag. It's just a star with a blue and red background.' It made sense to us at that point, but we got so much shit. People either loved it or hated it, but it went up.

26 April 1970: Concert at 'Cal Expo', State Fairgrounds, Sacramento, California.
Steve Avis (fan): It was a sunny afternoon. My friend Kent and I had bought tickets in advance for $3.75. There were a lot of people sitting on blankets and a sweet smell filled the air. The stage was directly in front of us so we sat down with some friends.

Craig Chaquico: All of us kids with paint all over our hands got drafted in at the last minute to help Hendrix's road crew carry the amps out of the truck and onto the stage. I got to be one of Hendrix's roadies for an afternoon.

Larry Hulst (fan): It was the largest show ever in Sacramento, which meant that everything was two or three times larger in scale—meaning more police, more hassle to get into the place, more area to figure out where you could stand and not be in front of somebody who'd yell at you.

Hendrix came in a white limousine and drove into the staging area and walked right up. He didn't have a soundcheck.

Craig Chaquico: It was the first time I'd seen him live. After his albums, what impressed me was that live, everything was noisy. The amps buzzed and hummed, things were out of tune and scratchy. I was so used to hearing immaculate recordings... the impression was, Wow! This stuff is really raw, live. I kind of dug it. It was super-loud.

Steve Avis: He wasn't jumping around too much. He'd left a lot of that flash behind him when he started playing with Billy Cox and Buddy Miles.

Craig Chaquico: At one point, a bunch of kids were trying to get in over the fence. The promoter drafted us to become security and said, 'Make sure those kids don't jump over the fence.' So I ran over and I'm looking at these guys on the other side of the fence and I think, What the fuck am I doing? I go to school with those guys! I'm not security. I'm outta here.

Steve Avis: In 'Machine Gun' he was doing things with the guitar I'd never heard before. I remember it sounding so mystical. But that was just like him. After you thought you'd heard everything, Jimi plays something completely different that just blows you away.

The wind was blowing. You know how it blows the sound around? And it made a flanging effect that reminded me of the record.

Craig Chaquico: A lot of it seemed unfamiliar. Some of the unfamiliar songs were taking people by surprise. Half the show, I was on stage, then I went out into the audience. I remember, it was either 'Foxy Lady' or 'Purple Haze', my friend said, 'Watch! Hendrix always jumps up in the air at this point.' And Jimi jumped in the air. I realized, Hey, these guys do these things every night!

John V. Hurst (music critic, the Sacramento Bee*):* Hendrix did get through to the crowd towards the end... with a searing rendition of 'Star Spangled Banner' complete with sound effects for the rockets and the bombs. That got the crowd excited, and it grooved with him as he closed out on a stately blues.

1 May 1970: Concert at the Milwaukee Auditorium, Milwaukee, Wisconsin.

2 May 1970: Concert at the Dane County Memorial Coliseum, Madison, Wisconsin.

Jim Craig (fan): I was 17, just finishing my last year of high school. Myself and two friends drove to the concert in my 1961 Volvo, because I was the only one who had a car. It was my first rock concert, and my friends assured me that it would be 'a shocker'.

Jimi came onstage, looked out into the crowd and said, 'Goddam! I didn't know there was that many people here!' During 'Fire', while he did a 'trill' (hammer-on / pull-off) on the guitar, he mimicked a machine gun with his left hand. I clearly remember he did 'Roomful Of Mirrors', because he said it was about being in a room and only seeing yourself, to which he added, 'Yeah, we've been there!'

3 May 1970: Concert at the Civic Center, St Paul, Minnesota.
John (fan who taped show): I remember listening to Hendrix warm up with the curtain down. When the curtain came up I was surprised to see that all of the speaker cloths, a substantial portion of them had been ripped, just torn, hanging down in shreds.

They stood quite far apart... essentially at different ends of the stage. Compared to what he did in the studio, I was disappointed... there wasn't the richness of sound that he would do in the studio. It compelled him to play more in the high registers, this fast Hendrix stuff. It felt a little more obligatory. I sensed that he was a little over the top... He had to work hard at maintaining interest in the show. He didn't really move.

Marshall Fine (critic, in the St Paul Dispatch*):*

> Hendrix was leaner and meaner than when he played here in November 1968. The most notable improvement is the cut-away of excess flash that used to be standard in his act. More appreciable now is Hendrix's amazing talent... there was a fluidity in his guitar work that he's never shown before... He also showed a Foxy sexuality in his singing and in his little introductions to each song.

Jimi Hendrix (onstage, to audience): I'd like to do a slow blues about this cat who feels kinda down, 'cause his old lady put him down, and his people and family don't want him around, so he had this big old long frown, and had to drag his ass down to the railroad station, waitin' for the train to come take him away on the road, be a voodoo child, magic warrior, come back, do it to his old lady one more time, give her a piece because she's all nice to him again. And that's what this song is... thank you very much. It's called 'Getting My Heart Back Together'.

8 May 1970: Concert at the University Of Oklahoma Field House, Norman, Oklahoma.

9 May 1970: Concert at the Will Rogers Coliseum, Fort Worth, Texas.

10 May 1970: Concert at the Hemisfair Arena, San Antonio, Texas.

14 May 1970: Recording 'Keep On Groovin'' at Record Plant, New York.
Billy Cox: We weren't playing by notes, we were playing by patterns. It was kind of weird, but that's how we thought. We were always trying to hook these patterns together to make songs. Jimi would just give you a look, and Mitch and I would know where he was going.

15 May 1970: Working on 'Freedom' at Record Plant.
Billy Cox: Originally, all Jimi had was just that opening riff. I remember him playing it to me at his apartment during the time of Band Of Gypsys We spent a lot of time working that song out before we finally recorded it at Electric Lady.

16 May 1970: Concert at the Temple University Stadium, Philadelphia,

"WE WEREN'T PLAYING BY NOTES, WE WERE PLAYING BY PATTERNS. IT WAS KIND OF WEIRD BUT THAT'S HOW WE THOUGHT. WE WERE ALWAYS TRYING TO HOOK THESE PATTERNS TOGETHER TO MAKE SONGS. JIMI WOULD JUST GIVE YOU A LOOK, AND MITCH AND I WOULD KNOW WHERE HE WAS GOING"

1970

Pennsylvania, supported by The Grateful Dead and The Steve Miller Band.
Steve Miller: I played a show with Hendrix at Temple University in Philadelphia and, at that time, the cat's scene was so far gone that he walked by me and smelled like he was dying... his band couldn't play...

22-24 May 1970: Three gigs—St Louis, Cincinatti and Columbus—are cancelled because of Hendrix's 'glandular problems'.

30 May 1970: The gig at the Community Theater, Berkeley, California, is filmed by Eric Saarinen. Carlos Santana hangs out backstage.
Carlos Santana: It was embarrassing because at that time there was like, uh, 'lady swapping', and his old lady (Devon Wilson) would check the rounds, and he knew that she was checking the rounds so... I dunno. It was awkward for me...

But there was a family that we used to call 'The Cosmic Family'. And it was the same family that hung out with Jimi Hendrix and Miles Davis—it was the same group of ladies. Uh, I won't go into names but it was like about, almost ten of them that like... uh, moons, they would just gravitate around certain things. I wanted to ask Jimi about everything and anything but with them it was kinda awkward.

John Wasserman (in the San Francisco Chronicle*):*

> The show was sold out and certain latecomers did not gracefully accept that fact, venting their frustrations on various entrance doors.
>
> When I arrived, a squadron of police had just disembarked in front of the building but were apparently not needed save for visual intimidation value. Up Grove Street, a small group was oinking at two cops who had just cornered a fleeing suspect, and Bill Graham was arguing, as usual, with some idiots in front of the auditorium doors.

Bob Levine: There was so much damage to the place that we had to release $8,000 to pay for it.

John Wasserman:

> Hendrix really is an exceptional musician. His playing appears effortless, even to the point of locking his right hand into a fixed position on the guitar's neck and then playing what seems to be thirty seconds or a minute varying only his finger-work, not his hand position.
>
> He played for an hour, did 'Purple Haze' and 'Foxy Lady' and 'The Star Spangled Banner'. He sang adequately and generally unintelligibly, slammed the neck up and down the microphone stand, went on his knees, to his back, picked with his teeth and indicated on a couple of occasions, that the guitar was not so much a guitar as an appendage of his lower body.

Eric Saarinen (film director): There was some problem with them not paying us in the beginning. I forgot if it was Jeffery or some other guy—there was some guy who was Jimi's manager—who said, 'If you don't send the film right away there's going to be a plane full of Black Panthers landing in Los Angeles today and they are going to kill you.' Whoever it was, was really really heavy duty.

Summer 1970

Early June 1970: Pleased with his studio work, Hendrix considers releasing a triple album.
Kathy Eberth: People, Hell And Angels was going to be the title. He couldn't settle on the songs or length of the album. In the early summer, *Straight Ahead* had emerged as a working title and then later *First Rays Of The New Rising Sun* made a comeback of sorts. At the very least, he definitely wanted to release a two-record set.

Gerry Stickells: He was starting to get some direction again... his enthusiasm was renewed and quite visible, especially by comparison to the fall of 1969 when he was desperately trying to write something creative and failing miserably.

5 June 1970: Concert at the Memorial Auditorium, Dallas, Texas.

6 June 1970: Concert at the Sam Houston Coliseum, Houston, Texas.
Luther Rabb: We went out on tour together. We were hanging out every night, doing the warm-up show. He'd watch our set, and we'd hang out and

watch his. We'd do the old Rhythm & Blues songs for the warm-up, and everybody in the room would be singing and clapping.

7 June 1970: Concert at the Assembly Center Arena, Tulsa, Oklahoma.

9 June 1970: Concert at the Mid-South Coliseum, Memphis; Jimi meets Larry Lee backstage and borrows his guitar for a few songs.

10 June 1970: Concert at the Roberts Municipal Stadium, Evansville, Illinois.

12 June 1970: The *Band Of Gypsys* album is released in the UK.

13 June 1970: Concert at the Civic Center, Baltimore, Maryland, supported by Cactus.

15 June 1970: Instrumental jams with Steve Winwood and Chris Wood of Traffic in Electric Lady Studios, New York.
John Veneble (assistant engineer): Shimon Ron and Kim King (engineers) worked to make Studio B operational, while Kramer and Hendrix had Studio A all to themselves.

Les Paul: When Jimi was involved in building Electric Lady Studios, he called me up with several questions, including an idea of miking a guitar amp from far away, across the room, while running the guitar directly into the board at the same time. He also wanted to know how I went into the board, and things of that sort.

During that talk, I told Jimi the story of my hunt for him, to snatch him up and get him to a record company. He really cracked up. He said, 'You mean I was that close and didn't know it?'

Eddie Kramer: Hendrix couldn't wait to get in and start recording. Right up until the time Studio A was functional, Jimi would call me and ask, 'Is it done yet? When is it going to be ready?' I would simply say, 'Almost, Jimi, as soon as we finish this and as soon as we finish that...'

It had been impossible trying to get work done during those sessions at the Hit Factory and the Record Plant. At one point, I remember there were 30 people in the control room. That would never happen at Electric Lady. I wouldn't allow it.

Dave Palmer (engineer): Kramer called me at 2am saying, 'Hendrix is down at the studio and we need a drummer. Get your ass over here and bang on those tubs.' When I got there, Hendrix and Kramer were showing Steve Winwood the place. Nothing was really set up, but Jimi and Steve had the itch to play, so Eddie set up a couple of microphones and I got behind the drums and jammed with the two of them.

Eddie Kramer: Steve was the perfect foil for Jimi and one of the very few musicians who could have kept up with him.

16 June 1970: Recording 'Nightbird Flying' and 'Straight Ahead'—the first real work towards the fourth album—at Electric Lady.
Eddie Kramer: 'Nightbird Flying' was a truly superlative effort. Mitch was great on that track, really on the mark.

That song was a bastard to mix, because we had so many guitar parts. There's one bit where Jimi displayed his country influence. He did it as a piss-take and was laughing when he played it. I loved when Jimi would throw bits like that in.

I think he finally felt at home in Electric Lady Studio. Electric Lady was his pride and joy. He even came to sessions early, which was unheard of in the past. He was so proud and it was his place. He was the boss.

17 June 1970: Recording 'Straight Ahead', 'Drifter's Escape', 'Blue Suede Shoes' and 'Astro Man' at Electric Lady.

19 June 1970: Concert at the Civic Auditorium, Albuquerque, New Mexico.

20 June 1970: Concert at the Swing Auditorium, San Bernardino, California.

21 June 1970: Concert at the Ventura County Fairgrounds, supported by Grin.

23 June 1970: Concert at the Mammoth Gardens, Denver, Colorado.

24 June 1970: Recording 'Astro Man' and 'Further On Up The Road' at Electric Lady.
Billy Cox: We used to love watching cartoons at his apartment. He enjoyed Mighty Mouse and

Steve Winwood often jammed with Hendrix. Eddie Kramer thought him one of the few who could keep pace with Hendrix

especially loved Rocky and Bullwinkle. That's what 'Astro Man' was all about... We were in a groove that night. 'Astro Man' was such a fun song to play. By that time, we knew those patterns extremely well.

25 June 1970: Working on various tracks at Electric Lady.
Linda Sharlin (Jeffery employee): Even when Electric Lady Studios was up and running, he (Mike Jeffery) would send Iris (studio receptionist) to the Bahamas to stuff wads of cash into the long boots she used to wear.

Bob Levine: I don't know how many times he came back from abroad with a paper bag full of money—English currency, West German marks—from wherever he went travelling, and would ask me to take it down to the currency exchange on Broadway. I never questioned it, but where the hell did those bags of money come from? We aren't talking about $1,000 here.

26 June 1970: Recording 'Earth Blues' at Electric Lady.
John Jansen (engineering assistant): 'Earth Blues' was a good track, but nobody upstairs wanted to hear those 'Everybody!' chants on a record by Jimi. When Jimi wasn't around, and Jeffery heard us working on it, he would wave his hands in the air and roll his eyes.

Eddie Kramer: While 'Earth Blues' very much fit musically into the framework of his new direction, we were never certain that it was ever going to make the final record.

Kim King (engineer): Some nights Jimi would arrive, head upstairs (to Jeffery's office) and not come down at all. We would wait and sometimes Eddie would get a phone call from upstairs saying that Jimi was not going to work that night. There were some serious politics going on up there, but Eddie forbade us from getting involved with it in any way. We were not to put our two cents in.

27 June 1970: While Hendrix plays a concert at the Boston Garden, Boston, Massachusetts, a band called Queen plays its first gig at the City Hall, Truro, Cornwall, England.
Roger Taylor (Queen): We came together through Hendrix. Freddie was a Hendrix freak. He once saw him 14 nights in a row, in different pubs.

29 June 1970: Recording overdubs for 'Drifting' at Electric Lady.

1 July 1970: Recording 'Dolly Dagger', 'Beginning' and 'Pali Gap' at Electric Lady.
Eddie Kramer: Hendrix cut 'Dolly Dagger' twice. He had recorded a rough demo at the Record Plant but that was scrapped entirely. We cut the new basic track in one evening, but spent three or four days overdubbing guitars and finishing the background vocals.

When we were cutting the basic track, Jimi put on a lead vocal at the same time he was recording his lead guitar to get into the mood of the vocal. Devon was in the control room at the time, and you can hear him sing, 'Watch out Devon, give me a little bit of that heaven.' It was a tribute to her, and a nice touch.

Jim Marron: Devon was just as cunning as Michael Jeffery. She was intensely into anything that she perceived as being good for Jimi. Jeffery would not take any shit from her but, at the same time, she used to try and see just how far she could push him.

Dave Palmer (engineer): She wanted to be there all the time, saying once, 'If you're going to be making music or mixing music with Jimi, I've got to be there.' That was weird—a necessary evil for Hendrix, I guess.

2 July 1970: More work on 'Ezy Ryder' and 'Dolly Dagger' at Electric Lady.
Billy Cox: We started 'Ezy Ryder' at the Record Plant (in December 1969) but it wasn't finished until the following summer at Electric Lady. Jimi had come up with the main pattern, but I had *da da da dum, da da did da da* and didn't know what to do with it. Jimi built on it from there and it became a living, breathing song, rather than just a combination of patterns.

Kim King: This was a symphonic guitar song. It was handled like string quartet parts, although nothing was written on paper—it was all improvised. We overdubbed eight tracks of guitars. Everything in pairs—four tracks of lead and four tracks of rhythm.

4 July 1970: Gig at the Atlanta Pop Festival, Byron, Georgia, with BB King, John Sebastian,

Mountain, Procol Harum, Poco, Jethro Tull, Johnny Winter and The Allman Brothers Band.

5 July 1970: Two shows at the Miami Jai Alai Fronton, Miami, Florida.

14 July 1970: Recording 'Come Down Hard On Me Baby', 'Midnight Lightning' and other tracks at Electric Lady.

15 July 1970: Working on 'Come Down Hard' and other tracks at Electric Lady.
Jim Marron: Jimi enjoyed recording at Electric Lady, but there were also times when he just wanted to cool out there. Devon was giving him a bitch of a time, so he would stay at the studio and listen to playbacks.

Kim King: Devon was more often part of the scene than not, but on some evenings, as per Jimi's instructions, we were not to answer the door to Devon.

Mid-July 1970: Hendrix confronts a New York gangster boss.
Arthur Allen: One particular gangster was a serious terror in Harlem and everybody knew it, including Jimi. This guy ran several big-time disc jockeys, had a few bodies under his belt and nobody fucked with him. We were on 59th Street and Jimi was pissed off because this guy was advertising that Jimi Hendrix was going to be at one of his shows.

Lo and behold, there was the guy with three of his henchmen. It was confrontation time. In his bell-bottoms, Hendrix turned around and started walking over to these guys in their gangster suits. He's waving the advertisement in one hand while carrying his guitar case in the other.

Hendrix was screaming, 'How dare you do this? You don't have the right to do this!' This guy was looking at him like he was crazy.

Hendrix wouldn't let up though, he was a man of principle. He kept pointing to the advertisement saying, 'What right do you have to do this?' We were waiting for the guns to come out, but Jimi never backed down. He stood his ground.

Finally, the guy told Hendrix that he was going to do the show with him or without him. As his crew escorted him away, Hendrix kept after him, yelling, 'My lawyer will be talking to you guys! You don't have a right to use my name on this.' They never hassled him again, but he was lucky he wasn't killed.

17 July 1970: Gig at the New York Pop Festival, Downing's Stadium, Randall's Island, New York, where a portion of the profits was to be donated to The Young Lords, a Hispanic version of the Black Panthers.
Don Friedman (promoter): He (Hendrix) was consuming drugs non-stop. He was mixing them. He was drinking. He was smoking grass and snorting coke. He may have had some heroin, because I know there was some in the room. I remember Mike Jeffery coming up to me over and over again. He kept saying, 'Put him on! Put him on or he won't make it!'

Ian Anderson (Jethro Tull): We were on the bill at Randall's Island but Hendrix now seemed like a different person than the man I'd met the previous year. I wanted to go and talk to him, but I couldn't get anywhere near him because he was surrounded by a phalanx of very sinister people. I saw him briefly as he made his way to the stage and he looked very out of it.

Gerry Stickells: It was a complete mess. We weren't going to go on, but the Young Lords held us at knife-point and wouldn't allow us to leave. When we finally did get out of there, we all jammed in a van, and the boat taking us over to Manhattan got stuck in the mud.

19 July 1970: Working on 'Nightbird Flying', 'Straight Ahead', 'Astro Man', 'Freedom' and 'Dolly Dagger'.
Eddie Kramer: Jimi would do a solo one night (on 'Dolly Dagger') and everybody would be completely knocked out. Then he would come back the next day and say, 'No, that was a piece of shit, let's re-do that.' And he would do it better.

20 July 1970: Working on 'Lover Man' at Electric Lady.

21-22 July 1970: Work on 'In From The Storm' and 'Hear My Train A'Comin'' at Electric Lady.
Billy Cox: That song was put together in one session in Jimi's hotel room when we were on the road. We had a little amplifier with us, and we

worked out the whole song. Room service came up with some steaks and trays of food, and I said, 'Jimi, do you remember the times when we used to share chili in Indianapolis?' He grabbed one of the dishes and said, 'Yeah, man. Look at us now, eating horsie doors!' I couldn't help but to break out laughing.

23 July 1970: Working on several tracks, including 'Drifting' and 'Angel' at Electric Lady.
Billy Cox: We didn't do much rehearsing of that song ('Drifting') before we recorded the basic tracks. That one just flowed from Jimi. It was very spiritual and didn't require many takes at all.

Before we had gone in to cut 'Angel', we had gone over and over it, because Jimi wanted to make it a nice sweet song. We made some adjustments here and there, just practicing in our hotel rooms on the road, but Jimi had it completed. The bassline for that track was inspired by an old record we loved called 'Cherry Pie'. That gave the record the feel of those great 1950's R&B ballads.

25 July 1970: Concert at the International Sports Arena, San Diego, California, supported by Cat Mother.

26 July 1970: Concert at the Sicks Stadium, Seattle, Washington.
Tom Hulett (Concerts West): Seattle had always been a big money market for us and Hendrix was up for the challenge. On the plane from San Diego, I spoke to Jimi about the weather forecast for Seattle. A steady rain was threatening our walk-up sales and I was afraid we were going to lose our ass. Remember, it was both Hendrix's own money and ours at stake that night. I was thinking about cancelling but Hendrix said no. He instructed Stickells to cover the stage floor with rubber, a process, he explained, to ensure that the band wouldn't be electrocuted.

Pernell Alexander (musician from Hendrix's youth): The last time I saw Jimi was when he came to Seattle for his last concert. I went out to the airport when he came in. Al and his family were there too. I went over to Al's with all of them, and then Jimmy came over to my house and met with my band. He was going to help us.

Al Hendrix: He told me he had some money put away somewhere. He was going to tell me more about it when he got back from Europe—but he didn't get back.

Pernell Alexander: I was never able to get through to him again. All my calls to him in New York got short-stopped by Mike Jeffery. Then my calls to England got short-stopped too. His management would not let me get through to him.

Eddie Hall (Jimi's cousin): He was so stressed out before that concert. I think he was burned out and frustrated. Before the concert he was sitting in the house, at his dad's, looking out the window. There was a limo out there waiting to take him to Sicks Stadium. He didn't want to ride in a limo, and that's what he told his manager. Then June and I drove him.

Leon Hendrix: You could tell Jimi didn't really want to be up there. It was like he was looking at people, seeing all those who were against him.

Bon Henderson (fan): It was an outdoor, all-afternoon event that started about 3pm. Typical for Seattle it was cloudy until the event began, at which time it started to pour down. People were drenched and miserable, opening bands had to wait until the rain let up a little. At dusk the moment we'd all suffered for was upon us.

Jimi played in a downpour. I was in such awe that he could have just stood there for 45 minutes and I would have been happy. But when he played it really was something special. That

"IT WAS CONFRONTATION TIME. HENDRIX STARTED WALKING OVER TO THESE GUYS IN GANGSTER SUITS. HE WAS SCREAMING, 'HOW DARE YOU DO THIS? YOU DON'T HAVE A RIGHT TO DO THIS!' WE WERE WAITING FOR THE GUNS TO COME OUT, BUT JIMI NEVER BACKED DOWN. HE STOOD HIS GROUND"

amazing sound we'd heard millions of times on records filled the stadium. I spent most of the time with my jaw dropping open.

Freddie Mae Gautier (who had looked after Hendrix as a baby): I was so upset. The acoustics were terrible, it was raining. This was Seattle's way of getting back at him. They resented it because he always talked bad about Washington and told how bad he was treated in school.

Bon Henderson: I remember him taking a few verbal jabs at Seattle, Garfield High School, and the fact that he had to move away to be noticed. He was absolutely right and the crowd agreed.

Janie Hendrix: I was on the side of the stage and it was pouring down rain, and they were all trying to keep the rain off his head, and I was fearful that he was going to get electrocuted. In the middle of the song ('Purple Haze') he turned around and he said, 'That girl put a spell on me,' and he was pointing at me, and all the audience was trying to look to see who he was pointing at.

Bon Henderson: During the show he said he'd spent a great day with his dad and family and dedicated one song to 'the girl dancing in the yellow pajamas'. The rain got so heavy that some people left! At that point I think Jimi was ticked off. He was risking being electrocuted and they didn't want to get wet! Despite the circumstances he put on an incredible show.

27 July 1970: Hendrix is re-united with 'Aunt' Freddie Mae.
Freddie Mae Gautier: Jimi came on over to the house... it was after midnight when Jimi got there, and he had never really done that before, so I felt something was bothering Jimi.

I said to him, 'How come you're back and you let those people put you on at the Sicks Stadium?' And he said it was a trick. He said, 'I started to break my contract, but my lawyers warned me that if I did, they'd clean me out.' Jimi had put it in writing that they could send him anywhere, but not the state of Washington—if they did, he'd break his contract.

I asked him where his money was. Well, he didn't really know, but they had it in different banks, and he thought some of it was in the Bahamas. Jimi's travelling manager called a lot of times during the morning... so I finally said, 'Quit calling over here. Leave him alone.' Because Jimi kept saying, 'I don't want to talk to him.'

Jerry Morrison (associate of Mike Jeffery): Jimi didn't want to have anything to do with it *(Rainbow Bridge)*. He didn't even want to be in the film. So Mike Jeffery ordered Gerry Stickells and two roadies to go to Seattle... He told them to get Jimi loaded and physically take him to Hawaii. And they did. Jimi was shanghaied.

28 July 1970: Hendrix entourage flies to Hawaii to film *Rainbow Bridge*.
Bob Levine: The money to make that movie represented Hendrix's involvement. *Rainbow Bridge* was Jeffery's vanity trip. Hendrix had some ideas, but Jeffery and Wein didn't ask for his input.

Gerry Stickells: Jeffery had fallen in love with the stoned California-Hawaii lifestyle. Just sit back, moan and smoke dope. This was the end of that era.

Chuck Wein's people were involved with surfers who would smuggle dope to the island. It was outrageous. We were staying at a girls' school in Maui which served only vegetarian food.

Pat Hartley: Chuck had rented the old Baldwin Mansion, which was a girls' school, and there were about 30 of us living in the dorm together. Most of the crew thought all these vegetarians were trying to poison them.

John Jansen: Warner Films had kicked in close to a million dollars on the premise that the soundtrack album would be every bit as successful as *Electric Ladyland* or *Smash Hits*. So Chuck Wein had money to begin shooting.

Chuck Wein (film-maker): Even though the album and video are called *Rainbow Bridge*, it was known as the Rainbow Ridge, because that's the name of the ridge on which the concert was held.

29 July 1970: Jimi injures his foot in a boating accident in Hawaii.
Bob Levine: We staged a big, formal dinner for some executives of Warner Films who had flown in to check up on the movie's progress. Unknown to any of us, Mitch Mitchell had gone into the

kitchen and dumped a potent mix of marijuana and hashish into the batter of the dessert.

After dinner and dessert, as we sat drinking coffee, we all started tripping. I got up, so I'm told, and yelled, 'Does anybody want to do the chicken dance?' These Warner Films representatives, stiff and very proper in their three-piece suits, started screaming, 'Yes!' Hendrix was under the table laughing, but he decided to do me one better. He started clucking like a chicken behind me.

Gerry Stickells: The (Warner Film) crew would be sleeping in the middle of the night when someone would rush in saying, 'The vibrations are right in the church! Come right now!' They thought you could just rush right in and film it. It was a complete shambles. Hendrix wanted nothing to do with the entire thing but, again, it was a case of Jeffery convincing him to do it. Hendrix was hanging out and smoking dope, but this was ridiculous.

Mitch Mitchell: They couldn't organize a piss-up in a brewery.

30 July 1970: Filming begins on the *Rainbow Bridge Vibratory Color-Sound Experiment*, at Haleakala Crater, Maui, Hawaii.
John Jansen: In the end, when all the money had been spent, and they realized that this movie wasn't a movie, Jeffery had to talk Hendrix into performing. Up until that point, he had refused to write a note of music for the film.

Chuck Wein: We went through every kind of why-are-we-here riff until finally Jimi and (Pat) Hartley got into an argument, and I said, 'Listen, the crew's been up there for eight hours. We have to do this now.'

John Jansen: Of course, now that a concert was necessary, it had to be shot atop one of the highest points in Maui. With nothing but blue sky behind him, they could have filmed him playing in Staten Island and no one would have known the difference.

Gene McFadden: We were in this meadow atop the mountain. The wind was howling, with gusts close to 50mph. We didn't have any wind screens, so I cut foam out of the instrument cases and wrapped them around the microphones.

Mitch Mitchell: We got there, and there's the director asking the audience what star sign they are. They're going, 'OK, all the Aquarians over this side, thank you very much. Cancers, stage left, that'll do very nicely.'

They'd hired a basic, straight Hollywood film crew, who were just killing themselves laughing every time the director told the audience to link arms of chant 'Om' or whatever.

Gerry Stickells: We started having trouble with the multi-track tape machine. I said, 'Whoa, stop! It's not recording properly!' Barry DePrendergast, standing next to me, was livid. 'You can't stop it now,' he told me. 'Chuck is creating the vibrations to make everything good.' I looked out the back of the truck and there, as thousands of dollars were rolling away, was Wein chanting, 'Om' on the edge of the stage.

Mike Neal (sound engineer): The whole thing was an unmitigated disaster and certainly not much of a show. No one, neither the band nor crew, were happy with what had gone down.

1 August 1970: International Center Arena, Honolulu, Hawaii.
Tom Hulett (Concerts West): I walked into his dressing room before the Honolulu show and Hendrix grabbed me. He said, 'Tom, you have to get me out of here. I'm staying over in Maui and I'm not happy. I have to do this film, I haven't eaten any meat and these people are making me eat this crazy shit.' I had never seen him like this, so I told him to jump in my station wagon after the show and I would take him to a hotel.

Mike Neal: That was a great show, but no one was there to film or record anything.

Tom Hulett: After the show, we hopped into the station wagon and took off. Backstage, everyone was panicking. They thought that Hendrix had gotten lost. Meanwhile, we had checked him into a hotel. Hendrix went upstairs, showered, changed and wanted to go out. He was as straight as a whistle and in great spirits, as if we'd sprung him from jail.

14 August 1970: Doing rough mixes on 'Dolly Dagger' and 'Freedom' at Electric Lady.
Billy Cox: Jimi wanted Eddie to set mixes up,

because he knew he had that ear. Eddie could hear things that we couldn't. Mitch would occasionally want his drums to sound a certain way, or I might suggest an idea, but once Eddie got things started for him, Jimi could really do some things behind that board.

15 August 1970: Proposed starting date of a Hendrix World Tour.
Bob Levine: Hendrix originally wanted to do a big concert at Stonehenge, and said that if that couldn't be arranged, he wanted to tour Mexico and the Yucatan peninsula as well as Japan. Japan seemed the most likely and, while individual dates were never booked, John Morris and Harold Davison (tour promoters) had set August 15, 1970 as the tentative start date.

18 August 1970: Doing overdubs on 'Dolly Dagger' at Electric Lady.
Billy Cox: Jimi and I were most comfortable doing our overdubs at the board. You didn't have the obstruction presented by those earphones. You could get right into it when you heard the music through those speakers. That was another benefit of working at Electric Lady—Eddie understood that this was our way of doing overdubs. We didn't have to fight or explain why we were doing them. We just did them.

Eddie Kramer: Ultimately, 'Dolly Dagger' was complex track with many layers of sound. Hendrix's lead guitar somehow floated through the whole thing and locked it all together. We recorded his guitar in stereo, combining direct feeds from both his guitar and amplifier. Since both Jimi and Billy were playing basically the same riff, it kind of locked the rhythm in.

20 August 1970: Jimi completes recording of 'Room Full Of Mirrors' at Electric Lady.
Eddie Kramer: Some of the material, such as 'Room Full Of Mirrors', required a great deal of work. I was never happy with the drum sound on the original master, as it sounded squashed. Therefore that track required a considerable amount of time. In a continuing series of overdubs and re-mixes, we added guitars and created some intricate panning effects before finishing.

22 August 1970: Electric Lady Studios, New York, working on 'Belly Button Window'.
Billy Cox: Jimi told me that 'Belly Button Window' had been written about the baby Mitch and his wife Lynn were expecting. He used to say that the baby was looking out Lynn's belly button window at us.

Jim Marron: I don't feel that Hendrix had peaked creatively. Drugs were not only screwing him up, they were destroying the environment he needed to create. With Electric Lady set to open, I didn't want to be the guy who procured drugs or women for him. Hendrix sat through many paternal lectures about his drug use from all of us, but I doubt it had any long-term effect.

24 August 1970: Monika Danneman travels from Düsseldorf to London, and books in at the Samarkand Hotel, 22 Lansdowne Crescent, Notting Hill. She stays in the basement flat.
Noel Redding: All those people who say they knew Jimi—well, it's ridiculous. All those chicks who say they knew him. He was very close to a chick he dug in Sweden, but the chick he met in Düsseldorf... well, he spent three days with her. They say they knew him, but they don't.

25 August 1970: Official opening party in New York for Electric Lady Studios, attended by Yoko Ono, Johnny Winter, Noel Redding and members of Fleetwood Mac.
Jim Marron: We had a hard time getting him to come. I appealed to him directly, telling him that I had been breaking my balls trying to open this place for him. I said, 'You can't have an opening party for Jimi Hendrix's studio without Jimi Hendrix.' He complained about having to go on tour and I cut him off, asking what exactly—between him and me—it would take to get him to the party. He said, 'Well, I have to leave for England after the party and I've never had a police escort to the airport...' For me,that was simple. I knew a lieutenant in the Village police precinct who had been co-operating with me and I called him, asking for a favour... My connection said, 'No problem, I'll arrange for two motorcycles.' With that, I got Hendrix to come.

John Veneble: Just before Hendrix was to leave, I saw him in Jeffery's office upstairs. I remember thinking to myself, Boy, this guy doesn't want any part of this tour. I couldn't say anything, as Hendrix barely knew I worked there, but I'll never forget that feeling. That was the last time most of us saw him.

26 August 1970: Electric Lady studios open officially for business.
Eddie Kramer: When we started recording at Electric Lady, there tended to be multiple choices of guitar solos. It's quite a desirable problem to have, really—you've got six fantastic Jimi Hendrix solos, so what do you do? We did quite a lot of taking bits from each to get the best overall. But it was hard, because they were all valid. Y'know, Jimi would always want to go one better. He was never completely happy with everything he'd done... like all true artists, I think.

27 August 1970: Hendrix flies to London, moves into the Londonderry Hotel, is interviewed by *The Times*, spends the evening at The Speakeasy, and ends up in bed with Angelia (Angie) Burdon and another girl.
Eric Barrett (road manager): We were still drunk after leaving the reception and the hostess woke us up—in London. He hadn't played England for two years. The press were all there to meet us, and he was very happy.

28 August 1970: Hendrix assaults his sleeping companions in the Londonderry Hotel. Later, he does interviews with *NME, Music Now* and *Record Mirror* in his suite. Danish model Kirsten Nefer drops in to meet him.
Kathy Etchingham: Angelia phoned me at home about eleven in the morning and said they were up in the hotel with Jimi, and Jimi had gone bananas. Their clothes were in the bedroom and they were in the sitting room and that they were frightened to go back in... Angelia said that he suddenly went bananas and started banging their heads together.

Rob Partridge (journalist): I was doing him for *Record Mirror*, and mine was the last interview on a day of conveyor-belt interviews and, by the time I got to Hendrix in the early evening, he seemed to be giving the answers by rote. I remember noting how thin he was, but he certainly didn't look or behave like a man who was about to die, or a man who was depressed or suicidal.

Kirsten Nefer: I was taken to meet Jimi by my friend Karen Davies who had known Jimi in New York. I was really into the music, but I didn't like the man. He looked small and ugly in his pictures and there was all this stuff about girls and everything. We knocked on Jimi's door, he opened it and I couldn't believe it—he was tall, he was skinny and he was beautiful.

We talked until three in the morning and then crashed out for the night.

29 August 1970: Press interviews at the Londonderry Hotel.
Kirsten Nefer: In the morning, I left and went to Eaton Square where I lived. About an hour later, Karen and Jimi turned up at the house. We then went to El Tusso for lunch and then later to a club. Jimi wrote me the directions to the Isle of Wight.

30 August 1970: Isle Of Wight Festival, East Afton Farm, Isle of Wight.
Gerry Stickells: It was the end of the love and peace era. People broke down the fences, there was violence. It had run its course—the love and peace bit.

Pete Townshend: Hendrix was a psychological mess of a man. Nobody cared. People thought, He can play such great guitar, so he's obviously okay. What made me work so hard was seeing the condition Jimi was in. He was in such tragically bad condition physically, and I remember thanking God as I walked on stage that I was healthy.

Ralph McTell: I saw Joan Baez and Jimi Hendrix's roadies backstage. They said that Hendrix was very out of it in somebody's garden and they were worried that he wouldn't be able to play.

"HENDRIX WAS A PSYCHOLOGICAL MESS OF A MAN. NOBODY CARED. PEOPLE THOUGHT: HE CAN PLAY SUCH GREAT GUITAR, SO HE'S OBVIOUSLY OKAY. HE WAS IN SUCH TRAGICALLY BAD CONDITION PHYSICALLY, AND I CAN REMEMBER THANKING GOD AS I WALKED ON STAGE THAT I WAS HEALTHY"

Kirsten Nefer: The whole atmosphere was very weird... he was so afraid of going on stage.

Roy Carr (NME*):* In the weeks leading up to his death, Jimi's hair became flecked with grey and his skin took on an unhealthy pallor. This was most noticeable in the bright sunlight backstage at the Isle Of Wight. Jimi shared a catering-size bottle of vodka with friends and journalists, before giving a well-below-par performance.

Ian Anderson: By this time, Jethro Tull had performed with Hendrix on quite a few bills and our star was in the ascendant, while he was in decline. As a result, on many dates we were effectively co-headlining. The golden rule of festivals is never close the show. Nobody wants to play to an audience that is exhausted, doped, hungry and ready to go home. As a result, when The Moody Blues came off, there was a real battle between our road crew and Jimi's to see who could get set up first and get on stage quickest. We beat them to the punch, and left him to close the show, which he really did not want to do.

Mitch Mitchell: We'd been touring America for nine months and when we arrived in England for the Isle Of Wight gig, Jimi was knackered. We hadn't played for three weeks and it showed.

Jeff Dexter (DJ and Festival MC): I went out to introduce Jimi, and he said, 'Hang on, I'm not ready.' It took him about 40 minutes to get himself together. He was in a state. He didn't want me to introduce him. I was to say, 'This is Blue Angel music'—the Blue Angel was the parachute division he had been in the US Army. He went to go on in his new gear and said, 'Hey man, I can't play my guitar...' The sleeves were too big, and got in the way of the strings.

So I put another record on, went to one side and I sewed up his sleeve. I was trained as a tailor at school. By this time the audience had been waiting 70 minutes, so I said, 'Better get on, Jimi,' and I just ran on and said, 'Here's the man with the guitar!' He was about to come on, and his trousers split. So I pinned him up and he went on stage all pinned and stitched up.

Kirsten Nefer: They booed him because he didn't do what they expected him to do, you know, all these gimmicks.

Glenn Tipton (fan, later of Judas Priest): I'd come down from Birmingham in a car with a bunch of friends, and camped in a tent, because Hendrix was one of my big influences on guitar. He was very much out of tune for the first two or three numbers, but then he got in tune and the rest of the show was amazing. But with Hendrix, even being out of tune was pretty good.

Kirsten Nefer: After the concert, Jimi walked off the opposite side of the stage to where I was standing. It took me 30 minutes to find his caravan. When I got in there, there were 20 people, you know? It was packed with people. When we got out, Jimi said to me, 'Don't you ever leave the stage while I'm playing.'

Then we went back to his hotel, The Seagrove. We stayed there for a few hours, then Jimi had to take the helicopter and I had to go back to London. Jimi said that he would be playing in Denmark and, as I'm Danish, it was the big idea that, you know, I go to Denmark, and he gave me and Karen money so we could go there and everything was arranged.

Jimi Hendrix: I was so mixed-up there and at that time it got so confused, like, eh... I didn't have a chance to base any of my future on that one gig, you know?

31 August 1970: Flight to Sweden, for a gig at Stora Scenen, Tivoli Gardens, Stockholm, where he is seen by Chas Chandler. Eva Sundquist is also there and Hendrix asks about their son.
Sigurgeir Sigurjonsson (photographer): As soon as he appeared in the (dressing) room, everyone and everything focused on him. As soon as he entered the room, he grabbed a small bottle of whisky and emptied it just like he was drinking water. I suggested that (for the photo session) he hold a little child that happened to be there. He immediately agreed, saying 'Oh, I found my baby, I can see this one is mine.' It wasn't. Instead it was Ditta, daughter of George Clemons, an old friend of Jimi from the New York days.

Chas Chandler: He was wrecked. He'd start a song, get into the solo section and then he wouldn't even remember what song they were playing at the time. He'd come into a different song. It was a disastrous concert, it was really awful to watch.

A messed-up Hendrix gives a well-below-par performance at the Isle Of Wight Festival, for which he was booed by fans

Hendrix and Eric Barrett (roadie from May 1968 until the very end) make their way through another airport in another city

Autumn 1970

1 September, 1970: Billy Cox tries LSD before the show at Stora Scene, Liseberg Nojespark, Gothenburg, Sweden, supported by Cat Mother.

Gerry Stickells: He (Billy Cox) freaked out. He was scared to go out, scared to be alone. He was sure someone was gonna shoot him on stage. I had to be with him everywhere, day and night.

Mitch Mitchell: That night, I got a call from England. My daughter, Aysha, had been born. I chartered a plane and flew back to see Aysha, just for the day. In fact, I saw her for about an hour.

2 September 1970: The band flies on to Aarhus, Denmark. Hendrix is interviewed in the Hotel Atlantic by Anne Bjorndal of *Morgensposten*. Gig at Vejlby Risskov Hallen, Aarhus. Hendrix leaves the stage after three songs, saying, 'I've been dead a long time.'

Mike Neal (sound engineer): The first time most of us felt that Billy Cox had a serious problem was there. Cox was afraid of almost everyone, including the people he had been working with for six months.

Kirsten Nefer: Karen and I flew to Denmark early in the morning. We went to the hotel where Jimi was staying. While we were waiting for the lift, the door opens and Mitch comes out. He was surprised to see us. 'Well, you better go on up. He's in a funny mood.'

We got up to the room and there was the whole Danish press gathered. Jimi opened the door and he was staggering. He said, 'Oh my God, you're here. I don't want you to see me like this.' He was really out of it.

Anne Bjorndal: He was already talking about cancelling because he was not feeling well. Eventually it was decided that he should go on. I can't remember him eating anything. He drank some orange juice. He was talking a lot about the supernatural and mentioning Jesus. He said, 'Well, obviously religion must come from inside, it's your own religion.' And he called himself a traveller in electric religion. He was also talking about harmony and peace of mind. He said, 'the guitar is through which I speak, and I sacrifice part of my soul every time I play.' But what was quite something, which was to be my headline, was he said, 'I don't think I will live to be 28.'

Mitch Mitchell: I got back just in time for the gig that night… I was tired but really up.

Kirsten Nefer: When we got to the concert hall, we were in the dressing room… There was this whole scene where he couldn't decide what to wear and he couldn't tune his guitar. He was throwing people out of the dressing room and calling them back in again. It was crazy. In the end, I was alone with him and he was going on and on about his guitar, about how he didn't want to play… eventually he got up there, but I could see on his face there was something really, really wrong… I found out that he had taken some sleeping pills.

Anne Bjorndal: The few bits we saw (of the concert) were great, but then, all of a sudden, he collapsed.

Otto Fewser (hall manager): Hendrix collapsed in my arms (in the dressing room) and we sat him upon a chair. He was cold, cold fever, they asked for cocaine. 'We have not cocaine,' I say. Hendrix could not play more.

Gene McFadden: Stickells told me to put the guitars away without being conspicuous. They were all still in full view of the audience. I went out there, pretended to tune each one and then set them back in their cases. We got everything out of there, but it was very scary for a while.

Anne Bjorndal: Exhausted and scared. That's how he appeared to me. Scared, like a frightened child.

Kirsten Nefer: After this Danish girl left, Jimi said to me that we have to talk all night. I said, 'Talk all night? I'm so tired.' But he insisted that we talk. Then he said, 'Wanna marry me?' We talked until about seven in the morning.

3 September 1970: Concert at the KB Hallen, Copenhagen.

Kirsten Nefer: We woke about 11—we had to catch this plane about 12. We arrived at Copenhagen about mid-day… I called my mum up and we stayed with her. My mum made food and the family came over. Jimi couldn't believe it. He said, 'This is a family. You're all so good to each other.'

Bo Jacobsen (support band, Blue Sun): We did not see Hendrix backstage. He locked himself up with some really beautiful girls. He only came out when he had to go on stage. I sat and talked with Mitch. Mitch was fixing right next to me but he was extremely nice to everyone. It was kind of, uh, 'Yes, come here and let's talk,'no arrogance.

Then it was time for Hendrix to enter the stage. I remember that very clearly. Hendrix came out, walked by me, and just before he entered the stage he said, 'Huh, people,' then he entered the stage showing the peace/victory symbol. How could he do this? That must be the American way of show business.

I saw the show far away from the stage but still the sound was absolutely deafening. He had his 12 Marshall amplifiers, and the volume level must have been in top. I also remember he broke a string and put a new one on without pausing.

Sharon Lawrence (reporter): Jimi looked the picture of health and played breathtakingly well. The roller coaster was back on track.

Gene McFadden: Hendrix played for nearly two hours. He even came out and did 'Hey Joe' and 'Fire' for an encore.

Kirsten Nefer: After the concert, we went back to my place and stayed there overnight.

4 September 1970: The band fly in to Berlin for the Super Concert 70 at Deutschlandhalle, with Procol Harum, Canned Heat, Ten Years After and Cat Mother.
Robin Trower (Procol Harum): Berlin was a strange gig. Up until when Jimi came on, everybody was going down better and better. And then when Jimi was on, the audience just wasn't there. They weren't digging it. I think it was above their heads, you know? I mean, I couldn't take in a lot of what he was doing and I'm a musician, a guitarist, so you can imagine what it was like for them.

I was very, very choked, because I felt very annoyed at the audience. So, anyway, then I was walking up and down outside the dressing room after he'd come off, and I was sort of saying, 'Should I go in?' Then I burst into the dressing room all of a sudden and said, 'Er—I've gotta tell you, it was the best thing I've ever seen.' Which it was. And he said, 'Uh, thank you, but, uh, naw.' And I just went, 'Woops, that's it,' and walked out again.

5 September 1970: The band travel by train from Berlin to Puttgarden, Isle of Fehmarn, for a festival.
Mitch Mitchell: We got there mid-afternoon and were supposedly on at eight. By about six we heard this wind and then it turned into a gale. We knew by then there were other problems as well. The usual equipment trouble, plus Hell's Angels with guns. We were re-scheduled for mid-day on Sunday.

Gerry Stickells: All of the musicians and crew had been booked into one hotel. When the performances on the 5th were cancelled, the bar was a madhouse, people fighting and smashing chairs. Later that night, when the bar ran out of liquor, the owners packed up and left, leaving people to fend for themselves.

Cox lost it completely at this point. He swore that people were trying to kill him and wouldn't stay in his room on his own. He was so paranoid that he ended up sleeping on the floor by the side of my bed. To convince him to play the gig, I had to promise to stand behind him on stage.

6 September 1970: The band play the Love And Peace Festival, Puttgarden, then return immediately to London. Hendrix books into the Cumberland Hotel.
Mitch Mitchell: We heard that there had been real problems overnight—a lot of violence. We drove out to the site, got out of the car and this plank of wood with six-inch nails in it was thrown from a group of Hell's Angels and hit Gerry Stickells on the head.

Gerry Stickells: When we got to the stage I got hit by the Hell's Angels with a chain. It was one of those things where the feeling was, well, let's just play this and get out of here, because we ain't gonna get out of here unless we play.

We were the last to perform… It was so bad, we had taxis stand by backstage while he played, ran straight off stage, jumped in the taxis and took them all the way back to Hamburg and straight to the airport… as soon as our gear was off the stage, the Hell's Angels burned it down.

Mitch Mitchell: The night we got back (to London) Billy started going again and Jimi and Gerry took him to the doctor. They hadn't seen paranoia like this for a long time…

8 September 1970: Billy Cox's condition deteriorates further. In the evening, Hendrix goes to see the film *The Red Desert* with Karen Davis and Kirsten Nefer.
Kirsten Nefer: In the afternoon, me and Karen went up to the Cumberland Hotel to see Jimi. While we were there, Jimi got a call from the Airways Hotel saying that he'd better come over because Billy Cox was completely freaked out, so we went over and Billy was out of his head.

Billy would be groaning, 'Oh, I'm gonna die, I'm gonna die,' and Jimi would say, 'Nobody is going to die!'

Mike Neal: At this point, to communicate with Cox you would have to say, 'Billy, you remember me. We're friends. We did this and that together…'

Kirsten Nefer: There was Karen, me and Jimi in this weird little (cinema) in the West End with really old-fashioned seats. It was an incredible film and Jimi was just so happy afterwards, after seeing this film.

9 September 1970: Billy Cox is flown to Pennsylvania to recover at home with his parents.
Gerry Stickells: Finally, I had to convince him to get on an airplane, alone, and fly back home.

10 September 1970: Hendrix goes to a party for Mike Nesmith at the Inn On The Park.
Mitch Mitchell: On the Thursday, Jimi called me and told me he was OK and that he was doing some writing, and looking forward to going back to New York and the new studio.

Mike Nesmith: We spent most of the time just talking and reminiscing. I was surprised to see him in somewhat of a funk. He was not happy with the way his music had developed. He felt stultified somehow. He felt that what he was doing didn't have the substance it once had.

We were standing outside, alone, in a lobby, and I felt a great deal of compassion for him. As he stood there, his eyes kind of drifted off, and I could see him trying to come to terms with some devil or something in his own head. And he said, 'You know, I think I'm gonna start an R&B band. I gotta do something. I think I'm gonna work with some horns and put together something like Otis, cause that's really where it's at.' I put my arm around him and I said, 'Jimi, don't you understand, man, you invented psychedelic music. Nobody ever played this before you came along. Why are you going through this crisis of self-confidence right now?'

And he didn't say anything. He didn't respond to that at all, but it was a very extraordinary moment in my life, and I think in his as well. He nodded kind of in agreement to that, but in a very humble way.

11 September 1970: Hendrix is interviewed by Keith Altham for *Record Mirror* at the Cumberland Hotel.
Keith Altham: Jimi was fragile, but not in a depressed state. In fact he was very positive about what he wanted to do.

There were three girlfriends in the room and we watched Kenny Everett's *Explosion* TV show which Jimi thought one of the funniest he had ever seen. We drank Mateus Rose and Jimi made plans to dine out that night.

12 September 1970: Devon Wilson and Alan Douglas fly to London; a Hendrix interview appears in *Disc & Music Echo*.

"WHEN JIMI WAS ON, THE AUDIENCE JUST WASN'T DIGGING IT. I THINK IT WAS ABOVE THEIR HEADS, YOU KNOW? I MEAN, I COULDN'T TAKE IN A LOT OF WHAT HE WAS DOING AND I'M A MUSICIAN, A GUITARIST, SO YOU CAN IMAGINE WHAT IT WAS LIKE FOR THEM. I WAS VERY, VERY CHOKED"

Jimi Hendrix:

Marriage is a bit risky now… I'd really hate to get hurt. That would completely blow my mind. But I must admit, I'd like to meet a quiet little girl now—probably one from the country. But someone who doesn't know anything about me and my 'reputation'. I'd really like to settle down.

13 September 1970: Mike Jeffery arrives in London; Hendrix calls Monika Danneman at the Samarkand Hotel.
Alan Douglas: I saw Jeffery at Track Records on Old Compton Street. He burst in, saying, 'Alan, you have to get me in touch with Jimi.' I pretended not to know anything because I didn't want to get in the middle of it all. Jeffery was desperate, saying he had urgent business and had to see him. I said, 'Look, I'll try to get in touch with him.' I told Hendrix the next day and he blew me off.

Alvenia Bridges: He had an anxiety attack at Elvaston Place (Pat Hartley's apartment). He told me a story about being kidnapped and taken to upstate New York. He got really intense about his management. He said, 'Man, they'll just do anything with you.' He was real unhappy in London. He didn't seem like his old self. He needed a lot of love. I'm a kisser, so we'd hug and kiss. But it wasn't enough.

14 September 1970: Hendrix visits Monika Danneman at the Samarkand Hotel.
Kirsten Nefer: In the morning I got up and left, and that was it. I had to go back to work on a film with George Lazenby. Jimi told me to please call in that night. I called and left messages for him but he wasn't there.

Monika Danneman: Because things were still going so heavy in America, he checked into a hotel. But secretly we stayed in our flat so that nobody knew where he was actually staying and everybody would approach him from the hotel. Which they did. Only in the last week did people find out where we were, because word always seems to get around.

15 September 1970: Ed Chalpin of PPX flies into London; at Ronnie Scott's Club, Hendrix tells Eric Burdon he'd like to jam, but he is too stoned to play.

Eric Burdon: Jimi had locked himself up in this dreadful hotel here in London, and he wouldn't come across the door. His road manager, Eric Barrett, came to me and said, 'What can we do to help Jimi? He's in real bad shape.' I said, 'Well, you know, if he wants to talk to me, I'm at Ronnie Scott's club tonight,' because I've done enough running around trying to tell this guy what's gonna happen to him if he doesn't....

I mean, at that point in time, what am I? An acid-drenched fucking rock star who's over the hill, trying to tell this guy what the right thing is to do. Is he going to listen to me? No fucking way. Would he listen to anybody? No.

Monika Danneman: Jimi had a meeting at 8pm with Ed Chalpin.

Ed Chalpin: Jimi was having problems with his career. He wanted to pull out of the music business and had called me in New York, begging me to join him in London.

Daniel Secunda: It was an incredibly stressful time for Jimi. Things were falling apart. Billy Cox was completely freaked out with acid, and Jimi was doing all sorts of drugs to escape from the reality of things like the PPX legal actions. He really did not want to face Ed Chalpin.

Monika Danneman: In the early evening, we went to Judy Wong's birthday party. After, we went together with others to Ronnie Scott's club.

Sharon Lawrence: Jimi moved as though in a daze, and it took him a long moment to realize who I was. He was terribly pale and his eyes looked exhausted.

Terry McVay (road manager, Eric Burdon): I wouldn't let him jam. He looked disoriented.

Ron Wood: I saw him when he left Ronnie Scott's. He had his arm round this girl and he was leaning over and I shouted to him, 'Hey, Jimi!' He was really slow and I said, 'Aren't you gonna say goodnight?' He turned round and just said, 'Night.'

Chas Chandler: He came up to our apartment, the same one we used to share. He came up to see my son, because he hadn't seen the baby, and we sat and talked. He wasn't satisfied with the stuff he had done in the studio. He had come to the conclusion, 'I grudgingly have to admit you were right about producing the band.' I said, 'If you got stuff, we'll bring it over here, we'll do it in London, away from the fuckin' crowd.'

He wanted to put the old team back together—him, myself and Eddie Kramer. I offered to book time in Olympic and listen to what he had done... at that point he called Eddie Kramer in New York about coming over with the tapes.

Eddie Kramer: I distinctly remember the call from London... it was Jimi and he was asking if I could bring all the tapes over to England. I sensed something was up, but I said, 'Jimi, don't be crazy. We've built this beautiful studio for you. You'll be here on Monday.' There was long drawn-out pause on the line until he said, 'Yeah, you're right. I'll be back on Monday and we'll get it together'... He never mentioned Chas or Olympic—probably because he didn't know who might be around me in the control room—but I wish he had.

Albert Allen: I got the phone, and Hendrix small-talked, saying that he thought someone had drugged Billy Cox with LSD and, as a result, he had to stay over there a little longer than expected.

Chas Chandler: He ended the night by saying that he was going to go back to New York and bring all the tapes back to London. I told him that I had already made arrangements to bring the baby up to Newcastle and see my parents over the weekend. I told him I would see him Monday or Tuesday.

16 September 1970: Hendrix spends most of the day with Monika Danneman; in the evening he visits The Speakeasy and later returns to Ronnie Scott's to jam with Eric Burdon and War.
Terry McVay: He was alone (when he got to Ronnie Scott's), looking clean and sharp. With a smile, Jimi asked, 'Can I play now? I've even brought my own cord.' I told him I would consider it a pleasure.

Eric Burdon: He started off badly, as Jimi The Sound Freak, did one solo which died and was very bad. Later, he became better, real loose, but when the break (between sets) came he wasn't in such a good mood. In the dressing room, he said he wouldn't go back on but, after a bit of talking, he did and, after some good playing, he really got into the last number, 'Tobacco Road'. He wasn't sound-freaking, he was just gelling nicely with the band.

*Roy Carr (*NME*):* Restricting himself mainly to playing rhythm, Jimi later retired to the cramped basement dressing room. Whether it was exhaustion or his usual pleasantly zonked demeanour, Jimi seemed tired as he sat and joked with those present. Asked what his plans were, Jimi said that he would really like to 'find an island of coke somewhere in the Pacific and just float away, know what I mean?' Everyone laughed knowingly.

Daniel Secunda: I had dinner with Jimi, Devon Wilson, Alan Douglas and his wife Stella in a Moroccan restaurant on Fulham Road. Alan was living in my flat, and he was hustling to take over as Jimi's manager. Jimi was, by now, very worried about Mike Jeffery.

Jimi and the girls were so smacked out that, through the meal, they barely ate anything or even said a word. When we got back to my place, Jimi went off to bed with Stella and Devon. He loved a menage a trois. I knew he was stressed out, but there was no indication of him being suicidal.

Alan Douglas: Wednesday night, Jimi stayed over at Danny's house with us. We just talked all night long. And the plan was that I would leave next morning and go back and tell Steingarten and that

"MARRIAGE IS A BIT RISKY... I'D REALLY HATE TO GET HURT. BUT I MUST ADMIT, I'D LIKE TO MEET A QUIET LITTLE GIRL — PROBABLY ONE FROM THE COUNTRY, BUT SOMEONE WHO DOESN'T KNOW ANYTHING ABOUT ME AND MY 'REPUTATION'. I'D REALLY LIKE TO SETTLE DOWN"

whole attorney's group, that it was all over, that we were terminating. I was gonna personally talk to all the business relationships and tell them what we were about to do. Instead of touring, we would do four concerts a year, film those concerts and bicycle the print around the country to all the theaters. He loved that idea, it was all part of the plan.

17 September 1970: Alan Douglas flies back to New York; Monika Danneman photographs Hendrix in the garden at The Samarkand; Hendrix bumps into Kathy Etchingham in Kensington Market; in the late afternoon, he calls Henry Steingarten to discuss business. A jam is planned with Hendrix and Sly Stone at The Speakeasy.
Monika Danneman: The photographs of him in the garden show him very naturally the gardener. He just wanted to show his natural side and not his image that had been following him for years. He was very happy, making plans in regard to us getting married, having children.

Kathy Etchingham: I was looking at some things and he came up behind me. He said, 'I'm staying at the Cumberland Hotel. Come over later.' I went home, but Ray was terribly jealous and I couldn't go.

Mitch Mitchell: About quarter to seven I went to see Gerry Stickells, who said that Hendrix had called about 15 minutes previously: would I give him a call?

I called him up and he asked me what I was doing. I told him I was just off to visit Ginger Baker and then we were going out to Heathrow to meet Sly Stone, who was flying in.

Jimi was really excited about Sly and said, 'Is there any chance of a play?'

So I said, 'Funny you should say that, yeah, the idea is we're all going down to The Speakeasy for a jam.' Jimi was really up for it and agreed to meet us there about midnight.

Monika Dannemann: We did not spend a tiring day on Thursday and arrived home about 8.30 pm. I cooked a meal and had a bottle of white wine about 11.00 pm. He drank more of the bottle than I did. He had nothing to drink other than the wine. I had a bath and washed my hair and then we talked. At this time there was no argument or stress, it was a happy atmosphere.

Mitch Mitchell: He didn't show up (at The Speakeasy) which we all thought was very, very strange, 'cos no matter what situation was going on, for Hendrix to miss a chance of a play was very out of character—really completely out of character.

Monika Danneman: He told me that at 1.45am he had to go see someone at their flat. They were people he didn't like. I dropped him off in my car and picked him up an hour later. Just after 3am we went back to my flat. We talked.

18 September 1970: Hendrix is with Monika Danneman at the Samarkand Hotel.
Monika Danneman: I took a sleeping tablet at about 7am. I made him two fish sandwiches. We were in bed talking. I woke about 10.20am. He was sleeping normally. I went around the corner to get cigarettes, when I came back he had been sick. He was breathing and his pulse was normal but I could not wake him. I saw that he had taken sleeping tablets, there were nine of mine missing.

I knew Jimi's doctor's name was Robertson, because Jimi had taken Billy Cox to see him. I looked in his phone book but there were too many Robertsons listed.

I called Alvenia (Bridges) because she knew Jimi and had lived in London for some time. She didn't know Jimi's doctor's name either.

Eric Burdon then got on the phone and asked what was happening. I told him Jimi was sick and wouldn't wake up, and that I wanted to call an ambulance. He told me to wait, and that maybe he would wake up on his own.

Eric Burdon: I was thinking, Why would anybody want to wake Jimi up? He never woke up before noon. She was frantic, so I told her just to walk him round, coffee, splash some water in his face, you know?

Monika Danneman: I telephoned a friend and she advised me to send for an ambulance. I suppose the ambulance came about 20 minutes later.

Alvenia Bridges: I arrived just as the ambulance pulled up. Monika said she had hidden Jimi's guitar. She didn't want anybody to know who he was. She had Jimi's passport and other identification.

Sly Stone: Hendrix loved his music and was due to jam with him only hours before hefore his death, but failed to turn up

Reg Jones (ambulance man): It was horrific. He was covered in vomit. There was tons of it all over the pillow—black and brown it was... We felt his pulse between his shoulders, pinched his earlobe and nose, showed a light in his eyes. But there was no response at all.

Monika Danneman: I think he knew exactly what he could take in the way of sleeping tablets. When I last saw him before he went to sleep he was very happy. The tablets were in a cupboard, he would have to get out of bed to get the tablets.

He said he had had cannabis. There was no question of exhaustion on this particular evening. He was not a man to have moods. He was not tensed up. I have never heard him say he wished he were dead or that life was not worth living. He had business stresses but this did not worry him.

Ian Smith (Notting Hill Police constable): We went to a basement flat in Lansdowne Crescent, and Hendrix's girlfriend told us who he was. Hendrix was on the floor, lumped out. The ambulance people were already there and, as far as they were concerned, he was dead.

Alvenia Bridges: When we got to the hospital she (Monika Danneman) checked him in, using a false name. She was afraid he would get mad at her.

Dr John Bannister (surgical registrar, St Mary Abbots hospital): The ambulance had brought in a patient who was unconscious. He was taken out of the ambulance on a trolley and wheeled into Casualty. We attempted resuscitation and cardiac massage. Continual suction of his pharynx and larynx was performed.

On admission, he was obviously dead. He had no pulse, no heartbeat, and the attempt to resuscitate him was merely a formality, an attempt we would perform on any patient in that condition. I can recall to this day that his respiratory tract and his pharynx were full of red wine mixed with gastric contents. I still vividly recall this aspect of the resuscitation and how tragically this man had died, literally drowning himself in red wine.

Alvenia Bridges: We didn't believe it. We didn't want to. I said I wanted to see him and, finally, they agreed to let us go in. We asked for his possessions and they gave us what he had in his pockets. Then Monika became hysterical. She curled up on the floor and began crying. I ran to a phone and called Eric, and he sent someone to take us back to his hotel.

Professor Robert Donald Teare (who carried out the post mortem): There were no stigmata of drug addiction. Once these marks are there, they never go. In this case, there were no marks at all.

Robin Turner (journalist and friend): He snorted heroin, which is a fairly wasteful method. But, towards the end, he only took small amounts. I think he was coming together and, if he had stayed around, he would have made it.

Gerry Stickells: I identified the body at the hospital. It was not my idea of fun... But it was very different then. There was no general awareness that such a great talent had been lost.

Barrie Martin: That night I was working as floor manager on the BBC TV current affairs programme *24 Hours,* which was presented by Kenneth Allsop. We were all sitting in the bar at Lime Grove studios when this bloke rushed in with a new running order. It had been changed to include the news that Hendrix was dead. He'd been such a hero to me, that I remember shivers running up and down all over my body.

Mitch Mitchell: I got a call from Eric Barrett, telling me that Jimi had died. I just couldn't believe it. I couldn't release any emotion at all... it was hard to accept that he was dead; it still felt as though he was right there.

Miller Anderson: I was still with the Keef Hartley band at that point, and we came back from a tour of Denmark that night. As we drove through London in the van, we could see the newspaper hoardings with the headline about Jimi's death. We stopped the van in Leicester Square and ran over to get a paper. It was such a heart-breaking, tragic way for him to go.

Noel Redding: It was the first time in my life that someone I had known was dead. All these women came to my room and wanted to commit suicide—to throw themselves out of the window. I'm not religious but I went with all these women to church. Then we went to a cocktail bar and we got rotten. I was shook up.

Chas Chandler: I got on the train to Newcastle on the Friday morning. When I arrived, my father was waiting for me, which he never usually did. 'I came to get you away from all the reporters.' 'Reporters?' 'Don't you know?' 'Know what?' 'Jimi's dead.'

Al Hendrix: His death was a terrible blow. He was only young, 27. I was always scared about him going in those planes all the time. That was my great fear.

Mitch Mitchell: If Hendrix had taken all the drugs the papers and rock books say he took, he'd never have lived as long as he did. Jimi was the kind of person who'd push things to the nth degree, but I never saw suicidal tendencies there. He's painted as the tragic figure, but he wasn't. He died tragically, but that's not the same thing.

Jim Marron: I was in Spain with Jeffery, and we were supposed to have dinner that night in Majorca. He called me from his club in Palma, saying that he would have to cancel. I said, 'Mike, we've already made reservations.' He said, 'Well... there is good reason. I've just got word from London. Jimi's dead.' I said, 'What?' He said, 'I always knew that son of a bitch would pull a quickie.'

Eric Clapton: When they told me he was dead I felt fucking angry. I felt, shit, he's let me down. I felt betrayed even though it wasn't a conscious decision for him to die. I felt like the loneliest person on earth.

Barry Mitchell (then bass-player for Queen): I arrived at the flat to meet the others, and had just walked in when Freddie (Mercury), very pale-faced, asked, 'Have you heard? Jimi Hendrix is dead.' God, the stunned feeling was immense. He'd been our idol, and we were all absolutely shattered... at rehearsal, as our own tribute, we played nothing but Hendrix songs the whole session.

Mark Knopfler: When I quit my job as a newspaper reporter, they gave me one last story to write up an hour before I left. It turned out to be the story of Jimi's death.

Keith Emerson (The Nice): Our song 'The Barbarian' was kind of dedicated to Hendrix. We went on stage the night he died and announced to the audience, 'This song's for Jimi,' because that song started almost with the 'Purple Haze' chords.

Yngwie Malmstein: That was the day I started playing. I had been given a guitar for my fifth birthday and when I was seven years old they showed him on Swedish TV. I started playing straight away that day.

Joe Satriani: When he died, I made a decision that I would play. I was suited up and ready to start football practice, and one of the guys on the team just sort of casually mentioned that Hendrix had died. It devastated me. It was one of the first times I felt real loss. I turned in my equipment and told the coach I was quitting.

Neneh Cherry: I can remember being in a car where we lived in Hicksville, Sweden, outside a shopping center called Bestro. My father (jazz trumpeter Don Cherry) came out and told me that Jimi had died.

I can still remember sitting in the car and feeling the sadness and shock of being told about it.

Marianne Faithfull: I didn't have an affair with him. It's my only lasting regret in life.

Eric Burdon: The business killed him and I just can't put it any better.

Noel Redding: I never used to dream about Jimi, but one night I had a dream and Jimi came into the room. I said, 'But you're dead,' and he said, 'It's cool. I just wanted to see you again.'

"ON ADMISSION HE WAS OBVIOUSLY DEAD. HE HAD NO PULSE, NO HEARTBEAT, AND THE ATTEMPT TO RESUSCITATE HIM WAS MERELY A FORMALITY. I STILL VIVIDLY RECALL HOW TRAGICALLY THIS MAN HAD DIED, LITERALLY DROWNING HIMSELF IN RED WINE"

INDEX

PICTURE CREDITS :

The publishers would like to thank the following sources for their kind permission to reproduce the pictures in this book:

Main section:
Corbis/Bettmann 23, 85, 143, 158, 191, 240/Henry Diltz 205/Kevin Fleming 37t/Lynn Goldsmith 103/Hulton-Deutsch Collection 49, 153, 175, 239, 247/Neal Preston 126, 168, 180, 218, 230/Roger Ressmeyer 214/Ted Streshinsky 106, 165
Harry Goodwin 6
London Features International Ltd. 51
Pictorial Press 21, 40, 42, 46, 54, 56, 59, 80, 89, 138/Tony Gale 37b
Popperfoto 3, 70, 112
Repfoto/Barrie Wentzell 93, 172
Retna Pictures Ltd./King Collection 62/Photofest 4, 202/Ray Stevenson 1
Rex Features Ltd. 9, 12
Ronald Grant Archive/EMI/Famous/Starling 17
Sotheby's Picture Library 27
Vintage Magazine Archive Ltd. 148, 217, 225

Colour insert section one (pictures in order of appearance):
Corbis/Hulton-Deutsch Collection 14/Neal Preston 13/Mike Zens 16
Nic Dartnell 1
London Features International Ltd. 8, 9, 10, 12t
Pictorial Press Ltd. 3, 4, 5, 6
Rex Features Ltd./Bruce Flemming 2, 5/Richard Young 7
Retna Pictures Ltd./Photofest 12b
Scope Features 11
Vintage Magazine Archive Ltd. 15

Colour insert section two (pictures in order of appearance):
Corbis/Bettmann 2/Hulton-Deutsch Collection 1/Henry Diltz 16
Harry Goodwin 3, 4t, 6-7,
Image Bank/Archive Photos/Joseph Sia 9
London Features International 11, 15
Pictorial Press 4b/Tony Gale 13
Retna Pictures/Photofest 10/Michael Putland 14/Peter Smith 8/Ray Stevenson 12

Special thanks are due to Nic Dartnell and Harry Goodwin for their help.

Every effort has been made to acknowledge correctly and contact the source and or copyright holder of each picture, and Carlton Books Limited apologises for any unintentional errors or omissions which will be corrected in future editions of this book.

Bibliography :

Many books, periodicals and websites proved invaluable when putting this book together. I sincerely hope I haven't missed any out in the following list:

BOOKS

Are You Experienced? (Noel Redding and Carol Appleby, Fourth Estate, 1990)
The Hendrix Experience (Mitch Mitchell and John Platt, Mitchell Beazley, 1990)
Jimi Hendrix—A Visual Documentary (Tony Brown, Omnibus, 1992)
Hendrix—Setting The Record Straight (John McDermott and Eddie Kramer, Little, Brown, 1992)
Jimi Hendrix—Voices From Home (Mary Willix, Creative Forces, 1995)
Jimi Hendrix—Electric Gypsy (Harry Shapiro and Caesar Glebeek, Mandarin, 1995)
Hendrix—Sessions (John McDermott, Little, Brown, 1995)
Hendrix—A Biography (Chris Welch, Omnibus, 1982)
Jimi Hendrix—In His Own Words (Tony Brown, Omnibus, 1994)
The Jimi Hendrix Story (Jerry Hopkins, Sphere, 1983)
The Life Of Jimi Hendrix (David Henderson, Omnibus, 1978)
The Jimi Hendrix Companion (Chris Potash, Omnibus, 1996)
Hendrix—The Final Days (Tony Brown, Rogan House, 1997)
Jimi Hendrix (Curtis Knight, Star Books, 1975)
Jimi Hendrix—The Ultimate Experience (Adrian Boot and Chris Salewicz, Boxtree, 1995)
Jimi Hendrix—From The Benjamin Franklin Studios (Jimpress, 1996)
Hoot! (Robbie Woliver, St Martin's Press, 1986)
Fit Like, New York? (Peter Innes, Evening Express Publications, 1997)
Rockin' Croydon (Chris Groom, Wombeat, 1998)
Close To The Edge—The Story Of Yes (Chris Welch, Omnibus, 1999)
Fleetwood (Mick Fleetwood with Stephen Davis, Sidgwick & Jackson, 1990)
The Fillmore East (Richard Kostelanetz, Schirmer Books, 1997)
One More Saturday Night (Sandy Troy, St Martin's Press, 1991)
Rock On Wood (Terry Rawlings, Boxtree, 1999)
Woodstock—The Oral History (Joel Makower, Sidgwick and Jackson, 1989)
Bill Graham Presents (Bill Graham and Robert Greenfield, Delta, 1992)
One Is The Loneliest Number (Jimmy Greenspoon and Mark Bego, Pharos, 1991)

WEBSITES

Jimpress, Experience Hendrix, Hey Joe, Delerium's Psychedelic Web, Gabgab Camcam, Univibes, Rockmine, Gomemphis.

PERIODICALS

Jimpress, Mojo, Q, Daily Telegraph, Disc & Music Echo, Experience Hendrix, Fabulous 208, Fat Angel, Goldmine, Guitar, Guitar Player, Guitarist, Guitar World, Hit Parader, International Musician, Melody Maker, Mix, Musician, NME, Newsweek, Oz, Ptolemaic Terrascope, Rave, Record Collector, Record Mirror, Rock CD, Rolling Stone, Straight Ahead, The Times, Uncut, Vox, Univibes.

Thanks and acknowledgments: These are the people who, although they did not provide direct quotes for this book, kindly provided a variety of different and useful functions, from simply pointing me in the right directions to supplying names, addresses and phone numbers, offering the right advice at just the right moment, tracking people down on my behalf, supplying cuttings and just generally being there when I needed them. Thanks folks. Without your many unpaid kindnesses this book would not exist.

Joel Abbott, Richard Allen, Tony Bacon, Rick Batey at *Guitar Magazine*, Kirk Blows, Lloyd Bradley, Joel J. Brattin, Pete Brown, Phil Carson, Rob Chapman, Barbara Charone, Terry Coates, Rosalind Cummings, Tony Dukes, Alex Dykes, Marc Eliot, Mark Ellen, Bill Ellis, Brian Emerson, Kees de Lange, Nic Dartnell, Jeff Dexter, Paul Du Noyer, David Evans, Ben Fisher, Keith Fordyce, David Fricke, Eddie Gaines, Ken Garner, Jerry Gilbert, Germaine Greer, Mark Hagen, Jess Hansen, Colin Harper, Tom Heimdahl, David Henderson, James Henke, Michael Hobson, Barney Hoskyns, Patrick Humphries, Peter Innes, Tim Jones, Gibson Keddie, Mike Kellie, Dominic Kennedy, Ken Kessler, Spencer Leigh, Mariel Lubman, Phil McMullen, Bruce Meyer, Frank Moriarty, Douglas J. Noble, Dave Noonan, Myles Palmer, Mike Prendergast, Parke Puterbaugh, Terry Rawlings, John Reed, David Ritz, Steven Roby, Steve Roeser, Ann Scanlon, Joel Selvin, Harry Shapiro, Andrea Sheridan, David Sinclair, Mat Snow, John Steel, Nicky Stevenson, John S. Stuart, Kevin Swift, Judy Totton, Paul Trynka, Gemma Warr, Les Wilson, Caesar Glebeek.

The co-operation of Malcolm Stewart and Steve Rodham of Jimpress, the UK's most indispensible Hendrix fanzine, was invaluable, even if time didn't allow me to take all of their suggestions and corrections on board. True Hendrix buffs should check out Jimpress on the Net at http://www.u-net.com/~jimpress/, or write to them at PO Box 218, Warrington, Cheshire A5 2FG, UK.